A Comprehensive
Guide to
Enterprise Mobility

A Comprehensive Guide to Enterprise Mobility

Jithesh Sathyan
Anoop Narayanan
Navin Narayan
Shibu K V

CRC Press
Taylor & Francis Group
Boca Raton London New York

CRC Press is an imprint of the
Taylor & Francis Group, an **informa** business
AN AUERBACH BOOK

Infosys® Press

CRC Press
Taylor & Francis Group
6000 Broken Sound Parkway NW, Suite 300
Boca Raton, FL 33487-2742

First issued in paperback 2019

ISBN-13: 978-1-4398-6735-8 (hbk)
ISBN-13: 978-1-138-38212-1 (pbk)

Library of Congress Cataloging-in-Publication Data

A comprehensive guide to enterprise mobility / Jithesh Sathyan ... [et al.].
    p. cm. -- (Infosys press series)
  Includes bibliographical references and index.
  ISBN 978-1-4398-6735-8 (alk. paper)
  1. Information technology--Management. 2. Mobile computing. 3. Mobile communication systems. I. Sathyan, Jithesh.

HD30.2.C6395 2013
658'.05--dc23
                                          2012028866

Visit the Taylor & Francis Web site at
http://www.taylorandfrancis.com

and the CRC Press Web site at
http://www.crcpress.com

Contents

SECTION IV TECHNOLOGY CONSIDERATIONS IN MOBILITY

Foreword

There is so much buzz around mobility with newer devices, platforms, solutions, and providers and with the entire enterprise ecosystem changing rapidly. Over the years, organizations have been leveraging technology to help their employees in multiple ways and have started using it as a key lever to engage with their end customers as well. It is almost a no-brainer as to the impact that mobile devices can have on an enterprise. Although it is absolutely critical to have a strategy in place before you start, the adoption or proliferation rate of the strategy has also to be understood for the strategy to yield the required benefits.

This book *A Comprehensive Guide to Enterprise Mobility* provides an excellent coverage of the basics of mobility from an enterprise usage perspective, from strategy definition to deployment. In this book, the authors introduce the basic principles of enterprise mobility and then go into the depth of implementation guidelines including the most common use cases and development and technology considerations. Thus, this book makes two important contributions. First, it shows the role that mobility can play in the enterprise ecosystem, targeting B2E (business to employee), B2B (business to business), and B2C (business to customer) scenarios. Second, it provides a very realistic view on the use cases and implementation examples, illustrating how the aspects covered in the initial sections are put into practice.

The authors Jithesh, Navin, Anoop, and Shibu have used their experience of delivering mobility projects to explain the concepts of enterprise mobility across industry verticals through concepts, functionality descriptions, applicable use cases, and implementation guidelines. Each section touches upon the definitions and use cases, explaining complex concepts without losing simplicity or introducing technical jargons, and finally directs the user to further reading materials to enable a better and detailed understanding of the introduced concepts, if desired.

I am honored to have had the opportunity to work directly with the authors in the architectural design efforts for various mobility programs, and I am sure that this book is a valuable asset for academicians and professionals. I introduce this book with great pleasure, and I wish the authors success in this and their future endeavors.

Manesh Sadasivan
Infosys Limited
India

Preface

With more than 250 million mobile subscribers in the United States and about three billion short message service (SMS) messages sent every month in the United Kingdom, there is no doubt about the level of penetration of mobiles in the consumer segment. Consumers no longer see a mobile handset as a device just for making calls and sending text messages. Mobile handsets are used to satisfy a wide variety of needs such as entertainment, business, commerce, and better life style and to improve productivity. The increase in the number of mobile commerce transactions year-on-year is a clear example of this changing trend. The number of enterprises adopting mobility to achieve higher operational efficiency and to boost profits is also increasing exponentially.

Enterprise mobility is the term broadly used to mean any mobility solution that is launched by an enterprise to increase profits or to reduce costs. This covers both customer-centric applications and internal enterprise applications for employees and partners in a supply chain. Enterprise mobility ecosystem has a wide coverage and is used in several mobility contexts. With acceptance across the industry that mobile is the next stage of digital revolution, enterprise mobility has emerged as a topic of great interest to both professionals and academicians.

There are currently limited books on enterprise mobility, as it is an emerging technology, and almost none that offers an end-to-end coverage of the topic. This is what triggered me to take up the initiative to write a guide on enterprise mobility, with three of my colleagues who are also experts in this topic. This book offers a complete coverage of the concepts, applications, and implementation of solutions under the realm of enterprise mobility in multiple industry domains.

The book has four sections. The first section is about mobility concepts. The chapters in this section provide a good foundation of enterprise mobility. All topics from strategy definition to deployment of enterprise mobility solution are covered in this section. This section was authored by me. The second section is about mobile solutions and case studies. The chapters in this section introduce the reader to the applications of enterprise mobility in various industry sectors. The section helps to bust the myth on enterprise mobility as confined to improving the operation efficiency of field service agents. This section was authored by Shibu. He is a talented enterprise mobility architect who had the chance to work with various technology giants in the mobile industry.

The third section is about mobile application development. This section gives the reader an overview of the popular mobile platform and mobile programming languages. This section was authored by Navin. He is an enterprise mobility architect who has experience in developing applications on all popular smartphone platforms for a variety of clients. The fourth section covers the key topic "Technology Considerations in Mobility." Enterprise mobility has fused with other technologies such as cloud computing and digital signage to create new hybrid offerings, and adoption of enterprise mobility is not possible without considering supporting technologies such as security and device management. Hence, this section details the hybrid and supporting technologies in enterprise mobility and was authored by Anoop. He is a talented mobility researcher and developer.

This book was made possible not only due to the joint effort of the four authors but also due to the consistent support from our families, which has gone a long way in ensuring the timely completion of this book. I would like to thank all of them for their patience and support. I would also like to take this opportunity to thank the members of the Mobility Unit at Infosys for giving us numerous engagements in the enterprise mobility space with a variety of clients in multiple countries, which has helped us in acquiring the knowledge to write this book. Writing this book had been a very good experience, and I hope that you would enjoy reading it as much as I enjoyed writing it.

Jithesh Sathyan
Infosys Limited
India

MOBILITY
CONCEPTS

Chapter 1

Emergence of Enterprise Mobility

This chapter gives a brief background on the evolution of enterprise mobility and the factors that contributed to the growth of mobility. Initially, the mobile phone was considered as just a portable version of a land or fixed phone for satisfying the requirement of making calls while on the move. However, several technological advancements led to its emergence as a platform for improving office productivity and as an additional channel of marketing endeavors. This chapter will provide a good understanding of the factors that contributed toward the emergence of enterprise mobility.

1.1 Introduction

Mobiles have developed from being just a device that offers the ability to make calls to becoming a handheld instrument that has numerous applications that change a person's lifestyle. More and more enterprises are adopting enterprise mobility to enhance their marketing channels, improve office productivity, increase customer satisfaction, and offer shopping experience or sales through mobile. In order to stay ahead of the competition, some of the largest corporations are investing heavily in the development of m-commerce and mobile marketing. Technology is developing rapidly in the mobile industry, opening new unimaginable opportunities to enterprises.

The current enterprise mobile technology, as we know it today, did not emerge overnight. The ground-breaking revolution started with the wireless network and rapidly evolved first into simple handsets for making calls and later to feature-rich smartphones as we know it today. Though mobility adoption is now quite common in most enterprises, it must be noted that enterprise mobility poses overheads to the enterprise in the form of additional infrastructure requirements to support new channels including cost of hardware, software, integration, service, and support. Security concerns, mobile device and infrastructure management, and performance issues due to traffic from mobiles on existing back-end enterprise systems are other issues associated with enterprise mobility enablement.

The emergence of enterprise mobility is attributed to advancements in three significant areas:

- The developments in web standards
- The advances in wireless networking technology
- The innovations in mobile device platforms

This chapter details the advancements in these three significant areas. Web standards have impacted mobile web presentation, while improvements in wireless networking have led to more innovative enterprise mobility applications, and finally innovations in mobile device platforms have led to the development of functionality-rich enterprise mobility applications. While enterprise mobility concepts will be discussed in Chapter 2, this chapter is intended to give the reader a background on how enterprise mobility reached its current level of maturity.

1.2 Developments in Web Standards

Web 1.0 treats Internet as an information portal, where information can be accessed through standard web protocols and browsers, with limited interaction in the form of chat. Web 2.0 and Web 3.0 are two major advancements in web technology, which have been significant from the mobile context. Web 2.0 is the second generation of web technology with a host of services that facilitate collaboration and sharing of data between web users. Social networking and web-based systems of knowledge-sharing evolved as a result of Web 2.0. Wiki and YouTube are representative information-sharing applications of Web 2.0, while MySpace, Twitter, and Facebook are examples of social networking sites. Web 2.0, in addition to the information portal offered in Web 1.0, provides features that allow users to participate.

Blogging that resulted from Web 2.0 can take one of the following forms:

- Personal blog: This is used to share personal details, similar to a diary, related to specific events or activities done and noted on an ongoing basis. Personal data is not private any more. With the sharing of personal details through blogs, people are becoming more transparent. Celebrity blogs are now being increasingly followed by fans, and the current trend is to first provide the information in the personal blog before providing details to the media.

- Microblog: This terminology is used for social networking through which thoughts and feeling are shared with a larger community. Microblogs, through Twitter, are being used to get opinions and advice from the user community and to share information. While sites such as MySpace are focused on friends- or family-based networking, LinkedIn offers a forum for professional networking, and sites such as Facebook are used from both the corporate and noncorporate perspective.
- Query blog: These sites are mostly discussion forums for posting queries and getting responses from multiple users around the globe. Based on site authentication and usage terms, any user with sufficient permissions can blog a response to the query posted by someone. The person who posted the query can also blog to the responses posted by others.
- Corporate blog: This can be either internal corporate blogging or external corporate blogging. Corporates have started internal blogging sites for employees to get inputs on new policies, understand employee issues, and use internal blogs to disseminate information. Thus, internal corporate blogs help to achieve higher transparency between corporates and their employees. External corporate blogs are targeted toward better interaction with partners and for running marketing initiatives including posts to improve brand image.

Wiki web page has been another innovative application of Web 2.0. It designated to enable team work and collaboration by creating a collective knowledge base where members can contribute and modify content. Although Wiki is the shortened form of What I Know Is, with the huge popularity of Wikipedia, which is an online database or encyclopedia of Wiki pages, most web users have started using the term Wiki to mean Wikipedia. Another major application is Really Simple Syndication (RSS), which offers a web-feed format to publish updates like news headlines. An RSS document, which is also known as web feed or channel, is a summarized text and metadata for subscribing to content. By using RSS, a web application can subscribe for updates from single or multiple web sites.

To summarize, Web 2.0 resulted in the following areas of advancement:

- Better content presentation: While WML was the prominent markup language in Web 1.0, the web standards in Web 2.0 focused on xHTML as markup language and CSS for style sheets.
- Better integration: There was an increased adoption of open and standard technology, with the opening up of web services in solutions for better integration with other components.
- Richer user experience: Web 2.0 solutions provided interactive experience to the user. User participation leads to web-based social networking.
- Content synchronization: Features offered from RSS feed helped users to get relevant content from a server based on a subscription model. The user in

this framework has the flexibility to select and filter data subscription from multiple areas.

■ Innovative applications: Standardization of web syntax made data easily accessible and led to the development of innovative applications.

Web 3.0 is the next level of development in the web domain. There are five key areas of advancement in Web 3.0 that differentiate it from the previous generation. These areas are cloud, semantic web, artificial intelligence, personalization, and mobility. Web applications in Web 3.0 are more sophisticated and distributed. Use of autonomous agents for web mining and support for machine learning are the features of web artificial intelligence in Web 3.0.

Semantic web is the foundation of Web 3.0. Semantic web is centered at a resource description framework (RDF) together with the formal notations. The formal notations include RDF schema, web ontology language, and data exchange formats. The data exchange formats used are RDF/XML, N3, Turtle, and N-Triples. The underlying structure of any expression in RDF is a collection of triples, each consisting of a subject, a predicate, and an object. There is an explosive growth in the variety of information sources on the web. Web mining can be used to analyze and track the content and usage patterns on the web.

The advances in web from Web 2.0 and Web 3.0 had a major impact on enterprise mobility. xHTML:MP, the mark-up language for mobile web, ensured that web pages displayed on mobile handsets were lightweight, had an appealing look and feel, and were not limited to the features of WML. The recent developments with HTML5 have paved the way for mobile multiplatform development. The social networking and interactive capabilities in Web 2.0 had widespread applications in the mobile context. The mobile, being present with the user most of the time, served to be an instrument for use in social networking and to keep connected even on the move. Social networking sites such as Twitter and Facebook launched mobile web versions for displaying contents on small handset screens and offered intuitive interfaces to twitter and blog from the handsets.

Mobility is considered as a separate area of focus in Web 3.0 and has been given due importance. Enterprise mobility has spread fast with developments in web standards, and most enterprises have extended web site support for mobile devices. Although current enterprise mobile web implementations have a rendering platform to handle the display of web content of different types of handsets, it is hoped that with widespread adoption of HTML5, mobile web implementation would be less expensive and will require much less development effort. Web 2.0 and Web 3.0 has thus led to the development of several innovative mobile applications, and this has been a major contributor to the emergence of enterprise mobility. Advances in web space is seen to have a direct correlation with developments in enterprise mobility, as changes in web space, in general, will bring about changes in mobile web technology.

1.3 Advances in Wireless Networking Technology

Wireless networks made mobile communication possible and are the key contributor to the emergence of enterprise mobility. The improvements in speed, brought about by advances in the wireless network, resulted in various data services that form the backbone of enterprise mobility. Hence, wireless networking technology is given due importance in this chapter. The main operation of elements in a communication network is transmission of information (voice, data, media, etc.), where the information is transformed or evaluated to make communication between two equipments possible. Communication networks have evolved based on the need for "more information" transfer at a "higher speed." There are different kinds of communication networks based on the area of coverage, type of modulation used, speed of data transfer, type of switching, bandwidth, and type of interface used for data transfer between elements.

Wireless networking technology can be split into two phases:

- Traditional wireless technology: This phase comprises the second-generation (2G) mobile networks such as the Global System for Mobile Communication (GSM), the 2.5G network such as the General Packet Radio Service (GPRS), and the third-generation (3G) network such as the Universal Mobile Telecommunications System (UMTS). It should be noted that code division multiple access (CDMA) also had evolved based on telecom generations and captured the U.S. and Asian markets, while GSM and its successors were serving the European segment.
- Modern wireless technology: This phase comprises technologies such as Worldwide Interoperability for Microwave Access (WiMax), Wireless Fidelity (WiFi), Wireless Mesh, 3G network extensions such as Internet Protocol Multimedia Subsystem (IMS), and pre-4G and fourth-generation (4G) technologies such as Long-Term Evolution (LTE).

1.3.1 Traditional Wireless Technology

Let us start with GSM. It is a cellular (user coverage area defined in the shape of cells) communication network. It was developed as an attempt to standardize the European mobile telephone network and is now one of the most popular standards for mobile phones in the world. GSM networks usually operate in the 900- or 1800-MHz bands, and in some countries the 850- and 1900-MHz bands are used. The modulation schema used in GSM is Gaussian minimum shift keying, and the bandwidth is distributed among many users using a combination of time and frequency division multiple access (TDMA/FDMA).

As shown in Figure 1.1, the GSM network consists of the following features:

- Mobile station: This is the user/mobile equipment that helps the user to make calls and receive subscribed services.

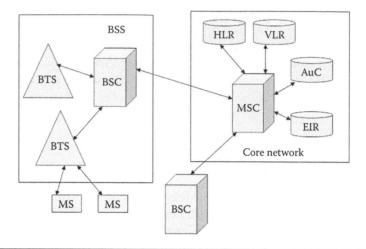

Figure 1.1   GSM network simplified architecture.

■ Base station system (BSS): It is linked to the radio interface functions and has two components:
  – Base transceiver station (BTS): The BTS is the signal handling node between a mobile station and the base station controller (BSC). Its main function is transmitting or receiving radio signals and encrypting or decrypting communications with the BSC.
  – BSC: The BSC is the controller for multiple BTS, and its main function is to handle handover (user moving from one cell to another) and allocate channels.
■ Switching system/network switching subsystem/core network: It does switching functions and is the main center for call processing. The core network is composed of the following components:
  – Home location register (HLR): HLR is a database for storing subscriber information. The information includes subscriber profile, location information, services subscribed to, and activity status. A subscriber is first registered with the HLR of the operator before he or she can start enjoying the services offered by the operator.
  – Mobile services switching center/mobile switching center (MSC)/call server: This is the main switching node of the GSM network and provides functionalities such as call switching to and from other telephones and data systems, call routing, subscriber registration and authentication, location updating, toll ticketing, common channel signaling, and handovers.
  – Visitor location register (VLR): It is a database for temporary storage of information about visiting subscribers. When a user moves to a location outside its MSC, the VLR in this new location queries the HLR and gets information about the subscriber to avoid querying the HLR each time

the user wants to access a service. The user in the new location is called a visiting subscriber.

- Additional functional elements in the GSM include the following components:
  - Authentication center (AuC): Handles security using authentication and encryption.
  - Equipment identity register (EIR): Database to store the identity of mobile equipments to prevent calls from unauthorized equipments.
  - Gateway mobile switching center (GMSC): A gateway integrated with MSC to interconnect two networks. It can be used for routing calls from a public-switched telephone network (PSTN) to a GSM user.

Many more components such as message center, mobile service node, and GSM-interworking unit can be seen in a GSM network. Some definitions specify operation and support system (OSS) as a part of GSM, although it is a more generic term that applies to operation and support for any kind of network.

The next entrant into the mobile communication network family is the GPRS network, which is more of an upgrade of the GSM network. The same components of the GSM network provide voice service, and the GPRS network handles data. Due to this reason, the GSM network providers do not have to start from scratch to deploy GPRS. GPRS triggered the transformation from the circuit-switched GSM network to the packet-switched network, and hence it is considered a technology between 2G and 3G, or commonly referred to as 2.5G.

Some of the benefits of GPRS over circuit-switched networks are as follows:

- Higher speed
- Instantaneous access to service ("always on")
- New services related to data communication
- Ease of upgrade and deployment on existing GSM network
- Can support applications that do not require dedicated connection

Compared with GSM, GPRS has three new components that are required, as shown in Figure 1.2:

- Terminal equipment: The existing GSM user equipments will not be capable of handling the enhanced air interface and packet data in GPRS. Hence, new terminal equipments that can handle packet data of GPRS and voice calls using GSM are required.
- Serving GPRS support node (SGSN): It handles mobility management functions including routing and handover. SGSN converts mobile data into Internet Protocol (IP) and is capable of IP address assignment.
- Gateway GPRS support node (GGSN): It acts as a gateway to connect with external networks such as public Internet (IP network) and other GPRS networks from a different service provider. It can be used to implement security or firewall in screening subscribers and to address mapping.

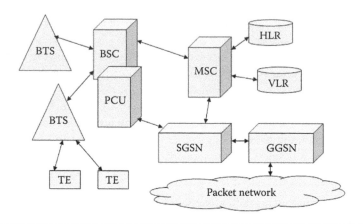

Figure 1.2   GPRS network simplified architecture.

The remaining components of GPRS are similar to GSM with minor software and hardware upgrades. The BSC in GPRS needs the installation of hardware components such as a packet control unit (PCU) to handle packet data traffic and some software upgrades, while components such as BTS, HLR, and VLR will only require software upgrades.

3G was a major leap in terms of communication network speed and has led to multiple services. UMTS is a 3G network that delivers voice, data, and media services. The media services that include pictures, video, and graphics are a new feature of 3G compared with the 2.5G networks such as GPRS. Some of the applications made possible with UMTS include video and music download, mobile commerce, messaging, conferencing, and location-based services. The air interface for communication in UMTS uses wideband CDMA (W-CDMA), and asynchronous transfer mode is the data transmission method used within the UMTS core network.

W-CDMA used for UMTS terrestrial radio access network (UTRAN) air interface is a modulation system where data is multiplied with quasi-random bits derived from W-CDMA spreading codes. These codes are used for canalization, synchronization, and scrambling. W-CDMA operates in both frequency division duplex and time division duplex.

UMTS has three major categories of network elements:

1. GSM elements: Core network (MSC, VLR, HLR, AuC, and EIR) and BSS (BTS and BSC)
2. GPRS elements: SGSN and GGSN
3. UMTS-specific elements: User equipment that can handle media and air interface and UTRAN consisting of radio network controller (RNC) and "Node B"

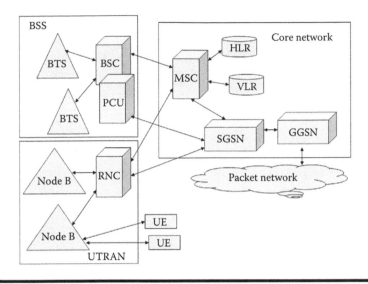

Figure 1.3 UMTS network simplified architecture.

"Node B" for the new air interface is the counterpart of BTS in GSM/GPRS (as shown in Figure 1.3). Based on the quality and strength of the connection, "Node B" calculates the frame error rate and transmits information to the RNC for processing. RNC for the W-CDMA air interface is the counterpart of BSC in GSM/GPRS. The main functions of the RNC include handover, security, broadcasting, and power control. The user equipment in the UMTS network should be compatible to work for the GSM/GPRS network.

During standardization activities for the 2G network, GSM was adopted in most parts of Europe, and CDMA evolved during the same time, capturing markets in the United States and Asia. The first major effort in the development of the CDMA network standard was from the Telecommunications Industry Association with an architecture named "cdmaOne" that could be used for commercial deployment of CDMA networks. While IS-95A of the Telecommunications Industry Association brought circuit-switched services using CDMA, the revised version (IS-95B) gave subscribers packet-switched data services. While networks based on IS-95B were considered 2.5G, the blueprint for CDMA-based 3G network came with CDMA2000 defined by International Telecommunication Union.

The following are the components in a CDMA2000 network (Figure 1.4):

■ Mobile station: This is the client equipment or user equipment, like a subscriber handset, that provides interface for the user to access the services.
■ Radio access network (RAN): It is the air interface component in CDMA for interacting with the core network. The RAN is similar to the BSS on GSM networks. The BSC and BTS are found in the GSM network. The RAN also

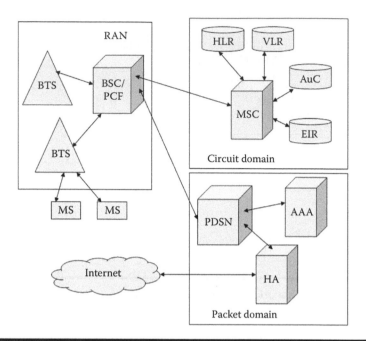

Figure 1.4   CDMA network simplified architecture.

contains a packet control function (PCF) that is used to route IP packets to a
packet data serving node (PDSN).
■ Packet domain: The packet domain in a CDMA network consists of the fol-
lowing components:
  – PDSN/foreign agent: It acts as a gateway for the RAN by routing packets
    to an external packet network such as the Internet. It can establish, main-
    tain, and terminate a packet link.
  – Authentication, authorization, and accounting (AAA): These are servers
    used to authenticate and authorize users for access to the network and to
    store subscriber call details for accounting.
  – Home agent: The interface component to the external packet network
    provides an IP for mobile messages and forwards it to the appropriate
    network. A PDSN can be configured to work as a home agent.
■ Circuit domain: The circuit domain is similar to the GSM network with
  components such as the MSC, GMSC, HLR, AuC, and EIR.

Third Generation Partnership Project 2 (3GPP2) is dedicated to the development of the next-generation standards for CDMA 2000. In addition to standardizing forums such as 3GPP2 that promote the evolution of CDMA, forums such as
CDMA Development Group work on adoption and ease in the deployment of 3G
CDMA wireless systems.

1.3.2 *Modern Wireless Technology*

Let us start with WiMax. WiMAX is a wireless broadband technology based on the IEEE 802.16 standard. It is a wireless alternative to cable modems, digital subscriber line (DSL), and T1/E1 links. The IEEE standard was named WiMAX by the WiMAX Forum to promote the IEEE standard for interoperability and deployment. It can support voice, video, and Internet data.

The spectrum bands in which WiMAX usually operates include 2.3, 2.5, 3.5, and 5.8 GHz, with a speed of approximately 40 Mbps per wireless channel. Based on coverage, WiMAX is classified under the metropolitan area network. WiMAX can offer both non-line-of-sight and line-of-sight services. In the non-line-of-sight service, which operates at a lower frequency range, an antenna on the personal computer communicates with the WiMAX tower, and in the line-of-sight service, which operates at high frequencies, a dish antenna points directly at the WiMAX tower. It uses orthogonal frequency division multiple access (OFDM) as the modulation technique.

WiMAX architecture can be split into three parts, as shown in Figure 1.5:

- Mobile station: This is the user equipment or user terminal that the end user uses to access the WiMAX network.
- Access service network (ASN): This is the access network of WiMAX comprising base stations and one or more ASN gateways. While the base station is responsible for providing the air interface with a mobile station, the ASN gateways form the RAN at the edge.
- Connectivity service network (CSN): This is the core network that offers services and connectivity with other networks. It includes the AAA server, the mobile IP home agent (MIP-HA), the services offered using supporting networks such as IMS, an operation support system, or a billing system, which can be a part of the core or a stand-alone application, and the gateways for protocol conversion and connectivity with other networks.

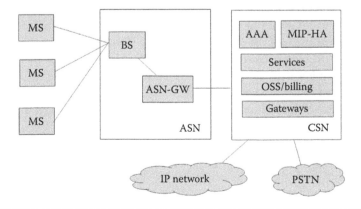

Figure 1.5   WiMAX simplified architecture.

WiFi refers to various IEEE 802.11 technologies used in mobile and video games. It is a packet-based network infrastructure and uses radio waves to communicate with handset devices. A wireless adapter on the end-user device translates data into a radio signal and transmits the same using an antenna on the device. The signals from the device are received by a WiFi router that decodes and sends the information to an external network, such as the Internet, or to an internal network. WiFi radios transmit at frequencies of 2.4 or 5 GHz.

WiFi has the following 802.11 networking standards:

- 802.11a: Transmits at 5 GHz and can handle up to 54 Mb of data per second.
- 802.11lb: Transmits at 2.4 GHz and can handle up to 11 Mb of data per second.
- 802.11g: Transmits at 2.4 GHz and can handle up to 54 Mb of data per second.
- 802.11n: Can provide a bandwidth of 140 Mb per second.

IMS is the next major development in mobile communication and is considered to be the backbone of "all-IP network." IMS was originally developed for mobile applications by the Third Generation Partnership Project (3GPP) and 3GPP2. With standards from the Telecommunications and Internet Converged Services and Protocols for Advanced Networking, fixed networks are also supported in IMS, leading to mobile and fixed convergence. Use of open standard IP, defined by the Internet Engineering Task Force, allows service providers to use IMS for introducing new services easily. With multiple standardizing organizations working on it, IMS will cross the frontiers of mobile, wireless, and fixed-line technologies.

IMS is based on open standard IP with session initiation protocol (SIP) used to establish, manage, and terminate connections. A multimedia session between two IMS users, between an IMS user and a user on the Internet, or between two users on the Internet is all established using the same protocol. Moreover, the interfaces for service developers are also based on IP. IMS merges the Internet with mobiles, using cellular technologies to provide ubiquitous access and Internet technologies to provide appealing services. The rapid spread of IP-based access technologies and the move toward core network convergence with IMS has led to an explosion in multimedia content delivery across packet networks. This transition has led to a much wider and richer service experience.

The IMS can be thought of as composed of three layers, as shown in Figure 1.6:

- The service or application layer: The end services reside in the application layer. It includes a host of application servers that execute services and communicate with the session control layer using SIP. It can be a part of the service provider home network or can reside in a third-party network. With open standards defined on interaction with the application server, it is easier to build applications on application servers. The power of IMS lies in easily

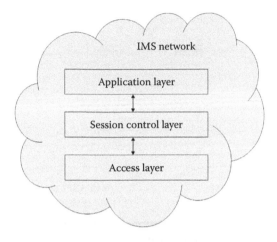

Figure 1.6   Three-layered IMS network.

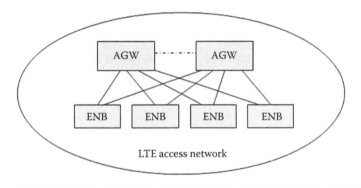

Figure 1.7   LTE simplified architecture.

rolling in or rolling out services on the fly in minimal time using application servers.

■ The IMS core or session control layer: Session control and interactions between transport and the application layer happen through the session layer. These are the main components of the core or session control layer:

   – Call session control function (CSCF): It can establish, monitor, maintain, and release sessions. It also manages user service interactions, quality of service policy, and access to external domains. Based on the role performed, a CSCF can be a serving-CSCF (S-CSCF), a proxy-CSCF (P-CSCF), or an interrogating-CSCF (I-CSCF).

   – Home subscriber server: Database for storing subscriber and service information.

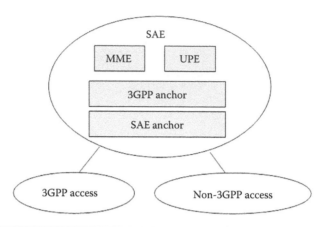

Figure 1.8   SAE simplified architecture.

- - Multimedia resource function plane (MRFP): It implements all media-related functions such as play media and mix media and provides announcements.
  - Multimedia resource function controller: It handles communications with the S-CSCF and controls the resources in the MRFP.
  - Breakout gateway control function: It mainly handles interactions with the PSTN.
  - Media gateway controller function: It is used to control a media gateway.
- ■ The access/transport layer: This layer is used for different networks to connect to the IMS using IP. It initiates and terminates SIP signaling and includes elements such as gateways for conversion between formats. The connecting network can be fixed access like DSL or Ethernet, mobile access like GSM or CDMA, and wireless access like WiMAX.

Some other IMS components include signaling gateways, media gateway, and telephone number mapping (e.g., ENUM).

Another key technology in modern mobile communication is wireless mesh network. Instead of simple wireless point-to-point or broadcast networks, radio nodes can form wireless mesh networks via IEEE 802.11, 802.15, and 802.16 technologies. In a mesh network, traffic from one node has multiple paths to travel to another node in the topology, and so in case of a path or a node failure, the network still provides services to applications.

Wireless mesh network has two types of nodes: mesh routers and mesh clients. A mesh router is usually equipped with multiple wireless interfaces built on either the same or different wireless access technologies. Mesh routers are static and form the backbone for mesh clients. Wireless mesh networks can be classified into three types:

- Infrastructure wireless mesh network: In this mesh network configuration, the mesh routers form a network infrastructure for mesh clients.
- Client wireless mesh network: In this mesh network configuration, the mesh clients provide peer-to-peer networks among mesh client devices.
- Hybrid wireless mesh network: This mesh network configuration involves a combination of infrastructure wireless mesh and the client wireless mesh networks.

Advanced LTE and mobile WiMax are two key drivers for 4G. So let us conclude the discussion with two initiatives that lead to 4G, which are LTE and system architecture evolution (SAE). The main difference between these two initiatives is that LTE is about enhancing the "access network" and SAE works on developing the "core network" architecture to support the high-throughput or low-latency LTE access system.

LTE is an effort to reduce the number of network elements, but it offers higher data rates and better quality of service on a packet-only network. It uses OFDM for uplink and SC-FDMA (single carrier-FDMA) for downlink. LTE access network has two types of components—the access gateways and Enhance Node B, as shown in Figure 1.7. While the access gateway does functionalities such as mode management, data compression, and ciphering, the Enhance Node B works on all radio-related issues and mobility management.

SAE is expected to provide an all-IP network solution with all services on the packet-switched domain and not on the circuit-switched domain. It will support mobility with multiple heterogeneous access systems both supported by 3GPP, such as LTE, and non-3GPP access systems, such as WiMAX. SAE consists of the following entities as shown in Figure 1.8:

- Mobility management entity (MME): It does functions such as user equipment authentication and mobility management.
- User plane entity (UPE): It manages and stores user equipment context, including ciphering, packet routing, and forwarding.
- 3GPP anchor: It is the mobility anchor between 2G or 3G and LTE.
- SAE anchor: It is the mobility anchor between 3GPP and non-3GPP.

Thus, it can be seen that there has been a tremendous improvement in bandwidth with the introduction of new technologies from different generations of communication. The upcoming generations are expected to offer even higher bandwidths, pushing user experience to high realms, with not just real-time media, but 3D holographic data transfer and projections similar to what is shown in *Star Wars* movies.

1.4 Innovations in Mobile Device Platforms

Mobile phones have turned out to be the fastest growing media device in terms of usage and sales. In 2007, the worldwide sale of mobile phones exceeded 1.5 billion. This is a huge number in comparison to 1.7 billion achieved by the television after years of deployment and approximately 1.3 billion units achieved by desktops.

Some of the key milestones in the mobile revolution are as follows:

1970s: Bell Labs started cellular revolution by developing the Advanced Mobile Phone Standard (AMPS).

1985: First transportable phone was developed.

1989: Personal cellular phone was launched in the market.

1992: First GSM mobile phone was launched.

1996: First personal digital assistant mobile phone was launched.

1999: First Wireless Application Protocol (WAP)-capable mobile phone arrives in the market.

2002: First smartphone was released.

2005: High-speed data access leading to features including 3G video calling was introduced.

2008: Apple iPhone 3G, App Store, and Android Market gave a new outlook to consumer mobility.

2009: Other platform vendors join the App Store race (BlackBerry App World, Nokia Ovi Store, Palm App Catalog, and Windows Marketplace for mobile), and enterprise mobility becomes part of enterprise strategy in most enterprises.

Present: Touch screens with qHD, iCloud, mobile payments, etc.

Future: Holographic mobile 3D displays, Unified Smartphone Platform standards, flawless speech and sensor-based mobiles, etc.

In developing countries, building wireline networking infrastructure is expensive and slow, making mobile technology a reliable and cost-efficient alternative option. In many Asian countries, there are more mobile phone users than the conventional wireline phone users. With the rise of smartphones having the capability of executing desktop or PC-like applications, there is an increased adoption of the mobile to satisfy personal and official needs. This change in perception has brought about a switch from the fixed-line phone to mobile phones as the main communication tool for users even in developed countries. The high processing power, extended memory, dedicated full-featured operating system, and the advances in wireless networks have ensured the development of innovative and appealing applications to meet the needs of mobile users.

The price of mobile phones has dropped considerably, making a handset easily affordable to all classes. Mobile devices have also become a part of a person's daily life. Even smartphones' prices have dropped significantly. Most executives in developed countries now have handsets from iPhone, BlackBerry, Palm, or Android. The launch of App Stores by mobile platform vendors was a game changer in the mobile technology space. This opened up a forum for many to upload applications built for specific mobile platforms, allowing easy distribution of applications. The practice of having handset applications developed only by the handset vendor was thus replaced by development by any enthusiastic developer. There has been an explosion in the number of applications that are published in App Stores, and the result is the availability of innovative applications that have made way to rapid developments in enterprise mobility space.

Google and the Open Handset Alliance brought out the most popular open mobile platform named Android. Android is an open-source software stack for mobile devices, which includes an operating system, middleware, and a suite of applications. The Android Software Development Kit provides the tools and application programming interfaces (APIs) for developers to create applications on the Android platform using the Java programming language. The open source nature that leads to absence of developer license costs in getting the development environment and publishing application has resulted in quick adoption of Android by many mobile application developers, leading to rich applications. The market share of Android has significantly grown, and it is now a major competitor with commercial platforms such as iPhone, BlackBerry, and Windows Mobile in the smartphone industry. The increase in Android developers and users and the free nature of the operating system have led many device manufacturers to launch Android mobile handsets.

Customers who want the Apple brand and those who look for the best user experience prefer iPhone. Apple continues to define new innovations in mobile space and ensures that customers are offered unique features for being loyal to the brand. However, BlackBerry still dominates the enterprise employee handset segment. This dominance in enterprise employee handset segment is due to the BlackBerry Enterprise Server that offers the ability to push corporate e-mails, the BlackBerry Mobile Data Service that enables applications to be deployed to mobile users, including developer tools and administrative services, and most importantly provides a secure framework for interaction between the BlackBerry handset and the enterprise server.

One of the significant developments in the mobile multiplatform development came with Java 2 Micro Edition (J2ME). J2ME is an edition of the Java platform targeted at mobile handset and embedded devices. J2ME consists of a virtual machine and a set of Java APIs tailored for mobile and embedded devices. Configurations and profiles make up the two primary components in the J2ME platform. Thus, an application developed in J2ME without the use of any platform-specific APIs can be executed on multiple Java-based mobile platforms such as Android and BlackBerry without any code level changes. Mobile device manufacturers install and prepackage their devices with the Java virtual machine and associated APIs to ensure that Java applications developed for target devices can be executed without further download of dependent libraries. These developments in mobile platform space have been a major factor for the current level of maturity in enterprise mobility.

1.5 Conclusion

Enterprise mobility is a topic of high significance in today's industry. Market research surveys suggest mobility adoption as top priority in the corporate strategy of most enterprises. The growth in sales of mobiles confirms that mobility will be a major channel for enterprises to reach customers. Mobiles provide instant access to information anytime and anywhere a user needs it. This has resulted in extensive use of mobile devices by customers for their daily information needs. The rise in mobile use has also resulted in multiple device vendors and tremendous reduction in the price of handsets. With multiplatform development tools, the lifecycle for mobile solution development has significantly shortened.

This chapter is intended to introduce the reader to the enabling technologies and major milestones in enterprise mobility. The chapter acts as an introduction to the complete book by explaining the history of enterprise mobility evolution. The three major factors that have made a significant impact on enterprise mobility (web standards, advances in mobile network, and handset technology) are discussed in this chapter. It is suggested to refer to the books listed under "Additional Reading" for a deep dive into the topics that are briefly covered in this chapter.

Additional Reading

1. Jochen Schiller. *Mobile Communications*, 2nd edition. Boston: Addison Wesley; 2003.
2. Rich Ling and Jonathan Donner. *Mobile Phones and Mobile Communication (Digital Media and Society Series)*. United Kingdom: Polity Press; 2009.
3. Mischa Schwartz. *Mobile Wireless Communications*, 1st edition. Cambridge: Cambridge University Press; 2005.
4. Syed A. Ahson and Mohammad Ilyas. *Mobile Web 2.0: Developing and Delivering Services to Mobile Devices*, 1st edition. Florida: Auerbach Publications; 2010.
5. Andrew Pearson. *The Mobile Revolution*, 1st edition. North Carolina: Lulu Press; 2010.

Chapter 2

Enterprise Mobility Landscape

Before delving deep into mobility, it is essential to understand some of the common terms used in mobility and the basic building blocks of enterprise mobility. This chapter is a must-read for those who are new to enterprise mobility, as it builds on a solid foundation for understanding the rest of the chapters in this book, and even a person who is new to enterprise mobility can easily pick up the details after reading this chapter. This chapter provides a high-level overview on enterprise mobility.

2.1 Introduction

Enterprise mobility is the term broadly used to mean any mobility solution that is launched by an enterprise to increase profits or to reduce costs. This brings us to the discussion of the types of mobile applications that come under the scope of enterprise mobility. Broadly, the enterprise mobility paradigm is classified into two groups:

- Customer-centric mobility
- Internal enterprise mobility

Customer-centric mobility relates to mobile solutions developed for use by the end customer. Customer mobile applications can serve different purposes. For example, a retailer may create a mobile application for mobile shopping to increase sales and attract more customers. With easy access to mobiles, purchases over the mobile would become more frequent. Mobile-based business also lowers the cost of serving the customer. The lowering of cost could be in the form of mobile customer support applications or reducing the visit of the customers to the physical store that needs support staff. For most enterprises, the fundamental purpose for launching mobile applications is to introduce a new channel for marketing and business. Internal enterprise mobility has several sublevels. The following are the different variations of internal enterprise mobility:

- Operational or field workforce mobility
- Partner or supply chain mobility
- Employee-centric mobility

Operational or field workforce mobility deals with mobile applications that are intended to bring down the operational expenditure of the enterprise. Bringing down the operational expenditure can mean different things to different enterprises based on the domain of operation. For example, for an enterprise that works on servicing equipments, reducing the operational expenditure can be achieved when the field service employee has a handset application that can help in collecting customer complaints, take images of faulty parts, connect to the office, check equipment manuals, take images of the bar code of the faulty part, check the availability of parts for replacement, place the order, and get service requests allocated to the location nearest to the current complaint's location. Similarly, for an enterprise in courier service, the operational expenditure can be reduced with a mobile application that reduces paper work and errors from manual entry, which is achieved using a handset application that can collect delivery details as well as get signature from the customer upon delivery and auto-update the details to the back-end server.

Partner or supply chain mobility deals with applications provided by the enterprise for channel partners. The intent is to increase sales and ensure better tracking. Let us discuss an example application under this category. An enterprise that specializes in car manufacturing could develop a mobile application for its suppliers who would use it to scan automobile parts that are sent with dates, which can be easily verified by the manufacturing unit on the arrival of the parts, and the production can be planned based on the shipment of parts. This makes it easier to keep track of the parts from different suppliers. It must be noted that a partner can also be a customer, for example, in scenarios where the enterprise creates a mobile application for its product service team to place orders for the end customer; although the application is for the partner, it is a means of getting business from the end customer.

Finally, we have employee-centric mobility that deals with mobile applications for employees at their work place. These can be simple applications that allow sharing of PC desktop data on the mobile device or applications that enable interaction with enterprise systems to generate critical reports for managers to make decisions even when they are on the move.

Through these different categories of mobile applications, it can be seen that enterprise mobility leads to higher productivity, improved data quality with less paper work, more business and satisfaction from customers, employee access to enterprise packages even when the employees are on the move, and a more productive workforce. Some of the overheads to the enterprise with enterprise mobility are additional infrastructure requirements to support a new channel, including the cost of hardware, software, integration, service and support, security concerns, mobile device and infrastructure management, and performance issues on back-end enterprise systems due to traffic from mobiles.

2.2 Mobile Solution Types

The mobile solution to a business problem can be of the following types:

- Short message service (SMS)
- Unstructured supplementary services data (USSD)
- Interactive voice response
- Thin application
- Thick application
- Hybrid application
- Subscriber identity module (SIM) application tool kit
- Combined package

The SMS is a popular method adopted for mobile-based customer support, mobile marketing, and multifactor authentication. An example of an SMS-based customer support is when we order an item from a retailer web site, and the retailer sends SMS messages to the customer to update the status of the order. Once the retailer has the customer's mobile number, this can be used to send SMS messages on promotions that might be of interest to the customer, leading to the use of the mobile as a marketing tool. Banks are increasingly using the SMS as an instrument for multifactor authentication, where the customer is sent an alphanumeric security code and asked to use the same, along with a web-based login or password for added security from hackers.

USSD is also a popular solution for customer support. Popular examples of USSD include dialing *123# to get the account balance message for a prepaid account with the telco service provider or *3445# to activate a service such as roaming or daily news. USSD is also being used to communicate promotional and advertising messages.

Interactive voice response is the traditional approach for customer support. Most enterprises provide a support number that can be called by the customer to get product information and customized responses to queries based on their product purchase or service subscription. The calls from a customer are first handled by an automated response system, which provides the caller with a predefined set of options, such as "Press 1 to know your balance," "Press 2 for activating new services," etc., and then it provides a recorded response based on an input selected by the user in the mobile handset. These automated systems also give an option for the user to reach a customer support executive and thus switch from automated response to response from an actual person.

Thin application (Thin App) is the term used for browser-based applications. The device diversity and multiple platforms make mobile web application development more complex than normal web site development for the desktop. Different mobile devices have different screen sizes, platform versions, memory capabilities, etc., which result in multiple device profiles to be supported by the mobile web server. In a typical mobile thin application implementation, the server side will contain a rendering engine. Based on the device making the request and the web format supported (WML, HTML, and xHTML), the rendering engine will create an appropriate page for presentation to the browser in the mobile device. So accessing a web site that is not mobile enabled will result in the content being presented in an unformatted manner based on the profile of the mobile device. Offering browsing capability and mobile shopping through a mobile browser involves thin application development. Thin application development relates to changes on the server by providing the capability to browse the enterprise site from a mobile.

Thick applications are application packages that need to be downloaded to a mobile. Thick applications can offer a much better user experience compared with thin applications. These also help the user to work in an offline mode. Offline mode means that the user can work on the application in the absence of network connectivity, which is not possible in the case of mobile web sites. The disadvantage, however, is the requirement to download and install the application, which is not required in the case of browser-based applications.

A hybrid application, as the name suggests, is a combination of thick and thin applications. The hybrid application is similar to a normal thick application, which needs to be downloaded. However, some screens in the application will have a browser page embedding. So clicking or selecting an option such as "button click" will launch the browser or web page inside the thick application container. This is usually a requirement when handling payment transactions, such as credit card information, where regulatory compliance requires that no card information is on the device, and the best way to handle security in such a case is to delegate the responsibility to the server. So by using a mobile commerce retailer hybrid application, the customer views products and performs checkout, and finally when the step to enter payment processing is to be handled, an embedded mobile web page is loaded in the thick application container.

The SIM application tool kit has a memory card that has details of the subscriber and is used to place calls by identifying the subscriber with the telco call servers. As address details and other information are stored on the SIM, applications can also be made available on the SIM card. The important part of working with applications for the SIM card is to understand that the storage capabilities of the SIM are limited. However, telco service providers who offer the SIM card can create value-added applications for the customer, which get loaded on starting up the mobile.

Combined packages are offered by most large enterprises, as a single mobile solution type will not satisfy the requirements of customers. The goal is usually to offer as many solution types as possible to address a business problem. For example, for mobile commerce, the retailer would provide the capability to browse mobile web pages (Thin App) and make a purchase; in the vendor App Stores, the retailer will launch a mobile thick application in which customers can save their favorite items and get customized promotions and other features leading to a purchase. To support the purchase, the retailer would complement an SMS service to provide delivery status and also provide interactive voice response support for handling queries. Also by offering an e-mail for support and providing the e-mail in the thick and thin solutions, the mobile mailing application can also be leveraged by the retailer.

2.3 Key Players in the Mobility Landscape

The mobile business landscape has the following players:

- Original equipment manufacturers (OEMs): Mobile handsets are manufactured by OEM vendors. There are both consumer handsets and handsets for enterprise requirements. Motorola and Panasonic are the two leaders in the enterprise handset manufacturing industry.
- Electronics manufacturing services (EMS) providers and original design manufacturing (ODM) companies: OEMs do not manufacture and design the electronic components that make up the mobile device. This is done by vendors who specialize in this space, which falls under the category of ODM/EMS. Compal and FlexMobile are the two popular players in the mobile ODM/EMS landscape.
- Mobile platform vendors: The operating system (OS) for a mobile is called the mobile platform. The inherent capabilities of a mobile handset depend on the OS in the mobile device. There are multiple mobile platforms, and Windows Mobile and Symbian are two examples of the mobile platform.
- Semiconductor vendors: The computational capability of the mobile handset depends on the processor chip. Market leaders in mobile chip technology, such as Intel, TexasInstruments, and Freescale, are coming up with smaller and more powerful processor chips that significantly improve the landscape of mobile applications that can be used in mobile handsets.
- Independent software vendors: Generic mobile applications for the mass market have been an area of key focus for independent software vendor giants

such as Google and Skype. However, Google has made a significant impact in the mobile space with its mobile OS named Android. Android is now eating up the market share of other mobile platform giants such as Research in Motion (RIM, BlackBerry) and Apple (iPhone).

- Content providers: Many content providers benefit from mobility. Media content providers such as Fonecta and MTV are just two examples of content providers from the media industry that benefit from mobility solutions. Enterprises that focus on consumer mobility use third-party content to provide value-added service to the customers.
- Operators: Telco operators play a key role in the enterprise mobility space. They come up with new service offerings for their enterprise customers. They are the leaders in innovation and change in the mobility industry by offering enhanced mobile middleware platform integrated with the telco service delivery platform, service application programming interfaces that can be used to create functionality-rich mobile apps, mobile cloud environment, etc. Vodafone, Orange, O2, and Telstra are some of the telco service providers who have made considerable contributions in the enterprise mobility space.
- Technology providers: Mobility client applications need to interact with mobile server components. The servers are supplied by technology providers such as HP, IBM, and Microsoft. Technology providers, such as Microsoft, are playing multiple roles with several mobility solutions: the Windows Mobile OS, the Windows CE for embedded systems including handsets, Azure as a hosting platform for mobile servers and middleware, and mobile synchronization solutions between the PC and the mobile.
- Enterprises: Enterprises require mobile applications for their customers and internal mobility needs. Enterprises interact with other players in the mobility space to meet their enterprise mobility needs.
- Mobile middleware providers: There are multiple mobile enterprise application platforms, mobile consumer application platforms, mobile web tools, and packaged tools for multiplatform application development. Some of the mobile middleware vendors are Netbiscuits, Volantis, Sybase, and Antenna Software. The use of middleware is not limited to multiplatform development. Mobile middleware also has capabilities of synchronization of data between the client and the server, built-in security, and quicker integration with back-end systems.
- Mobile application providers: The market leaders in back-end enterprise systems, such as Oracle and SAP, are effectively utilizing the opportunities coming up from mobility space, by introducing mobile applications that help enterprise users to connect with back-end systems. With the use of these mobile applications, enterprise users can get reports, alerts, and critical information and can work on enterprise applications even when they are on the move.

■ Enterprise mobile open-source software providers: Several operation support applications are required for mobile enablement. For example, for managing the mobile devices of the enterprise, mobile device management solutions such as Sybase Afaria would be required; for ensuring security, several mobile security packages would be required; for over-the-air deployment, solutions such as BlackBerry Enterprise Server or iPhone Configuration Utility can be used; for test management, solutions from TestQuest are available; and for multiplatform test, services are provided by DeviceAnywhere. Hence, multiple solutions satisfy specific operation support requirements in the enterprise for mobility enablement.

■ Cloud or managed mobility service providers: Enterprises are currently approaching managed mobility service providers to satisfy their mobile development, hosting, and maintenance requirements. Managed service providers give enterprises the ability to completely outsource their mobility activities. Cloud provider is a subset of the managed service provider and handles the hosting of the mobile solution. Mobiqa is a managed mobility service provider, and Kony Solutions is an example of a mobile cloud provider.

■ Information technology (IT) service providers and system integrators: IT companies such as Infosys Technologies Limited take up mobile application development as well as integration with existing back-end solutions. They act as full-service agencies offering mobile design, development, build, quality testing, and maintenance. These service providers would, in turn, partner with different players to meet the end-to-end solution requirements of the enterprise.

■ Consulting firms: Consulting service firms have added mobile strategy consulting to enterprises in their service portfolio to benefit from the immense opportunities in consulting. With multiple options on mobile platforms and vendors, most enterprises first introduce a consulting firm to define the mobility roadmap, before actually building the mobile solution in-house or outsourcing the development to an agency.

■ Mobility research: Research firms, such as ABI Research, which have dedicated teams working on mobility research, constitute another group of the key players in the enterprise mobility space. The research publications in mobility from ABI Research, Gartner, and Forrester are some of the key references for enterprises, agencies, consulting firms, and all the major players in planning their business and technical roadmaps.

■ Miscellaneous players: Apart from the major players discussed so far, several others are part of the mobility landscape. A few examples of other players include academic institutions, training centers, and certification centers that have started offering courses on mobility, considering its immense potential in today's industry. A mobile marketing firm is another example of a specialized firm that assists the enterprise to effectively use the mobile channel for marketing.

2.4 Mobile Handsets

It is not just the screen size and the external design that make mobile handsets different. A number of properties of the mobile handset need to be considered while designing applications to run on mobile handsets. Some of the typical properties that define the device profile, in addition to screen features, are as follows:

- Operating system
- Processor speed
- Memory
- Connectivity
- App implementation language

There are multiple handset OSs in the market, and the following are some of the popular ones:

- Mac OS: This is a UNIX-based OS. Different flavors of this OS are available from Apple. For Mac desktops and laptops, the Mac OS Snow Leopard is popular, iPod Touch uses OS X, and iPhone uses iOS.
- Android: This is a Linux-based OS from Google. This is an open-source OS, unlike most others in the market. Although the project is open source, it has powerful features that make Android one of the most popular mobile OSs. The entire source code, including network interface and telephony stacks, has been published by Google under the Apache License.
- Windows CE: Windows Embedded Compact is an OS from Microsoft for embedded devices. Windows CE is not limited to use in mobile handsets. It finds use in several embedded systems and is the core for Windows Mobile OS, which is a more specialized version for use in mobile handsets.
- Windows Mobile: As the name suggests, this is an OS from Microsoft. It finds extensive use in enterprise mobile handsets, developed specifically for rugged use. The ability to interface easily with Microsoft back-end systems makes this OS quite popular in enterprises. Documents developed using Microsoft applications can also be downloaded and viewed by installing Microsoft packages in the Windows Mobile OS.
- BlackBerry OS: This OS from RIM is specifically for BlackBerry handsets. A desktop package is provided by RIM to synchronize BlackBerry handsets with data in desktops. The OS supports multitasking and also provides support for input devices, such as track wheel, track ball, and track pad, which are used in BlackBerry handsets.
- Symbian OS: Symbian OS is an open-source OS. It is maintained by Nokia. As one of the leaders in handset manufacturing, Nokia was able to easily popularize Symbian OS as a successor of the Nokia Series 60 (S60). The code for this OS was published under the Eclipse Public License.

■ Others: There are several other mobile OSs such as Palm OS or Garnet OS, developed by Palm Inc., Bada OS, developed by Samsung Electronics, and MeeGo, which is an open-source Linux-based OS.

Mobile platforms are discussed in more detail in the section on mobile application development. Next, let us look into processor speed, which is another key factor that determines the type of applications that can be executed on the handset. The faster the processor speed, the better the performance. ARM processors with 400–600 MHz speed are the most popular processors for smartphone devices. Intel has introduced several types of processors for mobile handsets, such as Bulverde that is popular in Samsung handsets, PXA series in Palm devices, and Atom series supporting 1600 MHz to 2 GHz for high-end mobile devices including tablets. It can be seen from the examples that the processing capabilities of mobile devices are continuously increasing, and soon applications that can be run on the desktop can be easily executed on mobile devices as well.

Memory is also a differentiating factor and has two key components: RAM and storage. Most smartphones currently have a 128- or 256-MB RAM, while handheld devices such as iPAD have versions that support a 512-MB RAM. Storage involves both built-in storage and external storage. Built-in storage is usually limited to a few gigabytes; however, some handsets come with 32 GB and 64 GB built-in storage. External storages are usually detachable universal serial bus-based drives and secure digital cards.

Connectivity is another major differentiator limiting the handset capabilities. While a telco service provider offers connections through general packet radio service or code division multiple access handsets, in most enterprise scenarios, there is a need to connect to the corporate network directly by using wireless fidelity (WiFi) and perform data exchange transactions that might require Bluetooth. While most of the modern handsets have peripherals to support WiFi and Bluetooth, still a vast majority of customers do not have these features.

The next challenge is selecting the programming language that must be used for developing applications for handsets on which the applications should execute. iPhone, iPad, and other products of Apple, such as iPod Touch, all need applications that are developed using Objective C. Xcode integrated development environment (IDE) can be used for the development of applications in Objective C for Apple handsets. Java is the most popular programming language for a variety of handset OSs. Java 2 Platform Micro Edition provides the required components for developing handset applications in Java. Java is the preferred platform for both BlackBerry and Android application development. Java IDEs, such as Eclipse, have plug-ins for specific handset development as well as device simulation for testing purposes. C++ or CPP is also being used for application development to be run on some of the Linux-based mobile OSs. For Microsoft mobile OSs, such as Windows Mobile, Visual Studio IDE from Microsoft is used for application development with specific software development kits. Multiplatform development solutions and cross-platform porting packages have reduced the effort in application development for multiple mobile OSs.

Handsets also differ in their battery life, device peripherals, display capabilities, supporting browsers, and other software packages available, such as e-mail, chat client, etc. Hence, a lot of factors need to be accounted when developing applications for multiple platforms as is the case with consumer mobility applications. With internal enterprise applications, restrictions could be imposed on the types of handsets that can be used.

2.5 Challenges in Enterprise Mobility

While in Chapter 1 we discussed the immense opportunities for mobile technology in the current industry, there are also some challenges that most enterprises face as part of mobility enablement. The following are the key challenges:

- Dependency on connection availability: With mobile applications, continuous connectivity between the client in the handset and the mobile server may not be possible due to signal loss from the telco service provider. So field agents and sales executives might not be able to perform field operations effectively using mobile handsets during periods of connection unavailability.
- Extending enterprise functionalities across device platforms: Some of the back-end solution vendors, such as Oracle, Siebel, and SAP, have mobile solutions that interact with the back-end server module. However, the mobile solutions are limited to specific mobile OSs. For example, some Siebel modules have mobile solutions for Windows Mobile, and some SAP modules already have solutions that offer access from iPhone. This limits the choice of handsets that can be used by enterprises for enterprise mobility enablement.
- Multiple interfaces to support: Another issue in integration is the number of back-end interfaces to be supported. The solution for mobile support will need to interface with the billing system, the accounting system, and the customer support system. These back ends may be based on different interface specifications and standards, which limit the cost effectiveness and timely delivery of a functionality-rich mobility solution.
- Extensibility issues: The current enterprise policies need to be extended, which would require approval and inputs from various units in the enterprise. Enterprise IT policy for mobile platforms, content aggregation, and steps for new platform or technology adoption need to be well planned and executed without disrupting the existing business process and technology.
- Utilizing peripheral capabilities: Most enterprises develop mobile applications just to copy their competitors or with a narrow vision of satisfying a

set of business requirements. Often, device peripherals, such as camera, radio frequency identification (RFID) or barcode scanner, global positioning system, storage media, etc., are not effectively utilized in the making of a mobile application. A well-planned mobile application should be user friendly and make best use of device capabilities in satisfying business requirements.

■ Security: This is an area of concern in most enterprises. One of the key responsibilities of the mobility architect is to work with the IT security group in ensuring that all sensitive data are stored and transmitted in a secure way when enabling mobile access to enterprise data and systems.

■ Additional expense to support the mobile channel: The costs of new hardware, software, integration, service, and support need to be identified, and a cost-benefit analysis should be performed by the enterprise. Careful consideration should be given to defining long-term goals, benefits, and expenses of mobile enablement.

■ Specialized display capabilities: Display features (such as specific user interface controls) available for devices might not be effectively utilized when the application is not carefully planned. Each platform has its own display capabilities, and only when the user-interface controls of a specific platform are leveraged, the best look and feel can be achieved in a mobile application.

■ System alerts: Mobiles make it easier to provide alerts to sales, field, or customer personal. They would not be continuously connected to a corporate network in the absence of mobile technology. Alerts can help in quick decision making and in assigning field service work in an optimal way. The challenge is to ensure that the back-end system can push alerts to the mobile device, rather than field personal checking or querying (pulling) the server for any alert message.

■ Prioritized data transmission: Sending low-priority data, such as signature captured, supplementary documents, etc., over a cost-effective channel is a major concern for enterprises. Thick mobile applications reduce some of the data overhead, with the ability to have supplementary reference documents bundled in the installation. Thick apps can also maintain data storage, reducing queries to the server on information that has already been collected. For thin applications, caching and throttling need to be well planned.

■ Diverse devices: Complexity in mobile technology is introduced through the huge diversity of factors involved in mobility. There are diverse platforms, form factors, development environments, and middleware as well as multiple vendors. The real challenge is to understand all the available options and find out the best option to meet short- and long-term goals. Diversity poses challenges not just in development but also in testing an application for proper execution across all the devices it is expected to support.

■ Open-source software systems: Another hurdle is in planning the support systems for mobility enablement. New mobile platforms are being frequently introduced in the market, and to reach all the customers, enterprises would want support solutions that not only support all the current popular platforms but also evolve to support new platforms and standards. Consumerization, which involves the use of a single device for personal and corporate needs, has increased the mobile device management requirements from support for a single platform to managing all device platforms of employees when connected to a corporate network.

■ Data synchronization: The time to synchronize data between the mobile client and the server is dependent on the size of data as well as the signal strength or transfer rate. If huge data synchronization is required each time the application is launched, it can considerably affect the operational efficiency of the field executive. Loss of connection, as already discussed, will also be a challenge and will require local storage in the device for offline mode of operation, followed by synchronization of stored data with the server when connectivity is established. With multiple back-end systems and data size, managed data synchronization at regular intervals, as well as auto-synchronization based on events, needs to be planned.

■ Performance issues: For mobile enablement, usually the current online or web gateways and back-end systems will be leveraged. This would mean a considerable increase in the traffic to existing business gateways and requests to back-end systems for data. Hence, the infrastructure would need enhancements to scale based on the load requirements. The anticipated user traffic needs to be estimated, and infrastructure planning should also consider user bursts and peak-load scenarios.

■ Location- and context-based service: Providing service based on the current location as well as providing context-sensitive information is a challenge. For consumers, location-based service may be in the form of a map from the current location to a store or context-specific promotion. For field executives, location information can be used to allocate new tasks based on the shortest distance to the next customer service address.

■ Enterprise mobility strategy: Enterprise mobility solutions are complex, as their development is based on diverse technologies and requires considerable customization as no single solution fits every user or industry. The more diverse and complex the environment, the higher the associated costs and risks. Enterprise mobile strategy involves smart planning and adoption of roadmaps and policies that enterprises can use to communicate anytime and anywhere, while managing to keep skyrocketing costs under control. Hence, it is essential to clearly define the enterprise mobility strategy before engaging in any significant business investment for mobility enablement.

The challenges listed can be fixed with careful planning and need to be accounted while defining the technical and business roadmaps for enterprise mobility enablement.

2.6 Conclusion

There is a strong trend for business transformation as more and more enterprise roles demand mobility for productive work execution. IDC predicts an average of 18%–25% growth across mobile enterprise application. Mobility enablement has been incorporated as a key business strategy by most enterprises for 2010 and 2011, due to its immense potential in achieving two essential enterprise goals: increased profits and reduced costs.

It is essential for the reader to understand the business and the technical terminologies used in enterprise mobility, which are used extensively in the succeeding chapters in order to explain the concepts and give a comprehensive coverage of enterprise mobility. This chapter is intended to introduce the reader to these terminologies and provide an overview of the building blocks of enterprise mobility. Hence, this chapter acts as a base platform on which the concepts of enterprise mobility will be constructed. Most of the items briefly covered in this chapter, such as mobile middleware and mobile platforms, are discussed in more detail in the chapters that follow.

Additional Reading

1. Rich Ling and Jonathan Donner. *Mobile Phones and Mobile Communication (Digital Media and Society Series)*. United Kingdom: Polity Press; 2009.
2. Keri Hayes. *Going Mobile: Building the Real-Time Enterprise with Mobile Applications That Work*, 1st edition. California: CMP; 2003.
3. Bhuvan Unhelkar. *Mobile Enterprise Transition and Management (Advanced and Emerging Communications Technologies)*, 1st edition. Florida: Auerbach Publications; 2009.

Chapter 3

Enterprise Mobility Adoption

Enterprise mobility solutions are complex, as their development is based on diverse technologies, and require considerable customization, as no single solution fits every user or industry. The more diverse and complex the environment is, the higher will be the associated costs and risks. Enterprise mobile strategy involves smart planning and adoption of policies that enterprises can use to communicate anytime and anywhere, while also managing costs to keep them from skyrocketing out of control. This chapter provides an overview of the aspects to be considered while defining enterprise mobile adoption strategy.

3.1 Introduction

Enterprise mobility provides a threefold advantage of increased productivity, enhanced revenue, and reduced costs. Increased productivity is achieved by improved efficiency or effectiveness of mobile workers and better communication or collaboration that helps to turn downtime into uptime. Faster invoicing, automation, faster workflows, better decision making, and increased customer satisfaction lead to enhanced revenue. Factors such as telephony service, converging single-purpose devices, and significant reduction in data entry errors will bring about a reduction in costs through mobility enablement. Hence, several factors could drive the enterprise toward mobility enablement. The critical component that should not be missed by enterprises in the attempt to reap the benefits from mobility is to ensure that a mobility strategy that can address the short- and long-term goals of the enterprise is defined.

Enterprise mobility corporate strategy has two components:

■ Customer-centric mobility to increase profits: This is achieved by
  – Drawing more customers
  – Probing more frequent visits
  – Driving larger sales per visit
  – Driving more shared revenue from channel partners
  – Lowering the costs of serving customers
  – Drawing customers from more access points
■ Operation, distribution, and employee-centric mobility to reduce costs: This is achieved by
  – Improving efficiency
  – Making the overall process more effective and accurate
  – Achieving higher employee satisfaction
  – Providing more access points to enterprise data
  – Reducing the effort involved in operations and distribution

Many companies develop mobile solutions based on competitor offerings and mobility vendor offerings rather than their unique business needs and resulting mobile strategies. Thin, thick, and hybrid mobile applications, enterprise mobile platforms, and mobile cloud services are all available across a range of budgets and timing needs, based on the availability of the right resources. In general, there is no single mobile strategy that is suitable for all enterprises. The right approach is developed by aligning a set of key success factors against the business requirements, with due consideration on the environment variables. This chapter provides an overview of the ideal approach and the key factors to be accounted while defining an effective enterprise mobile adoption strategy.

Information is the cornerstone for preparing an effective enterprise strategy. Preparation of a mobility roadmap ensures that the required information is collected for defining short- and long-term strategies. There are several challenging questions from the business and in the technical context that the strategy team needs to answer in the mobility space. An effective mobility roadmap offers insights to address the challenges in the business and the technical context.

3.2 Key Decision Factors in Defining a Mobility Adoption Strategy

An enterprise runs into several hurdles when defining a mobility adoption strategy, with different stakeholders having their own view on the option to follow and with various decision factors that are vital for the success of enterprise mobility adoption. Some of the key factors that need to be accounted while defining the enterprise mobile strategy are discussed in this section.

3.2.1 Multiplatform Support

For enterprise applications developed for employees, the usual approach was to use a single platform. For example, the Motorola handset with Windows Mobile operating system was popular for mobile applications used by field personnel for scanning, and information technology employees used BlackBerry handsets to use the "push" and "security" features offered by the BlackBerry enterprise server (BES). This trend is changing with consumerization in the enterprise, and most enterprises allow its employees to use personal handsets for executing and accessing office applications. This has led to the need for a multiplatform approach in developing applications for employees.

For consumer applications developed by the enterprise, a multiplatform approach is mandatory. Shopping applications developed by retail giants such as Kmart and Walmart required multiple platforms to reach a wider consumer segment. Multiplatform support is a requirement for consumer applications in all domains such as telecommunication, health care, energy, utilities, and so on.

For telcos, targeting the top 80% of consumer handsets in the initial launch is suggested, and for enterprises, targeting iPhone, Android, and BlackBerry in the initial launch of consumer mobile applications is suggested. The devices supported need to be extended over multiple phases to incorporate additional platforms covering at least 95% of the target consumer segment.

Specific platforms should be adopted in the initial launch, and the evolution strategy needs to be planned to ensure maximum reuse in development. The usual approach adopted by enterprises shows the first launch to target iPhone and iPad, with applications for other smartphones following shortly in a few months. Multiple approaches to multiplatform development are discussed in Chapter 8. The roadmap for multiplatform support and development and the test methodology used for multiplatform support are critical factors to be looked into while defining an enterprise mobile adoption strategy.

3.2.2 Application Type

The application type(s) that will address the enterprise's requirements needs to be determined as part of the strategy. Thick client, thin client, hybrid, short message service (SMS), and unstructured supplementary services data (USSD) are some of the application types. While thick application provides superior user experience and is the most popular application type, most enterprises follow a staged approach of adoption starting with mobile enablement of their current web site, followed by other supporting channels such as SMS, thick applications, etc. The application type is dependent on the business and the technical requirements to be addressed in the application. For example, a mobile commerce application for shopping looks more attractive with a thick or hybrid application solution, which is more engaging for the customer, and to satisfy a technical requirement for a field application that needs offline support (work on the application even in the absence of connectivity), a thick client would be required.

The web- or browser-based thin application is the first step for most enterprises when introducing mobility, where access to enterprise web sites through the mobile is offered as an extension to their current web framework. Having a mobile web framework helps in the development of hybrid applications in the case of downloaded applications. It is the usual practice to delegate security functionalities as much as possible to the server side, including the need to comply with the Payment Card Industry Data Security Standard (PCI DSS) for payments from mobile applications; hybrid applications come in handy for security delegation to the server.

SMS, multimedia messaging service, and USSD can act as an additional marketing channel, along with thin and thick applications, in pushing information on promotions, discounts, and offers. These could also be used to provide information for thick application download when a new version is launched in an application store or to give the web link for accessing a thin or browser-based application.

3.2.3 Deployment

Mobile server deployment is another decision point to be carefully considered. The thin or browser-based application will require a server to format content and present it based on the device requesting the web page, while a thick mobile application would require a server component for data synchronization, analytics, and business intelligence.

The following are the typical deployment options for a mobile server that is mostly a middleware platform but also acts as a multiplatform server:

- Enterprise deployed: In this option, the mobile middleware infrastructure is owned and maintained by the enterprise itself. For large enterprises where infrastructure cost is not a concern and for server components that need high security due to handling of confidential information, this is the popular option. It is more costly compared with other options but offers maximum control on the infrastructure used to host or deploy the mobile server.
- Single-client hosted: In this option, the enterprise decides to host the server externally, thus reducing the initial costs related to building the infrastructure. The enterprise uses the infrastructure offered by a hosting service provider that offers a dedicated instance for each enterprise. In scenarios where a mobile enterprise application platform (MEAP) or a mobile consumer application platform (MCAP) is involved, a dedicated platform or middleware is available to support each enterprise in this option.
- Multiclient hosted: This is similar to the single-client hosted option where the server is hosted externally and not within the enterprise. The difference is that the hosted service provider uses the same mobile middleware instance to support multiple enterprise or small- and medium-business segments. This

option is popular with small- and medium-business segments where generating funds for achieving functional objectives is limited.

■ Managed service: This option involves complete outsourcing where the requirements are shared by the enterprise with a managed service vendor. The managed service vendor does all the development and deployment for a predetermined billing model. How the managed service vendor does the deployment is not of concern to the enterprise as long as the requirements are satisfied. Hence, managed service vendors can outsource the activity, work on a single-client or multiclient-hosted model with a middleware vendor, or host the server in their own data center.

3.2.4 Functionalities

The functionalities that need to be achieved and when they have to be made available are key inputs in defining the strategy. Budget constraints and functionalities anticipated in the mobile application can change a mobility roadmap that can be covered under a short-term strategy to extend to a medium- or long-term strategy. The business team needs to prepare the detailed list of functional requirements to be achieved and all the functionalities required in a specific release within a predefined time frame, based on the customer or market needs.

The functional requirements would involve user experience requirements, which at times can be tough to achieve, based on the middleware and rendering components used in multiplatform development. Applications, with multiple dependent integration requirements, that require a short time to launch can also lead to project deployment challenges. The business roadmap needs to be realistic in order to define an appropriate adoption strategy for the enterprise.

3.2.5 Comprehensive Security

Security is a key concern especially because the mobile server integrates with multiple enterprise systems. A comprehensive security framework is to be identified as part of defining the technical requirements for implementation. The presence of regulatory compliance standards, as in health care, m-commerce, etc., leads to the need for considering security as a key decision factor in mobility adoption strategy.

Enterprise mobile security has two key components:

■ Enterprise system security ensures that the server framework and the mobile network are secure. This ensures security in connection, communication, and data handling. BlackBerry leads the U.S. market in enterprise deployments because of the security advantage provided by BES. BlackBerry is not the only device targeted by the enterprise, and most enterprises now require a security framework that supports multiple platforms.

■ Commercial off-the-shelf (COTS) products are used to develop the enterprise system security framework. A variety of off-the-shelf products are available for addressing the mobile enterprise security requirements. Some of the popular ones are Sybase's Afaria for mobile device management, mobile security enterprise edition from Kaspersky lab for solving the issue of mobile antimalware and spyware, and Mobility XE from NetMotion Wireless for secure continuous remote access to enterprise applications and resources from mobile clients. Custom development of security platforms is also adopted by some enterprises, although it is best to procure COTS products and integrate them to build the mobile security platform.

■ Device and application security ensures that the mobile device and applications are secured from attacks. It includes authentication of the device, security of the content in the device, and device features such as encryption to ensure secure communication. The device and application security ecosystem consists of communication and transaction security, authentication and authorization, subscriber identity module (SIM) card security, security of software applications running on the handset, the phone's physical security, and end user security.

■ To address the most various threats and vulnerabilities, it is required to adopt multiple mobile security solutions. The most common practice followed by enterprises is to continuously assess the security risk and implement appropriate security measures to address threats.

Mobile enterprise security requirements for applications involving financial transactions (banking or financial domain) are much more critical in compliance of standards compared to that in other domains. An example of this is the mobile application compliance to PCI DSS when a financial transaction with a card is involved. PCI DSS relates to not just the financial domain but all types of m-commerce applications that handle information on customer payment cards. Examples of other policies include HIPAA, Sarbanes-Oxley, etc.

3.2.6 COTS versus Custom Development

One major decision that is critical for technical strategy in enterprises is whether to build the mobile solution in-house or to customize and integrate using COTS components. There are COTS middleware platforms and tools that support multiplatform development. For a rich user interface (UI) and to leverage the capabilities of a particular platform, custom development for a specific platform is performed, and porting using cross-platform built tools is done based on requirements. There are several middleware platforms offered by vendors such as Sybase, Kony Solutions, Antenna, Netbiscuits, etc., as well as tools such as J2ME polish, Cognito, Vaultus, etc.

The right choice of the platform and the tool is based on the devices to be supported, the type of application, the back-end integration, and the UI features

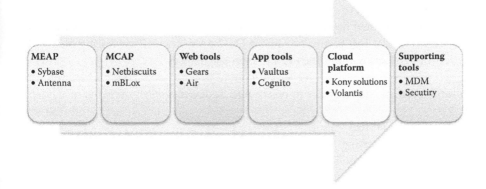

Figure 3.1   Major mobility solution categories where COTS products are available.

required. A detailed evaluation of the vendor based on the requirements is to be performed before selecting a specific vendor for COTS or custom development. There are multiple MEAPs, MCAPs, mobile web tools, and packaged tools for application development to choose from, as shown in Figure 3.1. This necessitates evaluation of the vendor offerings against enterprise requirements.

COTS solutions can reduce the time for development and also the maintenance complexity. However, there are license costs and intellectual property issues when using COTS solutions. The right vendor can not only support the business roadmap of the enterprise but also provide guidance and cost-effective options in realizing the requirements. Most enterprises buy COTS solutions and then customize the solution according to enterprise requirements.

3.2.7 Device Diversity Testing

Device diversity testing is important for mobile applications due to the wide range of device profiles that need to be supported for each of the mobile platforms. The device profile sets many constraints on the mobile application. While testing mobile devices, the following factors should be taken into consideration:

- Screen size
- Type of input devices available
- Resource constraints
- Diverse usage environments
- Limited user experience
- Physical movement of users

Local device diversity testing can be done using an in-house or outsourced laboratory with a limited number of handsets, where specific handsets categorized based on the mobile platform version are used. A staged test strategy for each platform needs to be defined for effective testing. Remote device diversity testing can be performed using multiplatform test services offered by vendors such as DeviceAnywhere. Test platforms such as DeviceAnywhere allow testing on a wide variety of handsets without the need to own the devices.

Device diversity testing is covered in detail in Chapter 9. At a higher level, the following are the main aspects to be covered in device diversity testing:

- UI look-and-feel testing
- Alignment testing
- Device native application programming interface (API) testing
- Device control testing
- Additional peripheral testing

3.2.8 Back-End Network Optimization

Mobile thick applications and web solutions need to be optimized to ensure quick delivery of quality content. The issue most mobility architects face is to include the mobile as an additional channel when the back-end enterprise system is already having a lot of latency in processing requests from existing channels. Running a separate server instance for responding to requests from mobile devices or using a middleware or service bus to queue messages is a common practice to solve latency issues. The back-end integration systems also need to be optimized to handle more requests. Throttling requests and caching data in mobile servers also are ways to ensure that the back-end systems are not overloaded with requests.

Network optimization is at times not given the relevant priority while formulating an enterprise mobile adoption strategy. This leads to complaints from clients on access delays and timeout in clients, when the actual issue would not be related to the mobile server or client but caused by back-end systems or connection network. Performance testing of the existing systems and assessment of the load needs of the mobile channel will help identifying additional investment requirements to enhance the existing infrastructure and ensuring their implementation within project timelines.

Cloud-based solutions for back-end systems are effective in enhancing the network capability to handle additional load. With the additional load requirements of mobile channels and based on advancements in cloud-based solutions, there is an increased interest across enterprises to switch to the cloud-based offering for server hosting needs. Hosting of the mobile server on a cloud is also an offering from the leading mobile middleware vendors such as Kony solutions to meet on-demand scaling.

3.2.9 On-Demand Scaling

The potential for significant increases in mobile content views as the subscriber or customer base increases needs to be estimated, and the middleware hosting or deployment environment should be able to scale to peak demands. For enterprises, this may not be a major issue due to limited users per unit of time. However, telcos and enterprises that provide hosting services for multiple other enterprises need to incorporate on-demand scaling as an important factor in their mobile strategy.

The need to offer on-demand scaling can be explained from the example of ticketmaster.com, which sells tickets using the online channel. Consider that a mobile client is available for mobile booking of tickets. When tickets for a pop star concert are open for sale, the number of users trying to block the tickets will be very high initially and then decrease. Having a mobile server framework that satisfies the peak demand would mean underutilization of infrastructure when the demand decreases; on the contrary, not having the required infrastructure for meeting the peak demand will lead to issues in booking and server-down scenario, resulting in dissatisfied customers. So the mobile server framework should be able to perform on-demand scaling, which involves both scaling up and scaling down as per load requirements.

3.2.10 Leveraging Mobile Capabilities

The device capabilities such as camera, Bluetooth print, touch, tilt, scroll, etc., need to be effectively utilized in delivering a unique experience to the customer. There are certain inherent features that are part of every mobile device, which need to be leveraged as much as possible in the solution offering. Mobile applications have the capability to work in an offline mode when there is no connectivity, which needs to be utilized in thick mobile applications where the user can work on the client, and the data will be synchronized with the server when connectivity is established.

For example, product information search using the image of a product or a bar code requires the use of camera APIs in the thick application. Enterprise mobile applications for inventory management applications use scanner APIs (a scanner as an add-on peripheral is attached to the mobile for this purpose) for decoding product tags. Global positioning system (GPS)-based nearest-store locator functionality is a common capability in most retail store applications that leverage the GPS system available in smartphones.

3.2.11 User Experience

A rich user experience is a winning factor for all types of consumer mobile applications. Wireframes should be analyzed for look and feel, ease of navigation, etc., as part of the processes in the requirements phase itself. The need to offer a consistent look and feel in all mobile platforms can be a challenge due to inherent features in one platform that might be missing in another platform. Also the use of cross-platform development tools puts considerable restriction on the UI, due to which several consumer applications are still developed using platform-specific APIs to get as much jazzy UI as possible rather than on an abstracted common development environment or with cross-compiler tools.

iPhone and iPad applications usually offer the best experience in consumer mobile applications, which is the main reason why enterprises and telcos usually choose this platform for the initial launch of their thick application solution. For enterprises' internal applications, ease of navigation and minimal steps for an operation are more important than offering an appealing look and feel.

3.2.12 Maintainability

The mobile solution should support system upgrades involving functionality enhancements or support for additional mobile platforms without changing the overall architecture. This is a critical requirement for consumer mobile applications where specific platform support would be introduced in stages (e.g., launching an iPhone application first, followed by BlackBerry a month later). For some enterprises and telcos that have multiple applications, the recent trend is to offer an umbrella application from which the capabilities in the other applications can be accessed. Hence, the integration interfaces should ensure reuse.

Maintainability is also impacted by the increasingly large number of devices to be supported with multiple version support in individual platforms. To reduce the complexity of maintenance and ensure maximum reuse, it is a common practice to use the multiplatform-integrated development environment offered by MEAPs or MCAPs.

3.2.13 Smooth Integration

The mobile server has to integrate with multiple subsystems. This should be a key factor in evaluating the middleware platforms and tools to be used in developing the enterprise mobile solution. Most mobile platforms support integration with popular interfaces such as web service, Siebel, and SAP. So time and cost of integration can be considerably reduced by choosing the right platform and tools.

From the enterprise perspective, this will be a key requirement as the enterprise will already have a preferred vendor for back-end systems such as Siebel-based inventory systems, a mobile platform to support Siebel integration or SAP-based customer relationship management, and the requirement to have support for SAP interfaces, and so on. The general trend is to expose web services, and in scenarios where a standard COTS middleware is not used, the general requirement is to work with a set of web APIs.

3.2.14 Enterprise Roadmap

The mobility adoption strategy is prepared to satisfy a specific roadmap that the enterprise wants to achieve. The enterprise needs to first formulate a set of well-defined goals to be achieved in the short, medium, and long terms. Then based on the roadmap, the adoption strategy is to be planned, keeping into consideration both the business requirements as well as the technical capabilities, both internal and external.

The mobility roadmap needs to account for planned enhancements to the solution. The possibility of opening up the mobile solution for customization and use by other enterprises or partners and the possibility of extending the platform to support enterprise applications and customer applications other than the current mobile solutions planned for the short term are use cases to be considered when preparing a roadmap. It can be seen that each of these goals could have a significant impact on the adoption strategy in terms of investment options that can influence the solution approach used in the strategy.

Defining the roadmap would require data collection from a variety of stakeholders, especially the end users. The data collection exercise helps to ensure that the roadmap achieves the perceived goals of the company and does not lead to unnecessary expenditure on an unfruitful business venture. Strategy definition brings out the best approach for achieving the mobility roadmap.

3.2.15 Other Considerations

Choosing the right mobile partners for solution development, middleware needs, and integration requirements is also important in addressing the complexity in technology and realizing long-term business goals. Hence, a critical part of the strategy is to identify the right partners for realizing the roadmap. Switching partners might turn out to be expensive. Hence, vendor evaluation needs to be covered in the strategy definition exercise.

The application types based on the end user targeted by the enterprise would also influence the solution identified in the technology strategy. The middleware platform options for enterprise applications (MEAP) can be different from those for consumer applications (MCAP). The investment needs would also get impacted, and the strategy might have a tactical solution defined to meet immediate needs, while a separate team works on the long-term optimal solution.

Targeted mobility channels (SMS, mobile web, thick app, etc.) and the timelines for the launch of the channels can also have an impact on strategy definition. As can be seen from this section, there are several secondary decision factors that can be key inputs in the enterprise mobility adoption strategy.

3.3 Steps to Define Mobility Adoption Strategy

The process of defining mobility adoption strategy is usually a six-step process (as shown in Figure 3.2):

- ■ Define scope or roadmap: The first activity is to either define the scope of the strategy definition exercise or outline a complete business roadmap. For some enterprises, the strategy definition will have a limited scope of simply identifying the best way to satisfy a mobility requirement, while for others, the

Figure 3.2   Steps in defining mobility adoption strategy.

strategy definition would be expected to satisfy a business roadmap. Hence, the scope or roadmap that has to be addressed by the mobility strategy should be clearly defined.

■ Detail requirements: The next activity is to detail the business requirements for the specific milestones in the scope or the roadmap. This activity helps in identifying the critical requirements and spreading the goals across multiple releases that correspond to realistically achievable milestones, matching market needs.

■ Analyze as-is framework: The mobility requirements in most scenarios are extensions of the existing functionality in the mobile channel. Hence, a proper analysis of the current framework is required to identify how best the existing investments involving software, hardware, and other resource investments can be optimally leveraged for enabling the mobile channel.

■ Outline key decision factors: As already discussed, there are multiple decision factors that need to be accounted in the mobility adoption strategy. The decision factors that are relevant to the enterprise scenario need to be identified and outlined for investigation.

■ Define to-be framework: A critical evaluation of as-is framework against business requirements and key decision factors leads to the definition of to-be framework. Hence, the to-be framework will be a logical extension of the current (as-is) framework and will satisfy the business requirements, taking into consideration the key decision factors.

■ Define adoption strategy: This is the culminating step for coming up with a mobility adoption strategy that works on the envisioned to-be framework in identifying the right milestones, right product vendors, right project plan, etc., and in creating an end-to-end adoption strategy.

3.4 Conclusion

Companies should not plan mobility enablement based on a narrow vision of competitor offerings and partner vendor offerings. When planning on mobility enablement, the focus should be on the unique business needs and the resulting mobile strategies. Thin, thick, and hybrid mobile applications, enterprise mobile platforms, and mobile cloud services are all available across a range of budgets and timing needs, based on the availability of the right resources. In general, there is no single mobile strategy that is suitable for all enterprises.

This chapter provides an overview of the decision factors and the steps involved in defining an effective enterprise mobile adoption strategy. It introduces the reader to the process followed and the thought process involved in mobility adoption planning.

Additional Reading

1. Keri Hayes. *Going Mobile: Building the Real-Time Enterprise with Mobile Applications That Work,* 1st edition. California: CMP; 2003.
2. Bhuvan Unhelkar. *Mobile Enterprise Transition and Management (Advanced and Emerging Communications Technologies),* 1st edition. Florida: Auerbach Publications; 2009.

Chapter 4

Mobile as an Effective Marketing Channel

Several features of the mobile make it an effective channel for marketing. There are several options for a marketer to utilize the mobile for marketing. With the growing number of mobile users, marketing using a mobile device (henceforth referred to as mobile marketing) has become an effective mass-marketing medium. This chapter provides an overview of the features and options that the marketer can leverage in mobile marketing.

4.1 Introduction

With more than 250 million mobile subscribers in the United States and about 3 billion short message services (SMSs) sent every month in the United Kingdom, there is no doubt that penetration of mobiles in the consumer segment will facilitate its use as an effective channel for mass marketing. The mobile is a personal device that is always carried by the user, and this makes it a powerful instrument for the marketer to reach the customer anywhere and anytime. Mobile marketing can be defined as the application of marketing communication techniques through mobile phones in promoting goods, services, and ideas.

Enterprises today are using the mobile to create web- and application-based advertising to get instant responses for sales promotions. The mobile channel has proved to be very effective for delivering direct marketing, where the contact information is provided in the mobile advertisement, and a push-to-click option is offered to immediately make a call to the support desk or to make a purchase.

Mobile marketers can also identify whether the messages to consumers are actually being read. In fact, most of the major brands have included mobiles in their integrated marketing communication (IMC) strategy, and mobile marketing has grown to be an indispensible part of marketing brands that target the youth segment.

However, it needs to be noted that mobile marketing is in its infancy. This is because current mobile marketers are limited to SMS or multimedia messaging service (MMS) and mobile web applications in most of the developing countries. However, in developed countries, some of the popular brands such as Adidas and Microsoft are increasingly using the mobile medium as a source of mainstream advertising. The current industry demands a coherent mobile marketing strategy that is fully integrated with the primary marketing strategy of the enterprise.

Mobile operators are now switching from consumer-funded models to advertiser-funded models for digital content. The previous, but prevalent, model involved charging of consumers to buy digital content from mobile portals. The new change involves operators sharing mobile media consumption insights with the enterprise to have advertiser-funded models. There are several mobile marketing organizations that perform the function of aggregating and buying mobile media in the same way that online media is bought and planned. Research has shown that consumers have only a short attention span in the mobile context. So mobile marketing communication must be compact, must have a high impact to catch the attention of the consumer, and must be repeated to facilitate recall. The diverse screen sizes of mobiles can make some communication messages inappropriate for proper view on the mobile handset. Hence, marketers should provide mobile solutions that render the mobile advertisement content suitable for the requirements of the mobile in which the advertisement will be displayed.

This chapter provides an overview of the mobile marketing fundamentals. It covers the features that the marketer must keep in mind while evaluating the option of using the mobile as a channel for marketing. The different techniques of mobile marketing are also covered so that the marketer can choose the most appropriate tools in developing a mobile marketing plan.

4.2 Key Features of Mobile to Be Accounted in Marketing

Like any other marketing medium, the mobile also has a set of unique features that makes it useful for marketing specific types of products and services. A summary of these features is shown in Figure 4.1. The marketer needs to understand and account these features not only while developing the marketing plan but also while

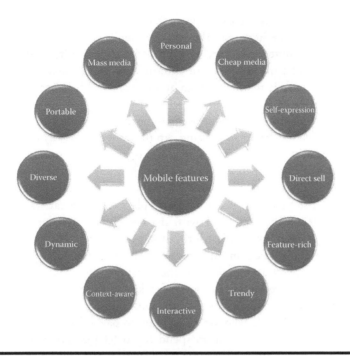

Figure 4.1   Features of a mobile from the marketing perspective.

executing the same. Let us analyze each of these features and understand their relevance in mobile marketing:

- Personal: The mobile can be considered a personal device because of the following factors:
  - The mobile is not shared with others, not even with friends and family, unlike a computer or TV, which would be used by others too.
  - The mobile is carried everywhere by the person who owns it. The mobile, unlike other marketing media, makes the customer accessible to the marketer anytime and anywhere.
  - The user of the mobile personalizes the initial screen, the screen saver, and the features.
  - The mobile stores personal details such as contact information, pictures, and media, which could be personal to the owner and not something that would be shared with the closest friends or family members. This necessarily implies that the marketer can get the information of a person's preference without intruding into the personal details available on the mobile. By sending different types of advertisements and promotions, the marketer will be able to clearly understand the marketing techniques to which the person or a specific market segment responds.

■ Cheap media: There are two aspects to this feature. One is affordability and the other is marketing costs. The cost of a mobile is much less compared with that of a computer, a laptop, or a TV. This affordability leads to the wide adoption of the mobile. Also an enterprise or small–medium business can work out a mobile marketing plan at a low cost. This is because sending an SMS costs much less and offers a wider reach compared with advertising in other mass media. However, it needs to be noted that mobile web-based and thick application-based advertising can turn out to be really expensive.

■ Self-expression: The mobile is a medium of self-expression. The color of the handset, the ringtone the person sets, and the wallpaper the person uses show the identity of the person. Most often, persons download wallpapers that show their self-identity. A car lover will place a trendy car wallpaper on the mobile screen. The same goes with the sleek looks and the branded handsets a person buys, which is a form of self-expression. The marketer can use the information based on the browsing pattern of the consumer and on the mobile commerce transactions of the consumer to get an idea of the self-identity of the user and use targeted marketing to show advertisements that will catch the attention of the user and will translate into a purchase.

■ Direct selling: People who are not willing to pay a dime for software applications on a PC are willing to spend $2 to $3 for application downloads from mobile App Stores. The same is true with music and other media downloads that people want for free on their PCs but are willing to pay for use on mobiles. As the mobile device is carried along most of the time, it can lead to impulse purchases, which cannot be the case with other marketing mediums. Compelling mobile advertisement banners can easily translate into a purchase through the mobile. A recent survey on shopping patterns during Christmas sales showed that a major proportion of teenagers in the United States made Christmas purchases using the mobile, and the percentage of purchases through mobiles on a festive day or when there are sales offers keeps increasing year after year. Mobile commerce has significantly increased in the past few years.

■ Feature-rich: The mobile device is feature-rich. With the flexibility and user experience offered in recent smartphones, marketers are able to create applications and advertisements that are not only attractive but also addictive. Mobile advertisements are mostly animated, and with widget-based applications and advertisement content management systems, marketers can keep changing the advertisements on a scheduled basis. Feature richness leads to the ability of developing advertisements that can easily catch the attention of the target customers, and it offers different ways to package the overall marketing message.

■ Trendy: Mobile handsets are trendy. For many, it is a fashion accessory. With the PC, the TV, and other mass media, the focus is on the features that are offered in the electronic gadget, with look and feel mostly being a secondary factor; however, in the case of mobile handsets, the most important factor is how fashionable and appealing the handset is. When the user makes a hypertext transfer protocol request to the enterprise server, the model of the device making the request can easily be identified based on the information in the request header. This information can be utilized to format the content to suit the specific handset. In addition to basic formatting of media and text, the marketer can also use color and designs that match with the specific handset model to directly appeal to the mind-set of the customer. Thus, the marketer can effectively exploit the technology by working with the development team to create marketing presentations that utilize a generic database of templates to be applied for specific handset models.

■ Interactive: Current smartphone applications are interactive and can be used to get the customer to make repeated visits to a web site or an application for purchase. Mobile advertisements are also being implemented as games where the level of interaction is more, and the promotion is presented as a gift the customer deserves for participating in a competition organized in a mobile application. Interactivity can also be in the form of the user selecting his or her favorite items for tracking in a shopping cart and the marketer offering promotions based on the items the user keeps in the tracking list. The level of interactivity differs based on the type of mobile marketing technique that is applied. The different types of mobile marketing are discussed in Section 4.3.

■ Context-aware: Context-based real-time marketing is a unique feature offered in mobile marketing. For example, a retail application that identifies the location of the customer in the store by mapping the person's movement within the store layout can provide context-based promotions based on the time spent in front of a specific category of items. These interactive applications provide context-based advertisements and promotions specific to the user by understanding their requirements. Context-based real-time promotions have quick impact and the potential to translate into an immediate purchase. Another type of context-aware feature using location information from the global positioning system (GPS) is to give the customer details of a nearby fast-food restaurant when the customer is taking a long drive, as identified by the location change information on the GPS. Thus, marketers have a key advantage by offering context-aware marketing with the mobile. A new variation is the augmented reality in mobiles, which is also being utilized by mobile marketers.

■ Dynamic: Mobile marketing solutions (mobile advertisement platforms) offer the capability to provide dynamic rule-based marketing. For example, the marketer can set a rule in the system to alter the discount dynamically based on the level of sales. If the number of sales is more than expected, the discount for sales promotion can be brought down, or after the first-day sales, the rule algorithm can dynamically update the advertisement to show a higher discount without the marketer changing the advertisement context as in static advertising mediums. An example of the same is depicted in Figure 4.2, which shows the value of discount changing based on the rule set in the advertisement platform.

◾ Diverse: Device diversity is a key feature that the marketer has to keep in mind while working on a mobile marketing framework. If a specific web page promotion is designed, it needs to be noted that the promotion will not show up the same way on all the mobile handsets. The way the marketing message is displayed is dependent on the capabilities supported by the mobile handset. Hence, the marketer needs to ensure that a rendering engine, which presents the data based on the capabilities of the handset, is used in front of the mobile advertisement platform to reformat the message based on the best template that suits the handset. There are multiple commercial off-the-shelf products that are available to solve this issue.

◾ Portable: The mobile handset is portable. This feature brings with it many capabilities that can be exploited by the marketer. Let us take an example to illustrate an application of portability. The mobile is effectively used by many to kill boredom during travel. This could be utilized to provide information to the customers on various products. To be more specific, many commuters while using the London Underground Rail Service have switched to the use of iPhones and iPads to read the morning news, and this change in behavior could be used by marketers to provide targeted advertisements in mobile news sites.

Rule 1 : For Week 1   Rule 2 : For Week 2

Figure 4.2   Rule-based sales promotion (illustrative and not an actual promotion from Dixie Plastic).

▪ Mass media: Mobile is a mass medium, and at the same time, it can be used to do customized and targeted marketing. Unlike other mass media where a single message goes to all, mobile marketing necessarily redefines mass media, as here the message can be easily customized based on the specific user. As already discussed, the customization could be handset-specific, rule-based, or based on the customer's self-identity.

4.3 Types of Mobile Marketing

There are several types of mobile marketing that are adopted by marketers. The 20 most popular types of mobile marketing are discussed below.

1. SMS: SMS is a text of a maximum of 160 characters, which is sent using an SMS gateway. SMS-based communication of marketing a message is widely used in developing countries. This is because a large majority of handsets in developing countries are of the legacy type, and they do not have advanced capabilities that are available in smartphones. The advantage of SMS is that it has a standard format, and hence, it does not require device-specific rendering. SMS-based marketing can take the following different forms:
   ▪ SMSs to stay in touch with customer: For example, an enterprise focusing on share trading can send proactive daily alerts on the best-suggested shares to purchase.
   ▪ SMSs to promote messages: For example, a retailer can send a message alert of the "promotion for the day" to customers who have a loyalty card.
   ▪ SMSs for market research: SMS messages can be used to get feedback, vote on items of interest, and responses on customer preferences.
   ▪ SMS to attract site visits: SMSs can be sent on headlines from a mobile web site, which would attract the customer to visit the site.
   ▪ SMSs to get leads on prospective customers: Generic SMSs for getting more details can be sent to a large set of mobile users with the details on the customer desk number. This technique helps in filtering out prospective customers from a generic set of mobile subscribers. It needs to be noted that there is a limit on the number of characters in an SMS message, and hence, the marketing message should be carefully drafted to ensure that it is appealing to the target audience.
   ▪ SMSs as a source of revenue: Many telcos and enterprises have the service of providing paid subscription for SMS alerts on dating, daily horoscope, news, etc.
2. MMS: MMS adds the capability to send media images and video rather than the limited text offered through the SMS. However, the MMS created in one handset model may not be entirely compatible with the capabilities of another handset. The telco rendering or adaptation framework plays a key

role in determining the way the MMS is displayed on a specific handset. Marketers can use the MMS to send slide presentations and video presentations with embedded text and images to intended recipients.

3. Mobile search: Search-based marketing in mobiles is similar to web-search marketing. By effective development techniques and by paying search engine providers, marketers can ensure that customers' search for an item leads them to the intended site of the enterprise. Care needs to be taken that a mobile web site is in place, which provides the customer an easy browse-and-buy option. Replicating the existing web site for a PC for view on the mobile is a definite situation for failure. The small screen size in the mobile, the rendering of content based on device capability, and formatting web site content to have limited text for easy browsing should be key considerations when mobile search is selected as an option for marketing. Mobile search can be purchased on a pay-per-click basis, if the intent is to have the search lead to an affiliate page that has a higher probability of getting hit during the search.

4. Mobile games: It is also known as Mobile Advergaming or Ad-funded mobile game. Mobile games are increasingly being used for advertising and promotional purposes. For example, a leading brand of soft drinks launched a mobile game that had weekly prize giveaways and a top-score board. The game had an average download of approximately 400,000 every week when the campaign was launched. It is not just enterprises that are using mobile games for advertising. Some of the recent movies have also started launching games, which prompt the user to download applications to solve a puzzle, rescue someone, or complete a challenge—all based on scenes in the movie. The interactive capability offered in mobile games can be an effective way for the marketer to promote a product or service. There is increased recall and a higher chance of repeated visits when mobile gaming is used for mobile marketing.

5. Mobile wallpaper and screen savers: Wallpaper and screen savers in mobiles work in the same way as those in PCs. Wallpapers and themes can be released by brands for promotional purposes. A car lover would place his or her favorite brand of car as the wallpaper on the handset, and the same would increase customer loyalty. Free downloads for loyal customers and revenue from paid downloads are applicable in mobile wallpaper- and screen saver-based marketing. Downloads of brand avatars to reflect the customer's personality match with the brand, and this has been a huge hit in mobile marketing campaigns conducted by many well-known brands. GeoPix, the location-based wallpaper tool launched by Myxer, which allows the user to choose mobile wallpapers for specific locations and which then changes the wallpaper image dynamically based on location, is an example of an innovation happening in the use of mobile wallpaper. Marketers need to come up with such innovations that can trigger massive downloads by the customer, and they can utilize the framework for brand promotion.

6. Mobile banners: Mobile banners are similar to PC banner advertisements, with a smaller size to fit on mobile screens. Banner advertisements need to be carefully linked with customer preferences such as keywords searched, sites visited, etc. Mobile banner advertisements are priced on a cost-per-click basis, and on clicking the banner the user is redirected to the mobile web site of the concerned enterprise. Most of the big players including Google and Microsoft are using banner advertising to reach customers. Google entered the mobile banner advertisement market with the launch of AdWords for mobiles. The Mobile Marketing Association has set specific guidelines on the size, format, and other specifications of mobile banner advertisements. Mobile advertisement banners can also be animated.

7. Mobile web site: The mobile web site can be used as an effective marketing tool both for the consumer and for industrial marketing. The web site can provide valuable information to the customer to lure the customer into making a purchase. Care needs to be taken to ensure that the web page has limited content to suit the mobile handset, and the enterprise needs to have a page-rendering engine that transforms the page to suit the device making the request for access or data from the mobile web site. Mobile web sites also act as tools for marketing research, where the browsing patterns and pages of interest can be identified and tracked. The web site can implement multiple marketing techniques as follows:

   ▪ Web triggers: This capability allows the user to enter his or her mobile number in the enterprise web site to get promotion- and product-related information. This capability helps the enterprise in identifying potential customers.

   ▪ Viral mobile marketing from a web site: The method of viral marketing using a mobile web site involves encouraging web site visitors to forward a link or a message to another user's phone in exchange for points or other promotional gifts when the person to whom the message is forwarded visits the web site or makes a purchase from the web site. This way, in addition to the visitor's mobile number, the enterprise also gets potential customer leads from existing visitors and customers.

8. Mobile applications: There can be different variations of mobile applications for the purpose of marketing:

   ▪ Applications designed for mobile commerce with marketing embedded: These applications are basically intended for shopping from a mobile but have features that save customer preferences and offer targeted promotions. Generic promotions on deals of low-price items and new products of demand that can be of interest to the customer can also be marketed using these applications.

   ▪ Applications with advertisements that can be downloaded for free and need payment from the customer for an advertisement-free version: Most customers would prefer an application that comes for free but has advertisements rather than an application that requires payment. The use of advertisements in the free version now comes without warning in many App Stores. The option of downloading a free trial version to evaluate the application before paying for full version is also a major factor for the increase in the download of applications with advertisements.

■ Applications intended for customer care with marketing embedded: Many service-oriented enterprises in the utility sector have launched customer care applications. These applications have in-built features for product and service marketing. For example, a telco service provider application that not only provides details of the current subscriber plan but also has the capability to switch plans or provides details of new handsets from the service provider, which can be purchased from the mobile application, is an example of thick applications that fall under this category.

■ Applications designed for the sole purpose of marketing: There are also applications that are designed for the sole purpose of marketing. Applications for information and branding that have content pulled from the server and updated automatically when connected to the service provider network are examples of applications in this category. Mobile games can be considered as a subcategory of this type of application, although games offer a framework for targeted promotion, and it is a mature area that needs separate treatment in mobile marketing. There are also vendors who develop solutions for consolidated marketing of multiple products, such as a mobile catalogue or a directory promoting multiple products, and who have to buy space in the application.

9. Mobile widgets: From a technical view point, mobile widgets are either small web components on a web site or web-based graphical user interface (GUI) applications that pull content from a server to show a marketing message. Although widget technically falls under the web site or thick application category, the context in which widgets are used is different from the way in which mobile web sites or mobile thick applications are used. The development and publishing process also has a significant difference. Now let us discuss the marketing strategy using mobile widgets. Mobile widgets can be added to an existing mobile web site, where the widget message can be a request to the user to register for getting promotions and discounts. The advantage of using the widget is that it can be added and removed to the existing web site without having to work on modifying the web site. IRIO is a vendor who offers customized mobile widgets for addition to an existing web site. Widget-based applications can be downloaded to provide new promotions, discounts, or offers that get updated on a daily basis. Clicking on the application widget will either show a larger view of the widget information or redirect the customer to the web site for further details on the information displayed in the widget.

10. Mobile marketing card: The card can take the form of mobile coupons, gift cards, vouchers, cash cards, brochures, membership or loyalty cards, etc.

The mobile marketing card is necessarily the mobile version of the physical sales promotion tools. Many leading retailers such as Target and Concurrent Versions System have adopted mobile marketing practices based on the mobile marketing card. There are specific firms such as Transaction Wireless that can be approached by other enterprises when they want to launch mobile gift cards. Applebee's and American Eagle Outfitters are some of the popular clients of Transaction Wireless, who specialize in mobile marketing cards.

11. Mobile audio marketing: Sound has been noted to be a great way to build brand recognition. The use of ringtones has been a popular method of brand promotion for quite some time now. Advertisement launch of many brands on mass media, such as TV and radio, are coupled with the release of the same tune as a ringtone in most of the marketing mediums to increase the recall of the brand. Ringtones have also been a source of huge revenue for telco service providers. Ringtones can also take the form of songs downloaded to mobiles, which can serve as tools for marketing, even though these may not be set as ringtones. Recent innovations in ringtone-based marketing have resulted in video ringtones, which fall under the mobile video marketing category.

12. Mobile affiliate marketing: Affiliate marketing involves working with affiliates of the enterprise to provide links on their web site to reach the web site of the enterprise. With affiliate marketing, the customer can get information about an enterprise product or service from affiliate member sites. Affiliate marketing is also applied in mobile marketing. AdMob can be used by affiliates to route traffic and also get the metrics on the number of users routed to the enterprise site. Affiliates usually get paid on a per-click basis or based on the number of redirects that transfer to an actual purchase.

13. Mobile proximity marketing: In this technique, hot spots are created where customers can download marketing messages packed in different formats. The customer can download ringtones, logos, and promotional pictures as mobile wallpapers, videos with promotional content, voice or audio marketing messages, mobile applications, games, and other type of files. There are different variations of proximity marketing in addition to hot spots using a wireless technology such as Bluetooth or Wireless Fidelity (WiFi). The user can also walk into a store and check out a poster that has information on a new trial application and download the same by placing the handset near the poster that has a wireless transmitter.

14. Mobile marketing with interactive voice response (IVR) and support desk: IVR is now a popular technique in mobile marketing. Most of the enterprises' IVR support lines start with a marketing message to the caller on a latest offering before providing options to the user to key in details from the mobile. In scenarios where the IVR cannot resolve the issue and the call gets forwarded to a support personnel, then after solving the customer's concerns, the support personnel also tries to market products that might be of interest

to the customer. For example, bank support personnel would probably suggest the customer to open a fixed deposit account or invest in some securities. Coupling marketing with customer support has been a technique of marketing not just in mobile marketing.

15. Mobile video marketing: This type of marketing is currently used extensively in industrial marketing. Solution demos with links to a web site for further details are used in corporate marketing, as most corporates are providing senior executives with enterprise handsets so that they would be productive even when they are on the move. Interactive mobile videos are also used in marketing presentations. Mobile video marketing also finds use in consumer marketing. It is used for developing video advertisements for the mobile and in creating interactive videos for mobile commerce. Mobile video advertisement impressions are growing at a tremendous rate over the past few years.

16. Marketing with the mobile version of traditional media: Mobile TV, mobile radio, mobile news, mobile mailing, etc., fall within this category, which are mobile versions of proven traditional media for marketing. The rules of marketing as well as the pros and cons associated with the traditional media apply to mobile versions of these media. Advertisements in video, audio, print, or digital formats can be sent using mobile services representing these media in the mobile context. Content adaptation needs to be done before these services are presented in the diverse set of consumer mobile handsets.

17. SIM tool kit (STK) and unstructured supplementary service data (USSD) marketing: Although STK applications can be used for marketing, there is very limited use of STK by marketers in mobile marketing. STK marketing is limited to presenting short messages or presenting links to the web site of the enterprise. USSD has found more applications in mobile marketing, where a response on the USSD gateway to a request from a customer is answered by a short marketing message. STK-based marketing as well as mobile marketing with USSD will require the involvement of a telco operator. Hence, it is mostly telcos that benefit from STK- and USSD-based mobile marketing. A key advantage in the use of USSD is that it does not require content adaptation and is cheaper when compared with SMSs. USSD and STK have the capability to offer menu-based user interaction and selection. Many telcos offer mobile customer care using a menu-driven USSD framework, which is cheaper than web-based or thick-application-based mobile care.

18. Mobile social marketing: With the increase in the number of subscribers who use the mobile for social networking, there is immense scope for social marketing in the mobile platform. Social networking sites such as Twitter and Facebook have released mobile versions of their web sites, which makes it easier for the user to browse and blog or tweet from these social networking sites. Marketers are now giving a higher focus to ensuring that marketing in the form of brand promotion is mostly done from these social networking

sites by creating special groups for brand users, blogging on new offerings, commenting on enterprise participation in a social cause, etc.

19. Mobile quick response (QR) code marketing: QR code is a two-dimensional code that can be read using barcode readers or captured by camera phones and processed using mobile softwares. Any information, such as a promotion text code or universal resource locator (URL), can be encoded and stored using QR codes. Current versions of Android handsets natively support the reading of QR codes. QR codes usually appear on print media, such as posters, brochures, visiting cards, etc., and can be scanned by the handset to get detailed information. QR codes are extensively used in mobile marketing where the mobile user does not have to search for information, manually type a URL, or remember a promotion code. By simply scanning the QR code, which is hardlinked or object-hyperlinked to the detailed information site, the mobile user directly gets to the marketing message that he or she is interested in.

20. Mobile integrated marketing: Mobile marketing is now part of the IMC strategy of most enterprises. It needs to be understood that the best marketing results are achieved in mobile-integrated marketing where the mobile is just one of the marketing channels used by the enterprise.

There are several other terminologies that are used in the context of mobile marketing, such as mobile location marketing, mobile marketing with augmented reality, and context-aware mobile marketing, etc. However, these can be considered as subtypes that are spread across the 20 key classifications of mobile marketing discussed in this section.

4.4 Integrated Mobile Marketing

With multiple ways of handling mobile marketing, there is an increased need for the enterprise to plan an integrated mobile marketing (IMM) campaign that ensures that all methods of mobile marketing are able to communicate the same position to the target customer. In most enterprises, initiatives on mobile marketing are introduced just to complement the current marketing channels, without much thought on how effectively mobile marketing can be implemented by utilizing its ability as a mass media that is also personal in nature.

Enterprises should prepare a mobile marketing plan involving multiple techniques of mobile marketing, which aligns with the objectives of the marketing campaign. The plan should ensure that the most appropriate mobile marketing types are used, and the plan should fit the target market segment. For example, the enterprise can develop a mobile web site to provide product information, use affiliate marketing to drive customers to the mobile web site, offer a mobile shopping application that also gives details on promotions, and have an SMS-based feature to provide customer support.

Enterprises need to understand that the mobile not only offers an electronic version of traditional marketing media similar to Internet marketing but also provides the ability to do customized marketing for a specific customer using predefined rules. The personal, and always reachable, nature of the mobile makes it a much more powerful marketing tool compared with other techniques of marketing.

While preparing a mobile marketing plan, enterprises should understand the best techniques of mobile marketing to be adopted in the IMM plan as well as identify how best the IMM plan can be fitted in an IMC campaign, along with other marketing channels. Significant research reports on new marketing models based on IMM and IMC campaigns involving IMM, is anticipated in coming years from market research scientists.

4.5 Conclusion

The personal nature of the mobile has made it a key resource for direct marketing (popularly called mobile direct marketing). The mobile offers the capability to reach a specific customer using a variety of marketing techniques. Almost all the major brands in the product and service industry are investing significantly on mobile advertising and have added the mobile channel in their integrated marketing strategies. Mobile marketing offers the dual advantage of reaching the customer anytime and anywhere as well as offering context-based marketing.

Considering the immense potential of the mobile in marketing, it becomes a key component to be covered in a discussion on enterprise mobility. This chapter is devoted to providing an overview of mobile marketing for the enterprise. It is suggested that enterprise marketers identify the marketing types that best fit their requirements and work out a mobile marketing plan to execute their marketing campaign.

Additional Reading

1. Cindy Krum. *Mobile Marketing: Finding Your Customers No Matter Where They Are*, 1st edition. New Jersey: Que; 2010.
2. Kim Dushinski. *The Mobile Marketing Handbook: A Step-by-Step Guide to Creating Dynamic Mobile Marketing Campaigns*, 1st edition. New Jersey: CyberAge Books; 2009.
3. Chetan Sharma, Joe Herzog, and Victor Melfi. *Mobile Advertising: Supercharge Your Brand in the Exploding Wireless Market*, 1st edition. New York: Wiley; 2008.

Chapter 5

Enterprise Mobility Layers

In this chapter we analyze the technical components that make up the enterprise mobility stack. There are several aspects that need to be looked into while designing enterprise mobility systems apart from the actual mobile application. Hence, a high-level view of the components that make up enterprise mobility is essential. This chapter provides an overview of the end-to-end solution components of enterprise mobility.

5.1 Introduction

Today's business environment demands optimized business execution that is not confined to the desktop but extends to offer business execution "on the go" using mobility. Mobile applications are playing a key role in a variety of business scenarios such as supply-chain management (SCM), sales-force automation (SFA), customer-relationship management, etc. Mobility needs to be approached as a strategic initiative that targets the consumer segment for increased profits, improves employee productivity, and optimizes the business process in enterprises using powerful mobile applications.

The number of enterprises using mobile applications to improve business agility and deliver superior customer service is increasing at a rapid pace. Mobility applications can capture information and provide quick delivery of information to relevant stakeholders and back-end systems for informed decisions and actions. The introduction of mobility should be considered as a logical extension of the existing systems by introducing web services on the mobile. A holistic view of mobility is not limited to the application and the communication framework. There are several other critical characteristics that are eminent to enterprise mobility, such as synchronization for off-line operation, power management, user/device authentication, etc.

This chapter splits the enterprise mobility framework into several layers to explain the different components that make up enterprise mobility. Each layer is made up of several building blocks that bring out the different technology options available to an enterprise in building an enterprise mobility solution. A three-dimensional (3D) model of enterprise mobility is used in this chapter to explain the components of a mobility solution, as incorporating the different facets of enterprise mobility in a single two-dimensional figure is not possible.

The model discussed in this chapter also incorporates the back-end systems with which the mobile application or the mobility server interacts to get and set information. The three-dimensional model captures the layers on one face of the model, the products and services on the second face, and the domains on the third face. An end-to-end system is set up using the components in the layers, with multiple vendor products and services available to realize the components, and the end-to-end system results in a solution for a specific domain. The products and services are spread across the different layers, showing that there are products and services available for each of the layers.

The domain is spread across the layers because the products or services making up the setup that comprises the different layers can be replicated for achieving the needs of the different domains. The replicated setup will only need customizations in the product or service and the component layers based on the needs of a specific domain. While the focus of this chapter will be on the different layers, a certain level of discussion on the other axis is also covered in this chapter.

5.2 Enterprise Mobility Model

The 3D model on enterprise mobility is shown in Figure 5.1. The model has two key blocks: the enterprise mobility block and the enterprise back-end systems block. Three faces of each of these blocks are shown in Figure 5.1. For the sake of simplicity, the visible face of the block and the invisible face (on the opposite side of the visible face) are assumed to be identical.

An enterprise mobility block has the following three faces:

- Enterprise mobility solution layers
- Enterprise mobility products and services
- Enterprise mobility domains

An enterprise back-end systems block has the following three faces:

- Enterprise applications
- Enterprise platforms and interfaces
- Enterprise domains

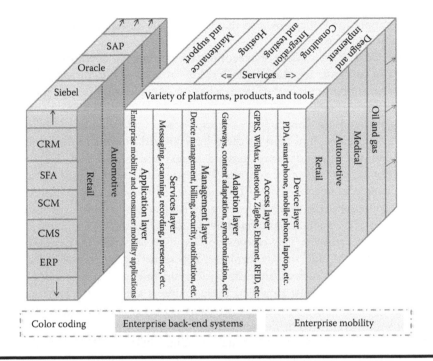

Figure 5.1 Three-dimensional model of enterprise mobility.

5.3 Enterprise Mobility Solution Layers

The face of the enterprise mobility block that captures the enterprise mobility solution layers consists of six layers:

- Device layer
- Access layer
- Adaptation layer
- Management layer
- Services layer
- Application layer

5.3.1 Device Layer

The device layer is quite complex due to the huge diversity in the display size, battery life, processing power, operating platform, etc. Some of the popular platforms include BlackBerry, iPhone, Windows Mobile, Android, Notebook, and Tablet. There are several versions of these platforms that make it difficult for a programmer to develop a generic application or for an enterprise to develop a multiplatform consumer application. It can be seen that the diversity exists both in the hardware as well as in the software.

Mobile devices are capable of executing a wide range of applications for both business and consumer use. Mobile devices are categorized into three levels by the enterprise for support purposes while developing an application:

- Legacy handsets: This category corresponds to traditional handsets that are WAP 1.0-based, and most of these have limited browser capabilities. Data rendering on these devices is limited to text and images, and these devices do not support advanced controls. Web pages for this category of handsets are simple text pages, and most often, external mobile thick applications are not supported. The device relies on a native platform, and its capabilities are limited to the applications offered by the device vendor.
- Mediocre handsets: This category of handsets is WAP 2.0-based. It supports xHTML and similar formats. Web rendering on these handsets can handle controls such as drop-down, text shading, and other text or media presentation controls. However, these handsets are limited by the applications provided by the vendor. They do not offer the flexibility and advanced look-and-feel offered by the next level of handsets.
- Advanced handsets: Personal data assistants (PDAs) and the ever-growing category of smartphones fall in this category. These handsets allow people to e-mail, do instant messaging, engage in web browsing, work on documents, download applications from App Stores, synchronize data from PCs, and do much more. The user experience offered by this category of handsets is much superior than that offered by its predecessors.

The advanced handset category is the market targeted for enterprise applications, and all three categories, from the legacy to the advanced, are targeted by the enterprise from the mobile web perspective. The category of advanced handsets includes the following three main types of devices:

- PDA: PDAs are also referred to as pocket computers. A typical PDA serves the purpose of making calls, sending fax, and web browsing, and it also acts as a personal organizer. PDAs were the first form of professional handsets, which unlike portable computers began as pen-based input interface solutions, using a stylus rather than a keyboard for input. Later generations of PDAs also responded to voice input by using voice recognition technologies. Current PDAs are similar to computers and have a datapad, which is a keyboard for PDAs. Palm Pilot, Sony Clie, Casio Cassiopedia, and Compaq iPaq are some popular examples of PDAs.
- Smartphones: Smartphones have revolutionized the mobile industry by combining mobile phones and handheld computers into a single device. The smartphone allows the user to run and to multitask applications that are

native to the underlying hardware. One of the key features that make this device so versatile is that it runs on a complete operating system (OS) software, providing a platform for developers to create compelling new applications. Palm Treo, BlackBerry, iPhone, and HTC Desire are some examples of popular smartphones.

■ Tablet PC: Tablet PCs represent a cut-down version of notebook computers. It has an LCD touch screen on which the user can write using a stylus. Tablet PCs may also have a keyboard and/or a mouse for input. This device has significantly higher computing power in comparison with the usual mobile handsets. Toshiba Portege, HP Compaq tablet PC, and IBM Thinkpad are some examples of popular tablet PCs.

Before we discuss the next layer of the enterprise mobility block, let us briefly discuss mobile OSs, which are important components in enterprise application development. The mobile OS, like any other OS, is the software platform over which other programs run. The device manufacturer decides the OS for a specific device. The applications that can run on the device are determined by the OS. Some of the popular mobile OSs include the following:

■ Symbian: This OS has the highest share among mobile OSs in the handset market. The Symbian platform is the successor of Symbian OS and Nokia S60. Symbian, which was previously managed as an open-source project, is currently maintained by Nokia.

■ BlackBerry: This OS and its related handsets are developed and maintained by Research In Motion. BlackBerry smartphones are popular for their ability to push mails to the handsets and for the security features offered by the BlackBerry enterprise server. BlackBerry was initially targeting the corporate segment. However, now the company also releases touch-based handsets with an appealing user interface for the consumer segment.

■ iPhone OS: iPhone OS, also known as iOS, is the mobile OS from Apple. It is used in the iPhone, the iPad, the iPod Touch, and other Apple handsets. The interface controls and user experience offered by iPhone are so compelling that it has a dominant market share in the consumer segment.

■ Windows Mobile: The Windows Mobile platform is available on a variety of devices from Dell, HP, Motorola, Palm, and i-mate. Windows Mobile-powered devices are available on Groupe Spécial Mobile (GSM) or code division multiple access (CDMA) networks.

■ Palm OS: The Palm OS platform provides mobile devices with business tools as well as the capability to access the Internet. Another key feature offered by Palm is the ability to access the corporate database using a wireless connection.

■ Android: This OS uses the Linux kernel and is currently owned and maintained by Google. Being an open-source product, Android has a large community of developers writing applications to extend the functionality of the devices using this OS.

◼ Others: There are several other mobile OSs such as MXI, Mobile Linux, etc. The presence of multiple OSs leads to much complexity for an enterprise developer to design applications for multiple platforms.

5.3.2 Access Layer

The access layer is the main communication or mediator network between the mobile device and the mobile server. Call establishment, maintaining the conversation line, and termination of a call in a telephone service are made possible using a mediator network such as the universal mobile telecommunications system (UMTS) or CDMA, which has a set of elements dedicated to perform a specific function and interoperate with other elements in the network to realize the call-handling service.

The main operation of elements in a communication network is transmission of information (voice, data, media, etc.), where the information is transformed or evaluated to make communication between two equipments possible. An example of "Transformation" is a protocol gateway in which the language for information exchange is changed from one protocol to another. "Evaluation" can happen at a call server that queries a register to find if the intended service can be fulfilled or at a billing gateway that evaluates the total bill a customer should pay based on service utilization.

Communication networks have evolved based on the need for more information transfer at higher speed. There are different kinds of communication networks based on the area of coverage, type of modulation used, speed of data transfer, type of switching, bandwidth, and the type of interface used for data transfer between elements.

The access layer can be supported by UMTS, wireless fidelity, GSM, general packet radio service (GPRS), CDMA, Internet Protocol (IP) multimedia subsystem, Bluetooth, or WiMAX, just to name a few of the communication networks that are used for establishing a connection and data exchange. Figure 5.2 shows the software and hardware support offered in the mobile device for connecting to the access layer. It can be seen from the figure that the device support for a specific access is important when designing applications. For example, while designing an implant device that communicates data to a handset application that, in turn, communicates to a hospital server, it is essential to ensure that both the access protocols for interaction with the implant device and the basic service provider network are supported by the handset. Mapping this specific scenario to Figure 5.2, the implant and the handset could interact using Bluetooth, while GPRS or enhanced data for global evolution (EDGE) can be used for communicating with the hosted server via Internet.

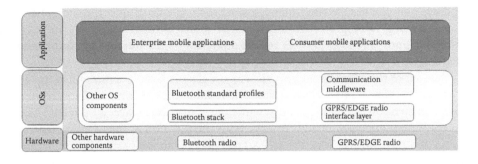

Figure 5.2 Software and hardware used in a mobile device to connect with an access layer.

5.3.3 Adaptation Layer

The adaptation layer is the first point of enterprise access from the customer's service provider network. This layer has the security gateways, WAP gateways, content adaptation modules such as rendering engines and synchronization components for data synchronization between the mobile application and server, as well as modules for messaging, queuing, brokering, etc. The adaptation does not directly contribute to the business logic of the mobile application but is composed of a set of components to ensure that the connection is secure, data are formatted, and all other basic functionalities are available to receive and transfer the message from the enterprise end. These are generic modules and are required for most mobile applications. Several standard commercial off-the-shelf (COTS) products that offer the functionalities of the adaptation layer are available.

Let us consider a simple web interaction to understand the purpose of the adaptation layer. When the user types a mobile web uniform resource locator, the request is sent to the service provider access network, and the first point of contact would be the firewall and the gateways of the enterprise network. The business gateway will have load balancers and will identity management servers to authenticate the user. Only after the request is handled by the adaptation layer, the request moves to the web servers and then from the web servers to the application servers for any data access. Original equipment manufacturers such as Cisco, Oracle, and Juniper are some of the key players in the development of components for the adaptation layer.

5.3.4 Management Layer

The management layer handles the management capabilities required for mobile services. It can be device management as would be required with enterprise-issued handsets for employees, application management in terms of software updates and patches, security management such as enforcing corporate policies and installing virus protection software, or management in the form of operational support modules such as online analytics of the number of connecting customers.

Similar to the adaptation layer this is also a generic layer in terms of its capability to be used for multiple applications. The main difference is that in most scenarios the adaptation layer is mandatory, while the management layer is optional based on the mobile application requirements. Also the function of the adaption layer is to act as a mediator between the access layer and the mobility servers (comprising web and application servers), while the management layer is not a direct contributor in the interaction and is more of a parallel support block that is built to manage the overall mobility framework.

Being a generic layer, there are several COTS components in this layer. Let us take security management as an example. A variety of off-the-shelf products are available from leading security solution providers for addressing the security requirements for mobile device management, content protection, securing the communication channel between the mobile device and enterprise systems, and creating a secure wall at the enterprise side to prevent unauthorized access. A few of the popular off-the-shelf mobile security products and their features, as discussed in the product documentation web page of the vendor, are discussed:

- ◼ Afaria: This is the most popular mobile device management product and enjoys a major market share in mobile device management. This off-the-shelf integrated mobile device management solution from the Sybase iAnywhere family has the following features:
  - − Corporate security policy enforcement
  - − Encryption of e-mail and Personal Information Manager
  - − Encryption of storage media
  - − Application run control policy
  - − Encryption of over-the-air data
  - − Compliance to FIPS 140–2 security standard
  - − Antivirus and firewall protection
- ◼ Mobicontrol: This off-the-shelf integrated mobile device management solution from SOTI has the following features:
  - − Remote device management for application deployment, user configuration, etc.
  - − Global positioning system (GPS)-based device tracking
  - − Authentication policy for administrative and user-level device operations
  - − Device lock-down support
  - − Application run control policy
  - − Out-of-contact device policy to manage security on "out-of-contact" devices that are not able to connect to the enterprise server

- File encryption policy for content protection
- Connection security policy for securing the communication channel between the device and the enterprise server
- Device feature control policy for selectively enabling or disabling device hardware features such as Bluetooth and WiFi
■ Kaspersky mobile security enterprise edition: This off-the-shelf antimalware and spyware solution, from Kaspersky Laboratory, for mobile clients has the following features:
  - Antitheft protection to protect important data stored on the mobile device in case of devices lost or stolen
  - Antivirus protection
  - Antispam protection for short message service (SMS)
  - Integrated IP firewall protection
■ Mobility XE: This off-the-shelf mobile virtual private network (VPN) solution from NetMotion Wireless for secure continuous remote access to enterprise applications and resources from mobile clients over an IP-based network has the following features:
  - Session persistence
  - Internet-work roaming support
  - Mobile network access control
  - Optimized wireless performance

5.3.5 Services Layer

The service layer is a set of capabilities that are offered in the mobile or provided by third parties, which can be utilized in the development of applications. The layer also includes some of the services offered by the telco service provider, which are open for leveraging in mobile applications. In many functional architecture diagrams, the mobile application layer is shown above the service layer, to show that although these services are used by the application, they are not part of the application.

Some of the examples of the components in the service layer include presence service, location service, messaging service, etc. Most mobile shopping applications from retail vendors have the capability to locate the nearest store of the user by entering the pin code or on the basis of GPS location of the user. This is made possible using location services from map vendors who expose application program interfaces that can be used in mobile applications to show the location on maps. The mobile application could also provide the user the ability to make a call from an application rather than use the main call interface.

Service capabilities are not necessarily limited to the software level. The hardware capabilities of the mobile device also contribute to the services. For example, to use the GPS capability, the device needs to support GPS. Another example is the use of barcode scanning in the application, which needs to have a hardware scanner module or a camera based on the barcode-processing methodology that is used in the application.

5.3.5 Application Layer

The application layer is the principal layer on the enterprise mobility stack and has the mobile application client and the server. This layer serves the purpose of providing a user interface to the customer from the mobile client and integrates with enterprise systems using the mobile server. The application layer thus offers enterprise mobility and consumer mobility applications. The application layer components can be developed using different programming languages. While the development of BlackBerry and Android is based on Java, iPhone development uses Objective C, and Windows development uses C#/.Net. Some of the device vendors offer software development kits that can be used for developing mobile applications for the platform supported by the vendor. For example, BlackBerry developers can either develop applications using the BlackBerry integrated development environment (IDE) or install the relevant plug-ins to work on an external IDE such as Eclipse.

Applications such as SMS, multimedia messaging service, media player, messenger, and browser are preinstalled in most mobile handsets. Then there are applications that the user or customer can download and install from an application store. Some applications are also pushed to the device from a server that controls the mobile device. While the preinstalled applications are usually called utilities that are packaged with the mobile device, the class of applications in the application layer mostly fall under the thin or browser-based application and downloadable thick applications.

The discussion shows that there are several layers that make up the enterprise mobility stack. The end-to-end interaction is not just limited to the mobility stack but also includes back-end systems. Figure 5.1 shows the mobility stack alongside the enterprise back-end systems stack. The mobility server interacts with enterprise back-end systems, which could be a CRM system, SCM system, or some other back-end system based on SAP, Siebel, Oracle, or any other vendor.

5.4 Conclusion

This chapter introduces the reader to the key players, other than the enterprise, who contribute in the development of an effective mobility solution for an enterprise. The intent of this chapter is to provide the reader a holistic view of enterprise mobility, which is achieved by presenting the enterprise mobility model along with the different layers that make up enterprise mobility.

This chapter provides an overview of the layers in the enterprise mobility stack and how the layers together make a complete suite enabling data access anytime and anywhere using mobile applications. The enterprise must focus on the different layers in the stack and ensure that the design of the enterprise mobility solution clearly brings out the components or solutions used in the different layers. An effective design at a high level needs to cover all the layers and should not be limited to just the mobile client application and the mobile server component.

Additional Reading

1. Andrew Pearson. *The Mobile Revolution*, 1st edition. Raleigh, NC: lulu.com; 2010.
2. Rich Ling and Scott Campbell. *Mobile Communication: Bringing Us Together and Tearing Us Apart*, 1st edition. New Jersey: Transaction Publishers; 2011.
3. Keri Hayes. *Going Mobile: Building the Real-Time Enterprise with Mobile Applications that Work*, 1st edition. California: CMP; 2003.
4. Brian Fling. *Mobile Design and Development: Practical Concepts and Techniques for Creating Mobile Sites and Web App*, 1st edition. California: O'Reilly Media; 2009.

Chapter 6

Mobility Solution Architecture

This chapter is a quick-review guide for a mobile-solution designer or architect to select the best approach while developing a mobile solution. The two main categories of mobile-solution development, for most enterprises, are limited to thin applications (browser-based) and thick applications (download required). This chapter explores the options as well as the components that make up the architecture of the mobile-application development solutions.

6.1 Introduction

Thick and thin mobile applications are the two major types of mobility solutions that enterprises mainly focus on, with regard to consumer and enterprise mobile-application development. Some enterprises evaluate the pros and cons of these two types of applications to decide on and develop the right type of application that meets their requirements in terms of functionality and look and feel. Larger enterprises (especially in the retail segment and telcos) prefer to reach their customers by using both mobile web sites (thin application) as well as thick applications. When mobile payment card transactions are involved, it is common to develop a hybrid application, where the application is a downloadable thick application but which uses an embedded web page to handle payments, thus delegating payment security to the server side and relying on a browser for payment to comply with standards such as the Payment Card Industry Data Security Standard (PCIDSS). To build hybrid applications, the enterprise needs to have a thin-application framework in place before building the hybrid application.

For small enterprises with a limited number of customers or those enterprises that build applications to improve employee productivity, a key choice is to decide whether they want to build a thin or thick mobile application. The advantages and disadvantages of these two application types are further discussed.

The advantages of thin applications are listed as follows:

- Thin applications do not require download and installation, as the application is displayed in a mobile browser.
- There is ease of application distribution, as only a server component that responds to requests from the mobile browser is required. This necessarily means that the application does not need approval for publishing in App Stores, thus reducing the time to market the product.
- Code maintenance is much easier, and there is no need to port the application across multiple mobile platforms.
- Development is not bound by the size limit. It is more an extension of the existing web framework for desktops.
- It is easy to make revisions and updates, as the same can be managed from the server.
- Security is mostly delegated to the server, and the design does not have to comply with client-specific security issues, as long as the communication channel and the server framework are secure.

The disadvantages of thin applications are listed as follows:

- Continuous connectivity is required. The browser needs to connect to the server to get the details. Hence, thin applications are not suggested for applications that need to work in an off-line mode, such as scanning tags or images and later synchronizing these with the server or collecting orders from customers in locations having no network access.
- There is limited use of device-specific capabilities.
- The user experience is limited.
- There is a high level of data exchange between the server and the browser client, as the client relies completely on the server to respond to client requirements.

The subsequent list provides the advantages of thick applications:

- Thick applications can leverage native capabilities offered by the platform application program interfaces (APIs).
- Thick applications offer a rich user interface (UI) and a much better user experience.
- Developing applications for off-line mode of operation (working even when there is no network coverage) is possible.

■ Thick applications allow the development of applications that leverage built-in external peripherals such as camera, external storage, etc., which cannot be done with browser applications.

The following list provides the disadvantages of thick applications:

■ Updates requires user to download the new version of software.
■ Application distribution, maintenance and version management is complex.
■ Platform dependency leading to less portability.
■ Higher total cost of ownership.

Once a decision is made on the type of application to be developed, the next step is to analyze the requirements and select an appropriate architecture that meets the requirements. The mobility solution architecture would be different for each enterprise; however, in most cases, the architecture is a customized version of the generic architectural options that are discussed in Sections 6.2 and 6.3 of this chapter.

6.2 Thin Client Solution Architecture

The enterprise has three architectural options when designing a thin-application solution:

■ Active Server Pages.net (ASP.net)-based solution: This method of solution implementation uses .net technology. It is used when the mobility server is an Internet information services (IIS) server. The server side uses Microsoft technologies for development and hosting.
■ Mobile JavaServer Faces (JSF)-based solution: This method of solution implementation uses Java technology. Mobile JSF provides the ability to render content on mobile handsets having different form factors.
■ Middleware-based solution: This method of thin-application development utilizes a middleware server that can perform content rendering based on the device making the request. Middleware solutions use open-source rendering solutions, commercial platforms, or commercial rendering stacks, and the following are some examples of middleware solutions:
  – Middleware using open-source stacks: An example for this category involves the use of the wall next generation (WNG) libraries for rendering and the wireless universal resource file device repository for identifying the features of the device from which the request for web content is sent.

- Middleware using commercial stacks: Examples for middleware using commercial stacks include SAP Netweaver server using Webdynpro to connect with SAP servers in the back end and Oracle application development framework (ADF) to connect with Oracle servers in the back end.
- Middleware based on commercial platforms: Examples include Infosys mConnect, MobileAware, and the mobility platform from Kony Solutions.

6.2.1 ASP.net-Based Thin Client Solution

This architecture utilizes adaptive control behavior in ASP.net. Adaptive control behavior helps to customize rendering for a specific mobile device. With this feature of ASP.net, generic controls can be intercepted and substituted with custom behavior. The presentation layer represents the UI layer for all the screens. ASP.net mobile forms are processed by respective control adapters (format controllers), and the contents are rendered as HTML, xHTML, or WML based on the device. The overall solution architecture is shown in Figure 6.1.

The steps in the interaction are as follows:

1. The mobile device or handset will send a hypertext transfer protocol (HTTP) request from the browser.
2. The request hits the enterprise gateway where any policy handling is performed.

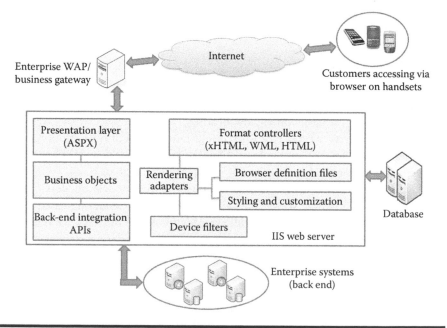

Figure 6.1   ASP.net-based thin client solution architecture.

3. The mobile page request will then be sent to the appropriate ASP.net server (IIS) that handles the request for the specific HTTP page.
4. The appropriate information to be displayed on the page is pulled from the back-end enterprise systems or from the static page repository.
5. The information is processed and formatted by the business objects and is given for presentation.
6. Based on the device making the request, as identified from the HTTP header, the rendering adapter creates the response page.
7. Rendering adapters use browser definition files and format controllers to create a response page in the format supported by the handset making the request.
8. The respective styles and themes will be applied into the controls before rendering content.
9. The device filters are applied on the response page to create a page that suits the specific handset.
10. The response page is then sent back to the mobile handset.

6.2.2 JSF-Based Thin Client Solutions for Mobile Applications

The JSF-based thin solution architecture has a clear separation of UI and functionality, where JavaServer Pages (JSP) or JSF packages are used while designing device-specific user experiences. The mobile presentation layer represents the UI layer for mobile-specific screens as shown in Figure 6.2. Device diversity is mostly handled by the device-rendering module as well as the styling and customization component. When an elaborate device repository is not available, it is common practice to classify devices based on a predefined set of categories, such as small, medium, and large, and create pages to suit the device categories rather than to support specific devices.

The steps in the interaction are as follows:

1. The mobile device or handset sends the HTTP(s) request from the browser.
2. The request hits the enterprise gateway where any policy handling is performed.
3. The request then reaches the Java controller servlet of the mobile presentation layer.
4. Once the request reaches the controller, the controller instance is created by the container, which, in turn, instantiates the device-rendering module.
5. The device-rendering module identifies the device, and the corresponding renderer is chosen.
6. The styling and customization utility chooses the appropriate cascading style sheets based on the device selected.
7. The controller servlet will then delegate the request to the business layer, and the response is prepared based on the data collected from back-end systems.

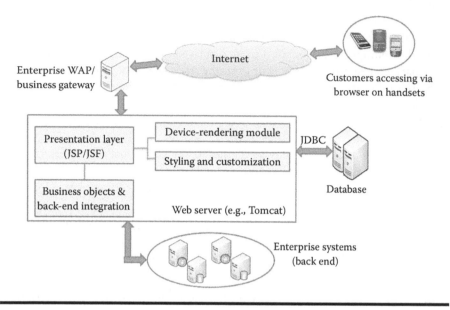

Figure 6.2 JSF-based thin client solution architecture.

8. The response is then formatted to suit the format supported by the device that originated the request.
9. The response page is then sent back to the mobile handset.

6.2.3 Middleware-Based Thin Client Solutions

Figure 6.3 shows the solution architecture involving a typical commercial mobile middleware platform. The following are the different components in the middleware server:

■ Device framework: This can be logically considered as the unit that transforms content to suit the handset making the request. Device framework has the following components:
  – Device rendering: This component performs content filtering and transformation. It performs content filtering such as removing links and images that cannot be rendered on the handset. It applies the transformation based on the styling and customization requirements of the device.
  – Device repository: This repository or storage has records of device types (device profiles). It also contains details of the capabilities or limitations of various handset models and specifies the rules for transformation.
  – Style-sheets repository: The device-rendering module uses style sheets to build the correct layout of the content for the handset.

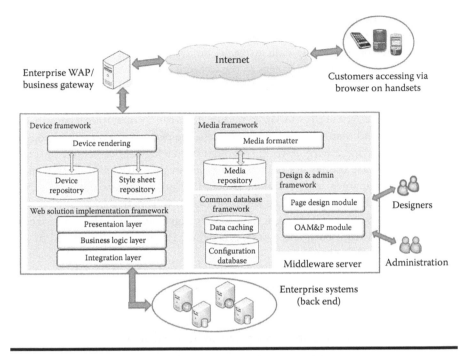

Figure 6.3 Middleware-based thin client solution architecture.

- Media framework: Media need to be transformed to suit the size of the handset and the format supported by the handset. The activity of transforming media is performed by this unit. It has the following components:
  - Media formatter: Media formatter retrieves and processes content such as images, audio files, and video clips according to the rendering decisions of the device framework.
  - Media repository: The media repository has algorithms for applying transformation rules on the media content.
- Web solution implementation framework: This is the main component that models the generic mobile web pages and associates the page controls with the back-end integration APIs to get data. Similar to the normal web and application server framework, this component has a presentation, business, and communication layer. In scenarios where the enterprise develops the web pages separately, this framework would reside on a separate server and use the middleware server only to change generic content and to device a specific format.
- Design and administration framework: This component is the interface for designers to create a generic mobile web page and offers the administrator an interface to perform operation, administration, maintenance, and provisioning (OAM&P). The following are the two main modules in this framework:

- Page design module: This is a UI wizard (designer interface) that can be used to design the mobile web page and to associate the controls in the page for interfacing calls to back-end systems. This interface helps the enterprise to make changes to the web site contents at runtime.
- OAM&P module: The administrator UI is offered by this module. The administrator can provision and configure the middleware server using the interface of the OAM&P module. Day-to-day operations, administration, and maintenance (OAM) can also be performed using this module.

■ Common database framework: Although from a logical perspective the common database framework is shown to reside in the middleware server, in an actual deployment this component could be on a separate database server. The following are some of the key components in this framework:

- Data caching: Caching of mobile web pages, session cache, and caching of data from back-end systems to reduce latency are all handled by the data-caching module.
- Configuration database: The configuration of the middleware server and the customization of mobile web for specific deployments are stored in this database.

The following are some of the key points to be noted about this approach:

■ There can be several variations of the middleware-based thin client approach, where specific libraries or commercial products could be used to satisfy the capabilities of a framework in the overall middleware server. For example, the device framework could be a solution such as WNG, while the rest is custom developed using a Java-based or an ASP.net-based approach. In custom development also, some of the integration libraries of SAP or Oracle might be utilized.

■ The interaction is mostly straightforward, where the request from the device reaches the middleware server after hitting the wireless application protocol (WAP) gateway. The middleware server interacts with back-end systems and sends back a response based on the device model from which the request is originated.

■ As the middleware server is mostly a commercial off-the-shelf (COTS) package, there is flexibility in the deployment of the middleware or mobile server. The enterprise could have a managed service model where the middleware server is managed and maintained by the middleware vendor. The managed service model could lead to significant cost reduction as the capital expenditure related to setting up the infrastructure with a mobile server is eliminated. Hence, this option is widely adopted in the small and medium business segment and is not just limited to the enterprise segment.

In addition to the Java-, .net-, and middleware-based approaches discussed so far, there are several other methods for thin client solution development such as the lightweight server to support only HTML5 and JavaScript or the server side based on some other high-level programming language. The three approaches discussed in this section are the most popular ones for multidevice and multiweb format implementation.

6.3 Thick Client Solution Architecture

Thick client mobile solution needs to be installed on of the devices, and consumer mobile thick applications need to be published in platform-specific App Stores for distribution. While using high-level applications, the enterprise has the following four architectural options to design a thick application client solution:

■ HTML5-based application development: Thick client development using HTML5 and JavaScript is becoming increasingly popular for cross-platform development. This method of development involves developing a thick client application using HTML by encapsulating the web pages inside a portable thick client framework. Device API frameworks such as PhoneGap can also be used for encapsulating the HTML-based web pages into a thick client framework.

■ Generic .net- or Java API-based application development: In this method of development, the client is implemented using .net- or Java-based generic APIs offered by the programming language and not device- or platform-specific APIs. This option can be used for single- or multiplatform development. Developing a .net application for Windows handsets or developing a J2ME application and packaging it for specific platforms such as Android, BlackBerry, etc., is an example of this approach.

■ Platform framework-based application development: This method is adopted for single platform development and leverages platform-specific APIs. Most platform vendors provide a development framework for application development. The BlackBerry mobile data system (MDS) studio application is one such example. The BlackBerry MDS is an ADF that provides tools to build and deploy applications on the BlackBerry.

■ Application development based on mobile enterprise application platform, mobile consumer application platform (MCAP), or multiplatform tools: Thick client solutions can also be developed using mobility enterprise application platforms such as the Antenna Mobility Platform, and Sybase Unwired Platform, etc., or MCAPs such as Volantis, Kony Solutions, etc., or using multiplatform tools such as J2ME Polish, MoSync, etc. This technique creates a layer of abstraction above the mobile platforms so that programs can be developed in a common language and can be seamlessly packaged for specific platforms.

It needs to be understood that the advantage of having a thick application is to have a more appealing look and feel and also to provide off-line support by synchronizing with the server. Hence, the architectural approach selected should be focused on developing client applications that have a server component for synchronizing and should also have a UI designed to support data collection from the customer.

The specific architectural approach selected depends on the business requirements. For example, a retailer developing a mobile shopping application would focus on the look and feel to ensure that the customer is able to not only get the product of interest easily but also have a fulfilling shopping experience. Hence, the retailer's best choice is to use a platform framework-based application development that utilizes platform-specific features to provide a superior look and feel. Leveraging device capabilities such as the global positioning system to provide the location of the nearest store is a requirement in most shopping applications on the mobile phone. Next, let us consider the use case of a car manufacturer wanting to provide mobile handsets to its dealers to search for replacements of parts and to place orders. The key focus of the car manufacturer is to provide this capability to the dealers and also maintain the solution at the lowest price; hence, a HTML5-based application would be a good option, as the handsets to be used and the browser application on the handset can be easily controlled by the car manufacturer.

Figure 6.4 shows a generic thin client solution architecture with the components that make up a thick client application. The following are the components in the thick client application:

- View: This module handles formatting and display of data to the user based on the type of the content. Both generic UI APIs or platform-specific APIs can be used for implementation based on the client platform. However, there needs to be consistency at the view level. For example, while designing

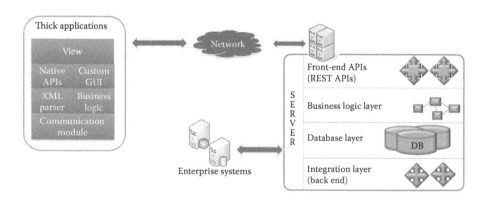

Figure 6.4   Generic thin client solution architecture.

BlackBerry clients, the same application should not use javax.microedition. lcdui (J2ME package) and net.rim.device.api.ui (RIM package).

■ Native APIs: This corresponds to the native components of the device, which will be used in the application. Native APIs help to leverage the features offered by the platform. The disadvantage of using Native APIs is that the application cannot be ported to other platforms easily.

■ Customized graphical user interface (GUI): This module corresponds to graphs, charts, and other UI components that are used in the application.

■ XML parser: This module parses the XML pages from the web service and retrieves the relevant data. The data from the server should be in XML format as is the case in most client–server interactions.

■ Business logic: The data collected need to be formatted, to present the relevant information on the application screen. Also the application should handle user events, initiate data refresh, autocomplete input entries, run background threads, and perform a host of other logical functions. These activities are performed in the business logic component.

■ Communication module: This module interacts with the server using exposed APIs. The establishment of a session with the server, sending a request, getting a response, and gracefully closing the session are performed by the communication module.

In addition to the generic components listed, there are several other components in a typical thick client application, such as a database module that locally stores data relevant to the application, a synchronization module that synchronizes data between the client and the server, a security module that ensures several levels of application-level security, etc. For employee mobile applications in an enterprise, a security agent might also be installed to track the device, audit device contents, lock the device, perform remote wipeout of date, make software updates, and perform other device security operations from an administrative console.

Application security is a key feature to be accounted in thick client solution development. Mobile enterprise security requirements are considered more critical in mobile applications involving financial transactions such as mobile commerce or shopping applications. There are specific standards to be followed in application development when financial transactions are involved. An example of this is the compliance of the mobile application to PCIDSS. Other security standards include HIPAA, Sarbanes-Oxley, etc. Some of the security best practices in enterprise mobility solution development are shown in Figure 6.5.

The appropriate mobile database selection is also a key activity in thick-application development. The following are some of the popular mobile databases:

■ DB4: It offers a very lightweight database management system with a footprint that is less than 500 KB. Although concurrency is handled in mobile db4, it needs to be noted that this database management system is not

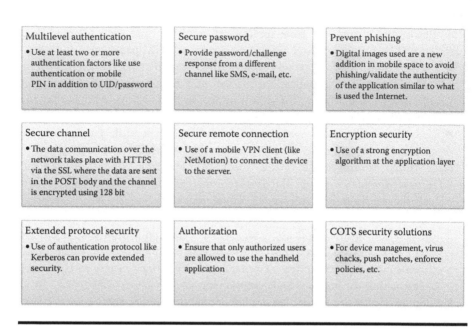

Figure 6.5   Enterprise mobile security best practices.

relational. Moreover, support for procedures is not available, although triggers can be defined. DB4 also supports encryption and is a preferred option for basic database management requirements.

- SQLite: Mobile SQLite offers an even lesser footprint compared with DB4. SQLite is a relational database management system. It supports concurrency and offers the capability to write database procedures and triggers. It also supports encryption, and its source code is available on the public domain. SQLite is the most widely used mobile database solution for mobile applications.

- Oracle Lite: This is a lightweight database solution from Oracle for mobile applications. Being a commercial product, it is rich in features. It offers support for encryption, replication, procedures, triggers, and concurrency. Its mobile server component provides secure, bidirectional data synchronization ability.

- SQL Server Compact Edition: This is an embedded database engine from Microsoft. The footprint of this solution is approximately 2–3 MB. It offers a robust relational database management solution for development of application intended to run on Windows handsets.

- SQL Anywhere: This is a mobile and embedded database management solution from Sybase. It is a relational database management solution. The database engine supports stored procedures, triggers, and encryption. Interface support is offered for open database connectivity, Java database connectivity (JDBC), and ActiveX Data Objects.

Thick client development options are discussed in much more detail in Chapter 20, and hence this chapter gives only the generic architecture for thick client mobile solutions.

6.4 Conclusion

The multiplatform scenario and device diversity in the mobility space have resulted in several architectural options a developer can choose while architecting enterprise mobility solutions. This chapter introduces the reader to the high-level architecture of mobile web- and mobile thick-application solutions. Popular screen resolutions in the mobile context are shown in Figure 6.6, which shows the need for designing applications to align content based on mobile form factors. With the rotation capability supported in smartphones, development also needs to account for realigning content on rotating the handset.

This chapter provides an overview of the components that make up the mobile-solution architecture. Most enterprise mobile implementations are customized versions of the generic architectures discussed in this chapter. The enterprise needs to analyze its business requirements and choose the appropriate platform and architecture to satisfy the functional and nonfunctional requirements of the business.

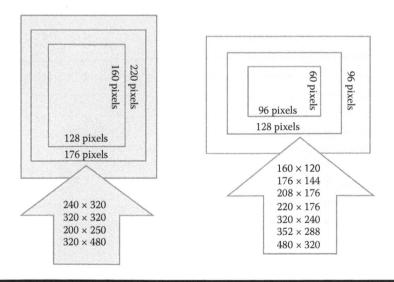

Figure 6.6   Common mobile screen resolutions.

Additional Reading

1. Valentino Lee, Heather Schneider, and Robbie Schell. *Mobile Applications: Architecture, Design, and Development*, 1st edition. New Jersey: Prentice Hall; 2004.
2. Maximiliano Firtman. *Programming the Mobile Web*, 1st edition. California: O'Reilly Media; 2010.
3. Gail Frederick. *Beginning Smartphone Web Development*, 1st edition. New York: Apress; 2010.

Chapter 7

Mobility Significance
and Solution Lifecycle

This chapter deals with the significance of mobility and the critical stages in the mobility solution lifecycle. Section 7.2 in this chapter deals with the application of enterprise mobility in different domains, giving a more complete picture of the significance of the mobility solution lifecycle. The mobility solution lifecycle can be based on the waterfall model or the agile methodology. The important part is how differently the specific stages in the lifecycle are handled compared with the stages in regular information technology (IT) application development lifecycles.

7.1 Introduction

Enterprise mobility has revolutionized the applications of mobile devices. From the basic capability of making calls, mobile technology has evolved to offer applications almost in all enterprise domains. There are pulse-monitoring mobile applications for the health care sector, mobile commerce applications for the retail sector, applications for reading meters in the energy and utilities sector, transaction applications for the banking sector, games and media players for the entertainment sector, and a wide variety of consumer mobile applications for both personal (torchlight, weather report, news subscriptions, etc.) and official purposes (calendar planner, office notes, electronic mail on the mobile, etc.).

Mobility adoption is approached from multiple angles by an enterprise. The primary focus initially from the consumer context is to generate sales by creating mobile consumer applications. The learning from this exercise is then applied to create mobile consumer applications that reduce customer support expenditure and also serve as channels for marketing. From the internal enterprise context, the primary focus is to use mobility for improving productivity with applications that reduce paper, help managers to take decisions and respond to mails even when they are on the move, provide connection to enterprise applications from the mobile, etc. This framework is then extended to offer mobile applications to suppliers and partners to achieve supply chain automation and ease of data exchange between enterprises.

This chapter details the significance of mobility from several angles such as user demand, business revenue context, productivity benefits, and innovation brought about from mobile applications. This chapter also covers the mobility solution lifecycle. The stages of mobile solution development are similar to those of the IT solution lifecycle. The key factors to be considered in the various stages of the lifecycle are discussed in this chapter.

7.2 Significance of Mobility

User demand for mobility has been steadily increasing over the years. Mobile handsets were initially used only to make calls, and hence the start of the mobility trend can be attributed to the laptop era. The mobility trend has been gaining momentum since the launch of laptops, which enabled people to work while on the move. The size of the laptops was seen as a drawback for mobility, and the industry was in need of a more lightweight solution that can run some of the critical applications. Another issue with the laptop was the need for network connectivity. To meet the industry's demands, the personal digital assistant (PDA) was launched, which was more lightweight and could have a telecom service provider subscription for network access. Cell phones and mobile handsets, which were limited to voice services, started offering data services for Internet access, and this facilitated the evolution of handsets to be a cut-down version of PDAs. With improvements in the computing and processing capabilities in the mobile handset space, smartphones came up as a combination of the PDA's capabilities and the ease and comfort of regular handsets.

The developments in wireless network technology also had a major impact on enterprise mobility. The solution for data mobility evolved in the mid-1990s in the form of wireless local area networks. The use of wireless network was not limited to enterprise applications. Even before wireless network technology caught up in the enterprise segment, it was used extensively in homes and in public Internet hot spots. The innovations in wireless network security in the form of new security protocols and secure routers led to the adoption of wireless network in the enterprise segment also. With the widespread adoption of wireless network technology, enterprise mobility players in the laptop, PDA, and smartphone industry integrated wireless into their products. The price of wireless networking equipment started to decline due to the huge demand, and new applications in enterprise mobility were developed, which utilized the wireless network technology.

Wireless network technology can be leveraged in many business use cases for reducing capital and operation expenditure in the enterprise segment. These business use cases in many industries contributed as a major driver for increase in mobility demand. Enterprise mobility not only leads to improvements in the operational efficiency and a reduction in costs but also offers improvements in sales and a competitive advantage for many enterprises. Soon mobility became an indispensable part of enterprises, especially for inventory tracking, order processing, and business applications. The availability of rugged handheld devices from market giants such as Motorola, with barcode scanners, resulted in the expansion of the mobility demand for both blue-collar and white-collar jobs. Thus, mobile handset scanner applications were used for warehousing and store inventory management and in mobile point-of-sale devices and consumer handsets for barcode search.

Let us look into a case study quoted by Sybase iAnywhere on its solution deployment in the retail segment. McDonald's replaced its paper-based inspection process in the United Kingdom with a mobile inspection solution built on Sybase iAnywhere technology. This resulted in a time saving of almost 3 h in the restaurant-assessment process per operational consultant and cost savings of over £140,000 pounds per year. The use of mobility also resulted in timely and easy access to historical inspection information, and operational consultants were able to spend more time analyzing trends with restaurant owners to create action plans to drive and support continuous improvement. Another case study from the same vendor in the utilities industry involves the South Florida Water Management District. Historically, the inspectors have recorded the data on paper forms, which they then manually entered into the agency's database when they returned to their offices. This paper-based process was inefficient, and so they implemented the iAnywhere-based mobile inspection system from Sybase. This mobility enablement eliminated manual data reentry, saving each field inspector approximately 1 h per day. There was dramatic improvement in the information accuracy of up to 99% and an annual cost reduction of more than $70,000.

In the health care sector, wireless technology can be used to enhance patient care and to reduce personnel expenses incurring from frequent hospital visits. With wireless monitoring implants and external devices, the doctors can get vital details on patients' conditions without the patient having to travel to see the doctor. Some hospitals have equipped doctors with laptops and tablets that can connect to the hospital network and instantly pull up any and all data on a patient. The doctor can order tests, send notes with patients' records as attachments to other doctors, and even change the settings on patient-care equipment remotely with the use of wireless technology. The implementation of wireless technology in health care reduces expenses and errors as well as improves patient satisfaction significantly.

Mobility demand has penetrated many industry domains including finance, retail, telecom, utilities, health care, transportation and logistics, manufacturing and supply chain, and academics. Each of these segments is finding new ways to leverage mobile technology to increase revenue and reduce costs. Mobility, no doubt, has been an effective technology, as it is indeed the third technology revolution after the Industrial Revolution and the Internet revolution.

Technical directors, business managers, and financial analysts have begun to calculate the cost savings that are possible with mobile networks. Let us consider a typical case to understand the business benefits and cost savings from enterprise mobility. For example, field service personnel often have to replace parts on customer systems. The parts are large and highly specialized. The field service executive (FSE) has to identify the correct part number to place orders for airfreight delivery to ensure rapid resolution of the customer's problem. The process involved in the paper-based system of data collection is shown in Figure 7.1, and the business process when all FSE data-entry operations are performed using mobiles is shown in Figure 7.2.

This shift in process to mobile-based data collection leads to several benefits as follows:

- Reducing the possibility of errors due to manual data entry, thereby resulting in improved data quality.
- Increasing the overall productivity of technicians through streamlined business flows on the handheld devices with automation (barcode scanning and integrated image capture).

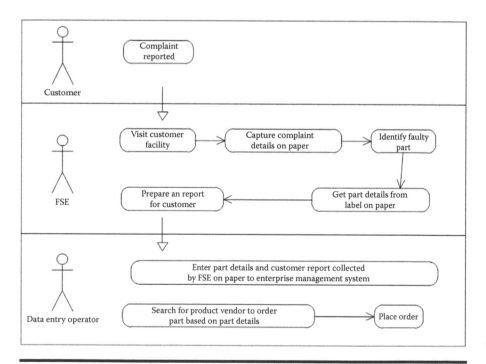

Figure 7.1 Business process for paper-based data collection.

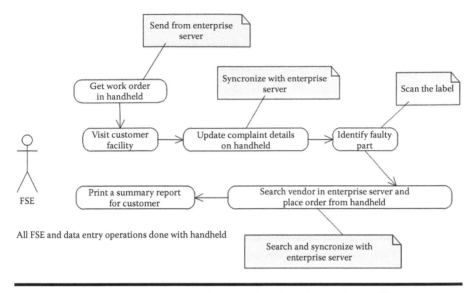

Figure 7.2 Business process with handheld mobile-based data collection.

- Lowering costs by reducing time, expenses, and errors associated with manual or paper-based processes.
- Automating the processes, which improves the total operational efficiency and reduces order completion time.
- Better customer satisfaction due to lesser time to fix a customer complaint.

Figure 7.3 shows a side-by-side analysis of the time required for paper-based order placement in comparison to mobile-enabled order handling for part replacement. The vendor search and ordering operation takes less time when mobility is enabled, because scanning of the part code (bar code or image) will initiate an autosearch that identifies the vendor and populates part details for placing the order by a single-button click on the handheld device. This comparison shows that approximately 1 h is wasted for placing a part order with the paper-based system compared with that in the mobility-enabled system.

In most high-tech companies, the FSE and data-entry operator are earning approximately $20 per hour. So mobility enablement results in a savings of $20 per person for every work hour associated to a request that involves ordering a replacement part. Even without considering the additional time spent in collecting the work order from the office and the delay in customer request completion due to data transfer between the customer, the FSE, and the data-entry operator, a saving of $24,000 per person is achieved every year in the mobility-based field service operation compared with the paper-based system (assuming that approximately 300 requests are handled per person per quarter). This example gives a quantitative assessment of the cost savings from mobility enablement for a specific use. Mobile

Paper based			Mobility enabled		
Actor	**Activity**	**Time**	**Actor**	**Activity**	**Time/Comments**
FSE	Getting the part details (code, manufacture date, specifications ...)	10 min	FSE	~~Making a rough sketch of the part to be ordered and getting the part details~~	Replaced with scanning and image capture
FSE	Collect complaint details on paper	10 min	FSE	Collect complaint details on handheld	10 min
FSE	Prepare a customer report on paper	10 min	FSE	~~Prepare a customer report on paper~~	Automatically generated with handheld
Data entry operator	Enter the data collected by FSE on paper to enterprise server database	20 min	Data entry operator	~~Entering the data collected by FSE on paper to Enterprise server database~~	Eliminated by synchronizing with server
Data entry operator	Search vendor and place order	30 min	FSI	Search vendor and place order (automated)	10 min

Figure 7.3   Time analysis for paper- and mobile-enabled ordering by FSEs.

applications have also made a significant impact in enhancing the significance of enterprise mobility. Although mobile thick applications can function even in the absence of connectivity, most applications for the enterprise segment are enabled by the mobile network, and these applications cannot function without connectivity.

7.3 Solution Lifecycle

Enterprise mobility has four quadrants created by its four key areas of focus as shown in Figure 7.4. It covers both mobility products and mobility services and deals with both solutions for enterprise customers (enterprise market) and end customers (consumer market). Thus, enterprise mobility has a wide spectrum of coverage. The discussion on solution lifecycle in this section is limited to the simple mobile application development lifecycle scenario.

Enterprises can adopt a waterfall model or an agile model when defining the solution lifecycle. The following key phases are involved in the mobility solution lifecycle, although the order in which they would be executed will depend on the lifecycle model adopted:

- Strategy definition: Involves defining the strategic roadmap or capabilities—both business and technical—to be achieved from mobility adoption or a specific release of the mobility solution.
- Requirements definition: Involves defining the business requirements, system requirements, and the user experience requirements (wireframes or prototype images). This could be for all the features required in a waterfall model or an agile model or a subset of features when working on an agile model.

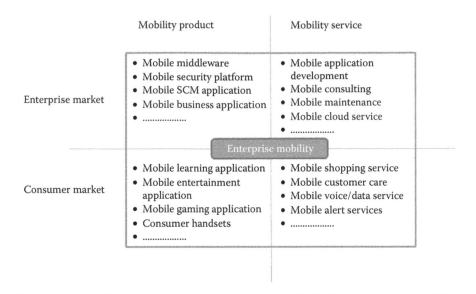

	Mobility product	Mobility service
Enterprise market	• Mobile middleware • Mobile security platform • Mobile SCM application • Mobile business application •	• Mobile application development • Mobile consulting • Mobile maintenance • Mobile cloud service • ....
	Enterprise mobility	
Consumer market	• Mobile learning application • Mobile entertainment application • Mobile gaming application • Consumer handsets •	• Mobile shopping service • Mobile customer care • Mobile voice/data service • Mobile alert services • ....

Figure 7.4 Enterprise mobility.

- ■ Analysis of requirements: This phase involves the analysis of the require-ments against feasibility both from the technical and business perspective and identification of the specific requirements to be taken up for design. A study of the existing literature to assist in the design phase is also covered in this analysis.
- ■ Design: The design of the solution is done in this phase and covers both the design of the mobile client side as well as the server side. The focus is on end-to-end solution design at a high level, followed by design of individual components that make up the solution. In an agile model, the scope of design would be limited, with changes introduced in an iterative way.
- ■ Implementation and test: Involves implementation of the solution based on the design and the testing of the components developed, integration, and system-level testing.
- ■ Deployment: There are two aspects to be factored under deployment in enter-prise mobility. One is client deployment, which involves multiple steps to get the application published in App Store, and the second aspect is server deployment.
- ■ Operation, administration, and maintenance (OAM): This phase involves maintenance operations and activities such as ensuring that the device soft-ware is updated periodically and the relevant antivirus package is installed, pushing new solutions based on enterprise needs, applying IT policies of usage on the mobile handset supplied by the enterprise, etc.

Having discussed the phases in high-level applications, let us focus on some of the key activities to be looked into in the mobile solution lifecycle, which may not be relevant for regular desktop or IT applications. It needs to be noted that mobile solutions are characterized by technology complexity, lesser control, and rapid evolution, which is not the case in IT solutions. Technology complexity is introduced because of device and platform diversity. There is a wide variety of handsets that differ in device profile, and added to this is the variety of operating systems for the mobile space. Hence, developing solutions for the mobile is more complex than developing desktop applications. The lesser control is because the solution is running on a device that is always moving. Hence, troubleshooting of bugs is a challenge. In addition to this, there are also chances of the mobile handset getting lost and the personal handset being used for office purposes, which would limit the level of control that can be applied. Rapid evolution is also a key factor in mobility. Every month, handset vendors are releasing new handsets with enhanced features and capabilities, making older versions obsolete, and every 3–4 months there is a new platform vendor or equipment manufacturer entering the mobility space with a revolutionary technology.

Strategy definition is the most vital activity in the mobile solution lifecycle. Unlike IT-based applications, mobile solutions are extensions of the existing IT applications in the mobility space. Hence, in addition to preparing a strategy for mobility adoption that satisfies business and technical requirements, there should also be focus on leveraging as much as possible the existing IT front-end and back-end systems of the enterprise.

Solution design is a key phase in the mobile solution lifecycle. Most mobile solutions, although initially targeted for a specific platform, will soon find the need to be supported in additional platforms. Hence, the need to support multiplatforms should be accounted in the design stage, as development should focus on the possibility of maximum reuse of developed components.

The deployment and testing phases in mobility also have significant differences compared with IT application deployment and testing. There are separate chapters detailing enterprise mobility solution testing and deployment (Chapters 9 and 10, respectively). Although administration of the mobility solution is not a key consideration in enterprise mobility, it is definitely an area to be factored in planning for enterprise employee mobile solutions. Administration covers the mobile server framework as well as the mobile devices provided to the employees. Unlike IT applications, remote management is a key capability required in the mobile solution administration framework. Mobile administrative functions are performed in enterprises using mobile device management (MDM) solutions. MDM solutions have the capability to perform mobile asset management, automatic update and patch management, and remote troubleshooting on mobile devices.

There is no single mobility solution lifecycle that applies to all customer needs. What can be defined are specific factors to be considered at various phases in the mobility solution lifecycle. Hence, vendors in the mobility product development and service industry need to ensure that they have a well-defined mobility solution lifecycle management approach that details the specific factors to be considered while developing mobility solutions.

7.4 Conclusion

The mobile industry is evolving so rapidly that the handsets that were used just a few years back are slated as legacy. The advent of smartphones and the developments in handset processor technology have helped in the development of mobile applications that perform the functions in most desktop applications. The immense number of stereoscopic games for three-dimensional handsets available for download is a clear indication of the processing capability that can be handled in mobile handsets.

Enterprise handsets are no longer limited to the BlackBerry platform. With consumerization of enterprise mobility, many enterprises are now allowing employees to use their personal mobile devices for accessing office applications. The mindset of both the consumer and the enterprise market is aligned to rapid adoption of the changes in technology in the mobility space. Mobility adoption has been rated as one of the key strategies of chief technology officers (CTOs) of most enterprises where it is still not implemented. Hence, there is no doubt that enterprise mobility has huge significance in today's industry for both productivity improvement and cost reduction.

While the primary focus of this chapter was to give the reader an overview of the significance of mobility, it also handles the mobility solution lifecycle. This chapter gives a high-level view on how the various phases in mobility solution lifecycle are significant for the end-to-end solution development and how different these are when compared with similar phases in the IT solution lifecycle.

Additional Reading

1. Rich Ling and Jonathan Donner. *Mobile Phones and Mobile Communication (Digital Media and Society Series)*. United Kingdom: Polity Press; 2009.
2. Keri Hayes. *Going Mobile: Building the Real-Time Enterprise with Mobile Applications that Work,* 1st edition. California: CMP; 2003.
3. Bhuvan Unhelkar. *Mobile Enterprise Transition and Management (Advanced & Emerging Communications Technologies*, 1st edition. Florida: Auerbach Publications; 2009.

Chapter 8

Cross-Platform Development

Mobile smartphone trends show that fragmentation is going to continue and is going to exist at least for the next decade. With multiple platforms such as Symbian, Android, BlackBerry (Research In Motion), iPhone, Windows Mobile, etc., in the mobile platform ecosystem, it is a challenge to develop an application that can be executed without code changes in other platforms. However, mobile solution developers need to address the concern on fragmentation and use techniques involving maximum reuse of development effort in offering multiplatform support. This chapter gives an overview of the different techniques of multiplatform development in enterprise mobility application development.

8.1 Introduction

Enterprises require different types of mobile applications such as B2B (business to business) applications, B2C (business to customer) applications, B2E (business to employee) applications, mobile web portals, mobile web apps, etc. From an App Store perspective, iPhone has the maximum number of applications, followed by Android, and, from an installation base perspective, Java 2 Micro Edition (J2ME) has the highest number. The key point is that for an enterprise there are multiple options to choose from, and in most scenarios, if consumer applications are being developed, then multiplatform support is a vital requirement to be satisfied.

Although multiplatform is the terminology commonly used to mean fragmentation in the mobility space, it needs to be noted that fragmentation is not just limited to the platform. Fragmentation in the mobility space is of the following types:

- Fragmentation due to the operating system (OS), for example, Symbian OS, iPhone OS, and Windows Mobile.
- Fragmentation due to programming languages, for example, Objective C for iPhone, Java for Android, C# for Windows Mobile, and C/C++ for Brew.
- Fragmentation due to OS versions, for example, Android 1.5, 1.6, 2.0, iPhone OS 3, iOS 4, and BlackBerry JDE 4.7, 5.0.
- Fragmentation due to device hardware, for example, screen resolution, communication peripherals, keyboard, and sensors.
- Fragmentation due to extensions and virtual machines, for example, extensions such as HTC Sense, Motorola API and virtual machines such as Google Dalvik, Myriad Dalvik Turbo, etc.
- Fragmentation due to device-specific differences, for example, Capture intent, OpenGL differences, camera package, and global positioning system settings.

Offering multiplatform support needs to ensure that the above factors contributing to fragmentation are addressed. Enterprises could also explore the option of building native applications for individual platforms without using cross-platform development techniques. However, building native applications would mean that the applications are developed for a limited set of platforms, and the code bases for multiple platforms are to be maintained. Also building applications specifically for each platform requires more time and effort. In spite of the effort involved in the native application development of multiple platforms, there is a probability that the chosen platforms might lose their customer bases and that several new platforms may come into market. Adding to all these issues, development on each platform needs a different programming skillset. Cross-platform or multiplatform development is thus a significant activity to be factored from strategy definition to implementation.

8.2 Custom-Development Approach or Cross-Platform Framework

Custom-developed point solution and cross-platform-based middleware development can be analyzed according to the following factors:

- Time to market: Custom development of native applications involves significant development time due to custom development of each and every module of the application. Because of this reason, when enterprises plan to do custom development, the usual strategy is to roll out a solution for different platforms in a phased manner. In most cases, iPhone app is launched first, followed by Android within the next three months, and the remaining platforms in a stage-wise release. However, with cross-platform development, there is a 40%–50% reduction in effort due to the reuse of the component repository across platforms, and most of the effort in supporting additional platforms goes into cross compiling and packaging. Hence, the time to market is significantly low with the cross-platform approach compared with the custom-development approach.

■ Technology transformation: Cross-platform development gives the flexibility to create technology- and platform-independent applications. It is based on the concept of "develop once" and "deploy multiple types." Hence, when new platforms enter the market, it is easy to transform the solution to meet market needs with the cross-platform approach. On the contrary, in custom-developed point solutions, there is a tight coupling between the device and the back-end technology. This makes adapting to new technology difficult with the custom-development approach.

■ User experience: The native approach or the custom development approach can offer a much better user experience compared with the cross-platform development framework. This is because a lot of platform-specific capabilities are compromised in achieving abstraction across multiple platforms. Hence, in the cross-platform approach, a lot of user experience components specific to a platform cannot be used as any platform-specific components cannot be directly ported to another platform. Many retail giants take up the additional cost and the effort of using the custom development approach to provide a unique and compelling experience to the customer, which cannot be achieved in a cross-platform framework.

■ Flexibility and extensibility: After developing the solution for multiple platforms, when a change has been done with regard to a fix or a new functionality, it is much easier to implement the change and repackage the solution with the cross-platform framework compared with the custom-development approach. This is because the core component is a single-code base with a cross platform, and the changes are to be made in a multiple-code base corresponding to each platform in the custom development approach.

■ Skillset, cost, and complexity: With native application development, the implementation team needs to have the knowledge of platform-specific APIs and the coding experience in the language used for the specific platform development, including the platform development environment. Thus, when developing a native application for multiple platforms, the skillset requirements are much more complex compared with development using a cross-platform framework. Managing the solution is also complex and requires more effort. The skillset requirements and maintenance complexity add up to a higher operational expenditure when following a custom-development approach. When user experience can be slightly compromised, it is always advisable to follow a cross-platform framework rather than a custom-development approach.

8.3 Multiplatform Development

Multiplatform development can be done in the following ways:

- A separate native application for each platform
- J2ME-based development
- Using cross-compilers for development
- Web-based development
  - Mobile web
  - Web-packaged app
- Middleware solutions, such as mobile enterprise application platform (MEAP) and mobile consumer application platform (MCAP)

Figure 8.1 shows a diagrammatic representation of developing a separate native application for each platform. A separate native application can be of help to effectively utilize platform features and to achieve a rich user experience. Also the skillset requirements are high when this approach is followed for multiplatform development. The effort and cost (implementation and maintenance) are also high, and there is no reuse achieved with separate development.

Figure 8.2 shows the application development using J2ME, which allows the running of the application on platforms that support Java. A majority of mobile platforms can be supported with this approach including Windows Mobile for which Java virtual machine is available. iPhone, however, does not support Java-based applications, and, hence, a native application needs to be developed for iPhone in J2ME-based development. It needs to be noted that the Java virtual

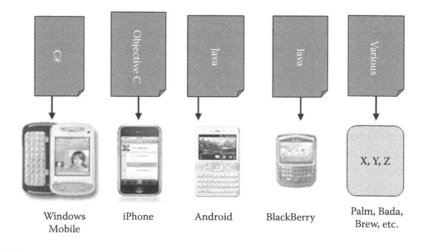

Figure 8.1   Separate native application for each platform.

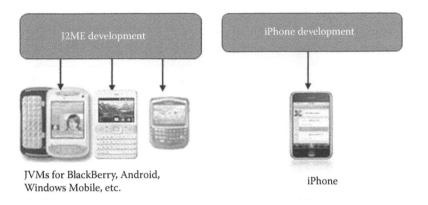

JVMs for BlackBerry, Android, Windows Mobile, etc.

iPhone

Figure 8.2   J2ME-based development.

machine version and its performance will impact the application's performance, and all platform-specific controls will not be available in J2ME.

Figure 8.3 shows the implementation using a mobile platform cross-compiler. In this technique, the application development is done in a common abstraction language, and cross-compilers are used to port the application to different platforms. This approach leads to reduced implementation effort and costs, as more component level reuse is involved. When changes are made in the base or in the abstract implementation, it is easier to fix bugs and propagate changes. The results of the compilation from the abstract implementation to a specific platform will usually have errors, and these need to be fixed manually.

The mobile web portal pages can be accessed from different device browsers. Based on the device sending the page view request, the response page will be formatted by a profiling engine. The profiling engine has information on the web format supported by the device and converts the response page to suit the device. HTML5-supported browsers have web tool kits that handle rendering; hence, wrapping HTML5 pages for specific mobile platforms is becoming a common solution followed by enterprises to achieve multiplatform capability. Mobile platforms provide coding flexibility to place the web view (embedded web page) in applications that can be used to delegate security or compliance requirements to the server and can also give multiplatform support by showing the mobile portal page in an application wrapper. Figure 8.4 shows the implementation architecture for a mobile application using HTML5, which uses the PhoneGap (phonegap.com) solution as a wrapper.

MEAP and MCAP from multiple vendors offer multiplatform development ability. These platforms have a development environment where applications can be modeled independent of the platform and then built for a specific platform. There is considerable reuse that can be achieved when the mobile middleware (Figure 8.5) is used for development, and it is also easier to maintain the solution when this

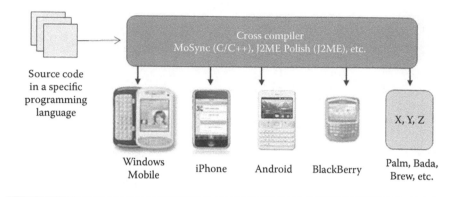

Figure 8.3   Using cross-compilers for development.

Figure 8.4   Model-view-controller architecture of a web wrapper to thick applications using PhoneGap.

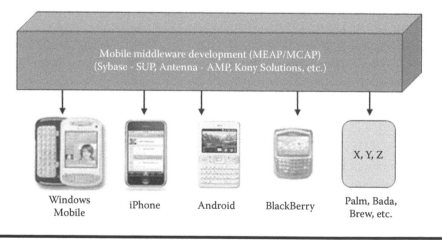

Figure 8.5   Mobile middleware-based development.

approach is used. Also the middleware server brings with it a set of server-level capabilities such as synchronization, application control, administrative capability, and analytics collection. The mobile middleware from most of the leading vendors provides the ability to integrate with multiple types of back-end systems such as Web Services, Siebel, SAP, Oracle, etc. This use of the middleware integration capabilities significantly reduces implementation and deployment effort. The downside of this approach is the license cost involved for multiplatform middleware and the limitations in user experience, as abstract implementation for multiplatforms leads to a compromise in platform-specific user experience controls.

Although this section details the five different approaches to multiplatform development, it needs to be noted that none of these approaches can be said to be the right solution in all scenarios of cross-platform development. The right solution is determined by the mobility road map and the requirements to be satisfied. For example, retailers would place user experience as their highest priority to ensure that customers not only feel comfortable with the application but the compelling experience also helps in generating more mobile sales. Hence, the retailer would most probably opt for a separate native application development approach. However, for an automotive chain that wants to supply handsets with the application for scanning and ordering spare parts, the HTML5 wrapping to the application would be a better approach, considering that the chain wants to roll out the solution at a minimum cost. The same automotive vendor when rolling out a mobile customer care application for its automobile customers would probably go for yet another application, where compelling user experience is not required but yet there is no control on whether the handset the customers use will support HTML5.

8.4 Conclusion

For enterprise applications developed for the employees, the usual approach was to use a single platform. For example, the Motorola handset with Windows Mobile OS was popular for mobile applications used by field personnel for scanning, and IT employees used BlackBerry handsets to use the push and security features offered by the BlackBerry Enterprise Server. This trend is changing with consumerization in the enterprise, and most enterprises allow their employees to use personal handsets for executing and accessing office applications. This has led to the need for a multiplatform approach in developing employee applications. For consumer applications developed by the enterprise, the multiplatform approach is a mandatory requirement.

The specific platforms to be adopted in the initial launch and the evolution strategy need to be planned to ensure maximum reuse in development. The usual approach adopted by enterprises shows the first launch to target iPhone and iPad, with applications for other smartphones following shortly in a few months. There are multiple approaches to multiplatform development as discussed in this chapter.

It is to be kept in mind that the road map for multiplatform support and the development and test methodology used for multiplatform support are critical factors to be looked into while defining an enterprise mobile adoption strategy. This chapter provides an overview of the techniques used in cross-platform development.

Additional Reading

1. Brian Fling. *Mobile Design and Development: Practical Concepts and Techniques for Creating Mobile Sites and Web Apps*, 1 edition. California: O'Reilly Media; 2009.
2. Keri Hayes. *Going Mobile: Building the Real-Time Enterprise with Mobile Applications that Work*, 1st edition. California: CMP; 2003.
3. Valentino Lee, Heather Schneider, and Robbie Schell. *Mobile Applications: Architecture, Design, and Development*, 1st edition. New Jersey: Prentice Hall; 2004.

Chapter 9

Mobile Application Testing

The number of mobile equipment manufacturers, mobile platforms, and handset models released by the equipment manufacturers has increased drastically over the past few years. This has lead to a lot of device diversity in the mobile industry. The testing of mobile applications is considerably more complex and requires more effort than PC-based software-application testing because of the device diversity that it involves. The same BlackBerry application is expected to enable the user to navigate irrespective of whether the specific model used supports track ball, touch screen, or track wheel for navigation, which can be guaranteed only after proper testing. This chapter gives an overview of mobile application testing. The methods and approaches of mobile application testing are covered in this chapter.

9.1 Introduction

Enterprises are currently adopting a multiplatform approach as part of their mobility enablement strategy. This has resulted in an increased focus on mobile application testing for the vast variety of devices. Also, mobile application testing has a definite testing life cycle similar to software testing for PC-based applications. This chapter is intended to introduce the reader to the test life cycle, the test approach, and the test tools adopted by enterprises for mobile application testing. Mobility applications are software applications, and, hence, much of the test strategies for mobiles are built on the generic IT test practices followed in the software life cycle.

Mobile application testing is not limited to manual testing or automated testing using in-house tools. There has been considerable progress in the field of mobile application testing with commercial off-the-shelf (COTS) products offered by market leaders such as Testquest, Mobile Complete, Argo, and Mercury Functional Testing for Wireless. While a discussion of all the COTS products in mobile testing is outside the scope of this book, the TestQuest Countdown platform has been taken as a specific example and discussed in this chapter. Remote-testing products, such as DeviceAnywhere, that aid enterprises to test applications on actual devices are also handled at a higher level.

9.2 Mobile Application Testing Life Cycle

The mobile application testing life cycle can be broken down into nine phases as shown in Figure 9.1. The phases are similar to those in usual software testing, except for some activities that are performed in these phases:

- Phase 1 (strategy definition): This phase involves the creation of a high-level test strategy. Based on the application requirements and test specifications, the test manager is expected to come up with a high-level strategy to test the functional and nonfunctional requirements in a comprehensive manner using the available resources, within the available budgets, and in the best quality possible.
- Phase 2 (test planning): Application testing on all platforms and associated devices cannot be done in parallel. Device sampling needs to be performed to identify which platform and models are of priority, and the test samples need to be clearly identified. At the end of this phase, a refined test specification along with a high-level test plan is ready for the testing team to perform the analysis.
- Phase 3 (test analysis): In this phase, the requirements are mapped to a matrix, and an analysis of the testability of the requirement is done. Generic requirements are broken down to a quantifiable set of subrequirements that can be validated. The result of this analysis is a functional validation matrix. Based on the validation matrix, test cases are prepared to test the requirements, and traceability is ensured to map the test to the requirements. The test plan is also revised based on the analysis performed in this phase.
- Phase 4 (test design): After the test cases are identified, the next step involves segregating the test cases according to the way in which testing will be performed. A common categorization technique involves splitting those that require manual testing and those that can be a candidate for automation testing. In mobility, there is scope for efficient test design based on the platform, the handsets locally available, the handset testing that needs a remote environment, a generic business logic test case, and a device-specific test case.

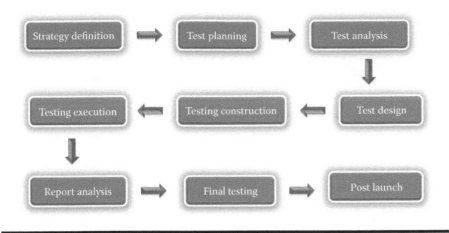

Figure 9.1 Mobile application testing life cycle.

Test cases can also be revised as part of the test design exercise. Another key activity in the test design is the preparation of test data sets and the assessment of the risks involved in the testing and the preparation of mitigation strategies for key risks at various stages of test execution.

■ Phase 5 (test construction): Based on the test design, the automation test cases are scripted in this phase. Suitable stub and drivers for test are designed, along with the formulation of manual test cases. Test scripting involves preparing test procedures for the mobile client, the server side, and the network, covering end-to-end solutions.

■ Phase 6 (testing execution): This is the most significant phase in mobile testing, and the actual difference between PC-based testing and mobile application testing becomes evident at this stage. High-level mobile test execution simply involves the completion of the execution cycle and obtaining the results. However, mobile test execution is performed in four methodical levels by most enterprises to ensure coverage of specific scenarios that are relevant in the enterprise mobility context. The following are the levels in the test execution of mobile applications, as shown in Figure 9.2:

    – Level 1: This level is intended to ensure that the test environment and the executable created from the build have undergone the required sanity checks before they are tested to satisfy the functional requirements. This level covers the following procedures:

        • Build-verification testing: The build reports are verified to ensure that the executable is stable for testing.

        • Deployment or installation testing: The mobile application is launched on a simulator or test device and checked for installation errors.

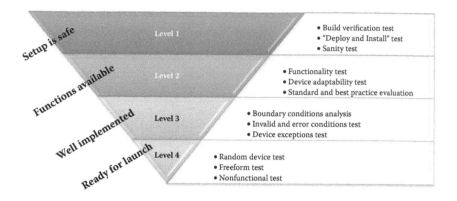

Figure 9.2   Mobile test execution.

- Sanity testing: These sanity test cases identified for mobile applications are executed to ensure that the application is ready for a detailed functional testing to be performed at the next level.
- Level 2: This level is intended to perform detailed functional testing of the application and also to perform device or platform testing of the application. The functionality is expected to work properly on all the targeted mobile platforms. This level covers the following procedures:
  - Functionality testing: A set of specific functionalities should be satisfied by the applications based on the functional requirements. These are tested as part of functionality testing.
  - Device adaptability testing: The mobile application needs to be tested for proper working on individual applications. This activity is verified as part of device adaptability testing.
  - Standards' evaluation: Mobile applications have to comply with specific standards based on the type of application. For example, if any credit card information is entered in the mobile application, then the application needs to be certified against the Payment Card Industry Data Security Standard (PCIDSS).
- Level 3: This level is intended to perform regression testing to test the different scenarios that would lead to exceptions or force close operations in the application during its execution on the mobile device. This level covers the following procedures:
  - Boundary conditions: The mobile application is tested against boundary conditions to ensure that the application handles all exceptional scenarios related to the boundary values.
  - Invalid and error conditions: The tester needs to aggressively check the application for possible error conditions. The enterprise or consumer application is expected to handle invalid and error conditions.

- Device exception testing: An application developed for the BlackBerry will not directly run on iPhone even if the application is developed on a middleware platform. The device-specific components need to be properly configured to be executed on a specific platform. The device-specific exceptions that arise from device-specific components are tested as part of device exception testing.
- Level 4: This level is intended to perform nonfunctional testing and experimental testing to ensure that the mobile application is robust and is ready for deployment. This level covers the following procedures:
  - Random device testing: In this testing, the tester works not on non-documented test cases with the intent of breaking the application on a specific platform but tries to identify all possible issues that could be caused in a specific device while running the application. Some low-end devices may crash while running the mobile apps because of limited resources, and optimization might be required, which can be identified under random testing.
  - Free-form application testing: In free-form testing, which is also a form of nondocumented testing, the tester experiments different scenarios that could possibly crash the application. Additional features that can be introduced in the application can also be in free-form application testing.
  - Nonfunctional testing: This test does a detailed validation of the nonfunctional test cases. This will include execution of test cases related to security, monitoring, latency, high availability, etc.

■ Phase 7 (report analysis): This phase is to analyze the results of test execution and understand whether the mobile application is ready for alpha and beta testing. The bug reports will help in identifying the list of open issues that could be skipped to the next release and the handset models and platform versions where the application is stable for test launch.

■ Phase 8 (final testing): This phase involves application testing with a set of users who may be internal or external to the enterprise. The main intent is to check if the mobile application is ready for commercial launch. Any cosmetic changes to make the product more appealing can be identified at this stage. In addition to the look and feel, many other attributes such as improving the usability, reducing the response time, and changing the layout for specific handsets can all be identified and raised for design consideration in this phase of testing. The marketing and sales team get the chance to use and provide their final suggestions at this stage. All solution-related document verification also needs to be completed before the end of this stage.

■ Phase 9 (post launch): This is the last phase in the mobile testing life cycle, and it deals with post launch. The intent of this phase is to evaluate the testing process and to improve it. The test efforts involved in the previous phases are analyzed to identify where the process could be optimized. For thin client and web-based solutions, monitoring the solutions at the server level is used to identify the number of hits on the mobile web page and the impact of the mobile solution on the market.

9.3 Enterprise Approach to Mobile Testing

Mobile testing needs to ensure that a proper strategy is in place for client and server-side testing. The client-side test could use real handsets or emulators. Both these options have specific benefits and constraints. The real handset provides exposure to the limitations and quirks present within the actual customer setup, which will not be directly evident while using emulators. The real handset-based test can help in validating the application for performance bottlenecks with network nodes. However, the entire testing on real mobiles will be a very expensive, laborious, and time-consuming affair. On the other hand, the use of emulators overcomes the limited processing power and the storage memory of real handsets, thereby providing an option for diagnostic software-isolating issues with the application. The optimal strategy used by most enterprises is to use emulator-based testing during development and initial testing and then to switch to real handsets once the application is stable for testing on actual handsets.

The server side also presents options for testing. Following the same scenario as in the client side, a real network or a proxy network can be used for testing in the server side. The real network-based tests help in analyzing real-time operational capability to ascertain the real-time feel of the platform and to emulate the effects of the timing of the network and the various network elements. Thus, with a real network, the quirks and the limitations of the platform on a particular network can be analyzed and rectified. However, real network-based test is a slow, expensive, and laborious process, and the platform-related specific issues will be difficult to isolate. On the other hand, with a proxy network, the complete platform can be thoroughly tested as a stand-alone product, and scenarios that involve verification of the platform's interoperability with the operator are best verified. Most enterprises use a proxy network as its main test environment and use real networks only for alpha and beta tests for analyzing capabilities in an actual setup.

A key issue to be addressed in mobility testing involves the handling of device diversity and ensuring that the mobile application runs on all the required platforms and associated handsets. The following are the main aspects to be covered in device diversity testing:

■ User interface (UI) look-and-feel testing: In this testing, the look and feel of the mobile application on the specific device is validated. This is to ensure that the data are rendered in the required format as expected.
■ Alignment testing: Different devices have different form factors. Even when the layout and general look and feel are correct, the alignment of content

may change due to a change in the size of controls such as buttons. This may block the content and, hence, this needs to be thoroughly tested on all the application screens.

■ Device native application programming interface testing: Devices might be calling different APIs for performing the same function. For example, the functionality of barcode scanning in a Motorola device is different from the functionality of another version of the device from the same vendor.

■ Device control testing: The control buttons on the devices differ. For example, a BlackBerry 9530 allows browsing through data with touch-screen technology, while BlackBerry 8700 would use the track wheel to browse data. When filling a form in the mobile application, the user might use the device controls available in his or her specific device. Hence, the applications need to be checked to work with different types of device control specific to the device.

■ Peripheral testing: Most enterprise mobile applications are designed to use additional mobile peripherals such as the secure digital card, smart card reader, or biometric reader. For example, law-enforcement professionals use handsets with biometric readers, and some enterprise BlackBerry handsets also have card readers for employee identification integrated with handset security. When the mobile application uses any peripheral components, these capabilities need to be tested on each device or platform level as part of device diversity testing.

9.4 Simulator Testing

There are several integrated development environments (IDEs) for application development. Two IDEs are given for each of the three popular platforms listed:

■ iPhone development
  – Xcode IDE
  – Dashcode IDE
■ Android development
  – Eclipse IDE
  – Dashcode IDE
■ BlackBerry development
  – Eclipse IDE
  – BlackBerry Java Development Environment (BlackBerry JDE)

To develop applications for the specific platform, the platform specific-software development kit (SDK) needs to be installed and configured with the IDE. The SDK will mostly contain the simulators for the platform. If not, most platforms also allow selective download and installation of simulators for a specific device.

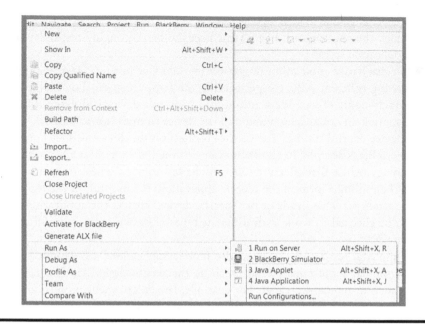

Figure 9.3 Launching the BlackBerry Simulator on Eclipse IDE.

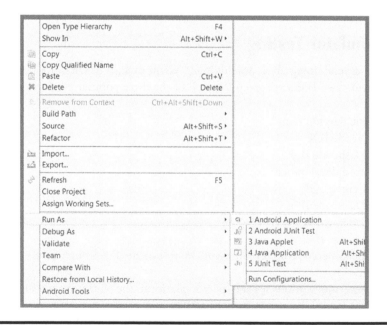

Figure 9.4 Launching the Android Simulator on Eclipse IDE.

The platform-specific emulators can be launched from the IDE. Figures 9.3 and 9.4 show how the simulator for BlackBerry and Android can be launched from the Eclipse IDE.

The simulator of the specific handset on which the application is to be tested can also be set from the IDE. The BlackBerry device profile on which the application is to be executed is selected, and the handset properties can be set as shown in Figure 9.5. It is possible to run the executable directly on the emulator, which will be provided as part of the SDK platform, without using the IDE. To do this, simply launch the required version of the device emulator from the command line and execute the "application install" command for the specific platform from the command line. The application package will be automatically installed on the launched emulator and can be tested.

9.5 Real-Device Testing

All enterprises test their applications on actual devices in addition to simulator-based testing. In most enterprise scenarios, a set of sample handsets are used in the enterprise for real-device testing. For extensive testing on a variety of handsets, either the test activity is outsourced to a testing service provider that has a mobility laboratory with an extensive collection of mobile handsets, which the

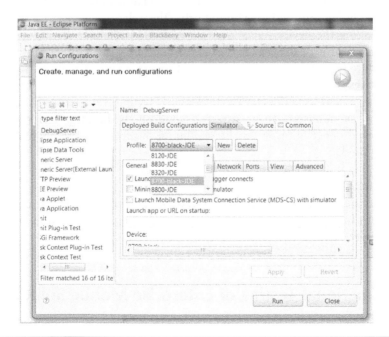

Figure 9.5   Selecting a specific device in a platform to be used as a simulator.

enterprise is targeting to launch its applications on, or an account is created with a service provider that allows remote testing of handsets. The use of a local laboratory with handsets in the enterprise or having the test activity outsourced to a service provider with required handsets is a straightforward activity. Hence, this section details remote testing using one of the leading market solutions or services for device diversity testing offered by DeviceAnywhere.

The steps for performing remote testing with DeviceAnywhere are listed:

■ Create an account: To work on DeviceAnywhere Test Center, an account needs to be available. Enterprises can contact DeviceAnywhere and set up an account. Trial users and all new customers are offered a free trial to DeviceAnywhere. To sign up for free trial, simply go to http://www.deviceanywhere.com and fill the sign-up form.

■ Launching the test studio: In order to deploy the application to a handset provided by DeviceAnywhere and test the application, we must first be running the DeviceAnywhere Studio and must have at least one device acquired. While working with DeviceAnywhere for the first time, the user needs to login to the account and download or launch the test studio from the link provided in the home page after login. The application can be installed to the tester's PC, and subsequent needs to work on DeviceAnywhere will only require the launch of the studio installed on the PC. Creating a shortcut while prompted during installation helps to launch DeviceAnywhere Studio directly from the desktop without using the web.

■ Selecting the device: Once the test studio is launched, the next step is to browse through the available handsets and select the handset on which the application is to be tested. Based on the enterprise subscription, the type of devices that can be selected will be different. The user has to select "Access Device" and "Acquire Device" to establish a connection with the real device. Multiple handsets can be acquired based on the subscription, with a predefined upper limit set on the maximum number of handsets that can be acquired.

■ Deploy and test the application: The final step is to upload the application to be tested onto the device. This can be done by transferring the application to a secure web server. Once the application is downloaded to the device, the user can run and test the application by interacting directly with the device from the remote desktop of the user.

9.6 Functional Testing of Enterprise Mobile Solutions

Functional testing on mobiles covers end-to-end business scenarios for a mobile application. The functional testing of a mobile application will involve the following components, as shown in Figure 9.6:

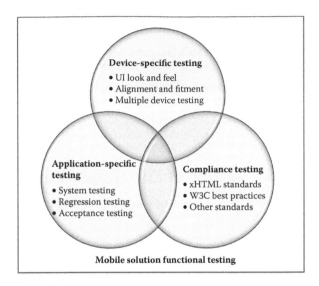

Figure 9.6 Components in the functional testing of a mobile solution.

■ App-specific testing: This testing involves testing the screens, the capabilities in each screen, interaction with the server, and interfaces used by the mobile application. This testing is similar to any software-solution testing and tests the entire system against the required functionality as identified in the requirement-gathering phase of the application development life cycle. The mobile solution system testing ensures compliancy with all the functional requirements. Regression testing on the system ensures that all bugs are identified. Finally, acceptance testing is performed to ensure that the required functionalities are available in the application to be published in the App Store in case of consumer mobile applications and pushed to mobiles in the case of enterprise mobile applications.

■ Device-specific testing: The wide variety of mobile handsets available in the market makes device-specific testing essential for mobile applications. In device testing, the emphasis is mainly on checking the UI look and feel on the mobile devices, ensuring alignment and fitment of the application on the devices that are in the scope of a specific project, and on multidevice testing to evaluate the performance and the customizations done to suit specific devices and platform versions.

■ Compliance testing: The mobile application functional standards can be web application standards for mobile web applications. Testing checks whether the web application complies with xHTML and W3C standards. Another category of standards deals with platform standards. The platform vendors define guidelines and standards to be followed for certifying the device and publishing the application in the App Store. For example, the iPhone human interface guide needs to be followed for iPhone application development. Based on the application transactions, there can be multiple mandatory compliance standards to be fulfilled, which can be grouped under the third category called "other functional standards." For example, PCIDSS defined by the Payment Card Industry Security Standards Council is usually to be followed when the mobile application has a financial transaction that takes payment card data as part of the inputs for completing a transaction.

9.7 Performance Testing of Enterprise Mobile Solutions

There are three levels of performance testing for mobile solutions:

- Server test
- Network test
- Device test

The server is tested for load scenarios involving requests from handsets; network testing is intended to validate coverage and latency; device testing will help to do performance tuning of the application on the device. Popular solutions for server-load testing include Load Runner, Web Load, Performance Studio, Silk Performer, and QALoad. These tools are not designed specifically for testing the server side performance to be loaded from mobile clients, but products such as iMobiload from Infosys and Mobile Master from Argogroup are solutions customized to perform load testing for mobile interaction with the server.

Another important aspect in mobile solution testing is the performance of the mobile solution to changes in the network latency covered under network simulation for performance testing. Test beds are offered by multiple vendors to test and analyze the performance of mobile or wireless applications in a controlled laboratory environment, which is independent of the application platform. The test setup constitutes access points such as 802.11b and WiFi to simulate the scenarios to be tested. These solutions can provide data on variations in the network coverage and in the bandwidth, including latency and 2.5G/3G/4G service emulation.

Devices differ in their memory and processing capability. Device performance can be determined by actually testing on the device. DeviceAnywhere can be used to test applications on real devices and measure the performance of the device while running the application. If the number of platforms or devices is limited, then in-house testing can be performed. The following are the performance test types:

- Best-case scenario test: The best-case scenario test entails measuring the performance of the server application under a load of a single mobile user. The response time of each and every possible transaction in the application will be measured for a single user under this test. No script will be used in this test, and a real user will be logging on through the mobile application, and the response time for all the transactions will be measured. The purpose behind this test is early detection of any obvious performance issue that may appear even when the application is subject to a load of as low as one user.

▪ Normal-load performance test: The scope of the normal-load performance test is to identify issues on the server side under normal load with multiple mobile users. This helps to identify performance deterioration and other issues in the server side due to the load.

▪ Production stability test: Stability testing is a variation of the load test run for an extended period of time, with the purpose of detecting slow-to-appear defects. For this test, the load test will be reexecuted during production for a minimum duration of 12 h and up to 48 h.

▪ Stress test: Performance test scenarios are run with maximum user volumes estimated on the basis of growth projections to ensure that the application and the interfaces continue to meet performance expectations.

▪ Volume test: For the volume growth test, the database is loaded with additional data volume to simulate scenarios that arise from huge data volume and to identify the system's response to corrupt data.

9.8 Stability Testing of Mobile Applications

The stability on the server side has been discussed in Section 9.7. Application-level stability testing involves identifying the possibility of crash of an application.

Mobile applications crash in the following scenarios:

▪ While executing
▪ During installation on the device
▪ On application launch

The main cause of crash of a mobile application during execution is due to exceptions that are not handled properly. When all exception scenarios are not identified and handled as part of the mobile application development, then the application will crash when the user performs an action that triggers an exception. Exceptions can also occur due to device-specific features that may not fit well with the mobile application. The approach to ensure exception-safe code is to have it listed as a nonfunctional requirement as part of coding requirements, which the vendor developing the mobile application has to comply with. Also straight coding guidelines ensure that each screen and the invoked functions have an exception-handling routine. Proactive testing will help to ensure that all exception scenarios are caught before use in live environment.

The main cause of application crash during installation is because the device capabilities may not support the system requirements of the mobile application. This could be due to a wrong application (platform or version) downloaded by the user, an application requiring more resources than what is available in the device, access issues to install the location on the device, etc. However, the mobile application published for a specific device is expected to run without any issues on the suggested device. This can be ensured using real-device remote testing.

The mobile application could crash on launch due to multiple reasons such as corrupt cache from previous launch or inadequate resources in the device. These issues can be easily identified and fixed as part of real-device testing. Real-device testing helps to identify the issues that can lead to application crash on launch, which may not be discovered as part of simulation testing. The application vendor needs to use mobile coding practices that ensure proper handling of crash scenarios, such as cleaning up the cache on exit of the application or when an exception occurs.

9.9 Mobile Security Testing

The security testing of mobile applications has four components:

- Functional security requirements testing
- Nonfunctional security requirements testing
- Vulnerability test of application in the device
- Vulnerability test on network access

The functional security requirements are specific to applications and are usually tested manually. In general, all mobility solutions will have authentication, authorization, and encryption of secure data as a mandatory requirement, which needs to be tested. The nonfunctional security test requirements cover aspects such as confidentiality, integrity, availability, intrusion prevention, control of enterprise devices, certificate exchanges, access controls, compliance to standards, etc. The nonfunctional requirements are mostly dependent on the application domain. The banking domain has more stringent requirements compared with other domains.

For applications that get installed on the mobile device, application footprint analysis is usually performed to ensure that the application is safe from vulnerabilities. The file system fingerprint of installed applications must be closely monitored and analyzed to ensure that the application is working as expected using safe directories and files that are protected and does not access or cache data, which it is not expected to perform.

Developers often assume that the phone memory is a safe storage location and use it to store sensitive information such as usernames, passwords, and other secure information. The main goals when analyzing the mobile device file system are as follows:

1. Identify the files created on the phone by the application during installation.
2. Identify changes made to the existing files over multiple application operations.
3. Analyze the information written to the phone file system during various stages of operation.
4. Analyze the impact of a driver application to corrupt the data or mobile application.

Most regulations enforce vulnerability tests on network access. For example, PCIDSS requires intended organizations to conduct annual or more frequent network and application penetration tests. The security rule of the Health Information Portability and Accountability Act requires a comprehensive security evaluation program, which on implementation would consist of security process audits, periodic vulnerability assessments, and penetration tests.

There are multiple vulnerability attacks such as Distributed Denial of Service (DDoS), ConFickr worm, Nimda, SQL Slammer, and e-mail viruses and their endless variants that can attack the mobile server framework. Vulnerability assessment solutions emulate thousands of attacks and variants. Some of the most popular solutions include the following:

- Rational AppScan Standard Edition is a leading web application security testing tool that automates vulnerability assessments and scans and tests for all common web server vulnerabilities including SQL-injection, cross-site scripting, and buffer overflow.
- Avalanche 2900 1G to 10G solutions from Spirent Communications emulate conditions such as DDoS, Worms, e-mail attacks, Viruses, Tojans, application penetrations, and evaded attacks.

Testing of client-level vulnerabilities involves manual testing by executing test cases for nonfunctional requirements. The server-level vulnerabilities can be tested by using existing enterprise security software or by utilizing the leading industrial solutions suggested in this section.

9.10 Usability Testing

The mobile application usability testing is important because there are a lot more constraints on mobile applications:

- Small screen size
- Type of input devices available

- Resource constraints
- Diverse usage environment
- Limited user experience
- Physical movement of users

With many constraints in mobility, there arises the need to test the usability of the application and ensure that the user is able to perform the required task in a minimum number of screens and with the least number of clicks and selections.

The following are the methods of mobile usability testing:

- Paper prototyping: This is the easiest way to prototype mobile application interfaces because most mobile interfaces are simplistic. The testers and alpha or beta users can have a look at it and give feedback about the ease of use. In the requirements phase, the UI screens should be reviewed, finalized, and approved. The UI screen shots prepared need to be carefully analyzed for usability.
- Working prototype: This can be done by proving a working prototype of the application and receiving feedback. The working prototype undergoes usability testing against the following parameters:
  - Performance: Measure the time and the number of steps required for completion of basic tasks (e.g., load time of application, exiting an application, moving to next screen, etc.).
  - Accuracy: Is the application giving the required results within a defined tolerance level?
  - Learn ability: How much does the user remember afterward or after periods of nonuse?
  - Errors: How many errors do users make, how severe are these errors, and how easily can they recover from the errors?
  - User satisfaction or emotional response: How does the user feel about the tasks completed? Is the user confident or stressed? Would the user recommend this application to other people?

Mobile devices differ not only in screen size and layout but also in the ways by which people input their information, whether it is a QWERTY keyboard, a stylus, a numeric keypad, or a dial wheel. These should all be taken into consideration while testing. The usability testing is always performed manually without automation.

9.11 Mobile Test Automation

Mobile test automation can assist in considerable cost reduction and improve the test efficiency for test activities in enterprises. Identifying and using the right test

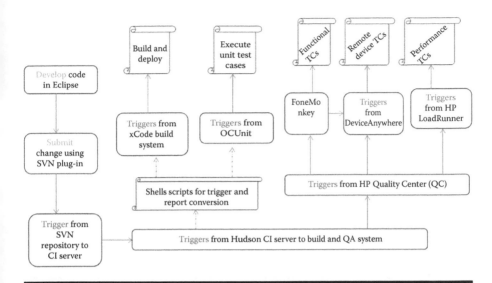

Figure 9.7 A sample mobile test automation framework for mobile web.

tools is the first step for test automation. There are tools that offer UI functional testing on mobile applications, leading to automation of test cases that need to be repeated, such as in sanity testing. For functional and UI automation, some of the popular tools for iPhone are FoneMonkey, UIAutomation Instrument, and EggPlanet, while the popular tools for Android are Robotium, Robolectric, and Monkeyrunner.

The activities for test automation start in the development stage itself with the use of tools such as OCunit or UnitKit for iPhone and Java tools such as Junit for Android, in preparing unit test cases that can be executed from the build framework itself. Considering the wide variety of devices on which testing is to be performed, it is a common practice to subscribe for remote device testing with providers such as DeviceAnywhere. With remote testing, the enterprise gets the opportunity to test on several mobile devices without procuring the device. Once the test case execution is automated, it becomes much easier to do remote testing, and this reduces manual test effort tremendously. Figure 9.7 shows a sample test automation framework for mobile web, while Figure 9.8 shows a sample test automation framework for native application developed for iPhone.

9.12 Conclusion

This chapter provides an overview of enterprise mobility testing. Mobility testing is similar to the usual software testing of enterprise applications, with specific considerations relevant to the mobility technology. The lack of standardization for mobile

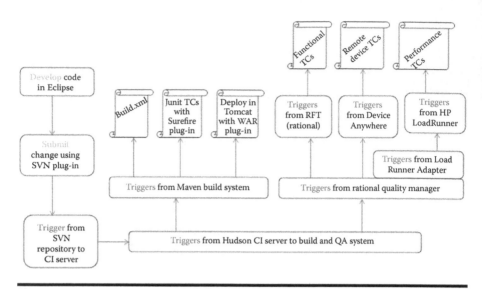

Figure 9.8   A sample mobile test automation framework for native applications (iPhone).

handset profiles makes mobility testing of enterprise applications challenging. Test engineers need to be trained in the mobility domain, and test scenarios are identified in the mobility domain to ensure that defects are identified and fixed before launch. The mobile application certification cycle done by the platform vendor also acts as an additional test before the application is made available on the platform vendor's App World/Store.

Mobility testing is an important component in the study of enterprise mobility. This chapter is intended to give the reader information on the essential topics in mobility testing, covering the life cycle, types of mobility testing, and the ideal test team composition for a mobility project. As part of the discussion, some of the leading products in the industry are also covered at a high level.

Additional Reading

1. Julian Harty and Mahadev Satyanarayanan. *A Practical Guide to Testing Wireless Smartphone Applications (Synthesis Lectures on Mobile and Pervasive Computing)*, 1st edition. California: Morgan & Claypool Publishers; 2009.
2. Hung Q. Nguyen, Bob Johnson, Michael Hackett, and Robert Johnson. *Testing Applications on the Web: Test Planning for Mobile and Internet-Based Systems*, 2nd edition. New Jersey: Wiley; 2003.
3. Brian Fling. *Mobile Design and Development: Practical Concepts and Techniques for Creating Mobile Sites and Web Apps*, 1st edition. California: O'Reilly Media; 2009.

Chapter 10

Mobile Solution Deployment

There are two parts to mobile solution deployment. One part is the client application deployment made available on the handsets, and the second part is the mobile server deployment. An overview of both these parts is discussed in this chapter. For simplicity, the application deployment options are discussed only for BlackBerry, iPhone, and Android. Most device vendors issue deployment guides that can be referred for detailed information.

10.1 Introduction

This chapter gives an overview of the deployment of mobile applications for Android, BlackBerry, and iPhone. Consumer mobile application deployment and enterprise mobile application deployment are covered separately in this document. This is required because enterprise mobility includes consumer mobile apps released by the enterprise to provide self-care, product information, to trigger mobile purchase, and to enhance sales. Consumer mobile application deployment mainly involves submission to App Stores, and enterprise mobile application deployment involves the use of the BlackBerry Enterprise Server (BES) for BlackBerry and a middleware platform to perform deployment for iPhone and Android.

There is a difference in deployment between consumer applications and enterprise applications because consumer devices cannot be controlled or managed by the enterprise, and hence, the consumer application cannot be pushed to the consumer devices. The consumer needs to download the application from the platform App Store or from the enterprise web site in order to install and use the application. On the contrary, enterprise devices and applications can be controlled by the enterprise, and the mobile application can be pushed to specific enterprise mobile devices that are monitored.

The server for mobile applications can be a custom-developed enterprise server or a customized mobile middleware from an external vendor. The enterprise has multiple deployment options for a mobility server, and the right option for a specific deployment is based on the capital and operational expenditure and the associated business process the enterprise wants to adopt.

10.2 Deployment of Enterprise Apps for Consumers

Let us start with Android, the open-source operating system (OS), which is eating up the market share of iPhone and other popular smartphones in the mobile industry. All Android applications must be signed before they can be deployed onto a device. Being part of the open-source project, the developer is not required to purchase digital certificates from a certificate authority. A personal certificate can be created and used by the enterprise to sign the Android applications.

To sign the Android application from a Windows machine, the following steps are involved:

1. In command prompt, go to JDK (Java Development Kit) bin directory. If JDK is not installed on the Windows machine, the installation package can be downloaded for free from Sun web site or any other popular free software site.
2. Next, in the command prompt, with the directory as "JDK bin," run the keytool command to create certificate:
   keytool –genkey –v –keystore <certificate name>.keystore –alias <certificate alias> –keyalg RSA –validity <no of days validity>
3. Fill in the enterprise details.
4. Enter the password for the keystore and a password for the private key.
5. Run the jarsigner command to sign the application using the certificate. Ensure to specify the "apk" path or copy the "apk" to the bin directory. APK is short for Android Package:
   ■ jarsigner -verbose –keystore <certificate name>.keystore <application name>.apk <certificate alias>
6. Finally, verify if the application is properly signed using "verify and ensure" so that there are no errors:
   ■ jarsigner -verify <application name>.apk

The next step is to publish the application in Android Market (App Store). Android Market is a hosted service that makes it easy for users to find and download

Android applications to their Android-powered devices and makes it easy for developers to publish their applications to Android users. The enterprise mobile applications for consumers need to be published in Android Market to reach a wider audience.

To publish an application in Android Market, the following process is to be followed:

1. Go to the Android Web site for publishing service (http://market.android.com/publish).
2. Register with the service and agree to the terms of service.
3. Upload the application to the service and then place a request to publish it.
4. Once published, the enterprise will be notified based on the details of registrations.
5. Users can then see the application, download it, and rate it using the "Market" application installed on their Android-powered devices.
6. To publish an application on Android Market, the application should meet the requirements published in the link, which are enforced by the "Market" server when the application is uploaded.

Enterprise Android applications can also be deployed on enterprise servers. Users can download and install the applications over a wireless network by browsing the enterprise web site using the browser on their Android device. Wireless application download using a web browser on the Android device is designed to provide a flexible way for users to install new applications. The publish process for over-the-air deployment requires hosting the compiled binary on an enterprise web server (can be hosted by external sites also). The link to download the Android package for the specific device needs to be provided from the hosted site of the enterprise.

Next let us look into BlackBerry, which is the most popular handset for enterprise internal apps for executives. When some sensitive application program interfaces (APIs) in the BlackBerry Java Development Environment (JDE) are used while designing the application, the BlackBerry consumer application must be signed using a key, or signature, provided by RIM (Research In Motion is a device vendor for BlackBerry handsets) before you can load the application.cod files onto the BlackBerry device. Code signing serves the purpose of tracking the usage of APIs. It does not indicate in any way RIM's approval of the application.

The process of signing a BlackBerry application involves several steps discussed as follows:

1. The first step is to get the "signing key." To get the signing keys, we will need to go to the BlackBerry Developer's Web site (http://na.blackberry.com/eng/developers/javaappdev/codekeys.jsp) and fill in the application form (https://www.blackberry.com/SignedKeys/).

2. The BlackBerry signature tool is sent by mail, which needs to be installed.
3. The application can then be signed from the development environment itself. The development environment can be the BlackBerry development environment (as shown in Figure 10.1) or any Java integrated development environment (IDE) for which the BlackBerry plug-in is available, such as Eclipse, as shown in Figure 10.2.

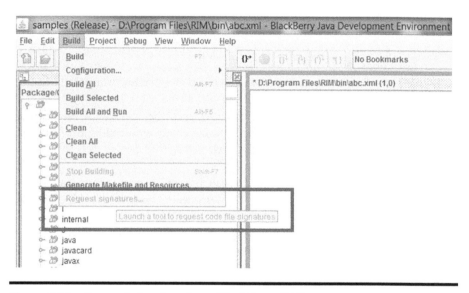

Figure 10.1 Request signature from BlackBerry JDE.

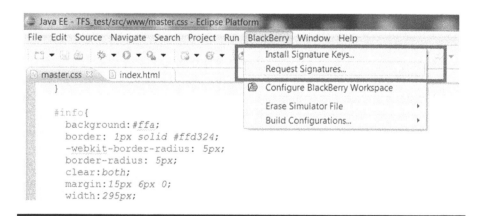

Figure 10.2 Request signature from Eclipse IDE.

Once the application is signed, the next activity is to make it available on App Store. The steps for publishing the BlackBerry application in App Store are listed as follows:

1. Ensure that the signature keys unique to the enterprise are used to sign the application.
2. The enterprise needs to have an account created at http://na.blackberry.com/eng/developers/appworld.jsp
3. Next the enterprise uploads and submits the application to RIM for approval.
4. RIM tests the application and publishes it in the App Store after checking that the application has cleared the checklists for publication in the BlackBerry App Store.
5. Once published, the enterprise is notified, and users can download the application.

Similar to Android applications, BlackBerry applications can also be deployed over air. This is a common distribution method for a lot of BlackBerry mainstream applications. To do this, first the application is to be signed using signature keys unique to the enterprise. Next the enterprise can host the compile binaries (.jar or .cod files) on a web server. Care is to be taken to provide specific multipurpose Internet mail extension types (application/java-archive jar, application/vnd.rim.cod cod). Once hosted, consumers can browse from their BlackBerry phone to access and directly download the application.

Finally, we have iPhone, which offers rich user interface (UI) features and is becoming increasingly popular in enterprises with consumerization. To develop and deploy a consumer application on iPhone, the following steps are involved:

1. The enterprise has to first sign-up for the iPhone developer program. This can be done online from the Apple development portal (http://developer.apple.com/iphone/program/).
2. The next step is to generate and submit a "certificate signing request." This can be done using the Keychain Access application located in the "Applications/Utilities/" folder of the Mac machine.
3. Obtain an iPhone development certificate from the iPhone Developer program portal.
4. Once the certificate is available, it can be saved in the keychain app. Use this to sign the application.

Signing can be done from Xcode, the development environment for iPhone apps. When your application project open in Xcode is to be signed, press Command-R to run the application. The developer will now be prompted for permission to access the certificate saved in your keychain. Click "Allow" (or "Always Allow") to go ahead with the signing.

Apple has very stringent guidelines to be followed in application development for publishing in the App Store. Even the UI needs to follow a "Human Interface Guideline for iPhone" published by Apple. The following steps are involved in publishing an application in the iPhone App Store:

1. Prepare the following documents for submission:
   a. Plain-text description of the application.
   b. Uniform resource locator (URL) that gives more information about the application.
   c. URL that can offer support and e-mail address that people can contact in case of issues.
   d. If the app requires a login, access credentials for Apple to review and test the application should be available.
   e. 512 × 512 pixel icon for the application.
   f. 320 × 480 pixel screenshots of the application.
   g. The distribution provisioning profile of the application.
   h. A zipped version of the application binary.
2. Submit the application:
   a. Log in to iTunes Connect (https://itunesconnect.apple.com).
   b. Click on "Manage Applications."
   c. Click on the "Add New Application" button.
   d. Follow the on-screen instructions to proceed with the submission process.
   e. Fill in the details or documents prepared and upload the application.
3. The application is listed in the "In-Review" status.
4. Mail notification is sent to the enterprise once the application is approved and published.

The typical steps for deployment are shown in Figure 10.3. The build server uploads the final package and the documents (required for submission of an application to the App Store) to the deployment database. There will be a daily or a weekly build of the package with the bug fixes, which will be automated and will use the existing build environment using a maven. The application packages are tested, and after the load is declared as sane and ready for release, the appropriate documents are prepared for the specific release that is required for submission to the platform Market Place or App Store. The packages for individual platforms and the required documents are uploaded to the deployment database.

The deployment database submits the application and documents to the App Store for publishing. This process needs to be followed for the initial submission as well as subsequent submissions. However, the script or manual process will involve more steps in the first-application submission compared with subsequent submissions of a different application or another version of the same application. Once the application is published, the enterprise is notified about the availability of an application in the App Store by mail. The enterprise exchange server receives the

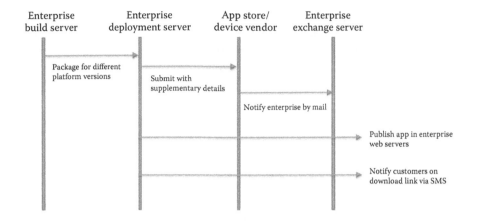

Figure 10.3 **Deployment of consumer mobile applications.**

notification from the App Store and then sends a notification to the deployment database on an approval mail from the App Store. The App Store sends the notification to the e-mail ID provided on submission when the application is approved or provides detailed information on why an application is rejected. The application ID in the mail helps in parsing and identifying the release that needs to be marked as approved for publication.

Once approved by the device vendor, the application can be published on the enterprise web server, and customers can be notified on the availability of the new application or a new version of the application. End users can download the mobile application from a web server using the browser in the mobile device. Once the application is marked approved, based on details from parsing the mail notification, a trigger or a function is invoked to publish the application on the web server. Another trigger involves a message to the short message service (SMS) gateway to notify registered users on the availability of the application to download it from the App Store as well as details of the web server link from where the application can be downloaded. The deployment can be automated to some extent. However, with consumer applications, considerable testing is required before publishing in the public domain App Store, and hence, a manual or semiautomated deployment process is followed by enterprises.

10.3 Deployment of Enterprise Internal Mobile Applications

BlackBerry is the most popular platform for internal mobile applications. The security features and device management capabilities provided by BES make it one of the most preferred platforms for employee applications.

In order to perform mobile application deployment on a BlackBerry using BES, the device should be able to run Java applications and have BlackBerry Device Software Version 4.0 or later installed. The BES Version should be 3.0 or later. The application files with alx and cod extension should be available, where *.alx file is an identifier file for the application and *.cod file contains the compiled and packaged application code.

The following steps are followed for pushing the application to the BlackBerry device:

1. Add the application files to a shared folder:
   a. Make sure the .alx and .cod files for the application are available.
   b. Create a folder maintaining the application's file structure in the network location that hosts the shared applications.
   c. Copy the .alx and .cod files to the created folder.
2. Next configure the application by editing the *.alx file. For example, if the IT administrator wants to ensure that the user cannot remove the application that is pushed to the device, then the application is configured as "required." To do this, open the .alx file and in the <application> element, type <required>true</required> and save the file.
3. Index the application (using "loader.exe/index"). The application loader builds the software index structure and adds any missing index file. If you modify a .alx file after you create a software index, reindex the applications (using "loader.exe/reindex").
4. Share the application folder and assign users to the defined IT and control policies of the enterprise.
5. Send the application to the BlackBerry device:
   a. In the BlackBerry Manager, select "Software Configurations."
   b. In the configuration name list that is shown, select the appropriate software configuration.
   c. Click "Edit Configuration" and select the check boxes beside the applications to push over the wireless network.
   d. From the Delivery list, select "Wireless."
   e. Click "OK."

These steps show that enterprise internal application deployment is different from consumer applications developed by enterprises for end customers. As the internal applications are not delivered to the App Store, the validations from the device vendor are limited, and they are usually pushed by the IT department directly to the handsets of the employees or the contractors who need to work with the specific enterprise's internal application.

Next, let us look into the application deployment for iPhone applications, which use iTunes, iPhone configuration utility, or a third-party mobile device management (MDM) solution such as Sybase Afaria.

But first to develop an iPhone application that is to be distributed within the enterprise, it must be digitally signed with a certificate issued by Apple. The enterprise should also provide the users with a distribution provisioning profile that allows their device to use the application.

The process for deploying iPhone applications involves the following steps:

■ Registration for application deployment: To develop and deploy enterprise applications for iPhone OS, the enterprise needs to register for the iPhone Enterprise Developer Program at http://developer.apple.com.

■ Signing applications using the distribution certificate: Applications to be distributed to users must be signed with your distribution certificate. The high-level steps to create a distributed certificate are given as follows:
   – Use the "Certificate Assistant" in the "Keychain Access Utility" available in the Mac machine to create a certificate signing request (CSR) file.
   – After creating a CSR file, next add the certificate in the iPhone developer program portal by navigating to "Certificates" => "Development."
   – The CSR needs to be approved by the administration. Once approved, the certificate (cer file) is to be downloaded and installed to the Mac machine.

■ Creation of distribution-provisioning profiles: A distribution profile is required for creating applications that need to be run on enterprise devices. The profile can be for a specific application or for multiple applications. The profile acts as an authorization for the user to use a specific application. The .mobileprovision file (enterprise distribution provisioning profile) needs to be securely distributed along with the application.

■ Deploy the provisioning profile: The two standard deployment options provided by Apple for iPhone apps is using iTunes or using the iPhone configuration utility. iTunes automatically installs provisioning profiles that are located in the provisioning profiles folder. Also, users can drag the .mobileprovision file distributed by the IT team to the iTunes application icon for installation. With iTunes, the installation is user-initiated, while with the iPhone configuration utility, the administrator can select an enterprise mobile device and force the installation of a provisioning profile to a specific device.

■ Installation of application: The application (.app file) is either distributed for installation using iTunes or the application can be directly installed by the administrator to a mobile device using the iPhone configuration utility.

There are several MDM solutions that can be used to manage enterprise mobile devices. Most MDM solutions support deployment for multiple platforms. Android-based devices are not so popular for enterprise deployments when compared with BlackBerry, Windows Mobile, and iPhone. Google is maturing on the security, compliance features, and deployment tools, which would enable the adoption of Android for internal enterprise mobile applications. As such, Android's major share is in the enterprise consumer applications due to the huge popularity of Android in the consumer segment where device management and centralized deployment from an administrator are not key requirements. However, there are several MDM solutions from MDM vendors that would enable the use of Android for enterprise applications.

10.4 Enterprise Mobile Server Deployment

There are several deployment options for enterprises in hosting their mobile server. The typical deployment options are discussed in the subsequent list:

- Enterprise deployed: In this category, the mobile middleware infrastructure is owned and maintained by the enterprise itself. This is the most common option for most enterprises when they have specific security requirements and expect the number of customers to be manageable internally by procuring the necessary hardware and software. The mobile application server instance is hosted internally on the enterprise infrastructure. The development and activity will be owned by the enterprise; however, it can be internally outsourced to external contractors.
- Single-client hosted: In this category, the enterprise uses the infrastructure of a hosted service or infrastructure as a service (IaaS) provider to run the mobile server instance. The hosted service provider offers a single mobile middleware instance for each enterprise to satisfy specific security requirements. This model is becoming increasingly popular even with large enterprises that do not want to spend on capital and on the operation expenditure of maintaining a huge infrastructure. A cloud-based platform for hosting also offers on-demand scalability. The development and test are owned in this case also by the enterprise, and the service is limited to using the infrastructure that will be owned and maintained by an external vendor. The actual billing model for use of the infrastructure can vary from a usage-based billing, subscription-based billing, or hybrid models that have a different initial cost, based on the number of anticipated users.
- Multiclient hosted: In this category, the hosted service provider uses the same mobile middleware instance to support multiple enterprises and small and medium businesses (SMBs). This is usually the case when the mobile application used by the different clients is a common enterprise application that can be supported by a single mobile server instance and just requires separate handling from the database perspective. SMBs many not have enough resources to invest in developing a new application and its server instance. So for SMBs that want to roll out new mobile applications with minimum investment quickly, the multiclient hosted scenario is a lucrative method.
- Managed service: In this scenario, only the requirements are shared with the managed service vendor. The managed service vendor does all the

development and deployment for a predetermined billing model. The managed service vendor could opt to deploy the mobile server instance in its IT infrastructure, use a cloud vendor, or outsource the different activities to different vendors. How the managed service vendor internally manages is not of concern to the enterprise, as they are only interested in seeing the application working and satisfying the requirements. It should be understood that clarity of requirements is a key success factor when opting for a managed service vendor. The functional requirements, nonfunctional requirements, and the UI screen mock-ups should be clearly identified, and compliance to the same should be guaranteed as part of the service-level agreement. This is a good option for enterprises that concentrate on branding and outsource almost all the other activities to external vendors. This option is also used when there are minimal dependencies on internal enterprise systems, and the application development and execution can happen without direct involvement of the enterprise.

The deployment option adopted by the enterprise is mostly based on the technology considerations, the budget constraints, the business model followed, and the long-term enterprise mobile road map the enterprise wants to achieve. The deployment options are shown in Figure 10.4, excluding the managed service option where the enterprise is not directly involved in the deployment activities.

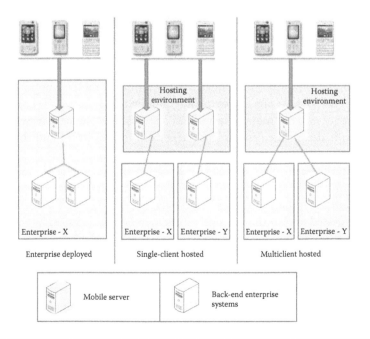

Figure 10.4 Mobile server deployment.

When multiplatform development is involved, a standard mobile middleware such as a mobile enterprise application platform or a mobile consumer application platform could be used to handle the device diversity and application porting. Most popular middleware vendors are coming up with a cloud offering or a hosted offering where the enterprises do not have to necessarily buy the middleware platform. The middleware vendor itself will host the mobile server instance that is developed to work on the middleware platform. This will help the enterprises to have a single vendor to take care of their development needs for multiple platforms as well as to look into the infrastructure requirements for hosting the solution.

The requirement for the mobile server is not limited to thick client applications in performing off-line synchronization and business functions. The mobile server is also required for thin or browser-based solutions. For browser-based applications, a mobile server serves the purpose of making requests to the back-end systems and creating a response page to the information requested from the mobile device from the device browser. The caching requirements and the need for having a rendering engine to support the different device web-page formats make it necessary to have a mobile server, whose deployment needs to be analyzed against the deployment options.

10.5 Conclusion

This chapter provides an overview of enterprise mobility deployment. The focus of the chapter was to break down and explain the technical jargons pertaining to and the complexities in enterprise mobile deployment. The client side deployment only considers thick client application deployment, where an application needs to be downloaded and installed on the device. Browser-based mobile applications (thin applications) do not have any deployment requirements as the mobile browser is the client that requests data from the server and displays the content sent by the server. The server side details the deployment framework for both thin and thick mobile applications.

Covering the deployment options for all the available mobile platforms will in itself result in a book, and hence, only three of the most popular smartphone platforms—iPhone, Android, and BlackBerry—have been taken up for discussion. The reader is suggested to refer the appropriate deployment guide issued by the platform vendor for an in-depth understanding on how enterprise deployment is performed for the specific platform of interest to the reader. Some quick references are given under "Additional Reading."

For enterprises that want a multiplatform deployment strategy, the best suggested option is to adopt an MDM solution that supports the platforms of their choice. This would be the scenario going forward as consumerization is catching up and enterprises are allowing their employees to use the personal handsets to work on internal enterprise applications.

Additional Reading

1. Guy Hart-Davis. *iPad & iPhone Administrators Guide: Enterprise Deployment Strategies and Security Solutions*, 1st edition. California: McGraw-Hill Osborne Media; 2010.
2. Dan Renfroe and Mitesh Desai. *BlackBerry Enterprise Server for Microsoft® Exchange: Installation and Administration*. India: Packt Publishing; 2007.
3. *iPhone OS Enterprise Deployment Guide*, 2nd edition. California: Apple Inc.; 2010.

MOBILE
SOLUTIONS AND
CASE STUDIES

Chapter 11

Mobility Solutions for the Retail Industry

Have you ever imagined designing your own pizza with the help of a mobile application and a professional pizza shop, such as Pizza Hut, which will make and deliver pizzas for you or your dearest, while you tweet about the recipe in Twitter or post the recipe to your Facebook wall? Smart mobile devices, mobility solutions, and the widespread adoption of the mobile social media have changed the way people shop. This chapter gives an overview of the mobility opportunities, the benefits of mobility, the various mobility solutions available for the retail industry, and a case study of a mobility solution for in-store operations management.

11.1 Introduction

The retail industry represents a group of diverse business organizations or merchants focused on selling a set of products or services. Retailers may be specialized in selling a specific set of goods or services, for example, apparel or fashion retailers (Macy's in the United States), footwear retailers (Payless Shoes in the United States), general merchandise retailers (Target, Fred Meyer, Walmart, etc., in the United States), office and home supplies retailers (STAPLES, Office Depot, Home Depot, etc., in the United States), pharmacy retailers (Rite Aid Pharmacy and Walgreens Pharmacy in the United States), wholesale retailers (COSTCO in the United States), and electronics goods or service retailers (BestBuy, Fry's Electronics, etc., in the United States).

The retail industry is fast-paced, constantly evolving, and highly competitive. Retailers must exceed the customer's expectations and should provide better personalized services to stay competitive in order to expand the loyal customer base. Retailers should be up-to-date on the inventory, product details, and pricing information to serve the customers' needs in real time.

Technology advances, especially in the areas of wireless networks (WiFi, 3G, 4G, and long-term evolution mobile networks) and mobile computing devices (smartphones, tablet PCs, etc.), have totally changed the way people shop. A recent survey reveals that more than 50% of consumers across the globe are interested in using their mobile devices for better shopping experiences (finding product information, product comparison, reviews, price checks, promotional offers, coupons, etc.). With the smartphone and tablet-PC revolution, most of the potential consumers are empowered with high-end smartphones or tablet PCs and are ready to explore mobile devices for shopping, comparing, and transacting. Hence, it is a potential business opportunity for retailers to unveil the untapped possibilities of mobility to transform the consumer shopping experience.

11.2 Scope for Mobility Solutions in the Retail Industry

When it comes to retail solutions, mobility has multiple dimensions. Depending on the type of services and the beneficiaries, mobility in the retail industry can be grouped into the following two categories:

- Mobility solutions for retailers (enterprise solutions)
- Mobility solutions for consumers

Mobility solutions for retailers primarily focus on the various mobile-enabled in-store operations and online services to provide a better and faster customer shopping experience. The various mobility solutions under this category improve retailer efficiency, leading to the efficient management of product outages, back-order management, efficient product management, easy checkouts, and increased customer satisfaction.

Retail mobility solutions for consumers are focused on providing a personalized shopping experience to the customers. Product information, new product alerts, product reviews, price checks, promotional offers, location- or store-specific advertisements, product-specific advertisements, store locators, etc., are typical examples of opportunities for mobility solutions. Figure 11.1 gives an overview of the various mobility solution opportunities for retailers and consumers.

11.2.1 Mobility Solutions for Retailers

The retail business requires timely monitoring of product inventory to prevent product outages and manage stock-ups. Most traditional retailers are heavily dependent on the human workforce for this activity, and most often it may end up in inaccurate inventory information, product outages, and back orders, leading to

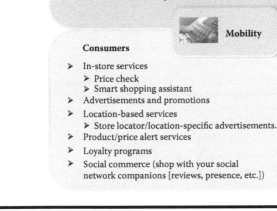

Figure 11.1   Scope for mobility solutions in the retail industry.

poor customer satisfaction and an impact on the turnovers. Also, today's consumers are highly tech savvy, and they expect more (product selection assistance, price comparison, virtual look and feel of the product, hassle-free checkouts, etc.) than the traditional shopping experience. This opens up tremendous opportunities for retailers to influence the shopping behavior of consumers.

Mobility solutions when combined with automatic identification and data collection (AIDC) techniques such as radio frequency identification (RFID) and barcode labels can effectively manage most of the in-store operations. Real-time inventory management, product availability and placement, price checks, easy returns management, smart shopping assistant solutions for customers, easy checkout solutions to avoid long queues at checkout stations, etc., are typical examples of in-store mobility solutions for retailers. Figure 11.2 gives an overview of the implementation of various in-store mobility solutions for retailers.

11.2.1.1 Store Solutions/In-Store Operations Management Solutions

Retail store mobility solutions empower store officials and staff with mobile computing devices to perform their duties on the retail store floor by extending the store's data and services to their handhelds. Typical use cases for retail store mobility services that can be mobile enabled are discussed in the following sections.

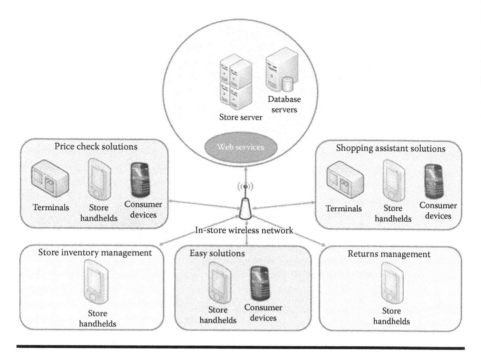

Figure 11.2 An overview of in-store retail mobility solutions.

11.2.1.1.1 Store Inventory Management Solutions

Each retail chain or store is unique in its operations. Depending on the type of the products sold or services offered (apparel retailer, footwear retailer, grocery retailer, electronic goods retailer, pharmacy retailer, general merchandise retailer, etc.) and the general demand of a product, the retailers may stock a large volume or a limited quantity of products, and it is essential to keep track of the inventory details for each product for on-time reordering of the products to avoid any possible product out-of-stock situations. AIDC technologies such as barcode labels and RFID tags can be easily combined with mobility solutions to implement efficient and cost-effective store inventory management solutions. RFID tags or barcode labels can be utilized as product identifiers (e.g., unique product code [UPC] for identifying a particular category of product and unique item identifier codes for identifying individual products among a particular product category). All information related to a product can be associated with a UPC in the store back-end database, and the details can be easily retrieved by a simple scanning of products' RFID tag or barcode label.

RFID tag-based store inventory solutions provide one more level of order-management automation. An RFID reader placed on the shelf holding the products can automatically scan the items at predefined intervals and can generate an automated reorder request for products whose stock count is below the threshold value.

Some retailers carry goods or products that are either perishable or may have limited shelf-life. Mobile-enabled inventory management solutions can alert the staff or sales person responsible for handling those products to move those products to another location with a price mark-down or remove the items immediately from the shelf, if the expiry date is over, by delivering alert messages or instructions at the handheld device of the concerned store personnel. The back-end stores management services or solutions can generate these alerts based on the expiry date or the shelf-life of the product.

Certain retailers specialized in selling specific products may have specific requirements for arranging product display based on specific occasions (e.g., a retailer network dedicated for selling greeting cards may have to rearrange the display of the cards based on the occasion such as New Year's Day, Mother's Day, Valentine's Day, Christmas, etc.). Such requirements can be easily implemented with mobile-enabled inventory solutions. The back-end systems can generate the product code and shelf location (combination of floor number, aisle number, row number, and column number) and can assign them to the sales person/staff handling this section and send the notification to his/her handheld device. The sales person or staff can use his/her handheld device to scan the cards to find out their intended display location and arrange them appropriately as per the requirement.

11.2.1.1.2 Price Checks and Smart Shopping Assistant Solutions

Personalized shopping experience is an important factor in building a loyal customer base in the retail industry. Most of the consumers today are looking for a better personalized shopping experience in terms of getting assistance in selecting the right product that meets their requirements at an affordable price. Retailers can deliver a wide range of mobility solutions and tools for an interactive and personalized shopping experience.

The price check mobility solution helps customers to find out the price of a product by a simple scanning or photo capture of the product tag. It eliminates the need for bringing the items to the final checkout station to find out the price. Similarly, the product-finder solution helps the customers to find a product of their interest through a simple keyword or brand-name search. The smart shopping assistant tools provide the option of viewing and comparing products from different manufactures and help the customers to decide on which product to purchase. For example, suppose a customer who finds a shirt from the manufacturer ABC in the apparel section and wants to know more about it as well as the other options and alternatives available for this shirt, can utilize the smart shopping assistant tool. With a simple scanning or photo capture of the product tag, the smart shopping assistant tool should be able to provide the options (color, design, etc.) available with the selected brand or the details of a similar product from a competitor brand along with reviews and recommendations.

Retailers can deliver these services through the handheld terminals placed at different locations of the store, through the handheld devices at the store (carried by sales associates or available to shoppers), or through the mobile devices of the shoppers. The retailers need to develop consumer mobile-specific applications for the different consumer device platforms (iOS App for iPhone and iPAD devices, Windows Phone App for Windows phone devices, Android App for Android devices, BlackBerry App for Research In Motion [RIM] BlackBerry devices, etc.). Consumers can download these applications from the respective device's App Store.

11.2.1.1.3 Mark Downs and Product Returns Management

Retailers can effectively utilize mobility solutions to manage price mark-downs and product returns. The product mark-down details can be delivered to the respective store associate's mobile device, and the store associate can scan the marked-down product to be moved to another location or a clearance section. Also, the store associate can generate mark-down price labels with the help of the mobile client solution.

The long-wait queue at the customer service department of the retailer for merchandise return is really a bad customer experience. Retailers can simplify the merchandise return process through effective implementation of mobility solutions. With mobility solutions for returns processing (receipt recalls), any store associate with a handheld device can perform a merchandise-return operation.

11.2.1.1.4 Easy Checkout Solutions

The long-wait queues at the retailer checkout terminal make in-store holiday shopping a nightmare for most of the customers. Thankfully, mobility has the right solution to address this issue. The mobile point-of-sale (mPOS) solution simplifies the checkout process. Consumers can utilize the mPOS-enabled handheld devices of the store for shopping and can perform a self-checkout at the end or can transfer the shopping cart list to a real point-of-sale (POS) terminal for fulfillment. Product scanning on the go by consumers during shopping saves the scan time at checkout counters and simplifies the checkout operation.

Consumers can alternatively seek the assistance of store associates to scan the products with the help of the mPOS-enabled handheld device of the store, which is carried by the store associate. Consumers can fulfill the order through the mPOS application using mPOS-supported tender options (such as credit, debit, or gift card payments). Consumers can alternatively complete the checkout process at the mPOS terminals. The store associate can transfer the shopping cart to the mPOS and can issue a transaction reference ID to the consumer. The consumer can later retrieve the shopping cart at the main checkout POS terminal through the transaction reference ID for order fulfillment.

11.2.1.1.5 Other Operations Management Solutions

Apart from the store management solutions, mobility solutions can be utilized for operations management such as workforce management (staff work and shift management), paperless solutions ("green" initiatives), supply chain traceability, etc.

11.2.1.2 Mobile Commerce (m-Commerce) Solutions

The widespread adoption of mobile devices for transaction fulfillment augments mobile commerce (m-Commerce) solutions. Retailers can extend their online services to mobile devices and open up a new channel for business. Typical online services such as Wish Lists, Baby Registry, Web POS, My Shopping Cart, etc., can be extended to mobile handheld devices. The online services can be extended to consumer mobile devices as portal services or thick and rich client solutions. m-Commerce solutions can also leverage the existing multichannel retail solutions such as Order Online Pick-Up at Store.

Latest consumer mobile devices are lined up to implement hardware support for mobile payment solutions to replace credit or debit card payments. Many retailers are experimenting with the near-field communication (NFC) technology-based mobile payment solutions. NFC-based payments are extremely faster in operation and can lead to significant labor and time savings.

Albert Heijn, the Dutch grocer, is an early adopter of the NFC payment solution. The grocer recently piloted the NFC-based payment solution using NFC-enabled consumer mobile devices from Nokia.

11.2.2 Retail Mobility Solutions for End Customers

Retail mobility solutions for the end customers (consumers) focus on delivering a personalized shopping experience to the customers. In-store services (such as product information, product reviews, price checks, shopping assistant tools, etc.), location- or store-specific advertisements, product-specific advertisements, store locators, etc., are typical examples of in-store services that use mobility solutions. Section 11.2.2.1 gives a detailed overview of the various retail mobility solutions for consumers.

11.2.2.1 In-Store Services

In-store retail mobility solutions help consumers in the decision-making process to select the right product that meets their needs and also deliver a personalized shopping experience. The following are examples of typical in-store mobility services for consumers:

- Price check: Helps the customers to find the price and promotional details of a product.
- Product finder: Helps the customers to check the availability and the location (combination of floor number, aisle number, row number, and column number) of a product in the store.

■ Smart shopping assistant: The smart shopping assistant tool helps the customers in the decision-making process of which product to buy. This tool provides information about the alternative products, reviews of the product, pricing comparison, and a virtual model illustrating the look and feel, if applicable (e.g., the virtual look and feel of an apparel).

As mentioned earlier in this chapter, retailers can deliver these services through the handheld terminals placed at different locations of the store, through the handheld devices in the store (carried by sales associates or the store handheld devices dedicated for the shoppers), or through the mobile devices of the shoppers. The retailers need to develop consumer mobile-specific applications for the different consumer device platforms (iOS App for iPhone or iPAD devices, Windows Phone App for Windows phone devices, Android App for Android devices, BlackBerry App for RIM BlackBerry devices, etc.). Consumers can download these applications from the respective device's Application Store.

11.2.2.2 Location Based Services

Most consumer mobile devices today are "smart" devices, and they incorporate multiple sensors and chips to implement features such as global positioning system or assisted-GPS (GPS/A-GPS), which can accurately sense the current location of the user. Retailers can leverage this feature to deliver location-specific services to consumers. The following gives a snapshot of the location-based retail services.

■ Store locator: The store-locator service can provide the details about the nearest store (distance to the store from the current location, store address, driving directions to the store, the products and services offered by the store, etc.) with respect to the current location of the user.
■ Store advertisements or promotions: This service can deliver details about the current store advertisements and promotional offers of the nearest store.

Both of these applications can utilize the GPS feature of the consumer handheld device to obtain the current location details. If the consumer device does not support GPS feature, the current location can be captured in the form of user inputs for ZIP code and address.

11.2.2.3 Context-Aware Alert Services (Products, Price, and Promotion Alerts)

Shopping behavior and spending habit vary across consumers. Some consumers may be eager to buy products at launch, whereas others may be stringent on price points and ready to buy the product only when the price falls within their budget.

Retailers can deliver context-aware or consumer-need-aware mobility solutions to address the diverse needs of the consumers. The following are examples of typical context-aware mobility services for consumers:

- Product alerts: The product alerts mobility solution can deliver notifications about new products and in-stock availability of products. Consumers can register to this service and can receive notifications about the product of their choice.
- Price alerts: The price alerts service provides notification about price drops and the current promotions of a product. Consumers can register to this service and can receive notifications about the product of their choice.
- Promotion alerts: Retailers may run online or in-store promotions and discount sales, and the promotion alerts or advertisements can be delivered to the customers through promotion alert services.
- Product recall alerts: Product manufacturers may recall certain products due to safety, security, and regulatory compliance requirements. It is likely that the customer may not get any notification about the product recall unless the customer registers the product with the manufacturer. Retailers can provide recall alerts of the products purchased from them to the consumers, through the product recall alert mobility solution.

Retailers can enable context-aware notification services on their mobiles through one or a combination of the following:

- Short messaging service (SMS)-based mobility solutions
- Stand-alone mobile client applications (thick or rich client solutions)

SMS is a cost-effective way of communicating with mobile users. SMS service is supported by almost all mobile handsets, and it facilitates a uniform way of messaging, which is simple and consistent across all mobile devices and mobile operators. Customers can subscribe to the SMS services during the registration process and can avail SMS service effectively for the services offered by the retailer.

Mobile client solutions (thick or rich client solutions) are another popular choice for delivering retail mobility solutions to end customers. Thick client solutions are mobile-platform dependent, and they need to be developed for individual mobile device platforms with the help of the supported software development kit (SDK) or the application development kit (ADK) for the corresponding platform (e.g., Windows Phone Developer Tools SDK for Windows phone devices and Android SDK for Android devices). Also, the solution needs to be deployed on the consumer mobile devices. Most smartphone mobile devices in today's market do not support side loading of applications to the device; rather, they support application hosting and download from the corresponding device's application store (e.g., Marketplace for Windows Phone devices, Google Play for Android devices, and App Store for Apple iOS devices such as iPhone and iPad).

11.2.2.4 Loyalty Programs

Loyalty programs help retailers to retain their loyal customer base through special promotions and offers. Loyalty programs can be implemented in multiple ways including reward points on every dollar spent, special discounts, and promotional coupons to be selected by regular customers. Consumer mobile phones can be used as a replacement for the loyalty cards. Also special promotions, coupons, discounts, reward points' redemption, etc., can be implemented through mobile applications.

11.2.2.5 Social Commerce

We are living in a world where social networking has significant influence on the day-to-day life of people. Retailers can leverage the social network media to provide a social network-oriented shopping experience to customers. "Shop with your Friends," "Share Review with your Friends," etc., are typical examples of social networking-oriented, personalized shopping programs. The trust on a product review is high if the review is from the consumer's known friend through a social network group than if it is from an unknown person through a website. "Shop with Your Friends" service enables you to share your shopping schedule with your networked friends so that anyone interested can join. Also, the person can set his/her location while in the store so that if any of his/her social-networked friends shopping simultaneously at the same or nearby stores can join, making the shopping experience a pleasure.

11.3 Benefits of Mobility Adoption in the Retail Industry

Mobility adoption in the retail segment is beneficial to both the retailers and the consumers in terms of revenue, cost, and shopping experience. A few important benefits among them are discussed in the following sections:

11.3.1 Employee and Shopper Productivity

With mobility solutions, store associates can effectively manage their day-to-day activities. The back-end store information system (SIS) with the help of mobility solutions can generate work schedules, important alerts, etc., and push them to the respective store associate's handheld device. The need for manual schedule management and the possible delays as well as extensive employer or employee communication requirements are eliminated.

Consumer-centric retail mobility solutions provide all kinds of in-store shopping assistance to the shoppers, leading to reduced search and wait times.

11.3.2 Better Inventory Management

Mobility solutions when combined with AIDC techniques, such as RFID and barcode labels, can fully automate the inventory management process, including keeping track of the store inventory, reorders, etc. A controlled inventory optimizes the store space requirements and prevents product outages.

11.3.3 All New Shopping Experience

With mobility solutions, the shoppers are in control of their shopping experience. Compared with the traditional shopping model, consumer-centric retail mobility solutions make the shopping experience a personalized and a fun-filled activity. Social commerce and loyalty programs add new dimensions to the shopping experience.

11.3.4 New Business Models and Revenue

Mobility opens up the window for grabbing the market share from competitors. Effective mobility implementations and innovations can greatly attract the mindset of consumers.

11.3.5 Green Stores

Bringing mobility into the store environment eliminates paper-based transactions and records. Saving paper is saving trees—a step towards the "green store" initiatives.

11.4 Choice of Mobility Solutions for the Retail Industry

The selection of a mobility solution in terms of architecture, business requirements, platform support, etc., is highly challenging, and it requires a thorough analysis in the decision-making process of mobilization. This section is intended to give the readers an overview of the different types of mobility solutions and the factors to be considered in the selection process while implementing mobility solutions in the retail industry.

11.4.1 Thin Client Solutions

Thin client solutions are applications that run on a supported web browser. The applications are developed as web pages that are hosted on a server. The client devices (mobile handhelds and personal digital assistants [PDAs]) can access these applications through the browsers. Thin client solutions are suited for applications that do not require any hardware resource access of the underlying platform and are always connected to the network. A typical example is portal services, which can be used for online shopping. Users can simply login to the portal through the web browser by accessing the corresponding URL. Thin client solutions always require connectivity to the hosted system and are known as "always connected" applications.

A thin client solution should address the features supported by the web browser of the client system (PDAs, mobile handhelds, etc.), the screen real estates (screen size and resolution, orientation, input support, etc.) of the client devices, etc. To address the devices of varying capabilities, the web pages may need to be redesigned for each client device, or a "device capabilities-aware middleware" should be used for rendering the pages on the device browser. A thin client solution is very limited in capabilities, when it comes to the hardware access of the client device (e.g., camera access for product tag scanning). It all depends on the client-side scripting support provided by the browser in use, which in turn may lead to potential security threats.

11.4.2 Thick Client and Rich Client Solutions

Thick client solutions are applications developed for a particular client device (mobile handheld or PDA) platform (Windows Phone or Windows CE operating system [OS], iPhone OS, Android OS, etc.). Thick client solutions reside in the memory of the handheld device, and it utilizes the platform support provided by the underlying OS and target hardware. The device manufacturers (commonly known as original equipment manufacturers [OEMs]) provide SDKs, exposing application programming interfaces (APIs) to access the platform-supported hardware for which the OS does not provide any standard APIs, which can be utilized in the thick client solution for leveraging the device's capabilities (e.g., barcode reading). Depending on the OS support and third-party products, a thick client solution may implement support for local data storage, syncing of locally stored data with standard databases such as SQL Server, Oracle, etc. This feature of thick client solutions qualifies them for "off-line data capture," which does not require a connectivity with the back-end system always. Thick client solutions are platform-dependent, and they are less portable to devices running different OSs. Application upgrades are bit challenging for thick client solutions.

Rich client solution is a variant of the thick client solution, which combines the architecture of both thin client and thick client solutions. The user interface part is developed as a rich thick client, and the integration with the back-end system or services is implemented through web services. The application is deployed on the handheld device, and it communicates with the back-end web services on a need basis.

Most of the in-store mobile applications are rich client applications, which connect the mobile application to the retailer's back-end systems through retailers'

WiFi network in real time. The in-store handheld device connects to the store's local network, and the different services are hosted as web services on the network.

Certain retailers still follow the thick client solution with off-line operations support. This requires scheduled syncing of the data with handheld devices and back-end systems before the start of store operations.

11.4.3 Off-the-Shelf Mobility Solutions versus Custom-Built Solutions

The choice on whether to adopt an off-the-shelf solution or a custom-built solution is dependent on multiple factors. A few important factors among them are listed below:

1. Availability of the off-the-shelf solutions for implementing all the required retail mobility feature requirements
2. Support for off-the-shelf solutions for extending to multiple mobile platforms
3. Customization effort for off-the-shelf solutions versus the effort for building a custom solution
4. Cost of off-the-shelf solutions versus custom solutions
5. Annual maintenance cost of off-the-shelf solutions versus custom-built solutions
6. Additional support features
7. Ease of operation

Most of the retailers already have a SIS in place, and the vendor of the SIS may already have a ready-to-use mobile solution for extending the existing SIS to handheld devices. If not, it may be possible to extend the existing SIS to handhelds through customized mobile solutions and web service infrastructure.

11.5 A Mobility Solution Scenario for In-Store Operations Management

SCOPE OF MOBILIZATION

Consider a retailer who wants to implement a store mobility solution for in-store operations management. The retailer currently uses an off-the-shelf POS solution and store retail information system (SIS) and they are not yet mobile ready. However, the retailer wants to implement the solution for a carrier-grade handset (Motorola MC75 taken as an example) device running Windows Mobile OS.

11.5.1 Usual Practice in the Absence of Mobility Solutions

The retailer is currently using an off-the-shelf POS solution and SIS. Most of the in-store operations like price check, product look-up, etc., are performed at the POS terminal with the help of the sales associate.

11.5.2 With Mobile Solution for In-Store Operations Management

Mobile handheld devices running a mobile client application, which interfaces with the existing SIS over the in-store wireless network, are used for in-store operations such as price checks, product look-up, stock-ups, auditing, receipt recalls, etc.

11.5.3 Requirements and Solution

The application is designed to address the following requirements:

- The retailer wants to use a rugged handset and is not looking to tablet PCs.
- The application should interface with the existing SIS to implement in-store operations such as price checks, product look-up, stock-ups, auditing, receipt recalls, etc.
- The application should implement user-level and supervisor-level access and prevent access to the system-level resources of the handheld device.
- The application should utilize the in-store WiFi network to connect to the existing SIS services.

The various services from the existing SIS are exposed through web services. The mobile client application running on the handheld device can access these services on a need basis, over the in-store wireless network.

The solution would involve a handheld application that is developed as a rich client application with front end in C#.net for execution on a handset in Motorola MC Series. Access to the web services hosted on the store network is controlled through user ID and password-based authentication mechanism. The rich client mobile application also implements restrictions to access other systems resources. Barcode reading feature is implemented in the handheld application to scan the barcode tags associated with the products.

11.5.4 Business Benefits from Mobile Enablement

- Improved business process
- Increased staff productivity

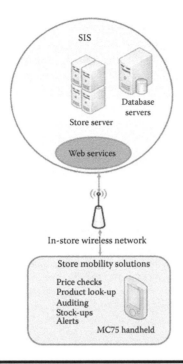

Figure 11.3   E2E solution architecture of in-store operations management mobility solution.

- Improved customer experience
- Reduced operations cost and increased revenue (Figure 11.3)

11.6 Conclusion

Smart mobile devices, mobility solutions, and mobile social media play a key influencing role in peoples' shopping behavior. With the smartphone and tablet-PC revolution, most of the potential consumers are empowered with high-end smartphones or tablet PCs and are ready to explore mobile devices to shop, compare, and transact. Hence, it is a potential business opportunity for retailers to unveil the untapped possibilities of mobility to transform consumer shopping experience.

This chapter was intended to provide a general overview of the mobility opportunities, the benefits of mobility, and the various mobility solutions for retail industry. As in the case of any mobility implementation project, retailers should identify the potential business opportunities for mobile enablement, the investment and infrastructure requirement, the challenges, and the right solution addressing their business needs.

Additional Reading

1. Ronald L. Bond. *Retail in Detail*, 4th edition. Irvine, CA: Entrepreneur Press; 2008.
2. Jan Kingaard. *Start Your Own Retail Business and More,* 2nd edition. Irvine, CA: Entrepreneur Press; 2007.
3. Bernie Brennan and Lori Schafer. *Branded! How Retailers Engage Consumers with Social Media and Mobility*, 1st edition. New York: Wiley; 2010.
4. Stephen L. Pearce and Rick Bushnell. *The Bar Code Implementation Guide: Using Bar Codes in Distribution*, 3rd edition. Tower Hill Press; 2010.
5. Hiroko Kato, Keng T. Tan, and Douglas Chai. *Barcodes for Mobile Devices*, 1st Edition. Cambridge University Press; (May 17, 2010).

Chapter 12

Mobility Solutions for the Transportation Industry

> Mobility is increasingly important since it has the inherent ability to drive new levels of efficiency ... in three years' time usage at the airport will be as commonplace as email is today.
>
> **Samuel Ingalls**
> *Assistant Director of Aviation Information Services,*
> *Las Vegas McCarran International Airport*
> *Source: http://www.airports.org*

12.1 Introduction

Mobility helps in improving employee productivity, reduce costs, meet regulatory compliance, and manage inventory for various transportation companies. Companies around the world are able to see upward revenue growth and productivity gains, and the extension of the mobile workforce is due to the increase in the usage of mobile solutions. Mobile operations currently represent the greatest opportunity to improve efficiency, responsiveness, and profitability through automation for the mobile workforce. From the company perspective, without real-time visibility, managing remote workforce is a challenge. To increase workers' productivity and minimize resource costs, the management needs to know where their workers are located and the different tasks that the field agents are doing at any point of time. Without real-time connection to the field force, the management lacks the information needed to maximize the utilization of their workforce and resources.

Mobility was once seen as an *ad hoc* solution or tool, but now mobile solutions have become key components of core business processes. The availability of a variety of converged mobile devices on different operating systems, the lowered cost of data plans, and the increasing availability of mobile applications are contributing to the growth of mobility. Enterprise mobility enables enterprises to conduct business more quickly, reliably, and cheaply through effective management of information. As the geographical spread of the workforce and customer base increases, enterprise mobility offers a means for organizations to have a unified workforce and maximize the return on mobility investments. Deploying enterprise mobility solutions requires efficient management of real-time capture and movement of information. Businesses need to handle the complexity of having to control numerous devices at multiple locations while maintaining a secure communication channel. Companies looking for mobility solutions need to find a technology partner who has comprehensive capabilities that not only make mobility work but also create a real advantage. Mobility extends enterprise systems to the field so that the workforce on the field can exchange information whenever and wherever it is needed. Mobility helps the skilled service staff and busy delivery drivers by eliminating time-consuming data entry.

In this chapter, the airline industry has been used to explain the concepts of mobility in the transportation sector. Baggage tags for cargo transportation and personal assistance for passenger transportation have been used as use cases.

12.2 Mobility in the Airline Industry

The airline industry is in a transformation phase with ever-increasing fuel prices, increased operational costs, and competition. Airlines are looking at new and innovative technologies to reduce cost and make existing processes more efficient and to help them generate revenues (Figure 12.1).

The airlines industry is evolving rapidly to exploit the growth of mobility. Various airlines are experimenting with bringing in personalized services with the help of mobility. Airlines are enabling employees to improve operational efficiency and are providing superior customer experience by using the latest technology trends including mobility. Mobility is considered as a critical technology area that will deliver integrated and more efficient operations by enabling airlines to have resources available at the right location, with right information at the right time. This will help the airlines in a significant manner, such that workforce management is handled by enhancing operational planning and decision making, which in turn leads to better allocation of resources. Some airlines are providing their employees

Figure 12.1 Areas that mobility can impact.

mobile devices for better customer service and for printing boarding pass, bag tags, etc. Airports and various airlines are using mobility enhancements in the areas of baggage tracking, maintenance, preflight and in-flight services, flight planning, employees' task allocations, and asset and spare-parts management.

Many airlines are providing its customers options to use mobiles for checking flight status, flight schedules, seat availability, seat selection, mobile check-in, boarding pass, mobile payment, baggage tracking, and making itinerary changes.

> By 2012, we anticipate that airports will be operating in real time, with a truly bi-directional flow of information between all operational stakeholders. Mobile technology most definitely plays a role here.
>
> **Martin Smith**
> *Director of Group technology and Innovation,*
> *Manchester Airports Group*
> *Source: http://www.airports.org*

12.3 Why Mobility?

For all the airlines, customer satisfaction is a major issue. Passengers selecting one airline over the other are not just dependent on lower cost. It also includes the

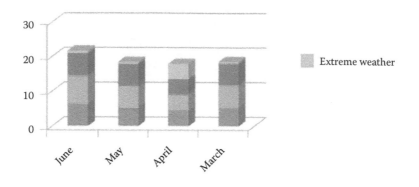

Figure 12.2 Flight delays by cause (Adapted from Bureau of Transportation Statistics).

overall experience (preflight, in-flight, and post-flight) that they have when they travel with the airlines. Preflight experience includes long waits in queues at check-in areas, crowded customer service desks, baggage handling, etc. In-flight experience includes providing in-flight entertainment in users' mobile, cashless cabins, etc. Post-flight experience involves the passenger experience at the final destination, which includes if the passenger received the bags, the amount of time waited for retrieving the bags, etc.

Figure 12.2 provides the main reasons that cause flight delays. On an average of 6%, the delay is caused by the carrier itself. The reasons for these delays are mainly because of baggage loading, fueling, maintenance issues or crew problems, aircraft cleaning, etc. Last-minute gate changes for a flight will also causes delays for the aircraft. These can be resolved using better real-time communications and tracking. This can be provided by using handheld solutions.

12.4 Mobility and Its Areas of Impact

Airlines will be able to provide mobility solutions that can be used for the customers as well as employees.

A customer-centric solution provides the following different options for customers:

- Viewing flight reservation
- Viewing flight status
- Itinerary changes
- Seat availability and selection
- Mobile check-in and payment
- Baggage tracking

These options for customers help them to spend less time in queues and receive reminders on flight-boarding gates and timings. Also, these will help them in keeping track of their baggage. Mobility will, to some extent, make traveling experience paperless. Airlines can send information and alerts to the customers on information such as travel time to the airport, average delays at security check line, etc.

For the solution provided for employees, airlines will have the following benefits:

- To keep track of employee shift and task details
- Dynamic task and work allocation
- Provide customer service anywhere in the airport, not just behind the desk
- Get information on gates and flights in real time for better customer service
- Provide better service for special assistance required by customers with timely data
- Provide better baggage handling
- Ability to burst queues at counters by providing check-in and boarding pass printing
- Reduce delays for aircrafts through better communication and real-time data such as gate changes
- Inventory tracking for repair and maintenance
- Option to provide better in-flight experience such as cashless cabins

Enabling mobility transforms the way an airline interacts with its customers beyond airports and flights. Using mobility, airlines can deliver real-time information, personalized services, offers, and discounts to its customers.

12.5 Mobility in Airport Ramp Operations

12.5.1 The Baggage-Handling Process

Most of the airlines have their own dedicated airport terminals, airline-specific bag tags with barcodes printed on them, which are then assigned to the passenger bags. The bag tags contain a six-digit numeric bag tag. When a passenger checks in a baggage at the ticket counter, a bag tag indicating the passenger's itinerary is put onto the bag. Then, it is placed onto a moving belt that takes the baggage to the bag room. All the checked bags are sorted in the bag room so that the bag will be loaded onto the correct flight. The bag tag that was affixed to the baggage during check-in will be read by the baggage handler and placed into the proper cart or into a unit load device (ULD). The bag cart or ULD is eventually taken from the bag room to the aircraft for loading by baggage handlers (Figure 12.3).

Figure 12.3 The baggage-handling process.

12.5.2 The Problems

As given in Figure 12.4, the major airlines in the United States handle approximately 600 million passengers each year. Current data for the airline industry show that the average occurrence of mishandled bags is five out of every 1000 passengers. For the top 10 airlines in the United States, the figure jumps to almost eight bags per 1000 passengers. Each lost or mishandled bag is an additional cost for airline in terms of cost occurring as part of transportation and labor for redirecting and delivering the baggage to the actual owner or the cost to reimburse the owner of the baggage if the baggage is lost. Another major issue because of mishandled baggage is loss of customer satisfaction, which in turn makes the customer move to another airline.

Airports and airlines work hard to offer their passengers a fast and efficient travel experience. Proper baggage handling is a major factor that leads to better customer satisfaction. Smarter baggage handling includes a fast and efficient option to check-in bags at the departure station, short transfer and turn-around times, no lost bags, and reduced waiting times at the reclaim point for the customer. Smarter baggage handling from an airline industry means optimized baggage and resource

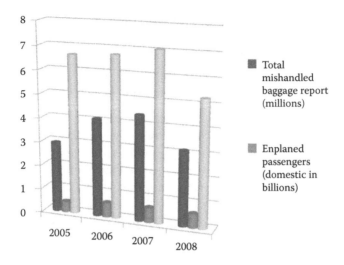

Figure 12.4 Mishandled baggage reports filed by passengers with the largest U.S. air carriers (Adapted from Bureau of Transportation Statistics).

planning, excellent process and resource control, and accurate management information to enable an excellent baggage-handling operation.

Most of the airlines' main choice for baggage handling has been the use of bag tags, which contain a barcode. By using bag tags, airlines will be able to accurately link the passengers to their baggage. Even this technology will fall short to directly link the bag to the correct aircraft at any point of time. The issues will be more challenging when the passenger's itinerary has multiple baggage transfers across different airlines. The Baggage Reconciliation System is used in identifying a bag, whose owner had not boarded the flight. In the current scenario, it takes around 15–20 min to identify the bags, which in turn delays the flight. Once a flight is delayed, further delay is caused as it is pushed down on priority. These delays from the scheduled departure will cause huge losses to the airline.

Handheld solutions provide ramp agents with up-to-date information required for their tasks. Using these solutions, ramp agents will get the latest status of bags that are supposed to be loaded onto the flight that is coming from the connecting flight. They will be able to know in advance whether the bags can make it to the flight, and then they will be able to plan for the bags if these are to miss the flight. This leads to lesser delays, faster problem resolution, and, further more, improved passenger satisfaction. Airlines are targeting to increase the weight and balance of the flight to "plus or minus" one bag accuracy. Also they are keeping track of the bags and cargo loaded onto the aircraft at the origin station, and therefore by the time the flight reaches the destination airport, the ramp agents at that airport are aware of what is coming in the flight.

12.6 Mobility in Customer Service (Gate Operations)

In today's business world, customer service is considered to be paramount. In majority of the airlines, customers interact with the airport or airline employees primarily at the counters in the front and behind security gates. Mobility applications help airlines to assist their customers better. These mobility solutions can act as queue busters and will be able to assist customers anywhere in the airport especially during off-schedule and bad weather scenarios. Handheld solutions provide gate agents for better customer service not just from behind the counter but from anywhere in the airport.

By providing handheld solutions and Bluetooth printers to gate agents, airlines can have the agents work as customer service agents as well as help the check-in desk in case of queues at check-in counters. The solutions will allow the agents to check-in passengers and print boarding passes when the check-in queue is long. Inside the airport, these agents will be able to help passengers by providing real-time information about flights and their connecting flights' information. These mobile applications should help airlines on frequently occurring scenarios such as flight cancellations, flight delays, and long queues at that particular gate with one or two gate agents trying to help the customers as fast as they can with the available computers. Usage of handheld applications and services of more gate agents could be used for customer services.

These devices could be used in providing vouchers or coupons to the passengers in case of flight delays or cancellations. These vouchers can be used by the passengers either for meals, traveling, hotel accommodation, etc. These applications can also act as a source of revenue for the airline. Many airlines across the world are using mobile applications for collecting fees for check-in excess and oversized bags at gates.

> Our customers are mobile by definition, and when we can equip our employees with real-time mobile technology that enables them to make better decisions on behalf of the customer, we all benefit. Our airport employees do an excellent job interacting with customers and meeting their needs—YADA enables them to come out from behind the counter and provide real-time information, bag tags, boarding passes and other answers wherever the customer is in the airport.
>
> **Monte Ford**
> *American Airlines (http://www.airlinetrends.com/2010/07/02/*
> *american-airlines-yada-handheld/Cached)*

12.7 Scenarios for Mobile Enablement

12.7.1 Scenario 1: Mobile Baggage Tracking System for Transportation and Logistics

---

SCOPE OF MOBILIZATION

Mobile baggage scanning solutions are available to expand the capabilities of the weight-and-balance system. These solutions load the cargo information into the weight and balance system by reading bag tags with bar codes with the aid of a scanning device. The solution allows users to manually enter bag tag information when bar codes cannot be read as well as in the case of manually entering actual weights. This information can later be used by the customers to track the bags in the track-and-trace systems. Moreover, the airline may want to reduce delayed delivery of booked cargo to the aircraft.

The initial state in most scenarios involves load planning being done manually on paper by crew chiefs. The information is then entered, verified, and finalized at the server. If there is no timely dissemination of data, the aircraft cannot take off resulting in an aircraft departure delay because of ramp issues. In addition, the existing load planning device may have stability and user-interface issues.

An application that has the ability to scan each bag or cargo that is loaded onto the aircraft can be developed. The application will need to display the graphical representation of the different compartment configurations for different flight types. The application has to be linked with enhanced back-end systems through multiple connectivity options. The application will expedite the process of cargo loading, will reduce load closeout delays, and result in saving fuel costs. The application will feed data into baggage tracking applications, which in turn provides information about baggages to customers and agents. The application can be service-oriented architecture (SOA)-based and ensures well-defined entry points for further enhancements. The potential benefits of the application are listed:

- Reduces maintenance, production support, and operating costs
- Expedites the process of loading cargo and baggage
- Saves fuel costs by reducing flight departure delays
- Increases accuracy in load planning by providing a user interface
- Cellular technology within the device provides long-term radio replacement
- The application is based on a distributed model that provides flexibility for future upgrades

12.7.2 Scenario 2: Passenger Assistance System

> **SCOPE OF MOBILIZATION**
>
> A mobile helpdesk solution assists passengers at the airports. Generally, passengers go to gate agents at the front desk to get information about connecting flights. There is usually no service provided for standby or upgrade requests other than at the airport front desk. During line-bursting, the services of the front-desk agents cannot be used effectively due to lack of infrastructure.

The airline's support staff need to be able to serve passengers by providing real-time flight status and gate information, allocation of seats, checking-in passengers and their bags, printing and issuing boarding passes, accepting upgrade requests, and providing other support functions.

12.7.3 The Solution

A mobile solution needs to be designed and developed to extend passenger assistance information to the personal digital assistant for better service and enhanced customer satisfaction. The application will display real-time flight status and gate information and provide services such as printing boarding passes, checking-in passengers and bags, and collecting excess bag fee. The application extends passenger assistance to any location at the airport. The solution can realize several benefits:

- Faster and effective services ensuring customer satisfaction
- Increased productivity by reducing the workload of the front desk
- Customers can avail of these services from any of the agents instead of waiting in queues
- System architecture based on a distributed model that provides flexibility for future upgrades

12.8 Conclusion

Mobility is a major trend that is changing the transportation industry. Mobility in transportation finds use cases for both cargo and passenger transportation. This chapter presents a focused approach on the airline industry to explain the use of mobility in some cases. The various mobile applications that are being developed by various airlines and airports change the way we go about with our day-to-day activities at the airport as a passenger or as an airport or airline employee. By putting together wireless infrastructures at the airports, airlines can improve the usage of data-centric intelligent applications supporting their staff including ground workers, ramp agents, gate agents, etc. The key business benefits that can be achieved from moving to mobile technology include faster aircraft turn-around times, better baggage tracking, and improved customer satisfaction with personalized assistance.

Additional Reading

Catherine Mayer. "Mobility: a major trend changing our industry" presented at the ACI World Annual General Assembly. Available at http://www.airports.org
SITA. Airline IT Trends Survey 2011. Available at http://www.sita.aero

Chapter 13

Mobility Solutions for the Manufacturing and Supply-Chain Industry

Increased customer demands and the new global economy force the manufacturing and supply-chain industry to follow improved business processes and automations wherever possible. Mobility solutions combined with automatic identification and data collection (AIDC) techniques such as radio frequency identification (RFID) and barcode labels are the first choice for manufacturing and supply-chain automation for various reasons. This chapter gives an overview of the mobility opportunities, the benefits of mobility, the various mobility solutions for manufacturing and supply-chain management (SCM), and a case study of a mobility solution for RFID-based bonded-warehouse management.

13.1 Introduction

The manufacturing and supply-chain industry represents a group of interconnected business entities (people, organizations, activities, technology, information, and resources) involved in the formation of a finished product or service and the supply of the same to customers or consumers. Based on the responsibilities and the involvement, the manufacturer, the distributor (supplier), the wholesaler, and the retailer are considered the four important role players of the manufacturing and supply-chain industry. Aerospace products, automotive goods, fast-moving consumer goods, food and beverages, etc., are examples of manufacturing entities.

The manufacturing and supply-chain industry accounts for a massive trillion-dollar business with stringent competition in each role. Manufacturers across the globe are being pressurized by retailers, wholesalers, distributors, and competitors to deliver better and faster at reduced costs. Regardless of their roles in the manufacturing and supply-chain industry, manufacturers, distributors (suppliers), wholesalers, and retailers are experiencing narrow margins, increased customer expectations, and the demand for quick turnaround. This leads to mergers, acquisitions, joint ventures, and outsourcing in the manufacturing and distribution process.

To stand out of the competition and grab a large market share, manufacturers and distributors have to always be above the industry's trends and should follow improved business processes and automations wherever possible, meeting high customer expectations and quick turnaround times.

13.2 Scope for Mobility Solutions in the Manufacturing and Supply-Chain Industry

Mobility has a significant role to play in a world where the manufacturing and supply-chain industry is looking for improved business processes and automations to reduce cycle times, overproduction, and underutilized resources and to beat the stiff competition. Traditional business processes in the manufacturing and supply-chain segment are heavily dependent on paper-based information processing (work orders, reports, order management, etc.), which is highly time-consuming and error-prone. Mobility solutions provide information access anytime and anywhere by transferring desktop computing to mobile handheld devices carried by the staff. Mobile enabling of the various operations and business processes in the manufacturing and supply-chain segment greatly improves the business process times, which is the root cause for many of the production or distribution delays. Mobility solutions when combined with AIDC techniques such as RFID and barcode labels can significantly automate the various business processes and operations involved in the manufacturing and distribution process, leading to accurate information and tighter coordination between production, supplies, and sales. Mobility implementation also provides real-time visibility to the supply chain, helping to identify the possible delays and fight against the intrusion of any counterfeit products in the supply-chain line. Figure 13.1 gives an overview of the various mobility solution opportunities in the manufacturing and supply-chain industry.

13.2.1 Mobility Solutions for Manufacturing

Mobility solutions for the manufacturing segment primarily focuses on mobile enabling of the various floor operations, warehouse management, asset management, and workforce management in the manufacturing environment. The

Manufacturing

➢ Floor operations management solutions
  ➢ Production line monitoring and automation
  ➢ Production line sequencing
➢ Warehouse management solutions
  ➢ Raw material reception management
  ➢ Storing, sorting, and pick-up
  ➢ Packing, storing, and shipping of finished products
➢ Asset management solutions
➢ Workforce management

Mobility

Supply chain

➢ Warehouse management solutions
  ➢ Product reception management
  ➢ Storing, sorting, and pick-up
  ➢ Packing, storing, and shipping of products to retailers
➢ Shipping and tracking solutions
  ➢ Pick-up schedules management
  ➢ Real-time shipment tracking
  ➢ Dynamic/optimized routing
➢ Asset management soutions
➢ Workforce management solutions

Figure 13.1   Scope for mobility solutions in the manufacturing and supply-chain industry.

various mobility solutions under this category help in production automation, leading to better utilization of resources, quick turnarounds, better control over the manufacturing process, and increased worker productivity.

13.2.1.1 Floor Operations Management Mobility Solutions

The shop floor forms the heart of any manufacturing or production environment. The shop floor contains a number of machines, assembly lines, control units, etc. As a typical example, let us consider a car manufacturing plant. It contains various machines for producing the parts and multiple assembly lines to assemble the various parts in a specified order. In the traditional manufacturing environment, the monitoring of the signals and data collected by the various supervisory control and data acquisition systems for plant automation is handled at a central control station, where the real-time information is displayed and recorded. This requires the presence and attention of a dedicated person at the central control station. Mobility solutions can easily extend this beyond the central control station to the handheld devices of workers for a quicker and efficient operation to fix any likely issues, minimizing the risk of machine outages and plant shutdowns.

Also, in the traditional manufacturing environment, most of the data-collection activities, such as work completion at assembly stations, capturing special notes and

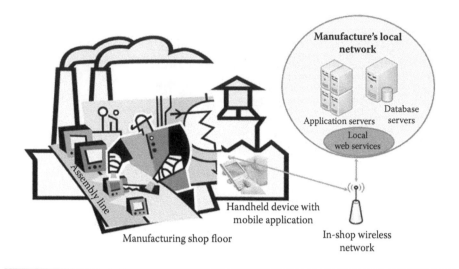

Figure 13.2 Overview of the manufacturing-floor operation automation with mobility solutions.

parts details, etc., are executed through manual paper-based data collection. This requires entering the paper-collected details to a central computer at a later time to report the work progress, status, and schedule updates. This doubles the effort, and any mistakes in recording the details lead to erroneous data, which may lead to production delays. Mobility solutions can be effectively deployed in the data-collection operation at the floor, where the floor workers can capture the details with the help of a mobile application running on a handheld, which is connected to the back-end systems over a wireless interface. Mobilizing the data-collection operation provides real-time visibility to information and status as well as it reduces the chances of errors associated with manual paper-based data entry (Figure 13.2).

Mobility solutions when combined with AIDC techniques such as RFID and barcode labels can effectively track the usage of the right parts in the assembly line and can also point out the wrong sequencing of parts for assembling, if any. Parts can be labeled with RFID tags and barcode labels, and the staff at the assembly line can scan the parts for verification, using an RFID reader and a barcode reader-enabled handheld device hosting the mobile application. Mobility solutions can instantly verify the parts and identify part sequencing in the assembly line to ensure proper sequencing of the parts in the assembly line. This will significantly reduce improper product assembly and rework effort.

13.2.1.2 Warehouse Management Mobility Solutions

The warehouse plays a key role in any manufacturing environment. It acts as a central hub for storing the incoming raw materials and parts used in the manufacturing

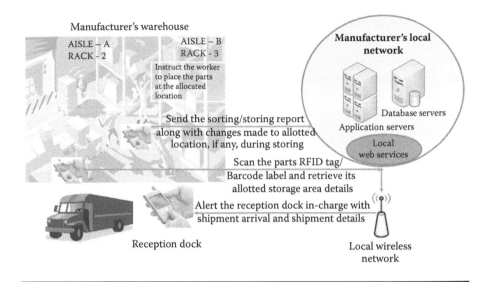

Figure 13.3   An example for warehouse operation automation with mobility solutions.

process and the finished products that are ready to be shipped to wholesalers and retailers. The warehouse at the manufacturing facility usually contains millions of raw materials and finished goods, and it is not an easy task to identify and manage them through manual processes. The day-to-day warehouse operations in a manufacturing environment involve multiple activities such as receiving raw materials and parts at the incoming docking station; sorting and arranging of the received raw material at the right shelves for easy access; stock counting of parts inventory; packaging, sorting, and storing of finished products; stock counting of finished products; and loading of the products at the outgoing docking station for shipping to the respective customers (Figure 13.3).

The shop floor and warehouse management mobility solutions empower the workers with mobile computing devices to perform their duties more efficiently, by extending the services to their handhelds and eliminating paper-based processes.

13.2.1.3 Unified Voice and Data Communication Mobility Solutions

Mobility solutions enable cross-communication between the various types of communication devices and techniques deployed in the organization. With mobility, it is easy to implement unified communications connecting the different communication equipments (handheld devices, desk phones, etc.). Cost-effective voice communication mechanisms such as voice calls over internal WiFi networks and push-to-talk features can be implemented through mobile solutions for communication among workers and supervisors in the work environment. Also handheld devices can act as an extension of desk phones to respond to incoming calls.

13.2.1.4 Asset Management Mobility Solutions

Any manufacturing environment contains hundreds or thousands of assets including machineries, pallets, and totes. In the case of machineries, it is essential to conduct scheduled or periodic inspections and maintenance to prevent any unplanned downtime on the production line. Mobility solutions can offer efficient and cost-effective asset management for asset tracking as well as asset maintenance. RFID-tagging and barcode labeling can be used for asset identification. RFID tags seem to be a better choice for asset tagging in a production environment due to their high-operating range. Barcode labels are based on line-of-sight technology, and they require close proximity between the barcode-reading handheld device and barcode labels; however, RFID tags are based on radio frequency technology, and they can provide an operating range varying from a few centimeters to hundreds of meters depending on the type of RFID technology, type of tags used (active or passive), and the RFID-reader handheld.

All machineries, pallets, and totes can be tagged with RFID tags, which gives real-time information about the asset movement (especially for totes and pallets) with the help of a fixed RFID reader or a close-proximity mobile handheld reader. A mobile client application can interface with the centralized manufacturing automation software for retrieving the details about the machine, its preventive maintenance schedules, calibration requirements, etc. The asset management team and field service staff can be equipped with a mobile handheld device hosting a smart client application, which can receive real-time alerts regarding machine status (online and off-line), alerts and reminders regarding the upcoming scheduled maintenance for an instrument, etc. Also the field service team can use this application to enter service details and inspection remarks about the machine during field service or regular inspection of the machine (Figure 13.4).

Adopting mobility for asset maintenance will reduce the risk of the outage of critical machineries, which may arise due to a missed preventive maintenance schedule or calibration service. It will also reduce the risk of missing service history, erroneous service data, etc., which may arise in paper-based service history tracking.

Implementation of asset tracking with mobility solutions and AIDC techniques for fixed assets (machineries) and mobile assets (pallets, totes, containers, etc.) reduces the manpower requirement for asset tracking. At the same time, it provides accurate tracking information about mobile assets in real time.

13.2.1.5 Workforce Management Mobility Solutions

Mobility solutions make workforce management easy and efficient. With mobility adoption, each worker can be equipped with a mobile handheld device, and work

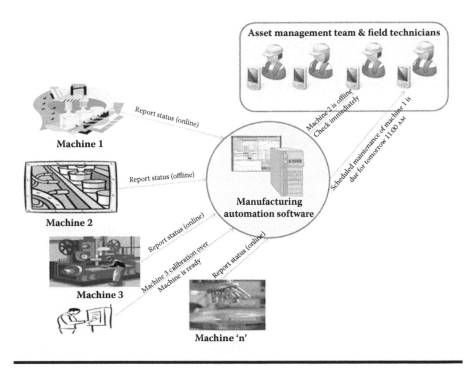

Figure 13.4 Mobility adoption sample use-case for asset management in manufacturing.

orders and shift details can be easily pushed to the handheld device of the respective workers. Workers can log their work hours and the time spent on the completion of each work item assigned to them. This will eliminate the paper-based workforce management and will provide real-time visibility on the work items assigned to each worker and the progress of work. With mobility solutions, workers can communicate with their coworkers for clarifications, assistance, etc., through cost-effective methods such as instant chats. Most of the manufacturing facilities work on a shift basis for round-the-clock operations. Manual shift management is the greatest pain point for many business organizations. With mobility, each worker can be alerted in real time on their work schedule, overtime allotment, and changes in schedule, if any, due to the absence of any worker.

13.2.2 Mobility Solutions for Supply Chain

Mobility solutions for the supply-chain segment primarily target on mobile enabling of the various operations in product and parts shipping and distribution, warehouse management, asset management, and workforce management. The various mobility solutions under this category help in product distribution automation, leading to better utilization of resources, quick turnarounds, better control over the distribution and stocking process, and increased worker productivity. The various mobility solution opportunities in the supply-chain segment are as follows:

13.2.2.1 Warehouse Management Mobility Solutions

The warehouse plays a critical role in the supply-chain process, facilitating the storage of products, goods, or parts on their way from the manufacturers to wholesalers and retailers and from parts suppliers to manufacturers. As explained in Section 13.2.1.2, warehouse operations involve multiple activities such as receiving finished products or parts at the in-coming docking station; sorting and arranging the received items at the right shelves for easy access; stock counting of inventory; packaging, sorting, and storing of items; stock counting; loading of the items at the outgoing docking station for shipping to the respective customers; and so on. Mobility can be adopted throughout all these core warehouse operations, resulting in improved business processes, real-time visibility into the supply chain, and faster turnaround.

Implementing mobility solutions at the product distribution stage and at the retailers' warehouse is advantageous because of improved worker productivity, easy access and handling of products, prevention of out-of-stock scenarios through automated order processing, etc. The paper-based manual stock-up and stock-counting process requires significant manpower efforts and is highly time-consuming, whereas advanced mobile data collection and AIDC techniques such as bar code and RFID techniques will significantly reduce the time and manpower requirements. Mobility when combined with AIDC techniques can easily identify product information during the storage and pickup process, helping the warehouse staff to identify fragile and perishable items, handle them appropriately, and store them at the appropriate location.

13.2.2.2 Shipping and Tracking Mobility Solutions

The supply-chain process involves lots of transportation activities such as moving raw materials from the supplier's warehouse to the manufacturer's warehouse, movement of finished products and goods from the manufacturer's warehouse to wholesalers or from the wholesaler's warehouse to retailers. Section 13.2.2.2.1 gives an overview of the various mobility solution opportunities for automating the shipment and transportation activities in SCM.

13.2.2.2.1 Real-Time Shipment Tracking Solutions

With the implementation of automated identification and tracking technologies such as RFID and global positioning systems (GPS), it is easy to track the shipment movement in real time and generate alerts, such as the time the product left the manufacturer's warehouse, the present location of the product of interest, the estimated delivery time of the product, etc., to the various concerned parties (Figure 13.5).

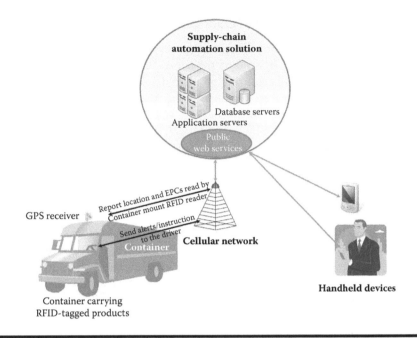

Figure 13.5 GPS- and RFID-based real-time container-tracking solution for SCM.

Products can be tagged with RFID tags, and a container- or vehicle-mounted RFID reader can scan the product tags periodically and send the tag details (electronic product codes implemented in RFID terminology) along with the current position (acquired by the GPS receiver present in the vehicle) in real time to the supply-chain automation software running at the central facility of the supply-chain provider. This solution provides real-time visibility into the supply chain and eliminates the probability of injecting counterfeit products during product movement. The real-time visibility into the supply chain also helps to identify the probable delivery schedule slippages and alert the concerned person about the situation and plan a work-around or take proactive steps to handle such scenarios. With real-time tracking, the security staff at the pickup or delivery point can be alerted in advance with the pickup truck details to avoid long waits at the gate for clearance.

13.2.2.2.2 Dynamic Routing

With mobility adoption, the delivery truck drivers can be equipped with handheld devices running mobility solutions, and the drivers can be alerted with special instructions, route change notifications, etc., in real time. Trucks can be tracked in real time with GPS solutions and in emergency situations such as a break down, the centralized dispatching system can send alerts to the nearest truck in the same locality to accommodate products that have immediate delivery requirements.

13.2.2.2.3 Electronic (Mobile) Data Collection

Implementing mobility solutions eliminates the paper-based process for pickup and delivery schedule generation, by sending the papers to the concerned persons (drivers, warehouse staff, etc.) and capturing proof-of-delivery, etc. Electronic data capture in the transportation process also helps to capture and record all the necessary information required to adhere to the local transportation laws. Mobile solution-based electronic data capture eliminates the double efforts in capturing data on paper and later converting it to electronic records at a central station. It also reduces the chances of data-entry errors.

13.2.2.3 Asset Management Mobility Solutions

Similar to the manufacturing industry, the supply-chain industry also contains hundreds or thousands of fixed and mobile assets including pallets, totes, container trucks, etc. Asset management and maintenance mobility solutions help to keep track of fixed and mobile assets as well as manage the maintenance schedules. Efficient fleet asset management solutions help to reduce the capital expenditure and operations cost.

13.2.2.4 Workforce Management Mobility Solutions

With mobility adoption, each worker (truck drivers, warehouse staff, etc.) can be equipped with a mobile handheld device, and pickup or delivery schedules and shift details can be easily pushed to the handheld device of the respective workers. Workers can log their work hours and the time spent on the completion of each work item assigned to them. This will eliminate the paper-based workforce management and will provide real-time visibility into the work items assigned to each worker and the progress of work. With mobility solution, workers can communicate with their coworkers for clarifications and assistance through cost-effective methods such as instant chats. With mobility, each worker can be alerted in real time on their work schedule, overtime allotment, and changes in schedule, if any.

13.3 Benefits of Mobility Adoption in the Manufacturing and Supply-Chain Industry

Adopting mobility in manufacturing and SCM brings benefits to manufacturers, distributors, wholesalers, retailers, and consumers in terms of revenue, efficiency, quality, and cost. A few important benefits among them are as follows:

13.3.1 Improved Worker Productivity

Automating the various operations at the manufacturing environment and at the warehouse enables the workers to handle more work easily. As a typical example, automating the warehouse management with RFID tags helps the warehouse staff to find the products quickly without the need for manually iterating through the aisles to find them. Also it will save the time required in stock counting, product placement, picking, sorting, etc., leading to increased worker productivity. Mobile data collection eliminates the double effort in paper-based data capture. Implementing mobility for transportation in the supply-chain operations greatly improves the driver's productivity. With mobile solutions, drivers can receive their pickup and delivery schedules in real time without waiting in long queues. This also helps the drivers from the hassles of paper-based data collection for proof-of-delivery, etc.

13.3.2 Better Inventory Management

Mobility solutions when combined with AIDC techniques such as RFID and barcode labels can fully automate the inventory management process, including keeping track of the warehouse inventory, reorders, etc., leading to the prevention of over and underproduction scenarios. A controlled inventory optimizes both the manufacturers' and distributors' storage space requirements and prevents product outages.

13.3.3 Elimination of Counterfeit Products

Counterfeit products* are one of the biggest problems faced by the industry today. As the supply-chain process involves lots of activities such as transporting the products, temporary storing, etc., counterfeit products may get injected into the supply chain at any point between the departure from the manufacturer's warehouse to the distribution point, if the products are not tracked in real time. Implementing product identification with barcode labels and techniques such as holograms, etc., may ensure the genuineness of the product. RFID-based identification can provide real-time tracking and real-time visibility into the supply chain.

13.3.4 High Return-on-Investment

Mobility solutions provide high return-on-investment (ROI) in the long run, through improved worker productivity, automations, control over the business process, etc.

13.3.5 Eco-Friendliness

Bringing mobility into the manufacturing and supply-chain environment eliminates paper-based data entry and records. Saving paper is saving trees—a step

---

* Counterfeit products refer to fake products that are deliberately and fraudulently mislabeled with respect to identity and source.

toward the "green" initiatives. Efficient implementation of mobility solutions for transportation and delivery optimizes the routes and thereby saves fuel consumption as well as reduces the carbon footprint.

13.4 Choice of Mobility Solutions for Manufacturing and Supply-Chain Industry

The selection of a mobility solution for manufacturing and supply-chain segments in terms of architecture, business requirements, and platform support is highly challenging. Many of the manufacturing and supply-chain providers may already have a legacy system in place, and it may be difficult to completely replace the existing system for various reasons such as the infrastructure changes required, the cost impact for replacing the existing system, the worker's familiarity with the existing business process, the software system, etc. Hence, it requires a thorough analysis in the decision-making process of mobilization. Extending the existing legacy system to mobile devices through custom-built mobility extensions and replacing the existing system with a custom-built or off-the-shelf full-fledged end-to-end solution supporting mobile devices are the various options to be iterated during the mobilization process. Each option should be weighted in terms of infrastructure requirements, investment, flexibility, training requirements, etc. Various manufacturing and SCM off-the-shelf solutions are available today from multiple vendors with varying functionality and feature support.

13.4.1 Off-the-Shelf Mobility Solutions versus Custom-Built Solutions

The choice on whether to adopt an off-the-shelf solution or a custom-built solution is dependent on multiple factors, and a few important factors among them are listed below:

1. Availability of the off-the-shelf solution for implementing all the necessary mobility requirements
2. Support for the off-the-shelf solution for extending to multiple mobile platforms
3. Customization effort for the off-the-shelf solution versus effort for building a custom solution
4. Cost for off-the-shelf solution versus custom solution
5. Annual maintenance cost for off-the-shelf solution versus custom-built solution
6. Feature addition support
7. Ease of operation

13.5 Scenario: Mobility Solution for RFID-Based Warehouse Management

SCOPE OF MOBILIZATION

Consider a logistics provider that is a partner for a leading supply-chain provider, dealing with the exporting and distribution of products, and that wants to implement an RFID-based mobility solution for the automation of tracking and movement of customs-cleared items at the bonded warehouse in its distribution hub at the cargo area of a major airport. The logistics provider wants to implement the solution for the existing handheld device used by its associates.

13.5.1 Sample Scenario before Introducing RFID Solution

The products that are exported are bonded items, and they require customs clearance before moving them to the distributor's warehouse. The in-bond items are kept in a bonded warehouse in the cargo area of the airport. The shipper will be notified about the list of items from the cage that has cleared the customs process. An operator at the bonded cage uses his/her handheld device to scan the product's barcode label to manually identify the products with cleared status and cross-verify these with the list of customs-cleared items and moves these out of the bonded cage to the distributors' warehouse of the retailer. The current process is highly time-consuming, and it requires manually scanning each item in the cage to find out the correct item. This process is also error prone as there is a high chance of moving a wrong item from the cage.

13.5.2 Scenario with RFID Mobile Solution

All the products will be tagged with EPC Gen 2 RFID tags. The list of the customs-cleared items is sent to the handheld device carried by the bonded-cage operator in real time from the centralized dispatch and inventory management station. The cage operator can figure out the location of the product through a simple aisle-wise scanning or a walk-through. A stand-alone RFID reader installed at the exit gate of the bonded cage reads the EPC of the products leaving the warehouse and sends the information to the central station in real time. If the EPC does not belong to the list of customs-cleared items, an immediate "wrong item" alert will be sent to the handheld device of the cage operator.

13.5.3 Requirements and Solution

The application is designed to address the following requirements:

- The logistics provider wants to use RFID-enabled (EPC Gen 2 standard) handheld device running on Windows mobile operating system as the enterprise device.

■ The application should interface with the existing dispatch and inventory management logistics solution used by the logistics provider.
■ The application should implement user-level and supervisor-level access and prevent access to the system-level resources of the handheld device.
■ The application should utilize both WiFi wireless network and cellular data connectivity (GPRS/3G/4G) to connect to the existing logistics back-end solution.

The various services from the existing logistics back-end solution are exposed through web services. The mobile client application running on the handheld device connects to the back-end logistics services over a wireless data network.

The handheld application is developed as a rich client application with front end in C#.net. Access to the web services hosted on the logistic provider's network is controlled through a user ID and password-based authentication mechanism. The rich client mobile application also implements restrictions to access other systems resources. The RFID tag-reading feature is implemented in the handheld application to read RFID tags associated with the products (Figure 13.6).

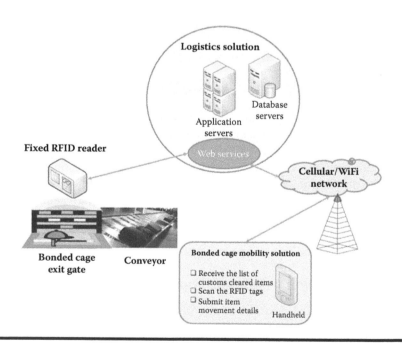

Figure 13.6 End-to-end solution architecture of RFID-based warehouse management.

13.5.4 Business Benefits

■ Real-time processing of cleared shipments
■ Reduction in shipment-handling errors
■ Reduced manpower requirements

13.6 Conclusion

Mobility solutions when combined with AIDC techniques such as RFID and bar-code labels greatly help the manufacturing and supply-chain industry to implement improved business processes and automation wherever possible, leading to efficient utilization of resources (machines, assets, and workforce), improved workforce productivity, and better control over the inventory.

Mobility adoption in the manufacturing and supply-chain process brings huge business benefits and at the same time lots of challenges. This chapter was intended to provide a general overview of the mobility opportunities, the benefits of mobility, and the various mobility solutions for manufacturing and SCM. The decision on which processes need to be mobilized and what type of mobility solution needs to be adopted is purely business-driven, and the concerned business organizations should perform a cost–benefit analysis during the decision-making process.

Additional Reading

1. Robert B. Handfield and Ernest L. Nichols. *Introduction to Supply Chain Management*, 1st edition. Upper Saddle River, NJ: Prentice Hall; 1998.
2. Michael H. Hugos. *Essentials of Supply Chain Management*, 3rd edition. New York: Wiley; 2011.
3. Klaus Finkenzeller. *RFID Handbook: Fundamentals and Applications in Contact-Less Smart Cards, Radio Frequency Identification and Near-Field Communication*, 3rd edition. New York: Wiley & Sons Ltd; 2010.
4. Tony Bradley and Satish Shah. *Unified Communications for Dummies*. New York: Wiley Publishing, Inc.; 2010.

Chapter 14

Mobility Solutions for the Healthcare Industry

The healthcare segment is the most information-intensive industry demanding real-time information exchange between healthcare providers, patients, and clinical diagnostic services. This chapter gives an overview of the key driving forces for mobility, mobility opportunities, the benefits of mobility, the various mobility solutions for the healthcare sector, and a case study of a mobility solution for patient management.

14.1 Introduction

Healthcare providers across the globe are facing high pressure and challenges due to increased patient volumes, resource crunches, and regulatory requirements to improve the quality of service and responsiveness. To meet these challenges, it is essential to have the right tools that would improve the workflow and staff throughput, to streamline the communication and interaction among the multiple stakeholders, and to provide quick and secure access to critical real-time information. The healthcare service industry is evaluating new ideas, strategies, and technologies to meet quality standards. The widespread consumer adoption of mobile computing devices for day-to-day life is proving that mobile devices are the best delivery channel for quick and convenient service access.

Mobile enabling of the healthcare services facilitates on-demand access to time-critical information, leading to accurate and timely patient assessment and right treatment and meaningful collaboration between healthcare providers, diagnostic service providers, and insurance providers, ensuring better care to patients at an affordable expense.

185

14.2 Key Driving Factors of Mobility in Healthcare

14.2.1 Addressing the Real-World Needs

The healthcare industry is heavily dependent on data. It is very essential for the doctors, nurses, or other healthcare professionals to access past and present data of a patient (such as current medications, treatment history, patients' vital statistics, allergic information, etc.) to make a quick decision on what treatment or medication needs to be done on a patient in an emergency situation. A paper-based recording system induces significant delays in finding the required information from a bunch of paper records, whereas electronic data storage and data retrieval mechanisms can provide the relevant data momentarily. Introducing mobility into the electronic data storage and retrieval system will act as a catalyst to provide near-real time response.

14.2.2 Consumer Empowerment

In today's information technology world, most of the people are "smart consumers," and most of them are heavily dependent on high-end smartphones (Windows Phone, iPhone, Android phone, or BlackBerry devices, etc.) or touch-pad devices for their day-to-day activities, and it is easy for them to receive information and access data or service through these devices and channels than through any other media or channels.

14.2.3 Convergence of Technology

As technology is advancing, we are witnessing technology convergences in many of the focus areas. The emergence of unified communications is a real-world example for this. We traveled a long way from an era where mobile devices were used only for voice calls to an era where it is used for both voice and data and to a step where voice can be transmitted over a data network (voice-over Internet protocol). Unified communications and technology convergences that provide desktop computing experiences in small form-factor mobile devices leading to data access anytime and anywhere are key driving factors for bringing mobility in the healthcare industry.

14.2.4 Meeting the Regulatory Compliance Requirements

As healthcare procedures are becoming more complex, government is imposing strict regulatory compliance guidelines to ensure patient safety and privacy, such as the electronic medical records (EMRs), the electronic health records (EHR), and the Health Insurance Portability and Accountability Act of 1996 (HIPAA) privacy rules, and healthcare service providers are forced to adopt electronic systems and mobility to comply with these regulatory requirements.

14.2.5 The Power of Cloud Computing

According to a Juniper Research study, the market for cloud-based mobile applications is expected to grow by 88% from 2009 to 2014. With the Software-as-a-Service cloud model, many healthcare-related requirements such as EMRs can be implemented quickly and safely with easy access anywhere.

14.3 Scope for Mobility Solutions in the Healthcare Sector

The healthcare industry represents a broad service segment that connects the general public with different healthcare-related services including healthcare service providers (primary care and specialty care hospitals), diagnostic service providers (clinical laboratories, radiology services, etc.), pharmacies, and health-insurance providers. Mobility can be adopted in every service segment under the healthcare industry to bring benefits to both the general public and the underlying healthcare service segment (Figure 14.1).

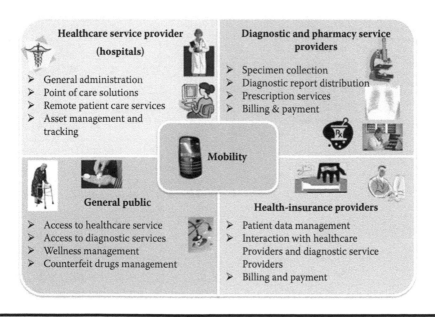

Figure 14.1 Scope for mobility solutions in the healthcare industry.

14.3.1 Mobility Solutions for Healthcare Service Providers

The healthcare service providers (hospitals and clinics) act as the central hub in connecting patients and the supporting healthcare services including diagnostic services (clinical laboratories and imaging and radiology services), pharmacies, emergency medical response (EMR) providers, and health-insurance providers. Figure 14.2 gives an overview of the various in-hospital services and the interaction with other supporting services that can be mobile enabled. The typical in-hospital services that can be mobilized are discussed further.

14.3.1.1 General Administration

Most of the hospitals today handle hundreds of cases ranging from first-time visit, follow-up visits, and emergency cases. It is extremely important to save the time of healthcare providers as well as patients through efficient patient administration and check-in methodologies. Automatic identification and data collection (AIDC) techniques such as barcodes and radio frequency identification (RFIDs) can be utilized for generating unique patient identification numbers and for associating the relevant personal and medical history of the patient with the unique ID. Following are some of the services in patient administration.

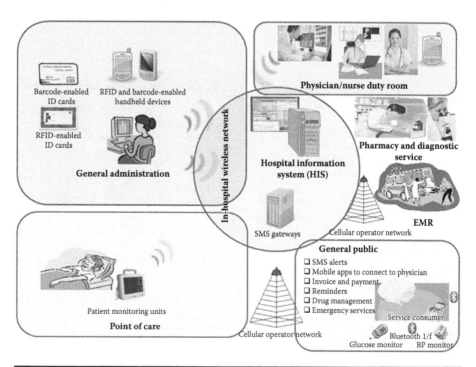

Figure 14.2   Overview of potential in-hospital services for mobile enablement.

14.3.1.1.1 Easy Check-In

The general administration staff can provide easy check-in to the patients through one-touch scanning of the patient barcode- or RFID-enabled ID cards using bar-code- or RFID-enabled handheld devices and a mobile client application that talks to the hospital information system (HIS) for retrieving or validating patient information and to the third-party systems such as the health-insurance provider network for authenticating the user. The easy check-in service helps in preventing long queues and ensures hassle-free check-in to the patients. The supporting units of the handheld device such as camera and touch screen can be utilized for document scanning and patient-signature capturing during the check-in process.

14.3.1.1.2 Intelligent SMS-Based Patient Interaction

Short messaging service (SMS) is a cost-effective way of communicating with mobile users. SMS service is supported by almost all mobile handsets and service providers, and it facilitates a uniform way of messaging, which is simple and consistent across all handsets and mobile operators. Patients can subscribe to the SMS services during the registration process and can avail SMS service effectively for the following processes:

- Appointment scheduling
- Appointment rescheduling
- Appointment reminder service
- Appointment confirmation
- Appointment cancellation

Once signed up for SMS-based services, the HIS can automatically schedule the SMS service for appointment reminders and confirmations and process the SMS request from users. No staff intervention is required for handling SMS-based services. The SMS gateway connects the HIS to the end users over the mobile operator's short message service center (SMS-C) or through an SS7 (signaling system no. 7) connectivity provider.

SMS-based services can effectively improve the service quality by preventing "no-shows." It also enables patient-friendly communication over telephone for scheduling, rescheduling, or canceling an appointment, thus alleviating the pain of staying on long-wait queues. The effective implementation of SMS-based services will lead to significant reduction in the number of call-center staff required for handling appointment management requests.

The only limitation of SMS-based services is that the communication may not be real time, if the underlying implementation of the SMS gateway is through an SMS aggregator, which routes the SMS through a mobile operator's SMS-C.

14.3.1.2 Point-of-Care and Remote-Monitoring Solutions

Among the medical staff, nursing staff and physicians are those who spend most of their time with patients. The high volume of patients and the shortage of the medical workforce is the highest challenge faced by the healthcare industry today. This may lead to a high-pressure work environment where the medical staff dedicate only a limited time for a patient. Mobile enablement empowers medical staff to take action at any time and to effectively manage the shortage of staff as well as the error proofing required to improve the safety and quality of care at the bedside or point of care.

Mobile enablement of patient monitoring helps medical staff to remotely monitor the vital statistics of a patient, and the staff do not need to return periodically to the patient's room for recording the statistics and analyzing the recorded vital parameters. Most patient-monitoring instruments today are "smart instruments," and they can transmit the collected information over the air with wireless interfaces such as WiFi, Bluetooth, etc. to the HISs. Handheld devices, smartphones, and touch-pad devices running a smart patient-monitoring client application, which communicates with the HIS, can provide the vital details of a patient to the medical staff who is in charge of taking care of the patient, regardless of the person's current location (Figure 14.3).

The mobile client application can provide real-time vital status of the patient including any potential life-threatening situation such as variations in ECG and abnormal dips or raises in blood pressure or heart rate, in real time. This service can even make smart and quicker response oriented by integrating global positioning

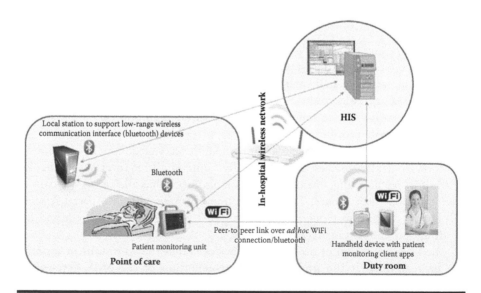

Figure 14.3 Mobility adoption usecase for remote patient-monitoring.

system (GPS) service where all medical staff who are currently located near the patient to provide immediate assistance in case of a life-threatening situation.

Most of the patient-monitoring equipment allows programmable digital control from a remote host, and the mobile client application can utilize this feature for controlling the devices as per the required situation.

One of the common instances of an emergency situation during treatment is the administration of wrong medicines or incorrect dosages. This can be easily prevented by combining AIDC techniques, for patient and medical-staff identification, and mobility application for verifying the current medications of the patient and its dosage, before any medication administration. This technique will greatly reduce the complications that may arise due to the administration of a wrong medicine or an incorrect dosage. RFID and barcode labels can be used for the unique identification of patients and medical staff. The RFID and barcode labels can be read using an RFID- or barcode-enabled handheld mobile device, and the mobile application running on the handheld can quickly retrieve the medication details of the patient including the medicines prescribed by the doctor, dosage, frequency of the medication administration, etc. Also the medical staff can electronically record the medication event and associate the medication administration to his or her name by a quick scanning of his or her RFID- or barcode-enabled ID card. This will eliminate paper-based data capture errors and will also create a precise electronic record for future verifications. Medical staffs can use the mobile client application to record observations or notes during routine patient rounds.

14.3.1.3 Remote Patient-Care Solutions

Remote patient-care solutions provide an optimal way for communicating between a healthcare provider (a primary-care physician or a specialist-care provider) and a remote user or a patient. The remote user can utilize this service for clarifying queries or concerns and for submitting data for analysis by the healthcare provider. Wellness-care management service and treatment follow-up are typical examples of this, where the end user can collect daily workout summaries, diet details, medication details, and vital statistics (such as blood sugar, blood pressure, etc.) in his or her mobile device and later send it to the physician with the help of the mobile client application running in the user's phone, which connects the user to the healthcare provider through the corresponding HIS.

Most consumers today are empowered with smartphones, which are capable of running native- or browser-based applications. Healthcare service providers can easily develop a smart client application for remote patient-care solutions for any of the smartphone platforms (Windows Phone, iPhone [iOS], Android, Symbian, etc.) and host it in the corresponding Application Store. The users can download these applications from the respective application stores (App Store for iPhone devices, Marketplace for Windows Phone devices, and Google Play for Android phones).

Most medical diagnostic instruments (blood glucose monitor, blood pressure monitor, etc.) are "smart devices," and they are capable of interfacing with the consumer's smartphones over wireless interfaces such as Bluetooth or infrared. These devices allow controlling it from the client application running on the consumer's smartphone, over the wireless interface and transferring the diagnostic data to the smartphone, device. The healthcare service providers who develop smart client applications for remote patient-care solutions for a given smartphone platform can select a set of diagnostic devices (e.g., Accu-Chek blood glucose monitor, OMRON blood pressure monitor, etc.) as the supported devices and can build the necessary interface to communicate with these devices over a wireless channel (Bluetooth or infrared) from the client application for collecting data. The end user can purchase the supported diagnostic device from market, connect it with his or her smartphone device hosting the remote patient-care mobile client application through simple steps, and collect and report the diagnostic data related to blood sugar, blood pressure, etc., to the healthcare provider.

Depending on the criticality of the response from the physician for a given request, the user can flag the requests as high-priority request, a medium-priority request, a low-priority request, etc. Any request that needs immediate attention and the response that is critical in deciding the course of action for a given condition falls under the high-priority category. For example, when a patient misses a dosage of the medicine and does not know how to handle the situation, he or she can send a high-priority request to the physician, seeking advice to handle the situation. HIS can alert the physician when a high-priority request is received from a user. If a physician is not available to answer a high-priority request from a patient, the HIS can route the request to another available physician who acts as a backup physician for the user. Normal requests can be handled within a reasonable time frame. This helps the healthcare provider to analyze the data off-line and provide suggestions or directions based on the data provided by the user.

To facilitate this system, the hospital should equip the healthcare provider with a handheld device or smartphone that runs a smart client application with features relevant to the healthcare provider. The provider can set the status as available, receive requests from remote users, respond to requests, or check the records related to a patient to serve the patient better, using the smart client application running on his or her handheld or smartphone (Figures 14.4 and 14.5).

14.3.1.4 Asset Management and Tracking

Any healthcare service-providing organization (hospitals or clinics) will have hundreds of lifesaving medical instruments installed, and it is extremely difficult to keep track of the details of these instruments, their service schedules, calibration requirements, etc., using a paper-based tracking system. The healthcare organization can tag these devices using bar codes or RFID tags and can associate their details to the HIS. A mobile client application can interface with the HIS for

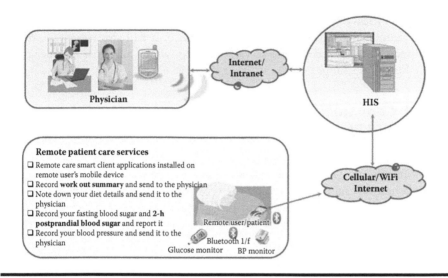

Figure 14.4 Mobility adoption usecase for remote patient-care solutions.

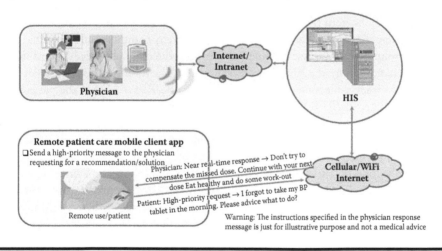

Figure 14.5 Mobility adoption usecase for near real-time remote patient-care needs.

retrieving the details about the instrument, its preventive maintenance schedules, calibration requirements, etc. The asset management team and field service staff can be equipped with a handheld device hosting a smart client application, which can receive real-time alerts regarding instrument status (online or off-line), alerts and reminders regarding the upcoming scheduled maintenance for an instrument, etc. Also the field service team can use this application to enter service details and inspection remarks about the instrument during the field service or regular inspection of the device. Adopting mobility for asset management will reduce the risk of outage of lifesaving medical instruments, which may arise due to a missed preventive maintenance schedule or calibration service. It will also reduce the risk of missing service history, erroneous service data, etc., which may arise in paper-based service history tracking.

14.3.2 Care Mobility Solutions for Diagnostics and Pharmacy Service Providers

Diagnostics and pharmacy services are another segment that comes under the healthcare system. Clinical laboratories play a key role in the assessment of the health condition and the decision on the type of treatment for a patient. The various operations in the diagnostic and pharmacy service segment where mobility solutions can be adopted are as follows.

14.3.2.1 Specimen Collection

It is true that most of the clinical laboratories are handling thousands of tests, and most of them involve manual processing that is prone to errors. Situations such as collecting specimens from the wrong patient, mislabeling of samples collected, etc., can lead to wrong diagnostics and wrong treatment, thereby compromising patient safety. A simple solution to avoid such a situation is to introduce mobility applications in the activities handheld by the laboratory technicians. Whenever the lab technician performs a specimen collection, simply scan the barcode/RFID label of the patient ID card with a barcode/RFID reader-enabled handheld device running a smart mobile client application which can talk to the HIS to retrieve the summary of diagnostic tests recommended for the patient. This will ensure that the right test is performed, and the right specimen is collected from the patient. Also the technician can enter the sample collection details to the HIS through the mobile application running on the handheld device. Further, the technician can use the mobile application to scan his/her barcode- or RFID-enabled ID card to record the details of the technician who conducted the specimen collection. Also the technician can attach an RFID or a barcode label to the specimen container and associate it with the RFID or the barcode label of the patient, with the help of the mobile application, for easy tracking of the diagnostic status and retrieval of results.

14.3.2.2 Diagnostic Report and Data Distribution

The diagnostic service providers can store the results of the tests in their servers or can send it to the hospital's information management system or can provide an interface in the form of a secure web service to access the results stored locally in the laboratory service provider network. The physician can access these reports through their handheld applications through proper authentication and authorization. This helps in electronics transfer of data and need-based quick access of test results.

14.3.2.3 Prescription Services

In today's busy world, it is very common that people forget their prescription refilling schedules, and it is also very difficult to manage schedules and find time to visit a pharmacy for ordering prescription refill.

Most of the pharmacy service providers are offering intelligent consumer mobile applications for all mobile platforms (Windows Phone, iPhone, Android, BlackBerry, etc.). Consumers can utilize these applications for prescription-refilling reminder service, ordering prescription refills by taking a snap of the current prescription bottle, prescription pickup scheduling, etc.

14.3.2.4 Billing and Payment

The diagnostic and pharmacy service providers can utilize the mobility channel for sending invoices for the service rendered and for acceptance of payment. The payment can be processed through secure payment gateways such as PayPal, Netbanking, Visa, MasterCard, Amex services, etc. The diagnostic and pharmacy service providers can integrate access to these secure payment gateways through their respective mobile client applications. This helps the consumers to make a simple one-click/touch payment through the mobile application.

14.3.3 Healthcare Mobility Solutions for the General Public

Mobile enabling of the services offered by healthcare and diagnostic providers helps patients to save their time and access the services at their convenience. A summary of the services that can be mobile enabled for the benefit of the general public is given below.

14.3.3.1 Access to Healthcare and Diagnostic Services

As discussed earlier in this chapter, the healthcare service provider can mobile enable some of the services for remote user's benefits. Typical examples are appointment management and remote patient-care solutions. The healthcare service provider can use mobile applications for these services by providing a mobile application that interfaces with the HIS and supports multiple consumer smartphone platforms (Windows Phone, iPhone, Android, BlackBerry, etc.).

Consumers can easily download this application to their smartphone from the respective provider's application store and can utilize it for appointment management, accessing remote patient-care service, wellness management service, etc.

The diagnostic service providers may also develop a consumer mobile device-centric application targeting multiple smartphone platforms (Windows Phone, iPhone, Android, BlackBerry, etc.) and can provide functionalities such as appointment scheduling, distribution of diagnostic reports, invoicing, and payment.

14.3.3.2 Counterfeit Drugs Management

Counterfeit medicines and drugs are a potential threat faced by the healthcare industry. Counterfeit medicines are fake medicines that are deliberately and fraudulently mislabeled with respect to identity and source. According to a recent survey, more than 10% of the pharmaceuticals in the global supply-chain are counterfeit medicines. It is extremely important to identify counterfeit drugs to protect health and wealth. Mobile applications when combined with AIDC techniques such as near-field communication (NFC), RFID tags and barcode labels can help to prevent counterfeit drugs to a greater extent. RFID labels help in the intelligent packing of medicines, thus preventing counterfeits in the supply chain. Mobile users and patients can scan the barcode labels or NFC- or RFID tags with camera capture and image processing or NFC/RFID reader-enabled smartphones, respectively, and the smart mobile client application can instantly verify the authenticity of the drug with the corresponding drug manufacturer.

14.3.4 Healthcare Mobility Solutions for Health-Insurance Service Providers

The health-insurance providers play a key role in connecting people with the healthcare providers in countries such as United States. Mobility solutions help the health-insurance providers to serve their customers in a better and efficient way. Health-insurance service providers can build consumer mobile applications to provide the following services to their customers:

- Finding the list of available providers for a particular specialization, within x miles of the user location
- Reviews and rating for a provider
- Finding the out-of-pocket expenses for a procedure
- Invoicing and payments

The insurance providers can implement interfaces with the HIS and the diagnostic service provider's database for real-time information exchange and can provide mobile applications for the use of medical providers and laboratory staff for accessing data and reporting patient-specific information.

The health-insurance providers can also mobile enable their workforce to efficiently handle customer requests anytime and anywhere.

14.4 Benefits of Mobility Adoption in the Healthcare Sector

Adopting mobility in the healthcare service industry brings seamless benefits to patients, healthcare providers, and other supporting services in terms of improving the management process. The following are a few among them.

14.4.1 Improved Patient Management Processes and Better Patient Experience

Mobility solutions when combined with AIDC techniques such as RFID and bar codes can significantly automate the patient check-in process and thereby reduce the time for the administrative process. Mobility-based automated appointment management solutions can further improve patient experience by providing a hassle-free environment where the patient do not need to stay in long-wait queues for appointment scheduling, rescheduling, cancellation, etc.

14.4.2 Improved Patient Safety

Mobility-enabled patient-care solutions help in positively identifying patients and patient tracking. This, in turn, will reduce the risks of administering the wrong medicine to the wrong patient, collecting diagnostic samples from the wrong patient, etc., leading to better patient security.

14.4.3 Increased Staff Productivity

With mobility solutions, the medical staff can effectively manage their time and provide the right care to the needy patient at the right time. The remote patient-care solutions will help to reduce the need for in-hospital services and alleviate the work pressure of medical practitioners.

14.4.4 Cost-Effective Regulatory Compliance

Most of the countries are insisting on various regulatory compliances in patient care to ensure privacy and safety of the patient. Electronic patient records (such as EMRs and EHRs) and the 1996 HIPAA privacy rules are some of the compliance requirements set forward by certain countries in providing healthcare services. Also certain countries insist on recording all medication events (details of who administered what medication at what time to a patient). Mobility solutions when combined with AIDC can easily provide a cost-effective solution for adhering to these regulatory requirements.

14.5 Choice of Mobility Solutions for the Healthcare Sector

Selecting a mobility solution for healthcare service is a very tough task. Whenever healthcare service providers think about mobile enabling their services, some of the important questions that may arise are as follows:

■ What is the need for this initiative?
■ What is the expected return on this initiative?

- Who should be the targeted audience to provide these services? Doctors, nurses, administrative staff, maintenance and asset management staff, patients, any other relevant category of people?
- What services need to be extended to mobile devices?
- What mobile devices (laptops, tablet PCs, smartphones, other touch-screen devices, etc.) and what mobile platforms (Windows Phone, iPhone [iOS], BlackBerry, Android, etc.) should be considered for extending these services?
- What infrastructure investment is required for this initiative?
- What level of security is required for this solution?
- Do we need to develop our own solution for this initiative or can we use an industry standard off-the-shelf mobility healthcare solution?
- If we choose to go with an off-the-shelf product, will it support interfacing with our current systems or data? If yes, how easy it is?
- What is the time line to implement this solution?
- What is the training requirement to the staff and users to implement these services?

Finding the right answers to these questions is the first step toward implementing a right mobility solution for healthcare services.

To start with, analyze the existing systems and the infrastructure, the new requirements, and then perform a cost–benefit analysis (CBA) for developing an in-house mobility solution or adopting an off-the-shelf healthcare mobility solution. It is better to seek the service of an expert consultant who is well versed with the healthcare mobility solution requirements and off-the-shelf healthcare mobility solutions.

A number of off-the-shelf mobility healthcare solutions and mobility healthcare platforms are available today, and the following are some of the important points to be taken into account while making a decision on which off-the-shelf product to go with:

- The support offered by the platform to interface with the existing legacy systems
- The extensibility of the platform for future needs
- The scalability of the platform
- The security offered by the platform
- The support offered by the platform for different mobility client platforms (Android, Windows Phone, iOS, Symbian, RIM BlackBerry, etc.)

Motorola mobility solutions, Ericsson mobile health, Philips Motiva, McKesson HIS, BL Healthcare, etc., are examples for off-the-shelf healthcare solutions.

Motorola and FUJITSU are the pioneers in delivering handheld computers (rugged mobile devices, touch pads, etc.) for the healthcare industry.

Cisco is a pioneer in providing various wireless networking products for building in-house wireless infrastructure to augment mobility.

14.6 Mobility Enablement Challenges in the Healthcare Sector

Mobility opens up a big world of opportunities in the healthcare industry. However, there are enormous challenges in converting these opportunities into reality. A few of the important mobility enablement challenges specific to healthcare industry are listed below.

14.6.1 Infrastructure Investment

Mobility adoption requires lot of infrastructure investment in terms of hardware and software. Handheld device procurements, servers and network infrastructure requirement, and firewalls for extending the data or services to staff and patients add to the hardware cost, whereas investments on extending the current system for mobile enablement, integrating a new healthcare platform, or building extended mobility solutions, etc., add to the software cost. It is always advised to conduct a CBA and return-on-investment (RoI) calculation before proceeding with mobility enablement.

14.6.2 Addressing the High-Availability Requirements

Most of the in-hospital services (patient monitoring, medications, etc.) are life-saving, and they need real-time response and data. Hence, all the services should be up and running all the time. There should not be any outage in the network or nonavailability of data due to server failures. Unlike any other service segment, the failure or nonavailability of services in the healthcare segment is catastrophic, and any network outage or issues in connecting to the server to retrieve the status or data during remote monitoring of a patient is critical and may result in a life-threatening situation (e.g., a duty nurse remotely monitoring the condition of a patient with the help of the mobile application running on the handheld device supplied to the nurse needs to be connected all the time). There should be proper fail-over mechanisms in place, including backup servers to address high availability requirements. Also frequent inspection of devices and network should be conducted to avoid any unexpected failures. Of course, this will increase the operating cost.

14.6.3 Lack of Unified Standards for Interoperability

There are no uniform standards available for interfacing diagnostic devices. Most of the diagnostic system manufacturers use proprietary standards or commandsets for device communication. This is a big limitation in integrating such devices into the healthcare platform. It ends up in customizing the platform for providing support to the devices from a selected manufacturer. One way of addressing this issue is to evaluate the popular and precise diagnostic devices in each category, build the interface to these selected devices in the platform, and publish these devices as the preferred or supported devices by the platform. The same issue pertains to interfacing portable consumer diagnostic devices such as blood glucose monitor, blood pressure monitor, etc., with consumer mobile device applications for collecting the data and sending them to the healthcare platform.

14.6.4 Protecting Patient Privacy

Protecting patient privacy is an important requirement in any patient care. Certain countries have a well-defined set of rules for this. In the United States, all providers are required to adhere to the HIPAA privacy rule. This calls for additional requirements in mobility enabling, such as meeting the regulatory standard compliance, implementing enhanced authentication, and authorization to ensure that only intended users are accessing the patient details.

14.7 Scenario: Mobility Solution for Prescription Management

SCOPE OF MOBILIZATION

Consider a leading pharmaceutical company that wants to rollout a consumer mobile application for all popular smartphone platforms (Windows Phone, Android, iPhone [iOS], and RIM BlackBerry) for prescription management services (prescription refilling reminders, prescription refilling, payment, etc.).

14.7.1 Before Mobile Enablement

Patients need to keep track of their medicines and call the pharmacy to request prescription refill.

14.7.2 After Mobile Enablement

A prescription management mobile solution keeps track of the prescription refill schedule and alerts the user when the refill date is approaching. Users can initiate prescription refill by simply capturing the image of the barcode label present on the prescription bottle with the help of the mobile client application. Users can also schedule a pickup and make payments through the mobile client application.

14.7.3 Requirements and Solution

Some of the features in this application (especially camera capture function for scanning the prescription bottle for prescription refill service) require access to the native hardware; hence, the application is architected as a stand-alone application. Also the native hardware support for accessing the device-specific features (camera, GPS, sensors, etc.) is implemented as platform-specific application programming interface calls, and the application needs to be developed as separate client applications for the different platforms using the platform-specific application development kit (Windows Phone Developer Tools for Windows Phone, Android software development kit [SDK] for Android devices, iOS SDK for iPhone).

The pharmaceutical service company maintains a database for holding user profiles, their prescription details, etc. All the services provided by the pharmaceutical company are exposed through public representational state transfer web services, and the mobile client application should implement the web service interfaces to access these web services for accessing the required services. The web-service call can be routed through general packet radio service, 3G, 4G, or WiFi Internet. Figure 14.6 illustrates the end-to-end system architecture.

The access to the services offered by the pharmaceutical company is restricted to only registered users. The mobile client application implements the front end for

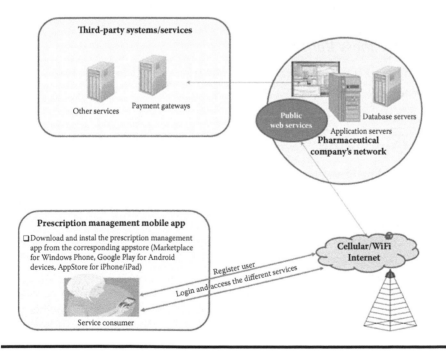

Figure 14.6 Prescription management mobility solution: end-to-end system architecture.

user registration and user authentication, whereas the web service performs the user registration and user authentication functions.

Users can subscribe to reminder services for prescription refilling through the mobile client application. Upon getting a prescription reminder service request, the back-end system will associate the request with the user profile. When the prescription refill date approaches, the back-end service will send reminder messages to the user's mobile client through an SMS or through another notification channel supported by the mobile device and mobile client application (e.g., push notification for live tiles for Windows Phone devices).

The mobile client application also implements automatic prescription refilling functionality. In order to perform a refill request, the user simply needs to capture the image of the bar code present on the prescription bottle with the help of the prescription management application running on the device. The prescription management application will process the image to retrieve the bar code associated with the bottle and will send the details to the back-end web service for initiating a prescription refill request. Upon successful processing of the request, the back-end system will send a prescription pickup confirmation to the mobile client application.

The user can schedule a pickup and make payments through the mobile client application. The web service will route the payment request through third-party payment gateways (PayPal, Visa, MasterCard, Amex, etc.).

14.7.4 Business Benefits

■ Improved customer experience and retention of loyal customer base
■ Increased revenue

14.8 Conclusion

Mobile enabling of the healthcare services facilitates on-demand access to time-critical information for accurate and timely patient assessment and right treatment, meaningful collaboration between healthcare providers, diagnostic service providers, and insurance providers to deliver better care to patients at an affordable cost.

This chapter was intended to provide a general overview of the key driving forces for mobility, mobility opportunities, the benefits of mobility, and the various mobility solutions for the healthcare industry. Protecting patient privacy, adherence to regulatory standards/compliance, and real-time information or data access are the three main critical requirements that need to be addressed in the mobile enablement of healthcare services. The mobility strategy should incorporate adequate plans to cover these requirements in the mobile enablement process of the various healthcare services.

Additional Reading

1. Hiroko Kato, Keng T. Tan, and Douglas Chai, *Barcodes for Mobile Devices*, 1st edition. UK: Cambridge University Press; 2010.
2. Klaus Finkenzeller. *RFID Handbook: Fundamentals and Applications in Contact-Less Smart Cards, Radio Frequency Identification and Near-Field Communication*, 3rd edition. New York: Wiley; 2010.
3. U.S. Department of Health and Human Services. Understanding HIPAA Privacy. Available at: http://www.hhs.gov/ocr/privacy/hipaa/understanding/index.html

Additional Reading

1.
2.

Chapter 15

Mobility Solutions for the Telecom Industry

Telecommunications or the telecom industry represents a group of service providers and organizations focused on enabling and delivering efficient communication across the globe. Radio, Voice Communications, Television, Broadband and Internet services, etc., are the major service offerings of the telecommunication industry. This chapter is specially designed to provide an overview of the mobility opportunities, the benefits of mobility, the various mobility solutions for mobile operators and mobile handset manufacturers, which represent a subset of the telecom industry. Mobility solutions for the telecom industry is a widespread topic, and it is impossible to cover all the mobility opportunities for the various service segments under the telecom sector in a single chapter. Hence, the discussions in this chapter are limited to the mobile communication segment only.

15.1 Introduction

The mobile communication industry is a fast-growing, highly technology-oriented business segment with operations across the globe, covering telecom mobile operators, software and solution providers, testing and measurement equipment providers, and mobile handset manufacturers (in other words, original equipment manufacturers [OEMs]). In the United States, AT&T, T-Mobile, Verizon, Sprint, etc., are some of the leading mobile operators. Nokia, Samsung, HTC, LG, Motorola, ZTE, Fujitsu, Apple, and Research In Motion (RIM) are some of the industry leaders in the mobile handset manufacturing segment.

The mobile communications industry has witnessed tremendous changes in technology, adoption, and services since its introduction to the present state (from the zeroth generation mobile phone (0G) of 1945, the analog-only first-generation mobile phone [1G] of the 1980s, the 2G, 2.5G, and 3G to the 4G long-term evolution phones of the present day). Although the mobile phone was initially invented as a means of transmitting voice over a wireless network, today it has transformed into not only a device for voice and data communication over a wireless network, gaming, media, and entertainment but also a powerful extension of desktop computing devices (personal computers). From an era in which processor clock speeds of kilohertz and memory of a few bytes were considered as the highest performers, telecommunications has reached an era where processor clock speeds of even gigahertz and gigabytes of memory are treated as insufficient for a high-performance smartphone. Today, single-core processors for smartphone devices are an outdated design; most of the smartphones are running on dual-core, power-efficient processors.

15.2 Mobility Solutions for the Mobile Communication Industry

As mobile communication technology is progressing, the world is also witnessing high competition in the mobile communication business. The scenario is totally changed from first-generation mobile devices, where there were only a limited number of handset manufacturers and mobile operators to the time when there is a wide range of handset manufacturers and operators to select.

Both mobile operators and mobile-device manufacturers are forced to think out-of-the-box and bring innovations in services and hardware to sustain the competition and to grab and retain the market share for a successful business footprint. Value-added mobility solutions are promising as a new revenue channel for both mobile operators and OEMs. Figure 15.1 gives an overview of the various mobility solution opportunities for mobile operators and OEMs.

Mobile operators and handset manufacturers can offer mobile-enabled services to the customers and subscribers through one or a combination of the following service delivery channels:

■ Short messaging service (SMS)-based mobility services
■ Downloadable stand-alone mobile client applications (thick and rich client solutions)

SMS is a cost-effective way of communicating with mobile users. SMS service is supported by almost all mobile handsets, and it facilitates a uniform way of messaging, which is simple and consistent across all mobile devices and mobile operators. Customers can subscribe to SMS services during the registration process and can effectively avail SMS service as part of the services offered by the mobile operator or handset manufacturer.

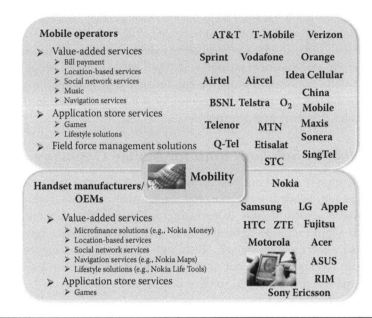

Figure 15.1 Scope for mobility solutions in the mobile communication industry.

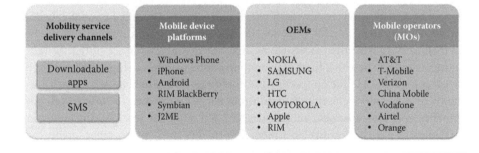

Figure 15.2 Mobility service delivery channels for mobile operators and OEMs.

Mobile client solutions (thick and rich client solutions) are the popular choice for delivering mobile operator and OEM-hosted solutions to subscribers (Figure 15.2). Thick client solutions are mobile-platform dependent, and they need to be developed for individual mobile device platforms with the help of the supported software development kit (SDK) or application development kit (ADK) for the corresponding platform (e.g., Windows Phone Developer Tools SDK for Windows Phone devices and Android SDK for Android devices, etc.). The solution needs to be deployed on the consumer mobile devices also. Most of the smartphone mobile devices in today's market do not support side-loading of applications to the device; rather, they support application hosting and download from the corresponding device's application store (e.g., Marketplace for Windows Phone devices, Google Play for Android devices, and App Store for Apple iOS devices [iPhone and iPad]).

Thick client and rich client-based downloadable applications utilize the data plan and are expensive when compared with SMS-based services. Thick client and rich client-based solutions can provide an abundance of information in a neat and user-friendly manner, whereas SMS-based services have limitations in the amount of data transfer as well as data presentation.

15.2.1 Mobility Solutions from/for Mobile Operators

The mobile communication business is highly competitive and dynamic. The telecom industry is growing at a fast rate, and the number of mobile communication service providers across the globe is increasing day by day. The competition in this segment has significantly brought down the call, SMS, and data service tariffs, attracting more and more subscribers. The tough competition among the operators compels them to think and act out-of-the box and redefine their roles in the telecom industry from the traditional voice or data service providers.

15.2.1.1 Value-Added Services

15.2.1.1.1 Bill Payment Services

Imagine a situation where in which you forgot your utility bill payment schedule and have a payment due for now, which falls on a non-working day and the bill payment service is neither accessible on-line nor through a service outlet. Sending payments round-the-clock from your mobile phone through a single click would be a wish come true. Mobile operators can collaborate with financial service providers (credit or debit service providers) and other service providers (utility, travel, government, etc.) to implement mobile-enabled bill payment services, thus allowing customers to pay their utility, insurance, mortgage, auto, government, credit card bills, etc., from their mobile phones through easy steps.

15.2.1.1.2 Mobile Payment Solutions

Most consumers across the globe today are using credit, debit, and gift cards as the most convenient payment option for their purchases and payments. Credit or debit cards are an easy replacement to currency notes and bills, and it is likely that most consumers' wallets contain more than one plastic card (credit, debit, or gift card). How about swiping your smartphone at the billing counter of the grocery store or food court? Interesting? The world is about to witness a similar scenario soon. Most high-end smartphones today incorporate near-field communication (NFC) hardware, which can act as both NFC reader and NFC card (contact-less smartcard). The NFC-chip present in the phone holds a unique identification number as well as secure storage. Credit and debit service providers can utilize NFC-enabled phones as a replacement to the current plastic cards. Mobile operators can collaborate with credit and debit service organizations to implement this mobile payment solution. Some of the major mobile operators in the United States have already partnered with leading credit and debit service providers to prototype and field trial the NFC-based mobile payment solutions in the place of the existing credit and debit card-based payment services. A successful implementation of this initiative may lead to the replacement of over one billion plastic cards in the United States.

15.2.1.1.3 Social Networking Services

Social networking services play a significant role in the day-to-day life of most of the people. Social networking web sites and applications have greatly changed people's lifestyles. In today's world, everybody wants to be always connected. Mobile operators can effectively leverage the social networking aspects to implement social networking-based value-added mobility services. This will open up a new revenue channel for the operators. Building networked groups, sending and receiving status updates and presence of subscriber's networked friends and family members and mapping the current location of a networked contact are typical usecases of value-added mobility services in the social networking segment (Figure 15.3).

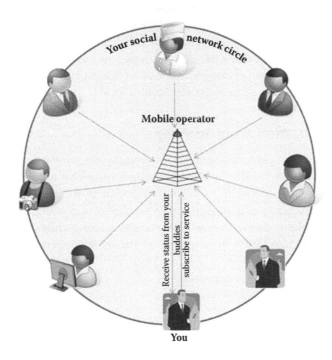

Figure 15.3   Social networking value-added service from mobile operators.

15.2.1.1.4 Navigation and Assistance Services

Navigation systems or global positioning systems (GPSs) device is an integral part of any ride in the United States, Europe, and other countries, where the roads are well mapped. Also, most vehicles contain a dedicated GPS device for navigation assistance. Latest smartphone devices integrate high-accuracy GPS hardware and large screens (ranging from 3.5 to 4.7 inches). Mobile operators can leverage the GPS feature supported by the smartphone device and can provide navigation services, such as maps, turn-by-turn visual and voice navigation, traffic advisory, points of interests, etc., to subscribers at a nominal rate. This helps subscribers to carry only a single device in place of multiple devices for each service. **AT&T Navigator** is an example of the navigation service offered by the mobile operator AT&T in the United States.

Mobile operators can also tie-up with other service providers to implement assistance programs to the subscribers. Accident or breakdown assistance, towing assistance, fuel refill assistance, tire replacement assistance, etc., are typical usecases for assistance services.

15.2.1.1.5 Lifestyle Solutions

Lifestyle solutions open up a new revenue channel for mobile operators across the globe. Mobile operators can create and deliver various types of lifestyle solutions to consumers on a subscription basis. Weather forecasts, market trends, price alerts, news services, horoscope, etc., are examples of lifestyle solutions. In addition, mobile operators can partner with various service providers such as retailers to deliver marketing solutions, advertisement solutions, etc.

15.2.1.2 Application Store Services

Today's smartphone platforms implement application programming support, allowing developers to build a number of applications, which utilizes the capabilities of the underlying platform. Most smartphone platform providers implement application store services to host applications for the corresponding platform, from where the smartphone users can download the applications either free or can purchase at a nominal rate. The App Store services offer mobile operators the opportunity to host their own App Store or dedicated hubs or zones in the App Store hosted by the handset operating system provider.

15.2.1.3 Field or Sales Force Management Solutions

Similar to any other business organization, mobile operators may also employ a number of field service or sales staff. Mobile operators can utilize mobility solutions for effective management of field or sales staff and improve their productivity.

15.2.2 Mobility Solutions from the Mobile Handset Manufacturers (OEMs)

The mobile handset market (especially, the smartphone and Tablet-PC segment) is highly competitive, and the handset manufacturers (also known as OEMs) are struggling to grab or retain the market share. Unlike in the past, where the role of OEMs in the telecom segment was restricted to manufacturing, selling, and servicing of handsets, today most of the smartphone OEMs are offering hundreds of services either free or on a subscription basis to their handset users.

15.2.2.1 Value-Added Services

15.2.2.1.1 Mobile Finance and Bill Payment Solutions

OEMs may partner with mobile operators, financial service providers, retailers, and other local service providers to deliver personalized services through mobile phones to the end customers. Such a solution will eliminate cash transactions and will benefit subscribers with a banking account as well as subscribers without a banking account. The typical personal finance services that can be mobile-enabled are listed below:

- Bill payment
- Cashless payments (payment to goods and services)
- Send and receive money to and from your family, friends, and business circle

It is likely that the major population, especially the rural population, of developing and underdeveloped nations is yet to have a banking account or is unaware of the banking services and may be dependent on local finance agencies or traditional financiers for day-to-day financial needs. It is an amazing fact that mobile communication has deep penetration into such population, and by tapping the potential opportunities in this segment, OEMs, mobile operators, and financial service providers can definitely open up a new revenue channel, benefiting both the public and the service providers. Microfinance solution is a typical example for such value-added services.

15.2.2.1.2 Location-Based Services

As mentioned earlier in this chapter, most consumer mobile devices today are smart devices, and they incorporate multiple sensors and chips to implement features such as GPS and assisted-GPS (A-GPS), which can accurately sense the current location of the user. OEMs can leverage this feature and may partner with other service segments such as retail, banking, etc., to deliver location-specific services to consumers. A summary of the useful location-based services is given below.

- Weather forecast
- Location-specific advertisements and deals

- ATM locator
- Places to eat and drink

15.2.2.1.3 Social Networking Services

As discussed earlier, social networking plays a significant role in most people's day-to-day life. OEMs can take advantage of this to deliver compelling social networking applications and services to their customers.

15.2.2.1.4 Navigation Services

OEMs can leverage the underlying GPS or A-GPS hardware support of the phone to provide value-added navigation services to their customers. Maps, turn-by-turn visual and voice navigation, traffic advisory, and points of interests are typical use cases for navigation services. OEMs can preinstall the navigation applications in the handset or can host them on the corresponding App Store and can offer the services on a registration basis.

OEMs may also partner with other local service providers to implement assistance programs to registered users. Accident, breakdown assistance, towing assistance, fuel refill assistance, and tire replacement assistance etc., are typical examples for assistance services. Nokia Maps and Nokia Drive are examples of navigation services.

15.2.2.1.5 Lifestyle Solutions

Mobile handset is becoming an unavoidable part of our day to-day life, and most of us are dependent on it a lot more than making phone calls. The role of mobile handsets has transformed from being a device to make phone calls and send text messages into a personal assistant and companion. Lifestyle Apps or solutions refer to a group of mobile applications that engage the mobile phone users in their day-to-day life, for leisure, to stay connected, and to gather information. A summary of the useful and desirable lifestyle solutions is listed below.

- Health and beauty (tips for a healthy life, expert advice, etc.)
- Hobbies (tips and things to do at leisure time, etc.)
- Entertainment (music, movies, news alerts, sports, etc.)
- Educational (learning, career planning, educational alerts, expert advice, etc.)
- Business (industry news, market trends and alerts, expert opinion services, etc.)

15.2.2.2 App Store Services

Many handset OEMs today host their own App Stores. Nokia's OVI Store and Samsung Apps, for its proprietary smartphone-operating system Samsung Bada, are examples of these.

In addition, most of the OEMs have dedicated hubs and zones in the App Store hosted by the handset operating system provider. HTC Hub and Samsung Zone in the Marketplace hosted by Microsoft for Windows Phone are typical examples of this.

15.3 Benefits of Mobility Adoption in the Mobile Communication Industry

Mobility adoption in the mobile communication segment is beneficial to mobile operators, OEMs, and consumers in terms of revenue, cost, and user experience. A few of the benefits are discussed below.

15.3.1 Convenience at the Fingertip

With mobility solutions, users can access information, data, and services anytime and anywhere—bringing convenience at the user's fingertip.

15.3.2 New Business Models and Revenue

Mobility opens up the window for grabbing the market share from competitors. Effective mobility implementations and innovations can greatly attract the mindset of customers, leading to a large customer base.

15.4 Choice of Mobility Solutions for the Mobile Communication Industry

The selection of a mobility solution in terms of architecture, business requirements, platform support, etc., is highly challenging, and it requires a thorough analysis, in the decision-making process of mobilization. This section is intended to give the readers an overview of the different types of mobility solutions for implementing mobility solutions in the mobile communication segment.

15.4.1 SMS-Based Solutions

When we talk about mobile applications, it is not necessary that they refer only to mobile application solutions running on smartphone devices; it can also be applications running on feature phones. As most of the feature phones do not provide end-user programming options or provide only limited end-user application development and deployment support, SMS-based service delivery is the most convenient and preferred option. SMS is a cost-effective way of communicating with mobile users. SMS service is supported by almost all mobile handsets, and it facilitates a uniform way of messaging, which is simple and consistent across all mobile devices and mobile operators. Customers can subscribe to SMS services during the registration process and can avail SMS service effectively for the services offered by the mobile operators or OEMs.

15.4.2 Preinstalled or Downloadable Thick and Rich Client Solutions

Thick client solutions are applications developed for a particular client device (mobile handheld and PDA) platform (Windows Phone, Windows CE Operating System, iPhone Operating System, Android Operating System, etc.). Thick client solutions reside in the memory of the handheld device, and it utilizes the platform support provided by the underlying operating system and target hardware. The device manufacturers or operating system providers (or OEMs) provide SDKs, exposing application programming interfaces (APIs) to access the platform-supported hardware for which the operating system does not provide any standard APIs, which can be utilized in the thick client solution for leveraging the device's capabilities (e.g., barcode reading). Depending on the operating system support and third-party products, a thick client solution may implement support for local data storage and syncing of locally stored data with standard databases such as SQL Server, Oracle, etc. This feature of thick client solutions qualifies them for off-line data capture, which does not require connectivity with the back-end systems always. Thick client solutions are platform-dependent, and they are less portable to devices running on different operating systems. Application upgrades are challenging for thick client solutions.

A rich client solution is a variant of the thick client solution, which combines the architecture of both thin client and thick client solutions. The user interface is developed as a rich thick client solution, and the integration with the back-end system or services is implemented through web services. The application is deployed on the handheld device, and it communicates with the back-end web services on a need basis.

OEMs or mobile operators may distribute the thick or rich client mobility solutions either as preinstalled applications on the device or host them at the respective zones or hubs of the App Store corresponding to each smartphone platform.

15.5 Scenario: Roadside Mobile Assistance Solution

SCOPE OF MOBILIZATION

A mobile operator wants to implement a roadside assistance program in collaboration with a local service provider for its subscribers. The mobile operator wants to implement the solution for the smartphone platforms—Windows Phone (smartphones), Android (smartphones and tablets), and iOS platform (iPhone and iPad).

15.5.1 Before Mobile Enablement

The driver or the copassenger needs to call the insurance provider, assistance service provider (e.g., AAA in the United States), or the local mechanic for assistance and describe the situation as well as the location in terms of the nearest landmark, in case of an emergency (breakdown, accident support, flat tire, fuel outage, etc.)

15.5.2 After Mobile Enablement

The driver or the copassenger can initiate a help request through the mobile application, which automatically captures the current location and routes the request to the nearest assistance service provider.

15.5.3 Requirements and Solution

The application is designed to address the following requirements:

- The service is offered on a subscription-based model. Subscribers need to register using a user ID and password to avail this service.
- All service requests (accident, breakdown assistance, towing assistance, fuel refill assistance, tire replacement request, etc.) are routed to the local service provider through the mobile operator's network, for monitoring and accounting purposes.
- The application should automatically capture the location details of the service-request initiator and should pass on these details transparently (without any user intervention) when a service request is initiated.

The registration process and request handling at the mobile operator side are exposed through secure web services. The mobile client application running on the smartphone device can access these services over the data connection (GPRS, 3G, or 4G) on a need basis.

The handheld application is developed as a rich or a thick client application for different smartphone platforms. Multiplatform development can be done using mobile middleware solutions.

The application implements predefined assistance request templates, and the location of the user is automatically captured using the GPS or A-GPS hardware support of the smartphone device.

The mobile operator's back-end service routes the service request to the local assistance service provider, and the routing algorithm at the local assistance service provider facility routes the request details to the nearest field service personnel's mobile device. The end-to-end architecture diagram (Figure 15.4) illustrates the solution implementation.

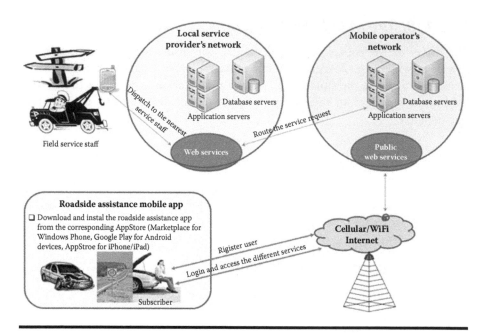

Figure 15.4 End-to-end solution architecture of roadside mobile assistance solution.

15.5.4 Business Benefits

The following are the business benefits achieved by the roadside assistance mobility solution

- Improved customer experience and retention of loyal customer base
- New revenue channel and increased revenue

15.6 Conclusion

The mobile communication industry today is highly competitive, and mobile operators and handset manufacturers or OEMs (especially smartphone and tablet manufacturers) are struggling to grab and retain the market share. Value-added mobility solutions are a promising new revenue channel for both mobile operators and mobile handset OEMs.

This chapter was specially designed to provide an overview of the mobility opportunities, the benefits of mobility, the various mobility solutions for mobile operators and the mobile handset manufacturers, which represent a subset of the telecom industry. As in the case of any mobility implementation project, MOs and OEMs should identify the potential business opportunities for mobile enablement, the investment and infrastructure requirement, the challenges, and the right solution that addresses their business needs.

Additional Reading

1. Leslie Haddon and Nicola Green. *Mobile Communications: An Introduction to New Media.* Berg Publishers; 2010.
2. Johan Zuidweg. *Implementing Value-Added Telecom Services.* Artech House; 2006.
3. Thierry Van de Velde. *Value-Added Services for Next Generation Networks,* 1st edition. Auerbach Publications; 2007.

Chapter 16

Mobility Solutions for Energy and Utilities

The utilities and energy industry is experiencing a widespread transformation, and it brings both challenges and opportunities. This chapter gives an overview of the mobility opportunities, the benefits of mobility, the various mobility solutions for energy and utility services management, and a case study of a mobility solution for automated metering.

16.1 Introduction

The energy and utilities sector is a broad service segment that generally comprises oil, natural gas, and petroleum sources; various power sources including nuclear power, coal, and renewable energies; and waste management and water industries. The term "utilities" refers to the set of services offered by various organizations under the energy and utilities sector, especially for electricity, natural gas, water, and sewage. Although the telecom services segment may also be considered as part of utilities, it is discussed as a separate entity as the opportunities in this segment are huge and that it requires special mention.

16.2 Scope for Mobility Solutions in Energy and Utilities Sector

Mobility can be adopted in the energy and utilities sector for almost all services in the areas of production, service, distribution, and transmission (Figure 16.1).

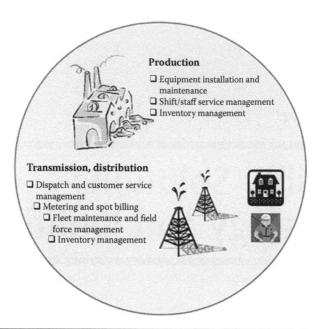

Figure 16.1   Scope for mobility solutions in the energy and utilities sector.

16.2.1 Mobility Solutions for Production Segment

The typical services that can be mobilized in the generation or production areas are explained below.

16.2.1.1 Equipment Installation and Maintenance

Equipment installation is an essential part in the setup of a new plant for energy, water, and waste management. Equipment purchase management, tracking, installation service progress monitoring, etc., are some of the key activities performed in the setup phase. Adoption of mobility for installation services will enable real-time progress tracking, saving of effort, and contribute to productivity improvements.

Routine equipment checkups and scheduled maintenance are very essential in a production environment to avoid any possible production outages. Deployment of mobility in this area can enhance accuracy and eliminate paper work and human errors in manual data collection by implementing electronic data capture and real-time communication with back-end service systems and operators to flag an emergency situation.

16.2.1.2 Shift and Staff Service Management

Most of the services in the production or generation environment (e.g., power plants) are round-the-clock services, and these require the core or support staff to work in shifts to operate on a 24 × 7 model. Shift management is a difficult task. Effective implementation of mobility for shift management makes work easier, by automating work allocation, thereby eliminating the last-minute rush for finding a replacement in case a staff is not available as per the schedule, provided the workers are equipped with the mobile shift-management solution and they respond proactively to the automated shift management service.

16.2.1.3 Inventory Management

Inventory management is essential for cost reduction, stock-out prevention, and production outage prevention. Adoption of automatic identification and data collection (AIDC) technologies such as barcodes, radio frequency identification (RFID), etc., along with mobility solutions can enable complete automation of inventory management. Barcode- or RFID-enabled mobile device in association with data collection software running on the device can capture the inventory details and can send the details in real time to a back-end order management or enterprise resource planning (ERP) system. This will enable real-time inventory tracking and automatic reorder of essential components to prevent production outage and emergency ordering. Implementation of AIDC and mobility solutions will also help in the usage trend analysis, restocking needs, and productivity improvements.

16.2.2 Mobility Solutions for Transmission and Distribution Segment

The transmission and distribution segment deals with end-user interfacing, new and existing customer management, service request management, logistics, and end-to-end system management (i.e., production house to end-customer and end-customer premise to disposal or recycle systems). The typical services that can be mobilized in the transmission and distribution areas are as follows.

16.2.2.1 Dispatch and Customer Service Management

Public life is heavily dependent on the energy and utilities sector. The volume of service requests in the day-to-day operation of this sector is of the order of millions. The request for a new service establishment (new electricity connection, water connection, sewage and trash management, etc.), request for termination of service, repair and maintenance service requests, and outage management service request are some of the typical examples. It is essential for a utility service provider to have a service management (dispatch and customer service management) system that can handle the high volume of service requests in an efficient way.

Introduction of mobility to the existing ecosystem of utility service management can bring about more value additions in terms of faster response to customer needs, intelligent dispatching of service requests based on the criticality of service requests and the availability of service technicians. The typical use case for mobility

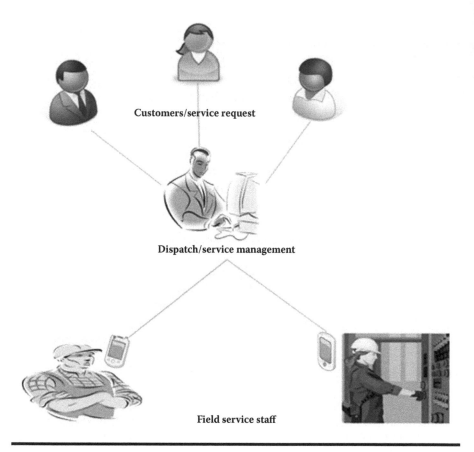

Figure 16.2   Mobility adoption use case for service request management.

adoption for service dispatch and management in the utilities service management can be visualized as in Figure 16.2.

Enablement of consumer mobility, by developing mobile utility service management consumer applications for the popular smartphone devices (Apple iPhone, Android phones, Windows Phone, etc.), will provide an enhanced customer experience. With consumer mobility enablement, users may be able to initiate their service requests, track the progress of their service request, and monitor their service history or usage, while they are on the move.

16.2.2.2 Metering and Spot Billing

Metering is an important task in the utility service management for usage monitoring and billing. The metering service includes installation, maintenance, and periodic recording of service consumption at a consumer premise. Typical examples are electricity and water metering. Meter recording can be a manual operation in which a field service staff manually records the readings at regular periods, or it can be an automated task in which the meter reading is automatically updated at the central service station. Power line carrier communication-based electricity metering is a typical example for fully automated meter recording. Mobility can be effectively applied to the metering service for implementing fully automated or partially automated meter recording. With the help of intelligent meters (e.g., Bluetooth-enabled electricity meter) and mobile solutions running on personal digital assistants (PDAs), a field service staff can automatically capture the meter reading by a simple walk-through of the area where the meters are installed. The data can be transferred to the central service station in real time using general packet radio service (GPRS), 3G, 4G or other wireless technologies. The metering field service staff can also generate spot billing. This eliminates the human errors in data capture, need for manual paper work for data capture and uploading as well as reduces service delays. Partially automated mobile solutions can be employed for recording of meter readings from meters that are not intelligent (typical examples are mechanical meters for water and electricity metering). A unique ID in the form of a barcode can be assigned to each meter, and the field service staff can capture the readings in electronic format, manually using data collection software running on a mobile handheld. Data can also be transmitted in real time to central service stations.

When implemented for service management, mobility solutions can be used for assigning meter installation and maintenance service requests to field service staffs in real time. This will reduce the service response time and improve the productivity of the field service staff.

16.2.2.3 Fleet Maintenance and Field Force Management

In the service industry, it does not matter how many service staffs are employed by an organization to manage service requests, but what matters is how efficiently and intelligently a service request is handled. Intelligent routing of field service requests, fleet maintenance, and field force management are the pillars of efficient service management. Modern mobile handsets and PDAs are not just electronic devices for mere communication and data transfer—they are "smart feature-packed goodies." Most modern handsets incorporate global positioning systems (GPS) and location services. The GPS service offered by the device can be utilized for reporting the current position of the field staff back to the central service dispatching station, and the dispatch service can intelligently map the service request from a user to the nearest available field service staff. This, in turn, efficiently manages the movement of field service staff and the fleet of service vehicles, leading to reduced fuel consumption, increased worker productivity, and reduced service request turnaround times (Figure 16.3).

16.2.2.4 Inventory Management

By adopting mobility, the field service staff can effectively capture, communicate, and check the availability of tools and consumables to complete a service request.

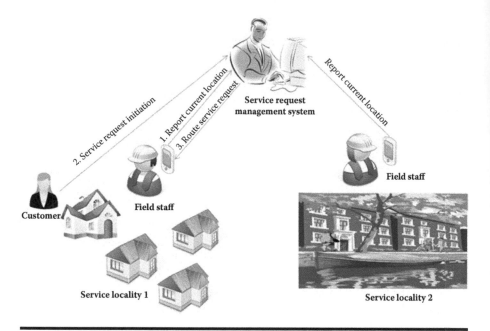

Figure 16.3 Mobility-enabled intelligent service request management system.

The field service staff can even check the availability of the required inventory among the other field staffs and locate the one that is nearest.

16.3 Benefits of Mobility for Energy and Utilities Sector

Bringing mobility into the current ecosystem brings a number of value additions and benefits to both the end customer and the utility service provider. A few important benefits among them are explained below.

16.3.1 Reduced Cycle Time and Faster Response Times

Mobility solutions leveraging the advanced features supported by mobile handhelds and PDA devices help in the efficient real-time handling of service requests and eliminate manual paper-based data capture and uploading of captured data to the central service station. The electronic data capture and restoration system improves the service request tracking efficiency, leading to faster turn-around times.

16.3.2 Increased Field Staff Productivity

With mobility solutions, field workers can be managed efficiently through location-based real-time dispatch of service requests, real-time reporting of service request completion, etc. Field service staff can also communicate with their co-worker in real time for any technical assistance, inventory enquiry, etc.

16.3.3 Reduced Operations Costs

Introducing mobility to the ecosystem leads to considerable cost reductions by reducing the fixed and variable facility costs. With efficient mobility solutions, the requirement for local offices and facilities can be significantly cut down by consolidating the facilities. This, in turn, will lead to the saving of the annual fixed facility costs (rent, utilities, etc.) and the consumables cost (paper, toners, stationery cost, etc.). Mobility also increases workers' productivity, which in turn will lead to the requirement for fewer number of field staffs to perform field services, leading to cost reductions.

16.3.4 Environment Friendliness

Mobility solutions implement electronic data capture and retention, which totally eliminates the conventional paper-based data capture and retention. Saving paper is saving trees—a true "green initiative." Mobility solutions also help in optimized fleet management, which in turn reduces the carbon footprint—another green initiative.

16.3.5 Seamless Customer Experience

The customer is the real catalyst in any business. Gaining customer confidence is a tough task, and it is the real driving force for any successful business. Mobility enablement in the utilities sector significantly reduces the service request turn-around time and provides easy access to user data and real-time status tracking of service requests, which brings seamless customer experience. Customers will be much delighted, if the utilities service organization can provide a unique application for their smartphone devices such as iPhone, Android Phones, or Windows Phone, with easy access to the services offered by the utilities service company, leading to access to information and services at fingertips while they are on the move.

16.4 Choice of Mobility Solutions for Energy and Utilities Sector

The selection of a mobility solution in terms of architecture, business requirements, platform support, etc., is highly challenging, and it requires a thorough analysis in the decision-making process of mobilization. This section is intended to give the readers an overview of the different types of mobility solutions and the factors to be considered in the selection process.

16.4.1 Thin Client Solutions

Thin client solutions are applications that run on a supported web browser. The applications are developed as web pages that are hosted on a server. The client devices (mobile handhelds and PDAs) can access these applications through browsers. Thin client solutions are suited for applications that do not require hardware resource access of the underlying platform. A typical example is the portal service, which can be used for tracking the status of a service request submitted. Users can simply log in to the application through the web browser by accessing the corresponding universal resource locator (URL). Thin client solutions always require connectivity to the hosted system and are known as "always connected" apps.

A thin client solution should address the features supported by the web browser of the client system (PDAs, mobile handhelds, etc.), the screen real estates (screen resolution, orientation, etc.) of the client devices, etc. To address devices of varying capabilities, the web pages may be redesigned for each client device, or a device capabilities-aware middleware should be used for rendering the pages on the device browser.

A thin client solution is very limited in capabilities, with regard to the hardware access of the client device (e.g., barcode hardware access for data capture). Implementation of a thin client solution depends on the client-side scripting support provided by the browser in use, which in turn may lead to potential security risks.

16.4.2 Thick Client Solutions

Thick client solutions are applications developed for a particular client device (mobile handheld or PDA) platform (Windows Mobile CE operating system, iPhone operating system, Android operating system, etc.). Thick client solutions reside in the memory of the handheld device, and it utilizes the platform support provided by the underlying operating system and target hardware. The device manufacturers (commonly known as original equipment manufacturers) provide software development kits, exposing application programming interfaces (APIs) to access the platform supported hardware for which the operating system does not provide any standard APIs, which can be utilized in the thick client solution for leveraging the device's capabilities (e.g., barcode reading). Depending on the operating system support and third-party products, a thick client solution may implement support for local data storage and syncing of locally stored data with standard databases such as SQL Server and Oracle. This feature of thick client solutions qualifies them for off-line data capture, which does not require connectivity with the back-end systems always.

Thick client solutions are platform-dependent, and they are less portable to devices running different operating systems. Application upgrades are challenging for thick client solutions.

16.4.3 Off-the-Shelf Mobility Solutions versus Custom-Built Solutions

In the utilities sector, the utilities service companies may already have an off-the-shelf ERP system in place. When a request for mobilizing the processes arises, obviously there are two choices: to use an off-the-shelf mobility solution or to build a custom solution. The choice is based on a number of factors. The following are a few important factors that help in the decision-making process:

1. Support for the off-the-shelf solution for extending to various mobile platforms
2. Customization effort for the off-the-shelf solution versus effort for building a custom solution
3. Cost of the off-the-shelf solution versus custom solution
4. Annual maintenance cost for off-the-shelf solution versus custom-built solution
5. Feature addition support
6. Ease of operation

Figure 16.4 gives an overview of extending the off-the-shelf ERP solutions for mobility enablement in the utilities sector. SAP is an example of an off-the-shelf

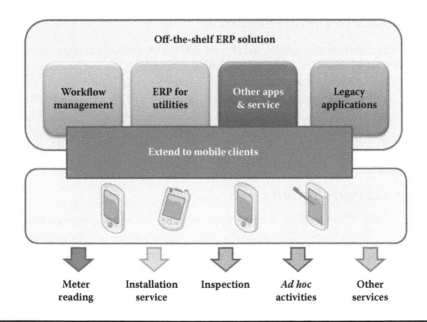

Figure 16.4 Extending off-the-shelf ERP solutions for mobility enablement.

ERP solution that offers mobility enablement. SAP supports mobility and also provides customization support.

16.5 Mobility Enablement Challenges in the Energy and Utilities Sector

Along with opportunities and business benefits, mobility enablement in the utilities sector brings various challenges also. A few of the important mobility enablement challenges are discussed below.

16.5.1 Infrastructure Investment

Mobility adoption requires a lot of infrastructure investment in terms of hardware and software. Handheld device procurements, servers and network infrastructure requirements, and firewalls for extending the data or services to field devices add to the hardware cost, whereas investments on extending ERP solutions to mobile or building custom mobility solutions, mobile device provisioning and management software add to the software cost. It is always advisable to conduct a cost–benefit analysis and return-on-investment calculation before proceeding with mobility enablement.

16.5.2 Lack of Unified Standards

Implementation of a fully automated end-to-end mobility solution requires the support of a unified standard interface for end devices including various meters. The end devices including smart meters manufactured by various providers implement proprietary interfaces and command response protocols for communication. It is rather difficult for a mobility solution developer to conceptualize a single solution for multiple end devices. It is high time to develop a unified communication system in terms of interfaces and command response protocols.

16.5.3 Ensuring Security

Extending the Corpnet (the corporate infrastructure hosting the services and holding the data) to mobile networks and devices opens up a way for injecting vulnerabilities, leading to security risk in the entire system. Proper security analysis must be carried out in the design, and the design should accommodate proper security implementations including virtual private network, firewalls, communication channel security (secure sockets, encrypted data transfer, etc.), mobile device security, etc.

16.5.4 Device Provisioning and Management

Field device (mobile handhelds and PDAs) provisioning and management is a challenging task in the implementation of mobility. The device may contain locally stored data that should be protected against unauthorized access. Also proper application access policies must be enforced on the device to limit the access of various applications in the mobile handhelds or PDAs by the field staff. The device must be updated with latest security policies and application upgrades, as and when they are available. Proper device provisioning, such as data wiping on lost devices and remote device lockdown of devices that are not sync'd with the server in a defined period of time, should be enforced for a successful mobility solution implementation. An off-the-shelf device management and provisioning software such as Mobicontrol from SOTI, Afaria from Sybase, Avalanche from Wavelink, etc., or a custom-built solution can be used for device management and provisioning.

16.6 Scenario: Mobility Solution for Automated Meter Reading

SCOPE OF MOBILIZATION

Consider a leading electricity service provider in a developing country implementing a mobility solution to automate the current process of manual paper-based recording of energy meter reading. All the energy meters are RS-485 enabled and support MODBUS protocol for communication. Meters are installed in locations including areas where cellular connectivity is intermittent or unavailable. The meter readings should be uploaded to a central database to which the OSS/BSS (operations support systems/business support systems) services are interfaced. The current cellular technology in the country at the time of implementation is GSM with GPRS and 3G data services.

16.6.1 Before Mobile Enablement

The current business process follows manual, paper-based recording of energy meters installed at various locations. A field service staff is assigned to each area, and he/she records the reading on paper on a periodic basis and later converts the data to electronic records at the central processing station.

16.6.2 After Mobile Enablement

A handheld device is allocated to all meter-reading recording staff, and the staff can automatically record meter-reading operation within a few meters of the meter cluster location. The readings are updated to the database of the central server in real time if Internet connectivity is available; else the readings are kept locally in the device and sync'd to the server database later when connectivity is available.

16.6.3 Requirements and Solution

As the application requirement explicitly calls for off-line data capture, a thick client solution with local data storage is the ideal solution for implementing this requirement. The locally stored data can later be synchronized with the central database, when network connection is available. GPRS or 3G network is used for data communication with the central station. Figure 16.5 illustrates the end-to-end system architecture. The RS-485 interface supports multidrop communication, and up to 32 meters can be connected to a single RS-485 bus. Each customer's meter is assigned a unique ID, and meters in an apartment complex are wired to a single RS-485 bus forming a meter cluster. Short-range wireless technologies, such as Bluetooth, ISM band RF, etc., can be used for building a wireless interface

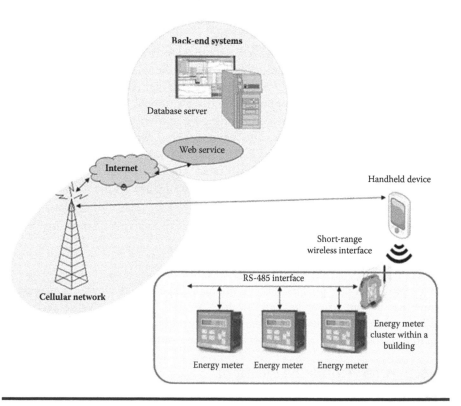

Figure 16.5   Automated meter reading solution—end-to-end system architecture.

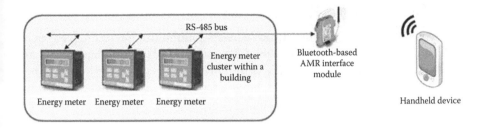

Figure 16.6 **Automated meter reading solution—handheld and meter cluster interfacing.**

between the RS-485 bus and the mobile device for meter recording. A custom-built or off-the-shelf interface converter module based on any one of the above-mentioned wireless technologies can be used for interface conversion at the RS-485 bus to which the meters are connected. In the current design, Bluetooth technology, which is the cheapest among the available short-range wireless technologies, is selected for building the automatic meter reading wireless interface. Any end device that supports Bluetooth communication interface and device programmability (such as smartphones, PDAs, laptops, etc.) can be used for collecting the meter reading programmatically (Figure 16.6).

A smartphone device with Bluetooth support is selected as the handheld device for capturing meter reading. The Windows Mobile handheld operating system supports local data storage in the device memory resident SQL Lite database. The automated meter reading software for the Windows Mobile device is developed in C# and .Net Compact Framework (.Net CF). The communication with the meter cluster is implemented over MODBUS protocol. A custom sync service is devised for syncing the locally captured data with the central server when cellular network connection is available. Connection manager API and secure socket layer enabled through the Windows Mobile operating system are used for implementing data communication over the cellular network.

16.6.4 Business Benefits

The following are the business benefits offered by the automated meter reading mobility solution.

- Automating the process eliminates the probable human errors in data collection
- Productivity improvement of field staff
- Reduction in the operations cost

16.7 Conclusion

Mobility solutions when combined with wireless communication techniques, such as RF communication, Bluetooth, WiFi, GPS, etc., and AIDC techniques, such as RFID and barcode labels, greatly help in automating the various services involved in the energy and utilities sector. Mobility adoption in the utilities and energy industry helps to achieve better turn-around time and improved service-level agreement timelines, improved worker productivity, and reduced operations cost.

This chapter was intended to provide a general overview of the mobility opportunities, the benefits of mobility, and the various mobility solutions for energy and utility services management. The decision on which services in the utilities sector needs to be mobilized and what type of mobility solution needs to be adopted is purely business-driven, and the concerned business organizations should perform a cost–benefit analysis in the decision-making process.

Additional Reading

1. MobiControl. *Enterprise Mobile Device Management for Smartphones, Tablets and Rugged Devices.* http://www.soti.net/mobicontrol/
2. Sybase Afaria. http://www.sybase.com/products/mobileenterprise/afaria
3. Wavelink Avalanche. http://www.wavelink.com/p/mobile-device-and-infrastructure-management
4. Modbus. *Modbus Specifications and Implementation Guides.* http://www.modbus.org
5. SAP Mobile Solutions. http://www.sap.com

Chapter 17

Mobility Solutions for the Financial Service Industry

The financial service industry (FSI) is a very competitive and evolving marketplace with tremendous opportunities for mobility. This chapter gives an overview of the mobility opportunities, the benefits of mobility, the various mobility solutions for FSI, and a case study of a mobility solution for paperless contract capture.

17.1 Introduction

The FSI represents a wide range of financial service providers including investment and commercial banking services, investment services, credit and debit card services, mortgage providers, brokerage firms, investment research providers, stock exchange services, debit and credit rating agencies, money transfer service providers, financial guarantor and assurance services, and microfinanciers, etc.

FSI is one of the early adopters of mobility solutions. Almost all services in the FSI are highly competitive, with multiple providers offering the same set of services. Hence, it is essential to understand the end customer needs and convenience for successful business in this segment.

Today, most of the service providers in the FSI are trying to create new revenue channels by leveraging mobility solutions that extend enterprise-centric services to mobile devices and optimize the sales process. Mobility solutions can effectively improve the productivity of the field staff and the sales force and the satisfaction of the customers. FSIs can realize real business benefits and grab potential business opportunities through mobility solutions that provide on-demand, real-time access to marketing data and sales tools.

17.2 Scope for Mobility Solutions in the FSI

When we talk about mobility solutions for the FSI, the first question that usually comes into mind is, who is the targeted audience (the financial institution's workforce or its end customers?) for these solutions and who is going to be benefitted out of this. Indeed the answer is—both. Mobility solutions can help both the FSI's workforce and its end customers. Depending on the targeted audience, we can visualize mobility in FSI as follows:

- Mobility solutions for the FSI enterprise users
- Mobility solutions for the FSI end customers

The targeted audience for the FSI enterprise mobility solutions is the workforce (employees; field, sales, and support staff) of the financial service providers. The mobility solutions in this category typically focus on extending the services, data, and operations, which a user can access or perform within the four walls of the financial service providers to the corresponding user's mobile devices, for anytime and anywhere access of data and resources.

The targeted audiences for the FSI end customer mobility solutions are the end customers who utilize the services offered by financial service providers. The mobility solutions in the end customer category focus on extending the services that an end user can access through only a traditional brick-and-mortar branch network (street-side business) of the financial service provider to the end customers' mobile devices for anytime and anywhere service access.

The FSI enterprise mobile solutions are limited to a small audience, whereas the FSI end user mobile solutions are open to a wide set of users who belong to the customer base of the financial service provider. Figure 17.1 gives an overview of the various services under the enterprise and end-user mobility solutions for the FSI.

17.2.1 Mobility Solutions for the FSI Enterprise Users

The typical enterprise financial services that can be mobile enabled for the consumption of the workforce of the financial service provider are operations management, workforce (sales and field force) solutions, and asset management.

17.2.1.1 Operations Management Solutions

Mobile enabling of the operations management services deals with building mobile solutions and extending the existing day-to-day operations management services of

Figure 17.1 Scope for mobility solutions in the FSI.

the financial service provider to mobile devices. The type and volume of operations management services that need to be mobile enabled are totally dependent on the primary financial service (banking, brokerage, etc.) offerings of the FSI.

Typical examples for the operations management services that can be mobile enabled for an FSI with banking as the primary financial service are listed below.

17.2.1.1.1 ATM and Kiosk Management

ATMs and kiosks play a pivotal role in banking services, where the customers can manage their cash withdrawal, check and cash deposits, etc., without visiting a regular operations branch. It is essential to have someone manage the operations of the ATM or the kiosk on a day-to-day basis and on a need basis to provide uninterrupted service. These operations management services can certainly be mobile enabled so that the concerned person or team can be intimated about service needs in real time (e.g., ATM is out of cash, need immediate cash refilling, the receipt printer is out of paper, the card reader is not functioning, etc.).

17.2.1.1.2 Shift and Staff Service Management

Most financial service providers work on extended hours, and they implement shifts to manage the work timings of the staff. Effective implementations of mobility for shift management can make life easier, by automating work allocation and, thereby, eliminating the final rush for finding a replacement in case a staff is not available as per the schedule, provided workers are equipped with the mobile shift management solution and they respond proactively to the automated shift-management service.

17.2.1.2 Mobile Workforce Enablement (Field and Sales Force Automation Solutions)

Most financial service providers employ a significant percentage of the field workforce who concentrate on marketing, sales, and field services. The marketing and sales team focuses on the demonstration of new products, providing support during beta trials, customer interactions, and expansion of the customer base. It is essential to equip the sales and marketing field staff by providing on-demand access to the sales and marketing tools for an effective marketing and sales campaign, leading to a successful business footprint.

It is not necessary and mandatory that the end devices used by field staff in customer interactions are always limited to a handheld mobile device (such as smartphones, personal digital assistants [PDAs], or tablet PCs). The end device used by the staff can be a laptop, a netbook, a tablet PC, or a smartphone. It depends on the type of information or data that need to be presented or collected both to and from the audience during field operations. For example, certain marketing operations and product demonstrations need to connect only to the financial service providers network to access protected data and tools and require a device with high-end processing and display capabilities to run the application and need not require any support for document capture, signature capture, etc., during field operations. A laptop seems to be a good choice to handle these situations.

On the other hand, most of the sales- and service-related field operations (e.g., new customer sign-up, new merchant contract capture, payments, etc.) require the peripheral support of the devices for performing operations such as document capture (through camera feature support), signature capture (using the touch-screen feature of the device for signature capture), barcode scanning or reading (through barcode scanner features or image capture and barcode decoding support with camera module and software), identity verification through smartcard reading (using the near-field communication [NFC] feature supported by smartphones or tablets), biometric identification (using the fingerprint reader or retina scan features supported by smartphones and tablet PCs), etc. A high-end smartphone or tablet PC supporting all the peripheral requirements is the best choice to handle these requirements.

Accessing enterprise data and services (intranet services, intranet web pages, etc.) varies across field operations. Certain categories of field staff may require access to only certain intranet applications, whereas others may require access to data and need a way to add, delete, or modify the data present on the enterprise network. Depending on the type of the end device and the application requirement, the field staff can connect to the financial service provider's enterprise network through one of the following methods.

17.2.1.2.1 Mobile VPN Client-Based Enterprise Resource Access

Virtual private network (VPN) connectivity is the best remote access solution for field service operations in which the field staff are expected to work from a premises that provides an "always connected to the Internet environment," and the field staff are dealing with operations that are a replica of the operations the field staff are supposed to perform from their enterprise computer when they are working from the enterprise network.

Mobile virtual private network (mVPN) solution is an optimized version of the traditional VPN solution. mVPN implements optimizations as well as specific features for handling connectivity requirements to address network access through mobile Internet-based connectivity. Session persistence, roaming support (network operator switching to a supported and agreed-upon network for uninterrupted connectivity in situations where network signal from the registered provider is unavailable), data compression, and link optimization to improve performance over wireless networks, application compatibility, enhanced authentication, etc., are examples of some of the mobile network-specific features and optimizations supported by mVPN solutions.

The end devices used by the field staff should be equipped with a mobile VPN client solution for accessing the enterprise network over VPN. Also the enterprise should implement infrastructure enhancements (VPN gateways, policy services, etc.) to support VPN connectivity (Figure 17.2).

It is not necessary that the mVPN client would support all mobile device platforms (Windows Phone, Apple iOS, Android, RIM BlackBerry, etc.). Hence, it is essential to identify the primary device of the enterprise's field service operations and then select an mVPN solution that supports the identified platform. Depending on the security requirements in the enterprise resource access, multiple authentication levels (user ID and PIN only, user credentials plus hardware- and software-based security token, etc.) can be configured in the mobile client for logging into the enterprise network.

17.2.1.2.2 Mobile Clients, Mobile Web Pages, and Secure Web Service-Based Enterprise Resource Access

Mobile web page-based solutions are an easy way of extending thin client- or browser-based enterprise applications or services to mobile devices. A typical example is the customer relations management application where the field staff just need to capture or update customer-related data, which can be done online through accessing the mobile web page. The challenges in mobile web

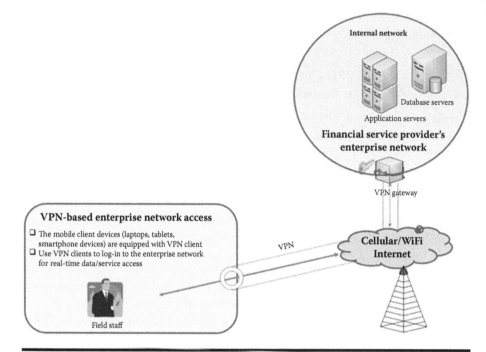

Figure 17.2 Accessing enterprise data or services: Mobile VPN client-based enterprise resource access.

page-based solutions are that most of the mobile devices in the market are with diverse screen estates (different screen sizes, different resolutions, and different input mechanisms such as touch or hardware keypad), and the mobile web pages need to be created for each set of devices, or a middleware needs to be implemented to render these pages appropriately on the device's browser, based on the device capabilities. A browser-based solution is not the right choice for field scenarios involving operations that require the hardware access of the device (such as invoking camera application to capture a document and upload the captured image, invoking the barcode scanner module for scanning a barcode label data, etc.). The underlying hardware access is device- and platform (OS)-specific, and the application programming interfaces (APIs) for invoking these features are nonuniform across multiple device platforms. Hence, it is not possible to invoke such an operation in a unique way from the browser-based application through techniques such as scripting. Also, most modern smartphone platforms block scripts that access hardware and other system resources due to security requirements. Another major limitation of browser-based applications is that they require an always-connected work environment and are not suitable for field scenarios with off-line data connectivity.

A mobile client (thick client) solution with a web-service model (Figure 17.3) is the most popular choice for field service operations that require device-specific hardware access (document capture through camera, signature capture through touch screen, etc.) and off-line data capture support (support for storing data in situations where no Internet connection is available for real-time communication with the enterprise network).

Thick client solutions are mobile-platform-dependent solutions, and they need to be developed for individual mobile device platforms with the help of the supported software development kit (SDK) and application development kit (ADK) for the corresponding platforms (e.g., Windows Phone developer tools SDK for Windows Phone devices and Android SDK for Android devices, etc.). Also, the solution needs to be deployed on the mobile devices. Most smartphone mobile devices in today's market do not support side loading of applications to the device; rather, they support application hosting and download from the corresponding device's application store (e.g., Marketplace for Windows Phone devices, Android Market for Android devices, and App Store for Apple iOS devices [iPhone and iPad]).

At the enterprise side, service and data access should be enabled and exposed beyond the enterprise walls, through secure web services. The web services

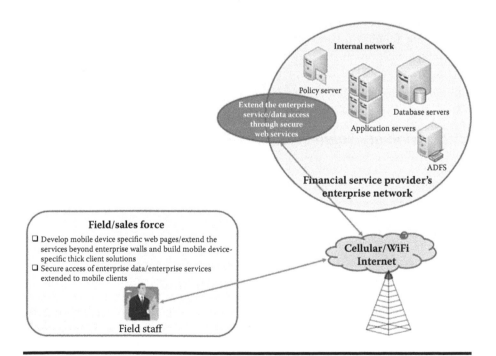

Figure 17.3   Accessing enterprise data or services: Mobile client applications and web services-based enterprise resource access.

should implement proper authentication and authorization to grant access to utilize the enterprise's resources. Claims-based authentications such as Active Directory Federation Services (ADFS) are the best choice for implementing authentications. The financial service provider may already have an active directory in place, and this can be easily extended through ADFS for single sign-on and authentication. The client application running on the mobile device can consume these web services over a secure socket layer for improved security. Additional security requirements can be implemented using client-side certificates and policy certificates, where devices with the client-side certificates provided by a trusted organization are only allowed to connect to the enterprise network and access the services.

In scenarios that include field operations where there is no real-time connectivity with the enterprise network, the thick client mobile applications can store the data locally on the device and can be synchronized later with the enterprise database when a network connection is available. A custom-developed or off-the-shelf data synchronization middleware can be used for syncing locally stored data with the enterprise system.

17.2.1.3 Asset Management and Tracking

Similar to any other industry, the financial service segment also has physical assets that require monitoring and tracking. Mobility solutions when combined with automatic identification and data collection techniques such as barcodes and NFC or radio frequency identification tags can provide a cost-effective, fully automated solution for asset management and tracking.

17.2.2 Mobility Solutions for the FSI End Customers

The typical enterprise financial services that can be mobile enabled for the consumption of the end customers (consumers) of the financial service provider are real-time financial service and data access on the go, mobile marketing utility and lifestyle solutions, etc.

17.2.2.1 Real-Time (Anytime and Anywhere) Financial Service Access and Information on the Go

In the traditional financial service solution, the end customers may have to visit a physical network branch of the financial service provider (e.g., branch office of a banking service provider) for accessing most of the services, whereas implementing mobility solutions provide anytime and anywhere financial services access to end customers and eliminate the need for visiting the conventional brick-and-mortar branch network (street-side business) of the financial service provider.

The financial service providers can mobile enable their consumer services to end customers through one or a combination of the following:

- Short messaging service (SMS)-based mobility solutions
- Browser-based application (thin client solutions)
- Stand-alone mobile client applications (thick client solutions)

SMS is a cost-effective way of communicating with mobile users. SMS service is supported by almost all mobile handsets, and it facilitates a uniform way of messaging, which is simple and consistent across all mobile devices and mobile operators (MO). Customers can subscribe to the SMS services during the registration process and can avail SMS service effectively for the services offered by the financial service provider. Following are the examples for the usage of SMS-based services in the banking financial services.

- Account balance and transaction alerts (deposits or withdrawals from the account)
- Balance and statement enquiry
- Loan repayment schedule reminders
- Funds transfer services
- Request for check book

The financial service provider can set up a specific number and text format for accessing the required services. Certain services such as reminders and alerts can be delivered on a registration basis. Once signed up for SMS-based services, the financial service provider can automatically generate SMS alerts or reminders based on the transaction scenario. No staff intervention is required for handling SMS-based services. The SMS gateway connects the financial service provider to the end users over the MO short message service center (SMS-C) or through an SS7 (signaling system no. 7) connectivity provider.

The only limitation of SMS-based service is that the communications may not be real time, if the underlying implementation of the SMS gateway is through an SMS aggregator, which routes the SMS through a MO SMS-C.

The financial service provider can extend the online services to mobile client devices for better customer experience. This can be provided through browser-based thin client solutions, which do not require the installation of any application on the device. The users can access these services with the built-in web browser of the device. The challenge is that the commercial mobile handhelds are of varying screen estates (varying screen sizes, resolution, and input capabilities) and browser support. To address the wide range of consumer devices, the financial service provider may have to develop web pages for each family of the end user's mobile handhelds or have to use a device agnostic middleware solution that renders the web pages based on the device screen estates.

Mobile client solutions or thick client solutions are another popular choice for delivering financial services to end customers. Compared with thin client solutions, thick client solutions can leverage the hardware features of the mobile device and can provide value-added services to customers. Location-based services is a typical use for leveraging device hardware features for delivering personalized financial services. Financial service providers such as banking and personal finance service providers can deliver personalized services to their customers with the help of global positioning system (GPS) hardware features and location-based services in terms of finding the nearest ATM, branch, and other service offerings in the current locality, which have tie-up with the financial service provider which gives better offers.

Thick client solutions are mobile-platform dependent, and they need to be developed for individual mobile device platforms with the help of the supported SDK or ADK for the corresponding platform (e.g., Windows Phone Developer Tools SDK for Windows Phone devices and Android SDK for Android devices, etc.). Also, the solution needs to be deployed on the consumer mobile devices. Most of the smartphone mobile devices in today's market do not support side loading of applications to the device; rather, they support application hosting and download from the corresponding device's application store (e.g., Marketplace for Windows Phone devices, Android Market for Android devices, and App Store for Apple iOS devices (iPhone and iPad)).

17.2.2.2 Mobile Utility Solutions

By adopting mobility solutions, the financial service providers can enhance the customer experience by providing a large number of utilities and tools, which may help the customers in the decision making of availing certain financial services. The number and type of utilities and tools that a financial service provider can provide to the end customer depend primarily on the focus area of the financial service provider. Loan or interest calculator, investment options, comparisons, etc., are typical examples for utility tools or solutions that a financial service provider, focusing on personal finance can offer to the end customers. The following gives a snapshot of the various utility solutions or tools that a financial service provider can offer to customers based on the focus area.

- Loan or interest rate calculators
- Currency converters and exchange rate calculator
- Surveys, promotional offers, etc.
- Investment options and comparisons
- Stock performance

- Income tax calculation
- Bill payment

17.3 Benefits of Mobility Adoption in the FSI

Bringing mobility into the current ecosystem brings lot of value additions and benefits to both the end customers and the financial service provider. A few important benefits among them are as follows.

17.3.1 Increased Field Staff Productivity

With mobility solutions, field staff can effectively perform their tasks. Electronic data and document capture eliminates the errors and the double efforts required in converting paper-based data capture to electronic data. The field service staff can access the required information and tools in real time from the financial service provider's enterprise systems, leading to faster turn-around time.

17.3.2 Reduced Cycle Time and Faster Response Times

Mobility solutions leveraging the advanced features supported by the mobile handhelds and PDA devices help in the efficient real-time handling of service requests and eliminate manual paper-based data capture and uploading of captured data to the central service station. The electronic data capture and restoration system improves the service request tracking efficiency, leading to faster turn-around times.

17.3.3 Reduced Operations Costs

Introducing mobility to the ecosystem leads to considerable cost reductions by reducing the fixed and variable facility costs. With efficient mobility solutions, the requirement for local offices and facilities can be significantly cut down by consolidating the facilities. This in turn will lead to the saving of the annual fixed facility costs (rent, utilities, etc.) and the cost of consumables (paper, toners, stationery cost, etc.). Mobility also enhances workers' productivity, which in turn will lead to the requirement for fewer number of field staffs to perform the field services, leading to cost reductions.

17.3.4 Environment Friendly

Mobility solutions implement electronic data capture and retention, which totally eliminate the conventional paper-based data capture and retention. Saving paper is saving trees—a true "green initiative."

17.3.5 Seamless Customer Experience

Most of the services in the financial service segment are highly competitive, with multiple providers offering the same set of services to end customers. Hence, it is essential to understand the customer needs and provide value-added service to stand out from the competitors. Mobility solutions are the best option to provide seamless customer experience (anytime and anywhere service access, personalized services, etc.). Mobility solutions such as loyalty programs are the best choice to expand the customer base, leading to a successful business.

17.4 Choice of Mobility Solutions for FSI

As discussed earlier, the services offered in the financial service sector are numerous, and they depend on the primary focus area of the financial service provider (e.g., banking services, personal finance services, mortgage services, etc.). There is no one-stop solution that can address the entire services in the FSI world. The financial service provider has to identify its focus area and the service within this area that can be mobile-enabled and then evaluate the option of using an off-the-shelf solution or a custom solution for mobile-enabling these services. The selection of a mobility solution in terms of architecture, business requirements, and platform support is highly challenging, and it requires a thorough analysis in the decision-making process of mobilization. This section is intended to give the readers an overview of the different types of mobility solutions and the factors to be considered in the selection process for implementing mobility solutions in financial services.

17.4.1 Thin Client Solutions

Thin client solutions are applications that run on a supported web browser. The applications are developed as web pages that are hosted on a server. The client devices (mobile handhelds and PDAs) can access these applications through browsers. Thin client solutions are suited for applications that do not require any hardware resource access of the underlying platform. A typical example is the portal service, which can be used for accessing financial information, such as in online banking. Users can simply login to the portal through the web browser by accessing the corresponding universal resource locator (URL). Thin client solutions always require connectivity to the hosted system and are known as "always-connected" applications.

A thin client solution should address the features supported by the web browser of the client system (PDAs, mobile handhelds, etc.) and the screen real-estates (screen size and resolution, orientation, input support, etc.) of the client devices. To address devices of varying capabilities, the web pages may be redesigned for each client device or a "device capabilities-aware middleware" should be used for rendering the pages on the device browser. A thin client solution is very limited in capabilities, with regard to the hardware access of the client device (e.g., camera access for document capture). It depends on the client-side scripting support provided by the browser in use, which in turn may lead to potential security threats.

17.4.2 Thick Client Solutions

Thick client solutions are applications developed for a particular client device (mobile handheld or PDA) platform (Windows Phone, Windows CE OS, iPhone OS, Android OS, etc.). Thick client solutions reside in the memory of the handheld device, and it utilizes the platform support provided by the underlying operating system and target hardware. The device manufacturers (commonly known as original equipment manufacturers) provide SDKs, exposing APIs to access the platform-supported hardware for which the OS does not provide any standard API interfaces, which can be utilized in the thick client solution for leveraging the device's capabilities (e.g., barcode reading). Depending on the OS support and third-party products, a thick client solution may implement support for local data storage, syncing of locally stored data with standard databases such as SQL Server, Oracle, etc. This feature of thick client solutions qualifies them for "off-line data capture," which does not require connectivity with the back-end systems always. Thick client solutions are platform dependent, and they are less portable to devices running different operating systems. Application upgrades are challenging for thick client solutions.

17.4.3 Off-the-Shelf Mobility Solutions versus Custom-Built Solutions

Depending on the financial service provider's focus area, certain services may already be using off-the-shelf solutions (e.g., customer relationship management software) for services, and it may be easy to extend this solution to mobile devices with less customization efforts than building a custom mobility solution from scratch to offer the same features. The choice on whether to use an off-the-shelf solution or a custom solution is dependent on a number of factors. A few important factors in the decision-making process are listed below.

1. Availability of the off-the shelf solution for the required service
2. Support for the off-the-shelf solution for extending to various mobile platforms
3. Customization effort for the off-the-shelf solution versus effort for building a custom solution
4. Cost for the off-the-shelf solution versus custom solution
5. Annual maintenance cost for off-the-shelf solution versus custom-built solution
6. Feature addition support
7. Ease of operation

17.5 Mobility Enablement Challenges in the FSI

Along with opportunities and business benefits, mobility enablement in the FSI has various challenges also. A few of the important challenges in mobility enablement are explained below.

17.5.1 Infrastructure Investment

Mobility adoption requires huge infrastructure investment in terms of hardware and software. Handheld device procurements, servers and network infrastructure requirements, and firewalls for extending the data and services to field devices add to the hardware cost, whereas investments on extending existing solutions to mobile or building custom mobility solutions, mobile device provisioning, and management software add to the software cost. It is always advisable to conduct a cost–benefit analysis and return-on-investment calculation before proceeding with mobility enablement.

17.5.2 Ensuring Security

Extending the financial service provider's enterprise network (the corporate infrastructure hosting the services and holding the data) to mobile networks and devices opens up a way for injecting vulnerabilities, leading to security risk in the entire system. Proper security analysis must be carried out in the design, and the design should accommodate proper security implementations including VPN, firewalls, communication channel security (secure sockets, encrypted data transfer, etc.), mobile device security, and authentication and authorization policies for data and service access.

17.5.3 Device Provisioning and Management

Field device (mobile handhelds and PDAs) provisioning and management is a challenging task in the implementation of mobility. The device may contain locally stored data, which should be protected against unauthorized access. Also, proper application access policies must be enforced on the device to limit the access of various applications in the mobile handhelds and PDAs used by the field staff. The device must be updated with latest security policies and application upgrades as and when they are available. Proper device provisioning, such as data wiping on lost devices and remote device lockdown of devices that are not sync'd with the server in a defined period of time, should be implemented for a successful mobility solution implementation. An off-the-shelf device management and provisioning software, such as Mobicontrol from SOTI, Afaria from Sybase, Avalanche from Wavelink, or a custom-built solution, can be used for this.

17.6 Scenario: Mobility Solution for Paperless Contract Capture

SCOPE OF MOBILIZATION

A credit service provider wants to automate the current paper-based merchant contract capturing system. In the current system, the sales person collects the data and documents from the merchant on paper, which are uploaded into the service provider's system once the sales person is back at the branch office. A decision on the approval or rejection of a merchant's application is intimated later, after the processing of the data. The current paper-based system is error prone due to multiple human interventions, and the turn-around time is high. Also the field staff are struggling to meet their day-to-day commitments, and this is reflected on their productivity due to the increased paper work.

17.6.1 Paper-Based System before Mobile Enablement

A paper-based data collection mechanism is used by field staff for new merchant enrollment. The approval or denial decision on the application is intimated later.

17.6.2 After Mobile Enablement

All field service staff will be equipped with a handheld device, and a mobile client application will be used for data collection. The approval or denial decision on the application is intimated instantly.

17.6.3 Requirements and Solution

The application is designed to address the following requirements:

■ The credit service provider firm is currently using Windows Phone as the enterprise phone, and the service needs to be built for the existing Windows Phone device.
■ The application should have provision for document capturing with the help of the handheld device's integrated camera.
■ The application should support merchant signature capture with the help of the handheld device's touch screen.
■ The application should support off-line data capture support to address situations where there is no Internet connectivity available.
■ The application should implement the highest possible authentication service utilizing single sign-on in which the field service staff can use his/her enterprise login credentials (user name and password) to authenticate.

As the application requirement explicitly calls for off-line data capture, a thick-client solution with local data storage is the ideal solution for implementing this requirement. The locally stored data can be later sync'd to the central database, when network connection is available. GPRS, 3G, or 4G network is used for data communication with the central station. Single sign-on requirement is implemented with claims-based authentication where the identity service is provided by ADFS. The credit service provider already has an active directory and an ADFS in place. Azure AppFabric's access control hosted service (ACS) can provide federated authentication as well as claims- and rules-based authorization to access any REST web services hosted in the credit service provider's network. ACS can be easily integrated with the credit service provider's ADFS for federated authentication. ACS brings the advantage of cross-platform support in which ACS can be accessed from applications running on any OS platform, provided the platform has support for hypertext transfer protocol secure (HTTPS). ACS uses HMACSHA256 signatures and symmetric keys for implementing authentication and authorization. Figure 17.4 gives an overview of the ACS-based authorization and access control implementation for utilizing field data capture processing and application approval or rejection service hosted in the credit service provider's network.

The proposed solution architecture implements the ADFS-based federated authentication and ACS. The service hosted on the credit service provider's network is exposed through Windows Communication Foundation (WCF) services and is registered with ACS for providing trusted claims. Figure 17.5 illustrates the end-to-end system architecture.

The Windows Phone application for data and document capture, and accessing the services hosted on the credit service provider's network, is developed in Silverlight (XAML) and C# .Net. The Windows Identity Framework (WIF)

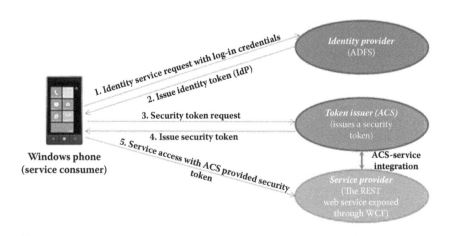

Figure 17.4 Implementation of claims-based authentication and access control with ACS.

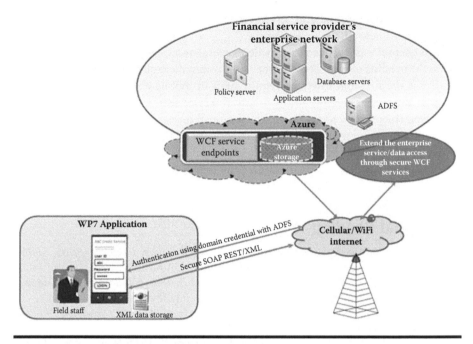

Figure 17.5   End-to-end solution architecture.

libraries provided by the .Net framework are used for implementing the active directory federation and ACS communication. Local data storage is implemented with xml files. A custom-sync service is developed as part of the solution to sync the off-line stored data with the back-end database residing at the credit service provider's network, in case of off-line data capture.

17.6.4 Business Benefits

- Improved business process
- Increased field staff productivity
- Improved customer experience and expansion of customer base
- Increased revenue

17.7 Conclusion

FSI is one of the early adopters of mobility solutions. Today, most of the service providers in the FSI are trying to create new revenue channels by leveraging mobility solutions, which extend enterprise-centric services to mobile devices and optimize the sales process. Mobility solutions help FSIs realize real business benefits and grab potential business opportunities. From an end-customer perspective, mobility solutions provide anytime and anywhere access to the various financial services, creating an all new customer experience.

This chapter was intended to provide a general overview of the mobility opportunities, the benefits of mobility, and the various mobility solutions for FSI. Ensuring security is the first and foremost requirement in mobile enabling of the financial services. The services offered in the financial service sector are numerous, and they depend on the primary focus area of the financial service provider. There is no one-stop solution that can address the entire services in the FSI world. The financial service provider has to identify the focus area and the service within this area that can be mobile-enabled and then evaluate the options and formulate the strategies.

Additional Reading

1. Alfred C. Morley. *Industry Analysis—The Financial Services Industry—Banks, Thrifts, Insurance Companies, and Securities Firms.* AIMR, CFA Institute, 1992.
2. Brett King, *Bank 2.0: How Customer Behavior and Technology Will Change the Future of Financial Services.* Marshall Cavendish Reference. July 15, 2010.
3. David W. Schropfer. *The SmartPhone Wallet: Understanding the Disruption Ahead—Volume 1.* CreateSpace. December 17, 2010.
4. Cisco Mobile VPN. *Enabling Cisco End-Device based IP Mobility.* Available at http://www.cisco.com.
5. MobiControl. *Enterprise Mobile Device Management for Smartphones, Tablets & Rugged Devices.* http://www.soti.net/mobicontrol/.
6. Sybase Afaria. http://www.sybase.com/products/mobileenterprise/afaria
7. Wavelink Avalanche. http://www.wavelink.com/p/mobile-device-and-infrastructure-management
8. Windows Azure AppFabric Access Control, Active Directory Federation Services 2.0. *Windows Identity Foundation Simplifies User Access for Developers.* Claims Based Architecture White Paper. Available at http://msdn.microsoft.com/en-us/security/aa570351

MOBILE APPLICATION DEVELOPMENT

Chapter 18

Mobile Platforms

Mobile computing has been growing in popularity over the years. The increasing capabilities of mobile phones, along with higher bandwidth networks available for these devices, have made the mobile platform very appealing for both consumers and enterprises. The term "platform" describes the hardware or software configuration of a system. The system can range from anything between a mobile device to tablets or computers. When a platform is referred in relation to the hardware of the system, it usually means the processor architecture such as Intel x86 platform, PowerPC platform, etc. When it is referred in terms of software, the term "platform" means the operating system (OS) that runs the computer or the mobile device.

18.1 Introduction

A mobile platform in a mobile device manages the hardware and the software resources of the device; in the same way, a computer OS manages its resources. Since the introduction of the first smartphone by IBM, mobile devices are evolving at a very high rate. Manufacturers are launching devices for various consumer segments, thus increasing the number of mobile platforms. In the current scenario, the OS on the device is as important as the device manufacturer. This mobile platform will determine the features in the phone, the applications available, and the user interface (UI) of the device.

18.2 Mobile Platforms in the Market

The different mobile platforms available in the market are as follows:

- Android
- iOS (iPhone, iPad, iPod, and Touch)
- Windows Phone
- Windows Mobile
- BlackBerry
- Symbian
- Bada
- Linux
- WebOS
- Brew
- MeeGo

In this chapter, few of the leading mobile OSs and their architecture and the key OS features are discussed.

18.2.1 Android

Android is a mobile device software platform and an OS that is codeveloped by Open Handset Alliance, which includes companies such as Google, HTC, Intel, Qualcomm, T-Mobile, Motorola, Sprint Nextel, and NVIDIA, etc. Android uses Linux Kernel 2.6 as its base and depends on Linux Kernel for its core services and is based on the GNU software. Android was initially developed by a firm named Android Inc., later purchased by Google. Figure 18.1 shows one of the Android handset model.

Figure 18.1   Android devices.

Android includes an entire set of software comprising an OS, a middleware, and applications. Android is an open source, and it has a large number of developers; already more than 300,000 applications are built on it. The key benefits in using the Android platform are as follows:

- Android is an open source.
- It is easily adaptable to emerging technologies.
- Programmers have control ranging from the hardware of the mobile to the UI of the web applications.
- All the applications installed in the phone have equal access to the phone's capabilities.
- Developers can customize their Android mobile device 100%.

18.2.1.1 OS Architecture

As mentioned earlier, Android is built on a foundation of Linux Kernel, which has a layered environment and includes rich functions. Android has an embedded browser built upon WebKit. There are different connectivity options that are available in Android including WiFi, Bluetooth, and wireless cellular connection for data transmission [e.g., general packet radio service, Enhanced Data rates for Groupe Spécial Mobile (GSM) Evolution (EDGE), and 3G]. Android also has location-based services [such as global positioning system (GPS)], camera, and accelerometers available in its software stack. In the Android world, original equipment manufacturers (OEMs) can decide the features that need to be included at the hardware level. A simplified view of the Android software layers is given in Figure 18.2.

18.2.1.1.1 Android Applications

Application components are considered as the building blocks of an Android application. Each of these components can be an entry point through which the system can enter the application. Not all components can be actual entry points for the user. In certain cases, the components depend on each other, but each will exist as its own entity and play a specific role; each will act as a unique building block that helps define the application's overall behavior. All application developments in Android are done using Java programming language. Applications run on Java core libraries on a Dalvik virtual machine. Dalvik is also an open-source software. Android applications are converted to compact Dalvik Executable (.dex) format. Each Android application is set to run within an instance of the Dalvik virtual machine. The Dalvik virtual machine resides within a Linux kernel-managed process, as shown in Figure 18.3.

Android software development kit tools compile the code into an Android package. The package is an archive file with an .apk suffix. The entire code in a single .apk file is a considered as one application. This file is used in installing the

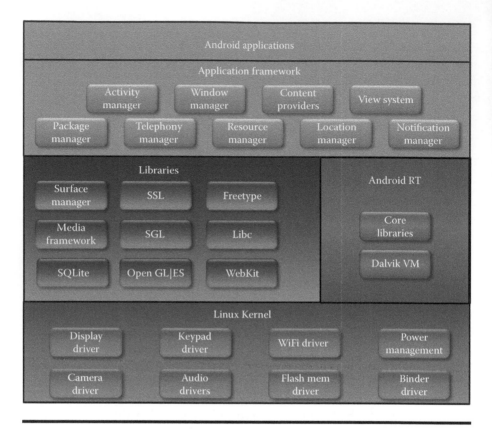

Figure 18.2 High level Android architecture.

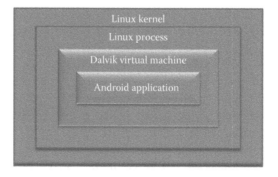

Figure 18.3 Android applications.

application in Android-powered devices. This .apk file includes all data and the resource files as well. When the application is executed, after the application installation, it will run on its own sandbox:

- The Android OS acts similar to a multiuser Linux system, where each application is a different user.
- The system assigns a unique Linux user ID for each application. Then, the system also sets permissions for all the files existing in an application. This makes sure that the user ID assigned to the corresponding application can only access it.
- Each process has its own virtual machine, which in turn makes sure that an application's code is running in isolation from other applications.
- Every application runs in its own Linux process. Android will start the process when any one of the components in the application needs to be executed. Android shuts down the process when it is no longer needed or when the system is recovering memory for other applications.

In short, each application has access only to the components that the application requires to do its work. This is known as the "principle of least privilege" in the Android system. This makes sure that the application cannot access any other module or part of the system for which it does not have required rights. Even though these restrictions are in place, there are methods available by which an application can share data with other applications, and applications can access system services:

- Multiple applications can share the same Linux user ID, which will help applications to access other applications files. Applications that use the same user ID can also run in the same process and share the same virtual machine so that system resources are conserved.
- Applications can request permission to access device data including the user's contacts, SMS messages, camera, Bluetooth, etc. All these application permissions should be granted by the user at the time of installation.

An Android application can be grouped into any of the following categories:

- Activities
    - The application has a visible UI and is implemented with an activity.
    - The activity starts when the user selects the application from the home screen or from the application launcher.
    - The activity is represented on a single screen with a UI.
- Services
    - The application can be categorized as a service if that application needs to persist for a long time.
    - The application runs in the background, performing long-running operations.

- – The application can also perform work for remote processes.
- – The service will not have a UI.
- ■ Content providers
  - – Content providers manage access to persistent data.
  - – Content providers are required if you are building a larger, complex application, or if the application provides data to multiple activities or applications.
  - – Content providers manage a shared set of application data.
  - – Content providers are useful for reading and writing data that are private to the application and not shared.
- ■ Broadcast receivers
  - – Broadcast receivers respond to system-wide broadcast announcements.
  - – An Android application can be launched to process data or respond to an event raised, similar to the receipt of a text message.
  - – Many broadcasts originate from the system.
  - – Applications can also initiate broadcasts.
  - – Broadcast receivers usually do not display a UI.
  - – Broadcast receivers can create a status bar notification so as to alert the user when a broadcast event occurs.
  - – The broadcast receiver is considered as a "gateway" to other components and is designed to do minimal amount of work.

A unique aspect of the Android system design is that an application can start another application's component. When the system starts a component, it starts the process corresponding to the component and also instantiates the classes used by the component. In Android, the system runs each application as a separate process with file permissions and restricts access to other applications. So applications cannot directly activate a component from another application. The Android system will be able to directly activate a component from another application. So, to activate a component in another application, a message must be delivered to the system that specifies the application's intent to start a particular component of an application. The system then activates the component for the application.

18.2.1.1.2 Application Framework

Parts of the Android toolkit are provided by Google, and some parts are extensions and services that developers write. The activity manager is a critical component of the application framework. The activity manager handles the application life cycle and a common "back-stack" for user navigation.

18.2.1.1.3 Libraries

The different components of the Android system use C and C++ native libraries. Developers have access to these capabilities through the Android application framework. These application programming interfaces (APIs) are called Java interfaces. Libraries for 2D and 3D graphics, SQLite database, Media codecs, and a native web-browser engine are available in this layer.

18.2.1.1.4 Android Runtime

Android consists of a set of core libraries helping the developer to use the functionalities available in the core libraries of Java language. All Android applications run with the assistance of the Dalvik virtual machine. The Dalvik virtual machine in turn runs .dex files, which are converted at compile time to .dex files from standard class and jar files. Dalvik enables the device to run multiple virtual machines efficiently, and .dex files are more efficient and compact than class files. They also aid in low-level memory management and battery management.

18.2.1.1.5 Linux Kernel

As mentioned earlier, Android is based on Linux kernel 2.6. System services are dependent on the Linux kernel, which acts as an abstraction between the software stack and the hardware layer. Developers cannot access this layer for programming.

18.2.1.2 OS Features

The OS features of the Android application are detailed as follows:

- The application framework helps in enabling reuse and replacement of individual components.
- The Dalvik virtual machine is highly optimized for mobile devices.
- The integrated browser is based on the open-sourced WebKit engine.
- The OS has optimized graphics by custom-2D graphics library.
- 3D graphics uses OpenGL ES 1.0 specification.
- SQLite can be used for structured data storage.
- The OS supports standard media formats.
- The OS includes GSM telephony.
- The application has EDGE, 3G, Bluetooth, and WiFi.
- The application has a compass, a camera, a GPS, and an accelerometer.
- A rich development environment, with a device emulator, debugging tools, tools for memory and performance profiling, and also a plug-in for the Eclipse integrated development environment (IDE), is available.

In Android Marketplace, fragmentation of devices is one of the key issues identified. Fragmentation is a scenario in which different versions of the software platform are available and start coexisting with the original. This can weaken interoperability mainly because applications built for one version of the platform might not work on others. The lack of consistency across platforms makes it difficult to create an application that integrates properly across all the platforms. This forces the packaging, compatibility testing, and certain platform integration tasks to be done by distros rather than by upstream application developers.

The challenges are more in the mobile space as the fundamental differences between the different devices also add to the fragmentation issue. For example, applications built to support a specific screen resolution, form factor, or input mechanism sometimes may not be compatible with devices that have a different specification in those areas. Another issue that arises in the Android space is that the handset makers and mobile carriers make their own changes to differentiate their products from a competitor's product. These changes can sometimes create additional compatibility issues.

Google's solution to the fragmentation issue is the Android compatibility definition document that defines a set of baseline standards for the platform. Google's control over Android Market forces device vendors to conform to the standard. The Market in Android platform is not open, and license has to be obtained from Google. For a device maker to obtain a license to ship Android Market, the vendor has to prove that the baseline standards are met for the product. This approach of linking market access to compliance of standards ensures that hardware vendors do not deviate much from the default code base. This approach is followed on virtually all mainstream Android devices (Figure 18.4).

18.2.1.3 OS Versions

Android has a received a lot of updates since its original release. Most of the updates to the base OS are typically for adding new features and fixing bugs. Figure 18.5 contains a detailed list of the most recent versions.

18.2.1.4 Market for Applications

Android Market is an online store for softwares, which can run in Android devices, developed by Google. An application program known as Market will be preinstalled on most Android devices. Only devices that comply with Google's requirements are allowed to preinstall Google's Android Market app and access the Market. This application allows users of Android phones to view, browse, and download apps published by third-party developers from Android Market. Developers have an option to publish paid or free applications on Android Market. For paid apps, a developer receives 70% of the application price and the rest 30% is distributed among carriers and payment processors. Currently, Android Market has more than 500,000 applications hosted. The Market filters the list of applications in the Market app to those that are compatible with the user's device.

Feature	Details
Handset display	Android is adaptable to larger, VGA, 2D graphics library, 3D graphics library based on OpenGL ES 2.0 specifications, and traditional smartphone layouts.
Database	SQLite (lightweight relational DB) is used fro data storage purposes.
Connectivity	Android supports connectivity technologies including GSM/EDGE, IDEN, CDMA, EV-DO, UMTS, Bluetooth, WiFi, LTE, NFC, and WiMAX
Messaging service	SMS and MMS are available forms of messaging, including threaded text messaging
Multiple language support	Android supports multiple human languages. The number of languages more than doubled for the platform 2.3 Gingerbread.
Web browser	Based on the WebKit layout engine, coupled with Chrome's V8 JavaScript engine.
Java support	While most Android applications are witten in Java, there is no Java virtual machine in the platform and Java byte code is not executed. J2ME support can be provided via third-party applications.
Media support	Following audio/video/still media formats are supported: WebM, H.263, H.264 (in 3GP or MP4 container), MPEG-4 SP, AMR, AMR-WB (in 3GP container), AAC, HE-AAC (in MP4 or 3GP container), MP3, MIDI, Ogg Vorbis, FLAC WAV, JPEG, PNG, GIF, BMP
Multitouch	Multitouch can be enabled natively.
Multitasking	Multitasking of applications is available.
Additional hardware support	Android can use video/still cameras, touchscreens, GPS, accelerometers, gyroscopes, magnetometers, dedicated gaming controls, proximity and pressure sensors, thermometers, accelerated 2D bit blits (with hardware orientation, scaling, pixel format conversion), and accelerated 3D graphics.
Bluetooth	Supports A2DP, AVRCP, sending files (OPP), accessing the phone book (PBAP), voice dialing and sending contacts between phones. Keyboard, mouse, and joystick (HID) support is available through manufacturer customizations and third-party applications.

Figure 18.4   Android OS features.

18.2.2 *iOS*

Apple's mobile OS is known as iOS (previously called iPhone OS). iOS was originally developed for iPhone but later extended to support other Apple mobility devices. iOS is the OS in iPhone, iPad, and iPod touch devices. iPhone is believed to be a revolution in mobile phones market because of its unique UI and deep integration with the web (Figure 18.6).

18.2.2.1 *OS Architecture*

iOS acts as an intermediate level between the hardware and the different applications that appear on the UI. Developer-created applications very rarely communicate with the underlying hardware directly. Developer applications communicate with the hardware through well-defined system interfaces that protect the developer

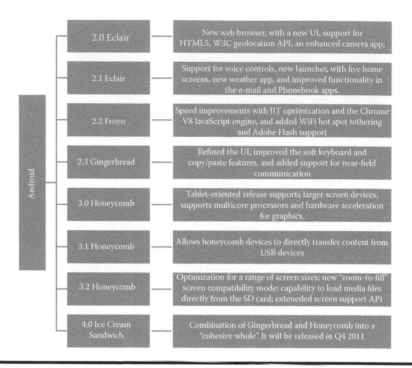

Figure 18.5   Android OS versions.

Figure 18.6   iPhone devices.

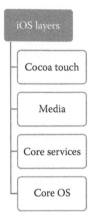

Figure 18.7   iPhone OS architecture.

application from hardware changes. This level of abstraction helps developers to write applications that can work consistently on various devices with different hardware capabilities.

The implementation of the iOS system resembles a set of layers, as shown in Figure 18.7. The bottom layers of the system are the basic services and technologies, which all the other applications rely on, and the higher level layers are used by more sophisticated services and technologies.

18.2.2.1.1 Cocoa Touch

The Cocoa Touch is the topmost layer and one of the key layers in the iOS stack. This layer contains the frameworks most commonly used by iPhone application developers. It comprises the UI Kit and Foundation frameworks. Cocoa Touch also includes other frameworks providing key services for accessing device features:

- UI Kit and foundation framework
  - It provides the basic tools and infrastructure that a developer needs to develop graphical and event-driven applications in iOS.
  - UI Kit framework is an Objective-C framework.
  - Every application in iOS uses this framework to implement this core set of features, which are as follows:
    - Application management
    - Graphics and windowing support
    - UI management
    - Event-handling support
    - Support for text and web content
    - Objects representing system views and controls

- UI Kit also supports some device-specific features and provides the basic fundamental code for building the application, such as the following:
  - Accelerometer data
  - Built-in camera
  - User's photo library
  - Device-specific information

18.2.2.1.2 Media

The graphics and multimedia technologies in iPhone mainly concentrate on providing the best multimedia experience on a mobile device. The high-level framework in iOS helps developers to create advanced graphics and animations quickly. The low-level frameworks provide developers with access to the tools that they need to do things exactly the way they want. The technologies mentioned below can be used to improve the application's graphical and audio contents:

1. Graphics technologies
   - High-quality graphics are an important part of all iPhone applications.
   - Graphics technologies comprise several key technologies to render 2D and 3D drawing.
2. Core audio
   - Low-latency C-based interface supports the manipulation of multichannel audio.
   - Core audio can generate, record, mix, and play audio in any application.
   - Developers can also use core audio interface to use the vibration feature on the devices that support it.
3. OpenAL
   - OpenAL is a cross-platform standard for getting 3D audio in applications.
   - Developers can use it to implement high-performance positional audio in games and other applications that need high-quality audio output.
   - Code modules written using OpenAL in iOS can be ported and can run on any other platform.
4. Video technologies
   - Full-screen video playback is supported through the media player framework.
   - The framework supports the playback of files with the .mov, .mp4, .m4v, and .3gp extensions and uses the following compression standards:
     - Video formats
       - H.264 baseline profile level 3.0 video
       - MPEG-4 Part 2 video (simple profile)
     - Audio formats
       - Advanced audio coding (AAC)
       - Apple Lossless Audio Codec (ALAC)

- A-law
- IMA/adaptive differential pulse-code modulation (IMA4)
- Linear pulse-code modulation (PCM)
- μ-Law

18.2.2.1.3 Core Services

The core-services layer provides the basic fundamental system services that all developer applications use. Most of the technology in the system is built over the core services, and so the developer applications directly or indirectly use these services. The following list describes the various frameworks of the core-services layer:

1. Address book
   - The address book provides programmatic access to the contacts on a user's device.
   - Applications that need access to this information can use this framework to access the data stored in contact records directly.
   - Programs can use the information internally or can provide custom UIs for displaying that data.
   - The address book UI complements the address book framework by giving a graphical interface for accessing the user's contacts.
   - Developers can use the Objective-C classes in this framework to present the system standard interfaces for reading the contact list or to create new contacts.
2. Core foundation
   - The group of C-based interfaces provides data management and service features for iPhone applications.
   - The framework includes support for the following:
     - Collection data types
     - Bundle support
     - String management
     - Date and time management
     - Raw data block management
     - Preferences management
     - Universal resource locator and stream manipulation
     - Thread and run loop support
     - Port and socket communication

The core foundation framework and foundation framework are closely related. The foundation framework provides an Objective-C interface for the same basic features. In situations where developers need to use both foundation objects and core foundation types, it can be implemented by taking advantage of the "toll-free bridging" that exists between the two frameworks. Toll-free bridging means that developers can use core foundation and foundation types interchangeably in the methods and functions in any of the framework.

1. Core location
   - Core location helps the user in determining the latitude and longitude of the location of the device.
   - It can use the available hardware to triangulate the device position based on nearby signal information.
   - The maps application uses the core location feature to show the user's current position on a map.
   - Developers can use this technology in their applications to display position-based information to the user.
2. CFNetwork
   - CFNetwork is a high-performance, C-based framework that provides a set of object-oriented abstractions for the users for working with network protocols.
   - CFNetwork gives the developer detailed control over the protocol stack.
   - This framework uses easy-to-use lower level constructs such as Berkeley Software Distribution (BSD) sockets.
   - The developer can use this to simplify tasks such as communicating with the file transfer protocol (FTP) or hypertext transfer protocol (HTTP) servers and resolving domain name system (DNS) hosts.
   - This framework is based both physically and theoretically on BSD sockets
   - Some of the tasks a developer can perform with the CFNetwork are as follows:
     - Usage of BSD sockets
     - Resolving DNS hosts
     - Creation of encrypted connections using secure sockets layer (SSL) or transport layer security
     - Working with HTTP and FTP servers
     - Authenticating HTTP and hypertext transfer protocol secure (HTTPS) servers
     - Publish, resolve, and browse Bonjour services
3. Security
   - Security provides an explicit framework that users can use to guarantee the security of the data that the application manages.
   - It provides interfaces for managing public and private keys, certificates, and trust policies.
   - It supports the generation of cryptographically secure, pseudorandom numbers.
   - It supports storage of certificates and cryptographic keys in the keychain, considered as a secure repository for sensitive user data.

4. SQLite
   - SQLite is a lightweight SQL database library.
   - From the application, the user can create local database files.
   - The application can manage the tables and records in these database files.
   - It is highly optimized to provide high performance and quick access to database records.
   - It is designed for general-purpose use.
5. XML support
   - LibXML2 and libxslt libraries provide support for manipulating XML content.
   - XML supports open-source libraries.
   - It can parse or write arbitrary XML data with high performance.
   - It can transform extensible markup language (XML) content to hypertext markup language (HTML).

18.2.2.1.4 Core OS

The core-OS layer includes kernel environment, drivers, and basic interfaces of OS. The kernel is based on Mac, and it is responsible for every aspect of the OS. Core OS manages the file system, virtual memory system, threads, network, and inter-process communication. The drivers available at this layer provide the interface between the hardware and the system frameworks. Access to the kernel and drivers is restricted to a limited set of system frameworks and applications as a security measure.

iOS also provides a set of interfaces that can be used for accessing low-level features of the OS. Developer application accesses these features through the LibSystem.

18.2.2.2 OS Features

Figure 18.8 illustrates the iPhone OS features.

18.2.2.3 OS Versions

Figure 18.9 illustrates the iPhone OS versions.

18.2.2.4 App Store for Applications

The iOS App Store is a distribution platform for iOS that is used for distributing a digital application. This is developed and maintained by Apple. App Store allows end users to browse and download developer applications from the store to their target device or to the PC Mac using iTunes. The application may be available

Feature	Details
Handset display	480 x 320 px (HVGA) OR 960 X 640 px,
Database	SQLite, lightweight relational database, can be used for data storage purposes.
Connectivity	iPhone supports connectivity technologies including GSM/EDGE, CDMA, HSDPA 3.6, UMTS, Bluetooth, WiFi
Messaging service	SMS and MMS are available forms of messaging
Multiple language support	Language support for English (United States), English (United Kingdom), French (France), German, traditional Chinese, simplified Chinese, Dutch, Italian, Spanish, Portuguese (Brazil), Portuguese (Portugal), Danish, Swedish, Finnish, Norwegian, Korean, Japanese, Russian, Polish, Turkish, Ukrainian, Hungarian, Arabic, Thai, Czech, Greek, Hebrew, Indonesian, Malay, Romanian, Slovak, Croation, Catalan, and Vietnamese Support for display of muliple languages and characters simultaneously
Web browser	Safari browser is used
Java support	Not supported
Media support	Audio formats supported: AAC (8–320 Kbps), protected AAC (from iTunes Store), HE-AAC, MP3 (8–320 Kbps), MP3 VBR, Audible (formats 2, 3, 4 audible enhanced Audio, AAX, and AAX+), Apple, Lossless, AIFF, and WAV Video formats supported: H.264 video up to 720 p, 30 frames per second, main profile level 3.1 with AAC-LC audio up to 160 Kbps, 48 kHz, stereo audio in .m4v, .mp4, and .mov file formats; MPEG-4 video, up to 2.5 Mbps, 640 by 480 pixel, 30 frames per second, simple profile with AAC-LC audio up to 160 Kbps per channel, 48 kHz, stereo audio in .mp4, and .mov file formats; Motion JPEG (M-JPEG) up to 35 Mbps, 1280 by 720 pixels, 30 frames per second, audio in ulaw, PCM stereo audio in .avi file format
Multitouch	With its large multitouch display and innovative software, iPhone lets you control everything using just your fingers. A panel laminated on the glass senses your touch using electrical fields. It can register multiple touches at once to support advanced gestures such as pinch to zoom, two-finger tap, and more. The panel then transmits the information to the retina display below it.
Multitasking	Multitasking of applications is available.
Additional hardware support	Three-axis gyro, accelerometer, proximity sensor ambient light sensor
Bluetooth	Bluetooth 2.1 + EDR wireless technology

Figure 18.8   iPhone OS features.

either free or at a cost. About 30% of the revenue from the store goes to Apple, and 70% goes to the developer of the application.

18.2.3 Windows Phone

Windows Phone 7 is the latest entrant into the mobile OS world. The OS is developed by Microsoft, and it succeeds the Windows Mobile platform. Windows Phone 7 platform is mainly targeted at the consumer market unlike its predecessor, which targeted the enterprise market (Figure 18.10).

Windows Phone 7 provides a standard platform that simplifies the design and development of applications that are designed to run on the devices provided by multiple phone manufacturers. Windows Phone 7 brings in the advantages of a standardized platform. Windows Phone 7 is the latest mobile device that incorporates

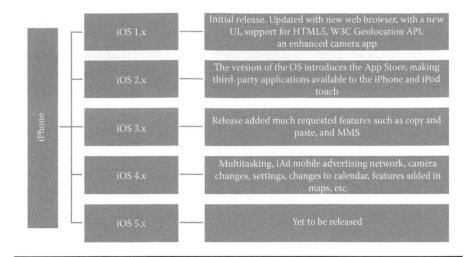

Figure 18.9 **iPhone OS versions.**

Figure 18.10 **Windows Phone devices.**

a comprehensive set of features, which is required to build applications that will satisfy the requirements of both the business community and consumers. It also allows developers to easily create powerful interactive and attractive applications reusing the skills and knowledge of the existing modern development environments. Windows Phone 7 supports most of the features that consumers now expect on a mobile device, such as the following:

- Stylish UI that supports gestures and smooth animation
- Cloud service and media integration
- Easy and safe application installation
- Device capabilities such as location awareness, sound recording, camera, messaging, and multitouch

18.2.3.1 OS Architecture

Windows Phone 7.0 utilizes a layered architecture that has a kernel space and a user space. Kernel space consists of the following items:

- Kernel
- File system
- Graphics rendering

Windows Phone OS kernel is completely based on Windows Embedded CE 6.0 as its core. It supports up to 32,000 simultaneous processes. Each of these processes can access up to 1 GB of virtual memory. Windows Phone OS is a 32-bit OS, and therefore, it can access up to 4 GB of RAM. The Windows Phone application platform architecture mainly consists of the following four components (Figure 18.11):

- Runtime on "screen": Silverlight, XNA Framework, and Windows Phone-specific features such as various sensors (accelerometer, GPS, and media options) together combine to provide a mature environment to build secure, graphically rich applications.
- Tools: IDEs used in Windows Phone development are Visual Studio and Expression Blend. These tools along with related tools and documentation, including the simulator and the online guides and samples, help the developer for creating, debugging, deploying, and updating applications.
- Cloud services: The various cloud services supported in Windows Phone 7 are Windows Azure, Xbox LIVE services, notification services, location services, and a variety of other web services. These different features allow developers to share data across the cloud. This in turn benefits consumers by providing a seamless experience without having to depend on the type of device they are using. Windows Phone OS also supports connections to third-party web services.

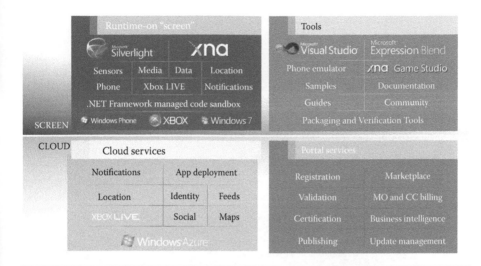

Figure 18.11   Windows Phone platform architecture components.

■ Portal Services: The Windows Phone Marketplace provides robust services, which allow application developers to register, certify, and market their applications.

18.2.3.1.1 Runtime on Screen

For Windows Phone, all the development happens in managed code, as the Silverlight and the XNA frameworks are used. This ensures that the managed code runs in a protected sandbox, which in turn allows a faster development cycle for safe and secure applications. All the applications that are written for the Silverlight and the XNA frameworks run on Windows Phone 7 with minor changes for screen size or for using device-specific features.

The two frameworks of Silverlight and XNA, the common base class library, and Windows Phone-specific components provide a large number of components for developers to develop applications (Figure 18.12):

■ Silverlight
  – Rich Internet application style UIs can be designed using the Silverlight framework.
  – Windows Phone Silverlight application UI is exposed through a set of pages.
  – The UI's look and feel can be enhanced by using Windows Phone controls that match the Windows Phone visual style.
  – Visual Studio or Expression Blend is used in designing extensible application markup language (XAML)-based interfaces.

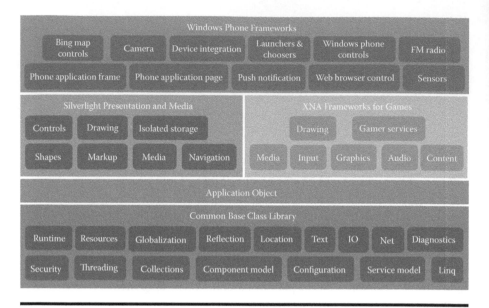

Figure 18.12 Windows Phone OS architecture.

- XNA Framework
  - Exclusively for game developers
  - Includes software, services, and resources required for developing on Microsoft gaming platforms
  - Provides a complete set of managed APIs for game development
  - Allows professional developers to quickly create games on platforms such as Windows Phone, Windows7, Xbox 360, and Zune HD
  - Includes 2D sprite-based APIs supporting rotation, scaling, stretching, and filtering
  - Also includes 3D graphics APIs for 3D geometry, textures, etc.
- Sensors
  - A variety of sensors supply data that can be consumed by applications.
  - The framework includes sensors for multitouch input, accelerometer, and microphone sensors, and all these sensors are accessible by APIs.
- Media
  - Used for building a rich UI that incorporates graphics, animation, and media
  - Available for both the Silverlight and the XNA framework developers
  - Variety of media formats are supported by managed APIs
  - Allow discovery and enumeration of media present on the device and also supports playback of that media
- Data
  - Isolated storage allows an application for creating and maintaining data, which is a sandboxed isolated virtual folder

- It prevents unauthorized access and in turn prevents data corruption by other applications.
- All input–output operations related to the application are restricted to isolated storage for that application.
- Applications do not have direct access to the OS file system.
■ Location
- APIs are available to access the physical location information from the device using Microsoft Location Service.
- Location APIs on the device work along with the location cloud services.
    • Using location APIs, developers have the option to query for the current location, set the desired accuracy of the location data collected, get access to device heading and speed, subscribe to location-changed events, and calculate the distance between points.

18.2.3.1.2 Tools

Developers can download and install the package that will include the necessary tools required to start developing applications for Windows Phone, and these tools are listed here:

■ Visual Studio 2010
- IDEs are used for building Windows Phone applications.
- Using the IDE, developers can create Silverlight or XNA Framework applications that can run on Windows Phone.
- The tool includes the project system, designer, debugger, packager, and manifest generation.
■ Expression blend
- It is used in creating the design of Silverlight-based applications on a Windows Phone.
- It allows developers to create XAML-based UI for Windows Phone applications.
- Behaviors for the XAML-based applications can be then implemented by developers in Visual Studio.
■ Windows Phone Emulator
- The Windows Phone Emulator is integrated into the Visual Studio and Expression blend.
- Testing and debugging applications are easier and faster.
- The tool supports application deployment, debugging, and application execution.
- Support for the graphics processing unit (GPU) emulation, orientation change, etc., is available.

- XNA Game Studio
  - Extends the Visual Studio tools in supporting the XNA framework
  - Used to build games for Microsoft Windows, Microsoft Xbox 360 system, Microsoft Zune, and Windows Phone
  - Managed-code class library in XNA framework contains functionality targeted specifically at game development tasks
  - Includes tools for adding graphical and audio content into the game
- Samples, documentation, guides, and community
  - Documentation, sample code, and applications are available.
  - Forums, blogs, and web sites are available for developers for query clarification and also for sharing information.
  - Visual Studio Help system allows developers to update their documentation sets.

18.2.3.1.3 Cloud Services

The Windows Phone Application development platform provides many features for building web-integrated applications. Windows Phone is powerful and rich, and the cloud makes it even more powerful. Cloud Services have the following advantages:

- Always available
- More scalable
- Not dependent on battery life
- Contains more functionality

For developer applications to get data on the phone, services built on Azure or any other third-party web services can be utilized. The Windows Phone Marketplace can be used by developers to certify and get their application distributed to consumers:

- Notifications
  - It enables efficient, dynamic, and latest information and communication channels.
  - Windows Phone Application Platform provides APIs to notify the application when relevant events occur.
  - It eliminates the need for polling and in turn reduces battery consumption.
- Location cloud services
  - These services work with the location APIs on the phone.
  - WiFi, cellular, and GPS provide data for position look-up.
  - Assisted GPS is available.
- Identity, feeds, social, and maps services
  - An extensive variety of web services is available in the cloud.

- It allows consumers to identify themselves.
- It allows interaction with social forums.
- It receives data feeds.
- Maps can be used for navigation and location-based services.
■ Azure
- Internet scale cloud computing and services platform that is hosted in Microsoft data centers.
- Supports functionality to develop applications that range from consumer web to enterprise scenarios.
- Includes a cloud OS along with developer services.
- Fully interoperable with support of industry standards and various web protocols (including representational state transfer and simple object access protocol).

18.2.3.1.4 Portal Services

The Windows Phone Marketplace is a central location for developers to submit and get their applications certified. It also acts as a centralized location for consumers, from which they can buy or update their applications.

■ Registration and validation
- Developers can get started on the App Hub by signing up with a Live ID.
- After successful registration, developers can obtain the tools in a single download.
■ Certification, publishing, and update management
- Developers can submit and certify their applications (in Marketplace) using the various tools provided.
- Applications are submitted in Marketplace in the .xap file format.
- Developers can track the submission status of their application and can also receive notifications on certification status.
- After an application is certified, it will be published on the Marketplace.
- Developers have the option to set the pricing and also select the markets (country wise) where they want to publish the application.
■ Windows Phone Marketplace and billing
- A common place where developers make their applications available for purchase by consumers
- Supported mode of payment for application includes mobile operator and credit card billing
■ Business intelligence: Business intelligence provides developers with information about their application in Marketplace.

18.2.3.2 OS Features

Figure 18.13 illustrates Windows Phone OS Features.

Feature	Details
Handset display	800 WVGA / 480 HVGA OR 480 WVGA / 320 HVGA
Database	SQLCE and SQLite can be used as local databases.
Connectivity	Various devices are available that supports technologies including GSM/EDGE, CDMA, HSDPA 3.6, UMTS, Bluetooth, Wi-Fi etc.
Messaging service	SMS and MMS is supported. Windows Phone combined messaging through "threads". Threads allow the Windows Phone user to engage with his contacts through Windows Live Messenger and Facebook Chat as well as traditional text messages
Multiple language support	Supports around 25 different languages
Web browser	Internet Explorer Mobile with a rendering engine that is based on Internet Explorer 9
Java support	Not supported
Media support	MP3, AAC, AAC+, eAAC+, WAV, WMA pro, AMR-NB, MIDI, H.263, H.264, WMV, MPEG4, MPEG4@ HD 720p 30fps, DivX, XviD
Multitouch	Multitouch gestures are supported
Multitasking	Multitasking is supported
Additional hardware support	GPS, Accelerometer, Compass, Light Proximity, Camera, GPU, CPU
Bluetooth	Window Phone supports Bluetooth 2.1 + EDR

Figure 18.13   Windows Phone OS features.

18.2.3.3 OS Versions

Figure 18.14 illustrates Windows Phone OS Versions.

18.2.3.4 Market Place for Applications

Once the developer completes the application development, the application can be made available to others using Windows Phone Marketplace. In order to publish the application to Marketplace, developers are required to submit the .xap file created for the application. The .xap file is a compiled Silverlight application that is in compressed format. The compressed file contains all the required information for the application. The XAP file includes an application icon, start tile, application manifest, and the necessary dynamic link libraries (DLLs) for the applications and the licensing terms that determine how the application can be used. Next, the developer signs into the App Hub and uploads the application package for certification.

The certification process includes static validation along with automated testing of the application to make sure that the application meets all the guidelines published. It also verifies that the application works for the languages and markets indicated. The certification process also verifies that the application does not adversely affect the working of the phone. Developers can publish applications to the consumers only through this way. Once the package has been certified for

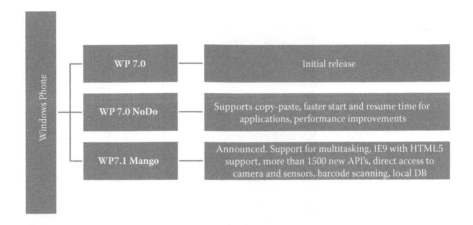

Figure 18.14   Windows Phone OS versions.

meeting the Windows Phone Marketplace certification requirements, the developers will be notified, and they can publish it to the Marketplace.

After a Windows Phone application is published to the Marketplace, the developer uses the App Hub to manage the versions of applications that are made available for purchase.

18.2.4 Windows Mobile

Windows Mobile is a mobile OS developed by Microsoft and was used in smartphones and mobile devices. Currently, it is phased out to support only specialized markets (Figure 18.15).

The latest version is Windows Mobile 6.5. Windows Mobile OS is based on the Windows CE 5.2 kernel. It is programmed in C++ programming language and features a set of basic applications developed with the Microsoft Windows API. There are three versions of Windows Mobile available for various hardware devices:

- Windows Mobile Professional (for smartphones with touch screens)
- Windows Mobile Standard (for phones with regular screens)
- Windows Mobile Classic (for pocket PCs)

The comparison of the different versions of Windows Mobile is given in Figure 18.16.

18.2.4.1 OS Architecture

Windows Mobile 6 works with the Windows CE 5.2 kernel. Windows Mobile 5 uses the Windows CE 5.1 kernel. The kernel in Windows CE 5.x is a fully preemptive and multithreaded kernel. Windows CE is a single-user OS. The read-only memory (ROM) stores the entire OS. The kernel provides the base OS functionality for a Windows

Figure 18.15   Windows Mobile device.

Classic	Professional	Standard
Touch screen PDAs	Touch screen devices with added phone capabilities	Nontouch screen Phones
One-tier security ✓Applications must be signed with privileged M2M cert to call privileged APIs ✓Applications signed with normal M2M cert can call normal APIs without user permission ✓Unsigned applications can make calls to normal APIs with user permission (prompt)	One-tier security ✓Applications must be signed with privileged M2M cert to call privileged APIs ✓Applications signed with normal M2M cert can call normal APIs without user permission ✓Unsigned applications can make calls to normal APIs with user permission (prompt)	Two-tier security ✓Drivers and pre-boot applications require privileged mode signing ✓Applications signed with normal M2M cert can call all APIs without user permission ✓Unsigned applications can call all API with users permission (prompt)
Compatible with standard touch screen Windows Mobile software.	Compatible with standard touch screen Windows Mobile software.	Will require standard smartphones software

Figure 18.16   Windows Mobile comparison.

Mobile device. The Kernel resides in the memory and also performs essential functions such as controlling memory and files and allocating system resources (Figure 18.17).

Windows CE kernel handles memory management along with process and thread scheduling. Most of these services are implemented within the nk.exe executable. Coredll.dll contains the entire OS core DLL module. Other kernel facilities such as the file, graphics, and services subsystems run as individual processes. Windows Mobile supports a 32-bit address space. Windows CE supports a maximum of 32 simultaneous processes wherein each process is considered as a single

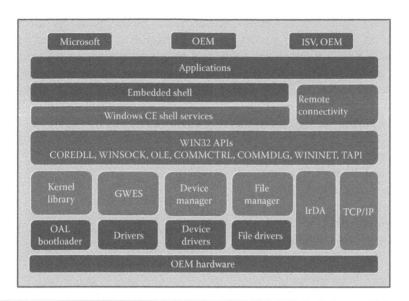

Figure 18.17   Windows Mobile OS architecture.

instance of the application. Each application can have any number of threads, which is limited only by the available memory. These 32 different processes include system processes such as nk.exe, file system (filesys.exe), device manager (device. exe), and graphical windowing environment system (GWES.exe).

Windows CE supports a single, flat virtual address space shared between all the processes. When a Windows Mobile device boots up, the kernel will allocate a single 4-GB virtual address space that will be shared by all the processes. The upper 2 GB of this virtual memory address space is assigned to the kernel and the lower 2-GB region is split into 64 slots of 32 MB each. The lower 32 slots contain different processes, except Slot 0 and Slot 1. Slot 0 will always contain the current running process, and Slot 1 will contain eXecute-in-place (XiP) DLLs. In short, processes can address up to 4 GB of memory:

■ Only the lower 2 GB is available for use by the process.
■ Memory allocations made by the process will return memory in the lower 2 GB of the address space.
■ Upper 2 GB will be used by the system for its own data.

For memory requirements that are less than 64 KB, an application will use local heap, which is provided to all applications or applications that can create separate heaps. The kernel allocates memory to the stack for a new process or thread. The kernel memory functions can be also used to allocate and deallocate virtual memory or to use memory on the local heap or to create separate heaps and to allocate memory from the stack. Processes can also use memory-mapped objects to share data.

The user mode and the kernel mode are the two primary modes of execution available on Windows CE 5.x devices. The current execution mode of an application is managed as per-thread basis, and privileged threads have an option to change their execution mode. All the application threads on most scenarios will run under the user mode. User mode threads will not have total access to the device and will have to depend on the kernel services to accomplish most of their work. The kernel mainly contains the following functionalities:

- Memory architecture
- Scheduling
- Real-time performance
- Loader
- System calls
- Kernel power management

1. Memory architecture:

When a process is initialized, the OS maps the DLLs and memory components according to the following process:

- The memory architecture includes XIP DLLs, read-and-write sections of other XIP DLLs, and all non-XIP DLLs.
- DLLs are controlled by the loader, and the loader will load all the DLLs to the same address for each process. Stack, heap, and executables are created and will be mapped from the bottom of the address space. Always the bottom 64 KB of memory will remain free. DLLs and ROM DLL read-and-write sections will be loaded to the top of the address space.
- Stack: Stack is the memory storage area for variables referenced in a function. In Windows Mobile, a separate stack for every thread is managed in the system. The default stack limit is 64 KB, with 8 KB reserved for overflow error control. Exceeding the stack limit will cause a system access violation that closes the application.
- Heap: Heap is the portion of memory reserved for the application to allocate and free on a per-byte basis. Heap can optimize memory use. When a process is created, a default heap is also created. The application can use this process heap for its memory allocations. This heap will grow and shrink according to the usage. Performance will suffer if the default heap becomes fragmented because of the amount of memory allocated in the heap.
- It also includes a data section for each process.

2. Scheduler:

Scheduler is a major component of the Windows Mobile system. During scheduling, the kernel will maintain a priority list of individual threads in the OS. The scheduling system will also control the order in which threads are arranged and also allow their paths to interact with each other in a predictable fashion. When an interrupt occurs in the scheduling system, the scheduler will take this into account and reprioritize threads accordingly.

3. Real-time performance:

Real-time OS is just an element of the real-time system. It will require the support of hardware, OS, and applications to give real-time performance.

4. Loader:

Windows Mobile loader loads modules, executables, and DLLs into virtual memory so that these modules can be executed by the OS.

5. System calls:

A system call is a function that resides in a different process, and the kernel is notified about this. The kernel will then call the proper server process to handle the system call.

6. Kernel power management:

The kernel operates in several power states and transitions between the power states when a trigger event occurs.

18.2.4.2 OS Features

Figure 18.18 illustrates the Windows Mobile OS features.

18.2.4.3 OS Versions

Figure 18.19 illustrates the Windows Mobile OS versions.

18.2.4.4 Market Place for Applications

Windows Marketplace for Mobile is a service supported by Microsoft for its Windows Mobile platform. This service allows users to browse, download, and install applications developed by third parties. This service is available for use directly on Windows Mobile 6.x devices and on personal computers.

As on July 2011, the Marketplace web site does not support Windows Mobile 6.x application download. Users can continue to download applications using the Marketplace Client in Windows Mobile 6.x phones.

18.2.5 BlackBerry

Research In Motion (RIM) manufactures the BlackBerry line of smartphones. The OS used in these mobiles is the BlackBerry OS. BlackBerry provides users with

Feature	Details
Handset display	Devices available with different resolutions. (320*240;640*480; 320 x 320 and 800 x 480 [WVGA])
Database	SQLCE and SQLite can be used as database
Connectivity	Various devices are available that supports technologies including GSM/EDGE, WCDMA, CDMA, HSDPA3.6 UMTS, Bluetooth, WiFi etc.
Messaging service	SMS and MMS is supported
Multiple language support	Supports muliple languages
Web browser	Comes with Internet explorer Mobile
Java support	Does not support Java
Media support	MPEG-4, H.263, H.264, AVI, WAV, MP3, MP4, MIDI, WMV, 3GP, 3G2, WMA
Multitouch	WM 6.5.3 version supports multitouch
Multitasking	Multitasking is supported
Additional hardware support	GPS and A-GPS
Bluetooth	Bluetooth® 2.0 with enhanced data rate and A2Dp for stereo wireless headsets

Figure 18.18   Windows Mobile OS features.

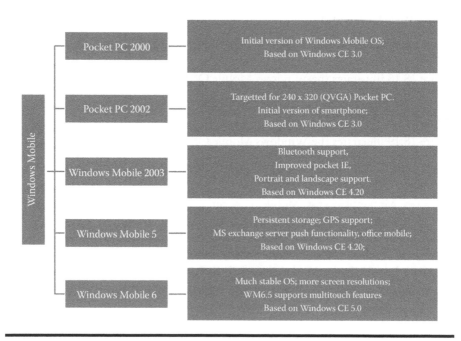

Figure 18.19   Windows Mobile OS versions.

Figure 18.20 BlackBerry devices.

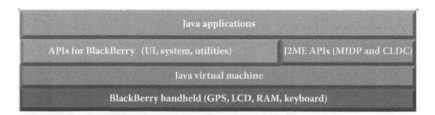

Figure 18.21 BlackBerry OS architecture.

wireless access to a full suite of business applications, including e-mail, corporate data, phone, SMS, web, and organizer (Figure 18.20).

18.2.5.1 OS Architecture

The BlackBerry OS is used in phones that are produced and marketed by RIM. The BlackBerry OS is programmed in the C++ programming language. RIM tightly controls the details of BlackBerry internals, making very few information publicly available. The BlackBerry OS is a modern OS that includes features such as multitasking, interprocess communication, and threads. The OS is developed by RIM, and it is designed in such a way to take inputs from input devices such as track pad, track ball, and track wheel (Figure 18.21). The BlackBerry OS supports the Java mobile information device profile (MIDP) 1.0 and wireless application protocol (WAP) 1.2:

- Java has MIDP as a specification used for mobile devices.
- WAP is a protocol supporting the WAP browser.

All OS and device features are accessed using APIs provided by RIM or by J2ME APIs. BlackBerry supports two types of memory:

- Flash
    - Nonvolatile and persists data even when the device runs out of power.
    - BlackBerry OS, applications, and data are stored within flash memory.
    - Flash memory chips are expensive.
    - Latest devices have 64 MB of flash.
- SRAM: SRAM is used for storing runtime object data and also holds information only when the device has power.

18.2.5.2 OS Features

Figure 18.22 illustrates BlackBerry OS features.

18.2.5.3 OS Versions

Figure 18.23 illustrates BlackBerry OS versions.

18.2.5.4 App World for Applications

BlackBerry App World is an application by RIM used for the application distribution service for a majority of BlackBerry devices. This service provides BlackBerry

Feature	Details
Handset display	Devices available with different resolutions like 320 × 240, 360 × 400; 640 × 480 (VGA)
Database	SQLite can be used
Connectivity	Various devices are available that supports technologies including GSM/EDGE, CDMA, HSDPA3.6 UMTS, Bluetooth, WiFi.
Messaging service	SMS and MMS supported
Multiple language support	Suppored
Web browser	BlackBerry browser contains portions of the WebKit Open-Source Project and JavaScriptCore Project
Java support	Yes
Media support	Audio: MP3, WAVE, WMA, AAC+, MIDI, AMR, eAAC+, FIAC, OGG Video: MP4, WMV, H.263, H.264, DivX, WMV, XviD, 3gp
Multitouch	Latest version support Multitouch
Multitasking	Supported
Additional hardware support	GPS
Bluetooth	Supports various Bluetooth 2.1 profiles that can be managed by IT policies A2DP; AVRCU; DUN; HFP; HSP; SPP; SIM access profile

Figure 18.22 BlackBerry OS features.

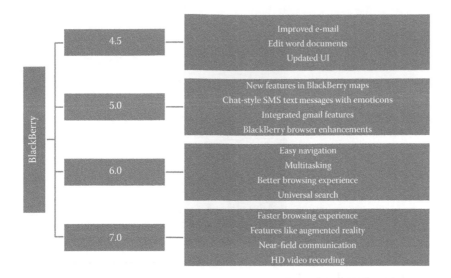

Figure 18.23 BlackBerry OS versions.

users an option to discover, try, purchase, download, rate, and review products for devices from a single location. BlackBerry App World provides vendors a location that is highly secure and accessible to distribute products to the consumers. App World 2.1 version introduced in-app purchases of digital goods and also allows for add-ons to be purchased within applications.

18.2.6 Symbian

Symbian is an open-source OS designed for smartphones and currently maintained by Nokia. Symbian OS is flexible and scalable as it is used for a wide variety of feature and smartphones. The Symbian platform is the successor to Symbian OS and Nokia Series 60 (Figure 18.24).

18.2.6.1 OS Architecture

Symbian has a microkernel architecture that supports the most basic functionality so as to maximize robustness, availability, and responsiveness. The EKA2 real-time kernel contains the most basic primitives. It will require an extended kernel to implement any further abstractions. It contains a scheduler, memory management, and device drivers (Figure 18.25). The overall model is divided into the following layers:

■ UI framework layer
■ Application services layer
   – Java ME

Figure 18.24   Symbian device.

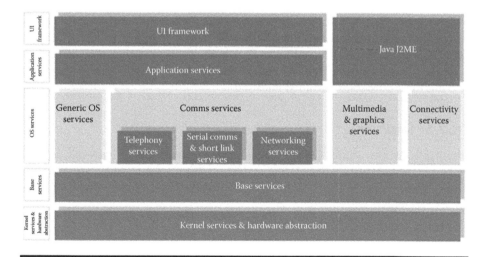

Figure 18.25   Symbian OS architecture.

- OS services layer
  - Generic OS services
  - Communications services
  - Multimedia and graphics services
  - Connectivity services
- Base services layer
- Hardware interface and kernel services layer

1. UI framework:
   - The UI layer is separated from the OS.
     - It helps the phone manufacturers to provide the required UI for their phones.
     - Series 60, UIQ, Foma, etc., are examples.
   - It contains graphics, text layout, and font-rendering libraries.
2. Application services:
   - UI-independent application support.
   - Personal information manager, office application engines, and multimedia protocols are other parts of this layer.
3. OS services:
   - Generic OS features
     - Includes system kernel, file server, memory management, and device management.
     - Manages system resources and is responsible for time-slicing the applications and system tasks.
     - Contains device drivers that provide the control and acts as an interface to hardware items such as keyboard, display, infrared port, etc.
   - Contains communication, multimedia, and connectivity services
     - Provides communication and extensive computing services.
     - Provides data management, communications, graphics, etc.
     - Has Bluetooth and browser engines.
     - Supports data synchronization and internationalization.
4. Base services:
   - Contains the lower level libraries providing abstractions of the kernel hardware.
   - Allows lowest level reachable by user-side operations
     - File server.
     - User library.
     - Plug-in framework managing plug-ins, store, central repository, database management system, and cryptographic services.
   - Includes the Text Window Server and the Text Shell.
5. Kernel services and hardware interface:
   - Contains the kernel of the OS.
   - Contains the physical and logical device drivers for hardware.

All native Symbian C++ applications are developed upon three framework classes that are defined by the application architecture: application class, document class, and application UI class.

These classes will create the fundamental application behavior. The remaining needed functions such as the application view, data model, and data interface must be created independently and will have to interact through the APIs with the other classes.

Some of the key features based on which Symbian OS is defined are given below:

- Minimal demands on batteries and to support low memory
- Applications are designed to work in parallel
- Runtime memory requirements are minimized
- Security mechanisms for secure communications and data storage
- Support for international environment using built-in Unicode character sets
- Optimized memory management

18.2.6.2 OS Features

Figure 18.26 illustrates Symbian OS features.

18.2.6.3 OS Versions

Figure 18.27 illustrates Symbian OS versions.

Feature	Details
Handset display	240 × 320 (QVGA); 360 × 640; 640 × 480 (VGA)
Database	SQLite can be used as DB
Connectivity	Various devices are available that supports technologies including GSM/EDGE, CDMA, HSDPA 3.6, UMTS, Bluetooth, WiFi, etc.
Messaging service	SMS and MMS is supported.
Multiple language support	Yes, supports multiple languages
Web browser	S60 browser, Opera Mobile, and a new browser with the release of Symbian Anna
Java support	Supports Java ME applciations
Media support	Audio: All file types Video: H.263, H.264, WMV, MPEG4, MPEG4@ HD 720p 30fps, MKV DivX, XviD
Multitouch	Supported in Symbian^3/Anna/Belle
Multitasking	Multitasking is supported
Additional hardware support	Integrated A-GPS, pentaband 3G radio
Bluetooth	Symbian Bluetooth stack runs in user space rather than kernel space and has public APIs for L2CAP, RFCOMM, SDP, AVRCP, etc. Profiles supported in the OS include GAP, OBEX, SPP, AVRCP, GAVDP, PAN, and PBAP

Figure 18.26   Symbian OS features.

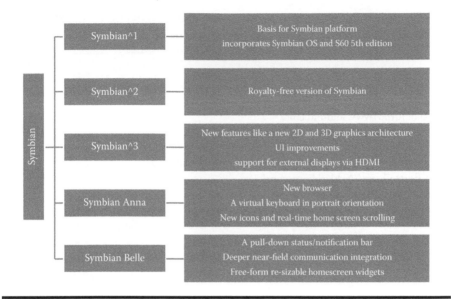

Figure 18.27   Symbian OS versions.

18.2.6.4 Ovi Store for Applications

Customers can download mobile games, applications, images, videos, and ring tones to their Nokia devices. As with the case of other markets, items are available free, and some others can be purchased through operator billing for selected operators or through credit card payments.

Ovi Store offers customers different contents that are compatible with their mobile devices. Customers can also share recommendations with their friends. Nokia offers a 70% revenue share of gross sales to the developers.

18.3 Conclusion

The mobile OS market is led by Android as it is open source and the number of manufacturers supporting it is large. iPhone and Windows Phone are next in line. Market researchers such as IDC and Gartner are predicting that Windows Phone will overtake iPhone by 2015. BlackBerry will be taking the next position. With Nokia moving away from the Symbian platform to Windows Phone, Symbian will slowly lose its market share mainly to Android and Windows Phone. Windows Mobile is not considered here as smartphones are no longer released on Windows Mobile.

With the number of applications available in the different market places, the Android market still leads by more than 500,000 active apps closely followed by iOS App Store with 470,000 apps. Windows Phone Marketplace and BlackBerry App World have around 32,000 apps for users to download.

Additional Reading

Android: http://www.android.com/
iPhone: http://www.apple.com/iphone/
Windows Phone: http://www.microsoft.com/windowsphone
Windows Mobile: http://www.microsoft.com/windowsmobile
BlackBerry: http://us.blackberry.com/
Symbian: http://symbian.nokia.com/
IDC Predictions: http://www.idc.com/getdoc.jsp?containerId=prUS22871611

Chapter 19

Mobile Application Designing

Wireless computing devices are proliferating rapidly, creating the need for software applications that can handle the realities of the mobile computing lifestyle. A mobile device that is used as a medium for making and receiving phone calls is a thing of the past. Currently, with the technological advances, we see mobile users doing anything from shopping on a mobile device to tracking their loved ones using mobiles. Technological advances are happening in different areas of the entire mobility ecosystem, including mobile device operating systems (OSs), hardware, carriers, device manufacturers, content creators, users, etc.

19.1 Introduction

In this chapter, we cover the various architecture and design considerations that need to be considered while developing a mobile application.

19.2 Mobile Application Technology

Mobile applications can be broadly classified into the following four categories:

- Thin client application (browser-based)
- Thick client application (downloaded or preinstalled in a device)
- Rich client application
- Message-based application

19.2.1 Thin Client Applications

Thin client applications or browser-based applications run in the web browser on a mobile device. All enterprises provide information that is useful for their mobile customers or associates on their web sites. When data specific to desktop environment are provided on to the mobiles, end users will get a less-than-satisfactory experience owing to the small screen sizes and keyboards on their mobile. To overcome this scenario, enterprises need to have strategies that optimize the capabilities of a mobile-specific user interface (UI) on a typical smartphone.

The key challenges in implementing a mobile browser-based application are because of the interoperability and usability problems. Interoperability issues are raised because of platform fragmentation happening in mobile devices, mobile OSs, and even mobile browsers. Usability problems are centered on the size of the mobile phone form-factors (limitation of small screen sizes, display resolutions, and user input or operation). HTML5 controls can support very rich, interactive, and compelling uses, except in some scenarios. These technologies are currently available in almost all the latest versions of smartphones such as Apple iPhone OS, Windows Phone 7, Google Android OS, etc. The key advantages are as follows:

■ Users need to develop the application once and deploy to a number of mobile platforms.
■ Web developers have an option of transitioning easily into mobile development.
■ The technology has the ability to support the UI optimized for mobiles.
■ The existing modules can be reused to integrate into back-end applications.

The key disadvantages are as follows:

■ Limited off-line capabilities
■ Limited support available for integrating with device hardware and calendars, which are becoming highly critical for mobile applications

19.2.2 Thick Client Applications

Thick client applications can also be downloaded, or they are native applications. That is, an application built for a mobile device is either downloaded to a device or is present when the device is purchased. Most of these applications provide a better user experience, as these applications are fully capable of taking advantage of the mobile device's unique capabilities.

But as these applications are device-specific, separate applications will be required for different types of device. This will increase the development costs exponentially. In addition to the development cost, when applications are upgraded or new applications are developed, mechanisms are required to deliver these applications to the devices on which they run. Almost every mobile OS vendor has created application stores (such as Apple's App Store, Microsoft's Windows Phone Marketplace, Google's Android Market, and RIM BlackBerry's App World) from where users can download applications written specifically for their phones.

Various solutions are available in the market that provides "write once, run anywhere" functionality for mobile device application development. These solutions help the developer to create applications, either for the customer or for the employees, once and deploy them on various mobile devices from different vendors and running different platforms. The evolution of mobile device technology allows cross-platform integration to ensure that all end users are treated equally. Handsets with near-field communication (NFC) chips provide a secure and simple application solution. These phones interact with contact-less terminals and other NFC devices, by sending and receiving data by tapping. The key advantages are as follows:

- Consistent performance
- Capable of having disconnected operation mode
- Close integration with all device peripherals such as global positioning system (GPS), camera, etc.

The key disadvantages are as follows:

- Development knowledge cannot be used across platforms. Applications developed are specific to a platform, which makes the developer write the same application for multiple platforms. JavaME-based apps are an exception to this.
- In most of the application markets, thick client applications will have to go through an approval process to be available to end users on the corresponding market.

19.2.3 Rich Client Architecture

Rich client applications also known as hybrid applications generally consist of both a native application layer and a web-based application content. The native application layer that runs on the device will provide the following features to the application:

- An executable of the application that resides in the device
- Acts as a web container for web content
- Can integrate with device hardware or services such as camera or calendar

The key advantages are as follows:

- Code reuse and can be shared across multiple mobile platforms
- Combines the power of native applications and the ease of web development
- Good integration with device peripherals and native services
- Supports off-line operations

	Thick	Rich	Thin	SMS
Usability	High	High	Moderate	High
Out of coverage	High	Limited	No	No
Security	High	High	Moderate	Moderate
TCO	High	High	Low	Low
Device range*	Few	Limited	High	High
Peripheral support	Yes	High	Low	NA
Time for deployment	High	High	Low	Low
Graphics presentation	High	Moderate	Less (emphasis more on text)	Less (emphasis more on text)

Figure 19.1 Comparison of mobile application development options.

The key disadvantages are as follows:

■ Complex business logic required by mobile enterprise applications will not be adequately supported by Java scripting.
■ No robust tools are available for supporting rapid application development for mobile enterprise applications.

19.2.4 Message-Based Applications

Message-based application uses short message service (SMS) or multimedia messaging service to exchange messages with the user. Message-based applications are not user friendly as other methods, and message-based applications work on the most of mobile phones including smartphones and feature phones. Almost all mobile phones support SMS for short messages.

Figure 19.1 gives a comparison of the various features of the different types of mobile applications.

19.3 Architecture and Design Considerations

Mobile application design and development is a complex act as it requires high levels of application performance along with usability, while working with many device-related constraints.

19.3.1 Thick Client versus Thin Client

While considering the development of a mobile-based application, one of the key architectural decisions that have to be made is the kind of application that needs to be developed. The distinction between mobile web and native applications is slowly diminishing as mobile browsers have now gained direct access to the hardware features of mobile devices, and the speed and abilities of browser-based applications are also improving. Persistent storage and access to sophisticated UI graphics functions might further reduce the need for the development of platform-specific native applications.

The key factors that are to be considered when users decide on a thick client application are when the application is supposed to have the following features:

- The application needs to support off-line scenario as well as occasionally connected scenario.
- The complex business process logic requires local processing.
- The application should provide access to device hardware resources.

The key drawback of thick client applications is the difficulty in maintaining the code for different platforms. Also separate distribution and upgrade infrastructure is required.

19.3.2 Network Communication

Network communication on the device is considered to be slow and costly. All network communications should be planned to have asynchronous mode of operation. During the design of the application, users should try to transmit data in bulk rather than firing individual requests for each action. This will help in reducing the network traffic greatly, which will further improve battery performance. Whenever a large amount of data is transmitted it needs to be compressed. The network delay will be more if the amount of data that needs to be transmitted is high. This will have an adverse impact on application performance. Data transfer should be in binary rather than XML or text format.

- Asynchronous, threaded communication design will improve the application's usability in occasionally connected scenarios.
- If the application is designed to run on a mobile phone, the application needs to allow suspend and resume features or even exit the application when a phone call or a message is received.
- Communication over untrusted connections should be protected.
- Web services can be used for communication if data are accessed from multiple sources and disconnected mode of operation is required.

19.3.3 User Experience

For mobile applications, user experience is the key to success. A UI should be rich, intuitive, and responsive. When the screen is designed, a developer should consider the fact that that user is focused on discrete tasks. A thorough understanding of the user's context and objectives is critical while designing a mobile application.

- Do not blindly reuse designs designed to run on desktop devices.
- Ensure that the UI elements are clearly visible in low light.
- Ensure effective and easy-to-read color combinations.
- Group related objects on the screen.
- Ensure that the UI is predictable.
- The user needs to enter only absolutely required data or information. The application should have all the essential data and functionality needed for the user to take action.
- User needs should be presented with the minimum number of options on any screen.
- Avoid using fixed and small font sizes. Enable options such as font size and idle-time settings.
- Avoid complex interaction patterns forcing close attention of the user for long periods of time.
- Provide adequate feedback on task progress and status of the tasks.
- Use simple navigation structures focusing on one task at a time.

19.3.4 Battery Power

The applications developed for mobile devices shall judiciously use the device resources to extend the battery power consumption. Few of the key strategies that are followed for mobile application development are given below.

- The mobile application has to be designed such that activities that require polling need to be avoided. When applications do polling, they should not allow the CPU to go to sleep, which in turn reduces battery life.
- The UI should not be updated if the application is in background.
- The number of background-processing threads should be limited.
- Idle time should be maximized by combining small work. Less power will be taken to perform a set of calculations at once. When the application does small bits of work periodically, the CPU needs to be waking up more often so as to do user tasks.
- Overaccessing the disk should be avoided.
- The applications should turn off the WiFi and cellular radios when there is lack of activity for some duration.
- The device should use much more power when it transmits data for a longer period of time than when it transmits the same data in a shorter duration of time.
- Connecting to the network using WiFi radios should be preferred as it uses less power.
- The UI should not be updated in the background mode.

- Nonessential network communication should be triggered only by manual input or when the device is running using external power sources.
- The communication protocols selected should be in such a way that only a very minimal amount of information is transmitted over the wireless network. This sustains battery life by less serialization and also improves performance due to lesser utilization of network bandwidth.
- Frequent turning on or off of various radios is not recommended.

19.3.5 Device Memory

Mobile device applications are limited to the amount of memory that is made available for the applications to use. Using large amounts of memory will seriously degrade system performance, potentially causing the system to terminate the application. In addition, as applications are running under the multitasking environment, the applications share system memory with all the other applications running in the device. Therefore, developers need to make it a practice to reduce the amount of memory used up by their application.

The amount of free memory available is directly related to the relative performance of the application. The lesser the amount of free memory, the more issues the application is likely to face because the system will face issues related to fulfilling the memory requests of the various applications. If memory issue occurs, the system can remove suspended applications and other nonvolatile resources from the memory. Removing those applications and resources from the memory can be considered as a temporary solution, especially if they are needed again later. It will be always better to minimize memory use and clean up the memory that was used by the application in a timely manner.

19.3.6 Security

One of the key aspects that concern any mobile user is the security of data stored in the consumer's mobile device. The device application should ensure that all the sensitive information is encrypted while it is transferred across the network or when it is stored on the phone's persistent memory. Also, the developer needs to design the application in a way that sensitive data stored in the device are removed as soon as the data are no longer required. Applications need to have an effective authentication and authorization strategy so as to improve the security and reliability of the application.

19.3.7 Layered Approach

Mobile applications generally follow a layered architectural design. It helps in improving the reusability and maintainability of the code. At the highest level, the architecture can be logically viewed as a presentation, business, and data layer.

19.3.8 Multithreaded Solutions

The main thread handles all the mobile application touch events and other user inputs. A developer will have to ensure that the application running on the device will always be responsive to the user. The application should not be designed to have the main thread performing long-running or unbounded tasks, such as tasks that access the network. Instead, all these tasks need to be moved onto background threads.

19.3.9 Minimal Processing on Device

Mobile devices act as an option to generate user input. Other than the basic validation of the data that are received, all data processing needs to happen in the back-end servers. This will help in increasing the battery life and the performance of the mobile devices.

19.3.10 Multiple Platform Versions

When developing an application, the user will need to select the platform version against which the application will be compiled. In general, users should compile the application against the minimum possible version of the OS platform that the application can support.

19.3.11 Forward Compatibility

Mobile applications are mostly forward-compatible with new versions of the OS platform. The application will run successfully on all later versions of the platform, except in cases where the application uses an application programming interface (API) or a part of the API, which is later removed.

19.3.12 Backward Compatibility

Applications will most unlikely be backward compatible with versions of the OS platform that precede the version against which they were compiled. Each new version of the mobile platform can include new APIs, which might give the applications access to new features provided in the platform, or it can be modifications of the existing APIs. The new APIs will be accessible to applications when they are running on the new platform and also when running on later versions of the platform. Conversely, earlier versions of the OS platform will not have new APIs, and, therefore, the applications that use the new APIs cannot run on previous versions of the platforms.

19.4 Conclusion

In this chapter, the different classifications of mobile applications are covered. With HTML5, thin client applications are very similar to thick client applications.

HTML5 can perform activities such as client-side database access, geolocation support, audio and video support, off-line application caching, etc. With almost all the major mobile OSs supporting HTML5, thin client applications gain prominence over thick client applications. The HTML5 specs will be finalized only by 2014. So until then thick client applications will dominate the mobility landscape. The various architecture and design-related considerations that a developer needs to remember while developing an application for mobile devices have been covered in this chapter.

Additional Reading

http://developer.apple.com/library/ios/#documentation/userexperience/conceptual/mobile-hig/Introduction/Introduction.html

http://msdn.microsoft.com/en-us/library/bb158602.aspx

http://msdn.microsoft.com/en-us/library/bb158602.aspx

http://msdn.microsoft.com/en-us/library/cc872774.aspx

http://download.microsoft.com/download/7/7/3/77371BBD-6613-4C1A-ACBF-08365C09D5FA/UI Design and Interaction Guide for Windows Phone 7 v2.0.pdf

http://www.forum.nokia.com/info/sw.nokia.com/id/5c419b14–75ff-4791-b1a8-db1e-0d72e36e/Symbian_3_UI_Style_Guide.html

http://docs.blackberry.com/en/developers/deliverables/17965/index.jsp?name=UI+Guidelines+-+BlackBerry+Smartphones6.0&language=English&userType=21&category=Java+Development+Guidelines&subCategory=

http://www.nrf.com/modules.php?name=Pages&op=viewlive&sp_id=1268

Chapter 20

Mobile Programming

Wireless computing devices are proliferating rapidly, creating the need for software applications that can handle the realities of the mobile computing lifestyle. Mobile devices that were used only for making and receiving calls are things of the past. Currently, with technological advances, we see mobile users using mobile devices for activities ranging from shopping to tracking their loved ones. Technological advances are happening in the different areas of the entire mobility ecosystem, including mobile device operating systems, hardware, device manufacturers, content creators, carriers, users, etc.

20.1 Android

The key steps in Android development are as follows:

- Installing the platform software development kit (SDK)
- Creating and configuring an Android virtual device (AVD)
- Creating the project
- Building the user interface (UI)
- Running the code

20.1.1 Development Environment

1. Eclipse integrated development environment (IDE) is as follows:
   - Android SDK needs Eclipse version 3.2 or later.
   - The latest version for Eclipse can be downloaded from http://www.eclipse.org/downloads.

2. Sun's Java development kit (JDK):
   - ■ Android SDK requires JDK version 5 or 6.
   - ■ The latest version can be downloaded from http://java.sun.com/javase/downloads.
3. Android SDK:
   - ■ The Android SDK includes the tools and APIs needed for writing creative and powerful mobile applications.
   - ■ The Android code is written using Java.
   - ■ Core Android libraries include features from the core Java APIs.
   - ■ Android SDK is completely open.
   - ■ SDK can be downloaded from http://code.google.com/android/download.html.

Android developer tool (ADT): Eclipse with the ADT plug-in for Android development is commonly used for Android app development. Eclipse is an open-source IDE commonly used for Java development. ADT plug-in for Eclipse simplifies Android development by integrating developer tools, which include the emulator and .class-to-.dex converter, into the IDE. By using the ADT plug-in, creating, testing, and debugging, the Android applications become faster and easier.

The ADT plug-in integrates the following different items into Eclipse:

- ■ Android project wizard
  - – For creating new projects.
  - – Basic application template included.
- ■ Forms-based manifest, layout, and resource editors
  - – Helps in creating, editing, and validating extensible markup language (XML) resources.
- ■ ADT helps in building the project, converting the .dex Android executable and packaging to .apk files, and finally installing the files to Dalvik virtual machines.
- ■ Android emulator
  - – Can control the emulator's appearance, network connection settings, etc.
  - – Ability to simulate incoming calls along with short message service messages.
- ■ Dalvik debug monitoring service
  - – Stack, heap, and thread viewing.
  - – Supports port forwarding.
  - – Screen-capture facilities.
  - – Process details.

- Access to the device or emulator's file system.
- Runtime debugging.
- All Android/Dalvik log and console outputs.

The SDK is presented as a ZIP file containing the developer tools, API libraries, documentation, and API demos highlighting the use of API features. The step-by-step instructions provided are for developers using Eclipse with the ADT plug-in without remote update site setup.

20.1.2 Project Templates and Setup Options

The project templates and setup options are detailed as follows:

1. Download the latest ADT plug-in zip from http://dl.google.com/android/
2. Start Eclipse, select help, and install new software.
3. Click "add" in the top-right corner.

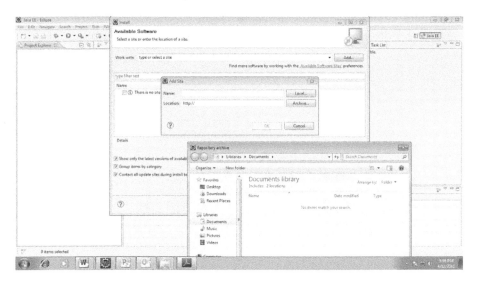

4. In the Add Site dialog, click "Archive."
5. Browse and select the downloaded ADT zip file.

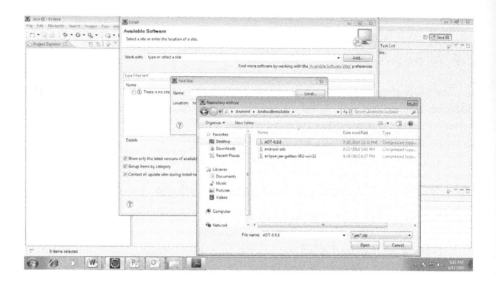

6. Enter a name for local site in "Name" field.
7. Click "OK."

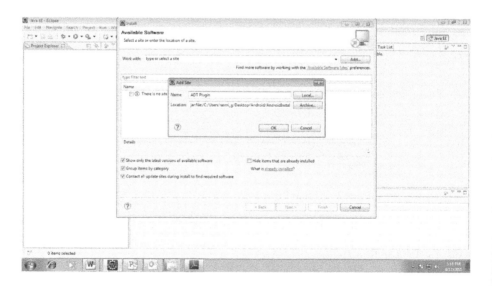

8. In the Available Software window, select the checkbox near Developer Tools, and click "Next."

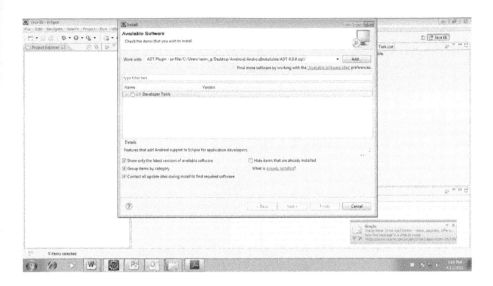

9. A list of the tools that need to be downloaded will be displayed in the next window. Click "Next."

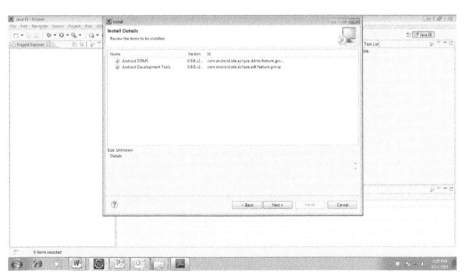

10. Read and accept the licensing agreements and then click "Finish."

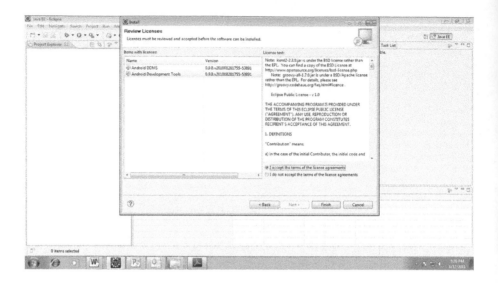

11. Restart the Eclipse IDE.

After you have successfully installed the ADT, the next step is modifying the "Update ADT preferences" in Eclipse to direct to the Android SDK directory.

12. Select Window → Preferences to open the Preferences panel.

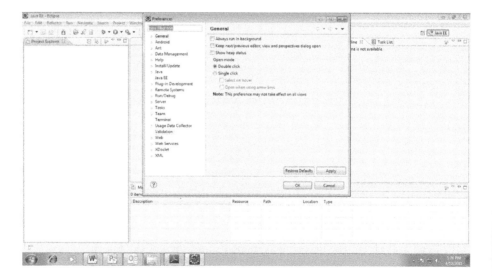

13. Select Android option from the left panel. Refer Figure 20.8.

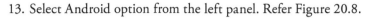
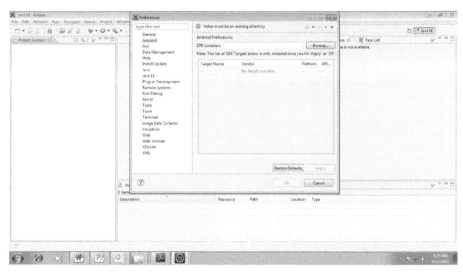

14. For entering SDK Location in the window, click "Browse" and locate down-loaded SDK directory.
15. Click "Apply," then "OK" (with this, all installation-related steps are complete).

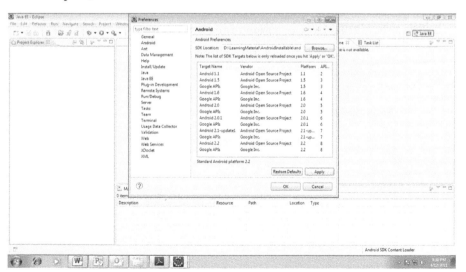

20.1.2.1 Creating an AVD

For running an Android application in the Android emulator, we need to create an AVD. It defines the system image and also the device settings that will be set up for the emulator.

1. In Eclipse, select Window → Android SDK and AVD Manager.

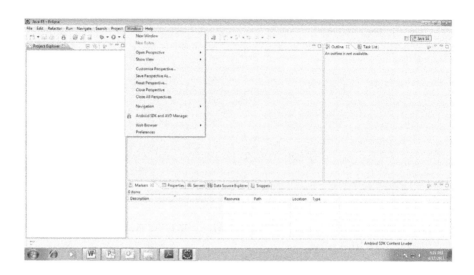

2. Select the Virtual Devices option in the left panel.

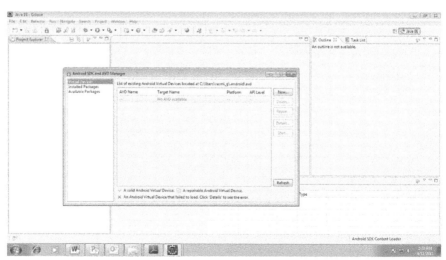

3. Click "New." Create New AVD dialog will appear.
4. Enter name of the AVD, such as "EMULATOR."
5. Choose a target version of Android SDK.
6. Click "Create AVD."

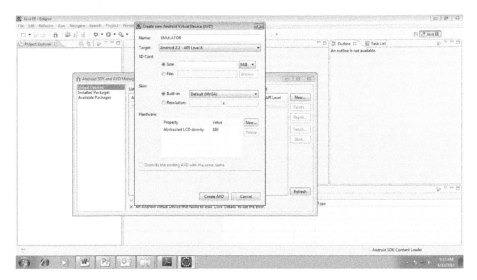

7. This will create an AVD.
8. Select the AVD that is created, and click on "Start Button."

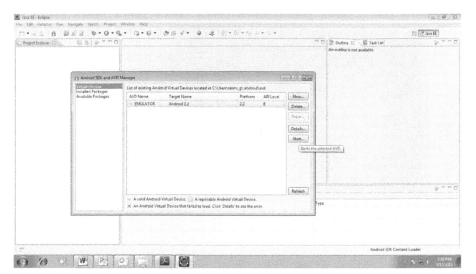

9. In the new window "Launch Option," click on the "Launch" button.

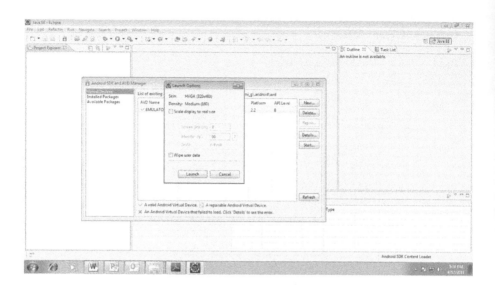

10. This will launch the emulator application.

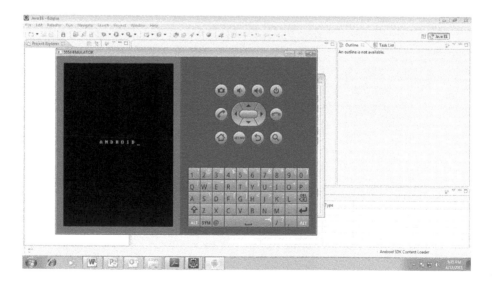

20.1.3 Creating a Hello World Project

1. In Eclipse menu, select File → New and select Project.
2. Choose "Android Project," and click on "Next."

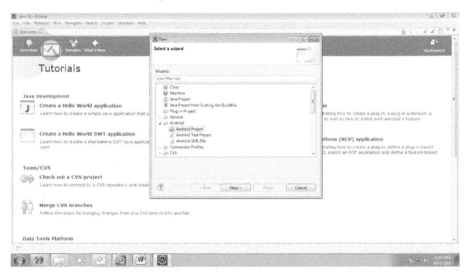

3. Create a project by giving the details.
4. Click "Finish."

Project Name: The user can enter the Eclipse project name, which will also be the name of the directory that contains these project files.

The checkbox for *Use default location* provides an option to change the project location.

Build Target: This is the Android SDK version that is used to build the application.

Application Name: This is the title for the application. This application name appears on the Android device as well.

Package Name: Package name space under which source code resides. The package name should be unique across all packages that are installed on the Android system.

Create Activity: Name for the class stub generated by the plug-in.

Min SDK Version: Minimum API level on which the application will run.

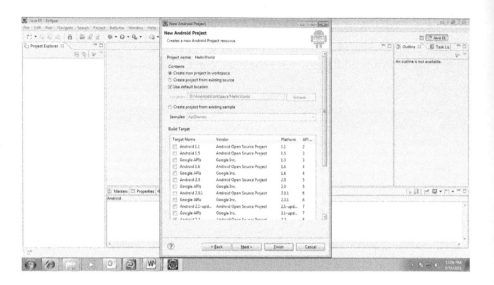

(After scrolling down)

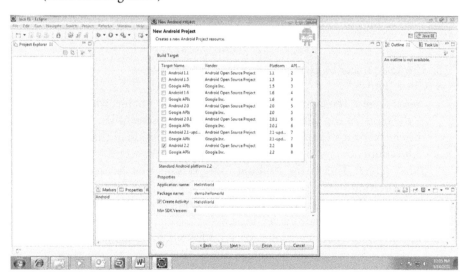

We will now add a TextView to the project and display a message in the emulator.

5. Add a TextView to the application screen layout.
6. Select the TextView property and set the text to "Hello World! Welcome to Android."

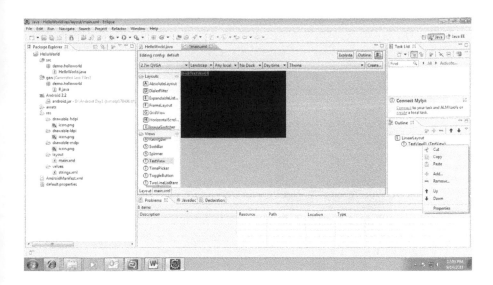

7. Select the project → Right click and Select "Run as Android App."

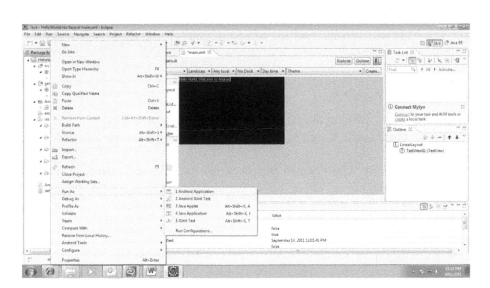

8. The emulator will then start running and will display the message.

20.1.4 Android APIs

The key APIs that can be used for accessing some of the features provided by Android are as follows.

20.1.4.1 Networking

Android supports different libraries to perform network operations.

Apache HttpClient: Preferred way of implementing network operations in Android.

Java Networking API: Even in this package, Android will internally use the Apache library.

Android HTTP client

- Available as from Android 2.2.
- Supports SSL.
- Utility methods for GZIP compressed data are available.

For accessing the Internet, the application requires the "android.permission. INTERNET" permission.

For XML parsing, Android provides "XmlPullParser" class, which is an XML parser specific for Android.

20.1.4.2 Location Services

20.1.4.2.1 Android Location API

Most Android devices allow determining the current geolocation. The various options for identifying the geolocation are via the following approaches:

- Global positioning system (GPS) device
- Cell tower triangulation
- WiFi networks with geolocation information

"Android.location" package provides the API to determine the current geoposition in an Android device.

20.1.4.2.2 Forward and Reverse Geocoding

The class "Geocoder" allows the application to determine the geocoordinates for a given address (forward geocoding) and the class also provides possible addresses for the given geocoordinates (reverse geocoding).

20.1.4.2.3 Google Maps

Google provides a library in the package "com.google.android.maps" for using Google Maps in Android. An additional key is required for using Google Maps. This is because Google Maps is not part of the standard open-source platform for Android.

20.1.4.3 File System

20.1.4.3.1 Android File System

- In Android, data can be saved in files, databases, and preference settings.
- Android creates a directory under the path "data/data/package.of.the. application" for each application.
    - Files are saved in the folder "files."
    - Application settings will be saved as XML files in the "shared_prefs" folder.
- Only the application can write into its application directory.
- Applications can create subdirectories in application directories.
    - For subdirectories, application can grant, read, or write permissions for other applications.
- Access to the file system is performed by Java.io classes.

- Helper classes are available for creating and accessing new files and directories.
  - getDir(String, int)
    - *For creating or accessing a directory*
  - openFileInput(String s)
    - *For opening a file for input*
  - openFileOutput(String s, int)
    - *For creating a file*

If the application creates a SQLite database, this is saved in the main directory under the folder "databases." The different levels of permission that can be used while creating a file in Android are as follows:

MODE_PRIVATE: Only the main application can access these files. Other applications cannot access these files.

MODE_WORLD_READABLE: All applications will have read access to this file.

MODE_WORLD_WRITABLE: All applications will have Write access to this file.

MODE_WORLD_READABLE | MODE_WORLD_WRITABLE: All applications have Read and Write access to the file.

20.1.4.3.2 SD Card

- Secure digital (SD) card access is supported in Android.
- All files and directories on the SD Card are readable and writable for all applications.
- For writing to the SD card, "android.permission.WRITE_EXTERNAL_STORAGE" permission is needed.
- SD card path can be obtained by Environment.getExternalStorageDirectory().

20.1.4.4 Sounds

Android provides multiple APIs for playing sounds.

20.1.4.4.1 Sound Pool

- Used for small audio clips
- Can repeat and play several sounds simultaneously
- File size played with Sound Pool should not exceed 1 MB
- Loads the file asynchronously

20.1.4.4.2 Media Player

- Suited for longer music and movies

20.1.4.5 Sensors

Android supports several sensors via the SensorManager. For getting accelerometer-related information, get a handle to the service manager via getSystemService (SENSOR_SERVICE). Once that is done, register a "Sensor EventListener" to the accelerometer to get the events from it.

```
sensorManager = (SensorManager) getSystemService(SENSOR_SERVICE)
sensorManager.registerListener(this
    sensorManager.getDefaultSensor (Sensor.TYPE_ACCELEROMETER),
    SensorManager.SENSOR_DELAY_ NORMAL);
```

To avoid unnecessary usage of battery, developers will need to register for the listener in the on-resume method and unregister in the on-pause method.

20.2 iPhone

Similar to all other application developments, an iOS-application development process generally follows the major steps that are given here:

- Create your project: A project template can be used for creating a project. Choose the template for the application type that needs to be developed.
- Design the UI: Design the application's UI graphically and save designs as resource files so that the application loads at runtime.
- Write code: Use Xcode features such as code completion, class and data modeling, refactoring, and direct access to documentation while writing the code.
- Build and run your application: Build the application on the computer and run the application in a simulator or on the device.
- Measure and tune application performance: After running the application, application performance needs to be analyzed for ensuring that it uses the device's resources efficiently and also provides satisfactory responses to a user's gestures.

20.2.1 Development Environment

To develop applications for iOS, we will require a Mac with an Intel processor, installed with Xcode and iPhone SDK:
  1. Xcode:
     - Provides the tools required for creating and managing iPhone projects and source files.
     - Provides options to build the code into an executable and then run it or debug it either in an iPhone device or a simulator.
     - Provides the launching point for testing the applications on an iPhone.

■ Can run applications in an iPhone simulator.
2. iPhone SDK:
   ■ Contains all the required code, information, and tools that are needed to develop, test, debug, run, and tune applications for the iOS.

20.2.2 Project Templates

Xcode provides several default project templates for developers for developing their application (Figure 20.1). The various options that are provided by Xcode are as follows:

■ Navigation-based application
  – Used for applications that present data hierarchically, using multiple screens.
  – Contacts application is an example.
■ OpenGLES application
  – An application that uses an OpenGL ES-based view to present images or animation.
■ Split View-based application
  – Application that displays more than one view onscreen.
  – iPad Mail application is an example.

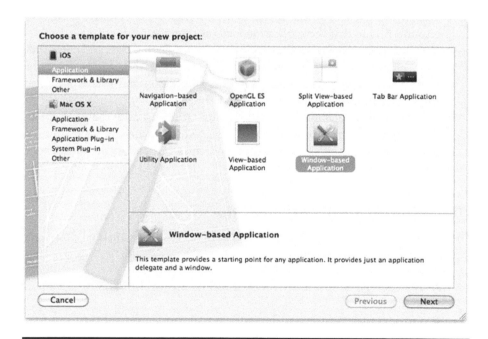

Figure 20.1 iOS project templates.

- Tab Bar application
  - Application that presents a radio interface, letting the user choose from several screens.
  - iPhone Clock application is an example.
- Utility application
  - Application that implements a main view and allows the user to access a flip-side view to perform simple customizations.
  - iPhone Stocks application is an example.
- View-based application
  - Application that uses a single view for implementing its UI.
- Window-based application
  - Serves as a starting point for any application.
  - Includes an application delegate and a window.
  - This template is to be used when developers want to implement their own view hierarchy.

20.2.3 Creating a Hello World Project

1. Launch the Xcode application.
2. Choose File → New and New Project.

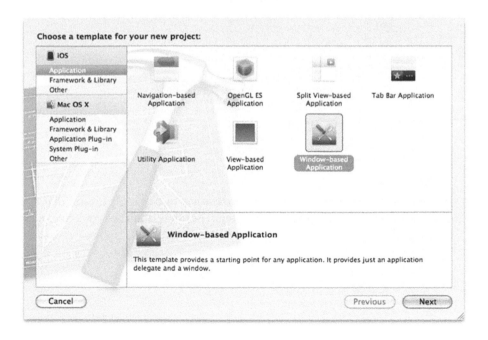

3. In iOS, select Application and then Window-based application, and click "Next."
4. Specify the options for the project.
   - **Product Name:** Book_Sample
   - **Company Identifier:** com.myBook
   - **Device Family:** iPhone
   - **Use Core Data:** No
   - **Include Unit Tests:** No

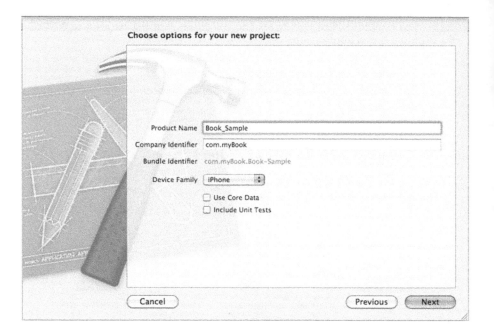

5. Click "Next."
6. Navigate to the location where the project has to be saved. Ensure that the "Create local git repository for this project" option is not selected, and click "Create."

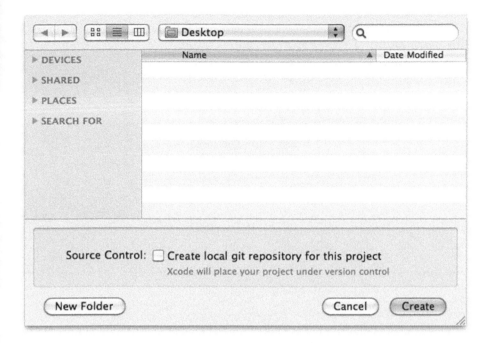

7. Project directory will be created and the project is saved. Xcode will open the project in a workspace window.
8. Project components will appear in the project navigator. The first item represents the project and displays the name given when the project was created. The project's components are grouped in three groups:
   ■ Book_Sample
      – Contains all the files that make the project
      – Files include source code files and a UI file
      – Contains subgroup, supporting files also with files used in supporting tasks
   ■ Frameworks
      – Identifies frameworks or libraries used by the project
      – UIKit framework is an example
   ■ Products
      – Contains the products the project creates
      – Here it will be the Book_Sample application

20.2.3.1 Create the UI View Subclass

Drawing in Cocoa Touch uses objects known as views. UI View class defines the basic drawing, event handling, and printing architecture of the application containing the view. After completing the above-mentioned steps, a class should be added to display the application message.

To create the UI View subclass in the Hello project:

1. Choose File → New and New File.
2. In the iOS section, select Cocoa Touch and then select the Objective-C class template. Click "Next."

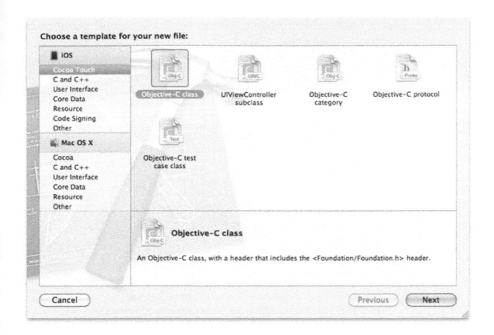

3. Specify new file as a subclass of UI View, and click "Next."

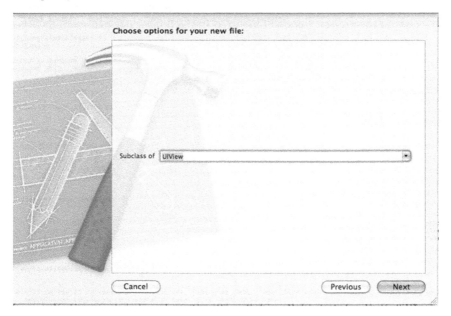

4. Enter HelloBook.m as the filename, choose the Book_Sample group from the Group menu list, and click "Save."

5. Xcode will handle adding header and implementation files for the HelloBook class to the project. Files will be listed in the project navigator along with all the other files in the Book_Sample group.

20.2.3.2 Write the Code

In Xcode, view and edit the source file by selecting it in the project navigator. The selected file will then open in the source editor.

1. Select View → Navigators → Project.
2. Select View → Utilities → Hide Utilities.
3. In the project navigator, select HelloBook.m to open the file in the source editor.
4. In the implementation section of the HelloBook.m file, insert the following code lines:
   - (void)drawRect:(CGRect)rect {
   NSString *hello = "Hello, World!";
   }
5. Complete the implementation of the drawRect: method.
   - (void)drawRect:(CGRect)rect {
   NSString *hello = @"Hello, World!";
   CGPoint point = CGPointMake(10, 20);
   UIFont *font = [UIFont systemFontOfSize:24.0];
   [[UIColor whiteColor] set];
   [hello drawAtPoint:point withFont:font];
   }

Now modify the Book_SampleAppDelegate class so that it adds a HelloBook object to its view hierarchy:

1. In the project navigator, select Book_SampleAppDelegate.m to open it in the source editor.
2. Include the following line of code below the #import line.
   #import "HelloBook.*h*"
3. Add below code snippet to the application: didFinishLaunchingWith Options: method in the Book_SampleAppDelegate.m:
   - (BOOL)application:(UIApplication *)application
   didFinishLaunchingWithOptions:(NSDictionary *)launchOptions {
   HelloBook *view = [[HelloBook alloc] initWithFrame:[self.window frame]];
   [self.window addSubview:view];
   [view release];
   [self.window makeKeyAndVisible];
   return YES;
   }

20.2.3.3 Run the Application

To run the Hello application:

1. Choose Product → Run. The program displays the message in a simulator or on a device.

2. Stop the program by choosing Product → Stop.

20.2.4 iPhone APIs

20.2.4.1 Networking

iOS includes several frameworks and libraries that allow developers to support networking and Internet-based features on their applications. Developers gain access to these protocols and services using the Foundation and Core Foundation frameworks, along with CF Network and Berkeley Software Distribution (BSD) sockets.

Core Foundation universal resource locator access utilities (CFURL) and NSURL APIs have the following features:

■ Provide the option to download files or resources from web servers and file transfer protocol (FTP) servers.

- NSURL Objective-C-based APIs are part of the foundation framework built over the CFURL.
- CFURL C-based APIs are part of the core foundation framework.

When these interfaces are used, developers do not have to choose between WiFi- and cell-based radios. The interfaces automatically access the device hardware and will choose the best transmission option and will seamlessly switch from one to the other as and when needed.

1. CFHTTPStream and CFFTPStream APIs
   - Used in scenarios where the application interacts with a web server or FTP server and requires capabilities that are beyond CFURL or NSURL APIs.
   - Supports complex hypertext transfer protocol (HTTP) and FTP requests.
2. Socket-based communication
   - Run-loop socket integration APIs are available in the core foundation.
   - Provides direct access to the BSD sockets.
   - The features are based on the CF Network API.
3. Register and discover network services
   - Users can register or discover a network service using Bonjour.
   - Users can use the C-based CFNetServices or Objective-C-based NSNetServices API.

20.2.4.2 Location Services

Location-based information in iOS comprises two parts: location services and maps.

1. Location services
   - Provided by the core location framework
   - Provides Objective-C interfaces for providing information about the device location and heading
2. Maps
   - Provided by the Map Kit framework
   - Supports both the display and annotation of maps

20.2.4.3 File System

The file system in iOS is one of the basic resources used by all processes running in an iPhone device. The file system in iOS handles the persistent storage of data files, applications, and also handles the files related with the operating system itself.

The iOS file system is configured in a way to support applications running on their own. iOS device users do not have direct access to the file system. All the applications are also expected not to have access to the file system. iOS applications interact with the file system that is inside the application's sandbox. During new application instal-lation, the installer will create a home directory for that application. The installer will also place the application in that newly created directory and create several other key directories. All these directories create the application's primary view of the file sys-tem. Some of the commonly used APIs in the file system are given below:

NSString: Used for text files, as the text file is an unstructured sequence of Unicode and ASCII characters

NSXMLParser: Used for structured data files consisting of string-based data

NSCoder: For archive file format used to store persistent version of the applica-tion's runtime objects

20.2.4.4 Sounds

iPhone supports APIs from the basic level such as iPod library playback and movie capture to advanced solutions for multimedia playback.

Media Player Framework: Used for playing the items from the user's iPod library or from local or streamed movies

AV Foundation Framework: For basic audio recording and playback

Open Audio Library (OpenAL) API: To add high-performance positional audio playback for OpenGL-based game or applications and for working with audio and video data for high performance or for advanced solutions such as VoIP, streaming, virtual music instruments, or Musical Instrument Digital Interface (MIDI)

Users can use the assets library framework, AV foundation framework, the vari-ous core audio frameworks, and the core MIDI framework.

20.2.4.5 Sensors

An iOS device generates motion events whenever the users move the device by shaking it or tilting it. All motion events originate in the device accelerometer or gyroscope. Every application has a UI accelerometer object that can be used to receive acceleration data. Users get the instance of this class by using the shared accelerometer class method of the UI accelerometer. Using this object, users set the desired reporting interval and use a custom delegate to receive acceleration events.

20.3 Windows Phone

Windows Phone 7 includes several tools to help users create and publish applica-tions. The latest version of Windows Phone OS contains a large number of features, new APIs, and performance enhancements.

20.3.1 Development Environment

Developers can download and install the package that includes the required tools that they require to start developing applications for Windows Phone.

1. Visual Studio 2010:
   - IDE for building Windows Phone applications
   - Includes a project system, designer, debugger, packager, and manifest generation
2. Expression Blend:
   - Design creative and unique applications based on Silverlight for a Windows Phone device
   - Designers can design extensible application markup language (XAML)-based interfaces for applications
3. Windows Phone Emulator:
   - Integrated into the Visual Studio and Expression Blend so as to make debugging and testing of applications easier and efficient
   - Fully supports application deployment, debugging, and execution
   - Supports graphics processing unit emulation and orientation change
4. XNA Game Studio
   - Integrated design environment that helps developers to build games
   - Extends the Visual Studio to support the XNA Framework
   - Managed-code class library that contains functionality for game development tasks
   - Includes tools for graphical and audio content into the game

20.3.2 Project Templates

This section covers the default project templates available while creating a Windows Phone 7 project. There are few more project templates available for Silverlight- and XNA-based application development in the Windows Phone OS 7.1 version.

For creating an application from an existing template, the following steps should be performed:

1. In Visual Studio, click "New Project" available on the File menu.
2. In New Project window, select language as Visual C#, then Silverlight for Windows Phone.

The list of project templates for developing Silverlight for Windows Phone will be shown in the window. The various project templates that are included in Visual Studio 2010 are described below. These templates are available both for C# and Visual Basic. Refer Figure 20.2.

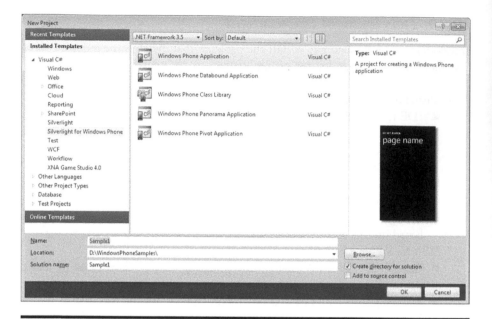

Figure 20.2 Windows Phone project templates.

1. Windows Phone application:
   - Creates a project used for developing Silverlight for Windows Phone application
   - Provides a single-page application that uses the PhoneApplicationPage and PhoneApplicationFrame elements
2. Windows Phone Databound application:
   - Creates a project using ListBox control and navigation features
   - Based on Model-View-View-Model design pattern
3. Windows Phone Class Library:
   - Creates a class library project that compiles to an assembly
   - No UI elements
   - Can be shared with other applications
4. Windows Phone Panorama Application:
   - Creates a project using a Panorama control
   - Allows users to view controls, data, and services by a long horizontal canvas
   - Canvas extends beyond the boundaries of the screen
5. Windows Phone Pivot Application
   - Creates a project using a Pivot control
   - Enables users to switch between views and pages within the application

20.3.3 *Creating a Hello World Project*

1. Start Visual Studio and Select File and New Project command.

2. Select "Silverlight for Windows Phone" option.

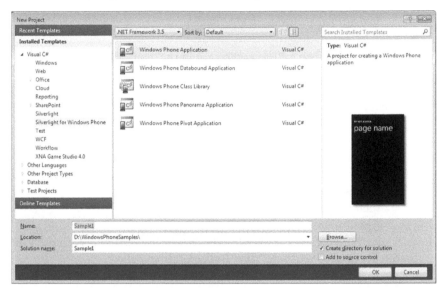

3. Select "Windows Phone Application."
4. Specify *<project name>,* and click "OK" button.
5. Wizard will create the project with all the files required for the application.

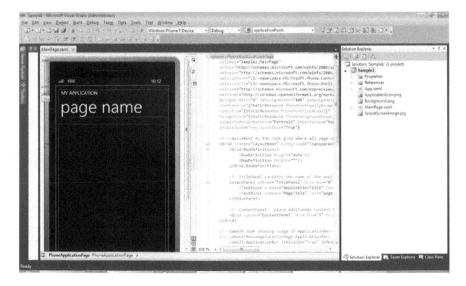

The key files generated by the wizard are as follows:
- MainPage.xaml
  - Default page with some UI element.
- ApplicationIcon.png
  - Holds the icon for the application in the application list.
  - Icon size: 60 × 60 pixels
  - Resolution: 72 pixels per inch.
- Background.png
  - Holds the icon for application in the start list.
    - Displayed as the background of the application's live tile
- App.xaml
  - Used to declare shared application resources
  - Code-behind file app.xaml.cs is used to handle events such as Application_Startup, Application_Exit, and Application_UnhandledException

6. Add Silverlight controls to the Windows Phone application. Open the Visual Studio Toolbox by selecting View Toolbox in the menu.

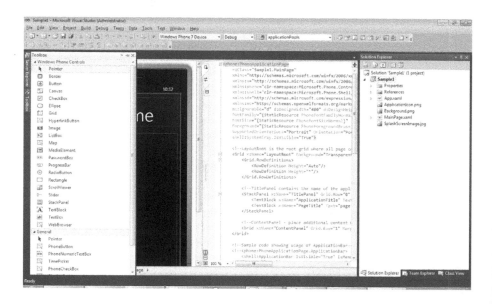

7. Add a TextBox control from Toolbox and also set the text as "Hello World."

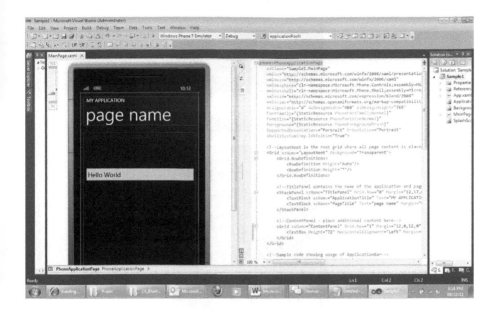

```
<Grid x:Name="ContentPanel" Grid.Row="1" Margin="12,0,12,0">
<TextBox Height="72" HorizontalAlignment="Left" Margin="0,135,0,0"
Name="textBox1" Text="Hello World" VerticalAlignment="Top" Width=
"460" /></Grid>
```

8. To build the solution, select Build → Build Solution on the Visual Studio menu.
9. To run the application, select Debug → Start Debugging.
10. Once the debugging starts, we will be able to see the emulator appearing and the application running in the emulator.

20.3.4 Windows Phone APIs

20.3.4.1 Networking

Web services generally enable the phone with access to data over the Internet. A data service will be able to implement the Open Data (OData) Protocol to expose data defined by a data model and addressable by uniform resource identifiers (URIs). Web service APIs are defined using an XML-based language. The web service description language (WSDL) describes the services offered by the web services.

The following list contains classes and utilizes it to generate optimized classes for web requests from WP7 applications:

Web client class: Provides common methods to send and receive data from a URI-based resource

HTTP web request class: Supports an abstract WebRequest class

Silverlight Service Model Proxy Generation Tool (SLsvcUtil.exe): Used to generate proxy classes based on the WSDL file

WCF Data Service Client Utility (DataSvcUtil.exe): Used to generate proxy classes based on the CSDL file

Visual Studio Add Service Reference Feature: Used to generate proxy classes based on the WSDL file

Open Data Protocol (OData)

- It is based on an entity and relationship model offering access to data in the form of REST resources.
- Provides state-less service but will be able to maintain the state of entities on the client between interactions with the data services.
- Can use OData Client library to execute queries and even manipulate data from a data service.
- DataServiceContext class and DataServiceCollection class are the main classes.
- DataServiceContext class encapsulates operations executed against a specific data service.

20.3.4.2 Location Services

Location service is the service provided by a managed interface. It is exposed through a dynamic-link library (DLL) in Windows Phone SDK. This interface supports the following features:

- Start and stop the location service
- Set the required accuracy level for the application
- Obtain location data from the native code layer as and when it is received

20.3.4.3 GeoCoordinateWatcher API

GeoCoordinateWatcher API has the following features:

- Obtain information about the device's geographic location by using a single API.
- Location information will be obtained by Windows Location Provider using WiFi triangulation and along with IP information or from other sources such as a GPS device.
- Windows.Devices.Geolocation API provides the accurate geolocation data from the available sources.

20.3.4.4 File System

In Windows Phone, all input–output operations are restricted to isolated storage. Applications do not have direct access to the operating system or to the isolated storage of other applications. Windows Phone applications can use isolated storage in multiple ways based on the type of data that is being stored:

- System.IO.IsolatedStorage.IsolatedStorageSettings (for Settings):
  - Store data as key and value pairs by using the IsolatedStorageSettings class.
  - Stores key and value pairs in isolated storage as a dictionary.

■ System.IO.IsolatedStorage.IsolatedStorageFile (for files and folders):
  − It represents an isolated storage area containing files and directories.
  − It stores files or folders with the IsolatedStorageFile class.
■ System.Data.Linq (for relational data):
  − Stores relational data in a local database by using LINQ to SQL.

20.3.4.5 Sounds

Users can use Windows Phone APIs, Silverlight, or XNA Game Studio to use media features in their application.

1. MediaPlayerLauncher class
   ■ Embeds audio or video using the device media player
   ■ Ideal for XNA applications
2. Silverlight MediaElement API
   ■ Embeds audio or video using a customizable interface
   ■ Ideal for Silverlight applications
   ■ Add sound effects using XNA game studio
3. MediaStreamSource
   ■ Used in scenarios where adaptive streaming solutions are necessary
4. Microsoft.Phone.BackgroundAudio
   ■ Used for applications that continue playing the audio when another application is in the foreground

20.3.4.6 Sensors

■ Windows Phone Developer Tools offers Accelerometer API as a managed library.
■ API is built over the general sensor framework.
■ AccelerometerReadingEventArgs class will pass Accelerometer data to application.
■ Class exposes properties for the X-, Y-, and Z-axis so that the application can read the data.
■ Accelerometer in Microsoft.Devices.Sensors provides Windows Phone applications access to the device's accelerometer sensor.

20.4 Windows Mobile

Windows Mobile 6 SDK tools are required along with Visual Studio and .Net Compact Framework for application development in Windows Mobile. The SDK provides support and templates for designing and developing applications for Windows Mobile platforms. Windows Mobile SDK also has tools that help develop and test applications without any need for real devices and infrastructure.

20.4.1 Development Environment

The IDE used for building, testing, and deploying applications for the Microsoft platform is Visual Studio IDE. The IDE also provides the same level of support to the development of Windows Mobile applications.

Visual Studio 2005 standard edition or above or Visual Studio 2008 professional edition or above is required for developing applications for the Windows Mobile environment. SDKs are required for each family of Windows Mobiles. The SDKs include emulators for a variety of Windows Mobile devices. Specific versions of SDKs are required, depending on the platform and the type of device.

20.4.2 Project Templates

The project templates are detailed in the following list (see Figure 20.3).

Device application: Creates a .Net Compact Framework windows Forms application
Class library: Creates a .Net Compact Framework class library (DLL)
Console application: Creates a .Net Compact Framework 3.5 nongraphical application
Control library: Creates.NET Compact Framework 3.5 custom controls
Empty project: Empty project for creating a.NET Compact Framework 3.5 application

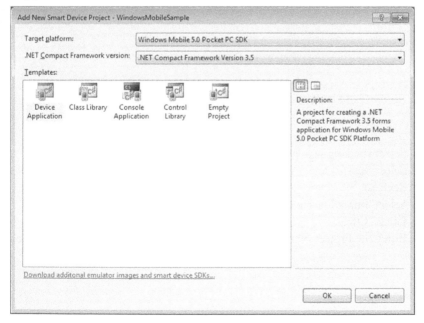

Figure 20.3 Windows Mobile project templates.

20.4.3 Creating a Hello World Project

Visual Studio 2008 allows users to build Windows Mobile applications for .Net and native apps. It supports a wide range of languages including C++, C#, J# (Java), and Visual Basic.

The following are the steps for creating a Windows Mobile project in Visual Studio:

1. Launch VS2008 and select "New Project" from the File menu.

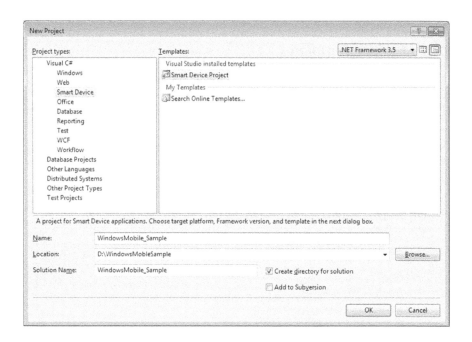

2. Select the language prefered (C#, VB) for application development.
3. Select Smart Device (the generic name for Windows CE or Windows Mobile devices).
4. Select Smart Device Project.
5. Click "OK."
6. Enter the Project Name, Solution Name, and the Location for the project.

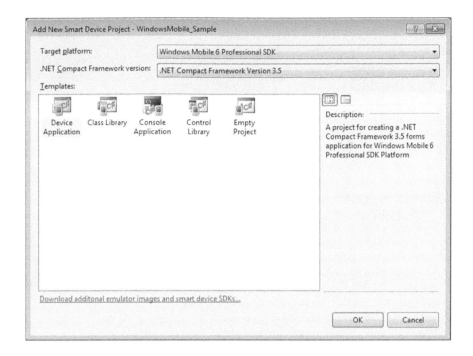

7. Choose "Windows Mobile 6 Professional SDK" for Target platform.
8. Choose ".Net Compact Framework Version 3.5" for .Net Compact Framework version.
9. Choose "Device Application" Template.
10. Click "OK."

Visual Studio will generate a complete smart device framework and open a blank application.

11. The next step is to add UI controls to the application. Open the Visual Studio Toolbox by selecting View Toolbox on the Visual Studio menu options.

12. Drag and drop a TextBox control from the Toolbox and set the text as "Hello World."

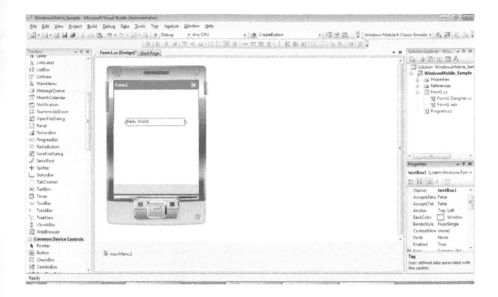

13. Press "F5" button for compiling and running the application.
14. Select the configuration you want to run the application, and click "Deploy."

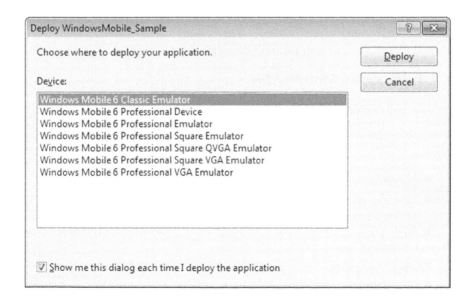

15. The application will be deployed on the device or on the emulator, and the application will be launched.

16. Hit "Shift + F5" to stop running the application.

20.4.4 Windows Mobile APIs

20.4.4.1 Networking

The following are the key name spaces for using the networking APIs in Windows Mobile:

1. System.Net namespace
   - Provides simple programming interfaces for many of the protocols used on the networks.
   - Web request and web response classes form the basis of an implementation of network services.
2. System.Net.Sockets namespace
   - An interface for Windows Sockets is provided by a managed implementation.
   - UdpClient, TcpClient, and TcpListener classes encapsulate the details of creating transmission control protocol (TCP) and user datagram protocol (UDP) connections to the Internet.

20.4.4.2 Location Services

Retrieving location information on a Windows Mobile device is fairly easy. The location information can be retrieved by either of the following options:

- GPS Look-up has the disadvantage of taking some initialization time and also drains additional battery power, but is very accurate.
- Cell Tower Lookup is fast, does not consume much battery power, but is not accurate.

The key APIs required for retrieving cell-tower information are described in the following list. For using these APIs in managed code, P/Invoke needs to be used as these APIs are in native code.

RIL_Initialize: (RIL—Radio Interface Layer): Initializes RIL to be used by the application.

RIL_GetCellTowerInfo: Retrieves information about the cell tower that the device uses.

RIL_Deinitialize: Correctly closes and cleans up resources after the application is finished using the RIL.

The key APIs that need to be used for retrieving location based on GPS are as follows:

GPS.Open: Creates a connection to the GPS Intermediate Driver (GPSID).

GPS.Close: Connection to GPSID will be closed. It will also close the internal handle to the underlying GPS hardware driver if that is the only connection to GPSID.

GPS.GetPosition: Retrieves location information, including latitude and longitude, by setting the required fields of the passed structure with the location information.

GPSGetDeviceState: Provides information about the current state of the GPS hardware by setting the fields of the passed structure.

20.4.4.3 File System

Windows Mobile provides support for a range of storage features:

- System registry for storing data about applications, drivers, user preferences, and other configuration settings.
- Databases including SQL-CE.
- Includes file system drivers for various systems such as several types of FAT file systems, the read-only memory (RAM) file system, and compact disc file system/universal disc file system (CDFS/UDFS).

■ Using managed code System.IO provides Basic file and directory support and Namespace includes types that enable synchronous and asynchronous reading and writing on data streams and files.
■ Using native code, many more APIs are available for file system access for the following:

Database reference provides reference information for the database APIs.
File I/O reference provides reference information for the file I/O APIs.
Registry reference provides reference information for the registry.

20.4.4.4 Sounds

System.Media namespace contains classes for playing sound files and accessing sounds provided by the system. The key classes that are used for working with sound files are as follows:

■ Sound Player: For loading and playing sounds in various file formats.
■ System Sounds: For retrieving sounds associated with Windows operating system sound-event types.
■ System Sound: For representing and playing a system sound.
■ There are native code implementations with WavOutOpen methods, which could be used for playing sounds.

20.4.4.5 Sensors

Windows Mobile Unified Sensor API provides developers with easy access to the hardware sensors that are available on various phones. These APIs are developed by codeplex team. The sensors that are supported include Light Sensor, Capacitive Touch Pad, and Accelerometer. There are also APIs provided by hardware vendors as part of their SDK, which supports accessing sensors.

20.5 BlackBerry

BlackBerry smartphone is Java-based and supports Java ME. The phone also supports a rich set of BlackBerry APIs for Java. In addition to Java ME APIs, BlackBerry-specific APIs are also made available for developers. These APIs provide access to more advanced UI functionality. This makes sure that developers can integrate and utilize the capabilities of BlackBerry smartphones.

20.5.1 Development Environment

Java Application Development approach can be used to create rich client applications for BlackBerry. In order to develop Java-based applications for BlackBerry smartphones, developers can choose either the Eclipse environment or the BlackBerry Java development environment (BlackBerry JDE).

20.5.1.1 BlackBerry Java Plug-in for Eclipse

This plug-in will extend the Eclipse framework to support Java developers to create applications for BlackBerry smartphones. Within both Eclipse and Eclipse-based IDEs, the plug-in provides the tools to create, debug, optimize, and localize Java applications for BlackBerry smartphones. The applications are listed as follows:

- Eclipse 3.6 classic
- BlackBerry Java plug-in
- Java SE development kit (JDK) 6, update 14, or later

BlackBerry Java Plug-in for Eclipse greatly improves the application development experience and productivity by providing an integrated BlackBerry smartphone-specific development, debugging, and simulation.

- BlackBerry JDE
  - BlackBerry JDE is a fully IDE and simulation tool that is used for building Java Platform Micro Edition (Java ME) applications for Java-based BlackBerry smartphones.
  - BlackBerry JDE is a legacy, stand-alone development environment.
  - The application includes BlackBerry JDE v4.5+: Java SE JDK v6.0.
- BlackBerry smartphone simulators
  - Users can run and debug applications as if they were on an actual BlackBerry smartphone.
  - Users can view and test the application along with checking how the screen, keyboard, track wheel, and track ball will work with the application.

20.5.2 Project Templates

The different project templates available in BlackBerry are given in the subsequent list (see figure 20.4).

1. BlackBerry application
   - Creates a basic UI application with a screen
   - Also creates two Java source files, one for the application and one for the UI screen
2. Hello BlackBerry template
   - Creates a UI application with a screen populated with simple UI components
   - Creates two Java source files, one for the application and one for the UI screen
3. Empty application
   - Creates an empty BlackBerry device application
4. Empty library
   - Creates an empty BlackBerry device library

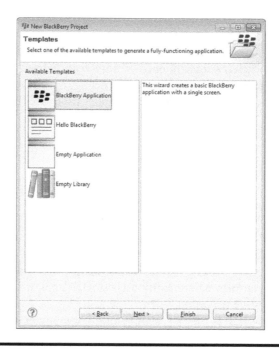

Figure 20.4 BlackBerry project templates.

20.5.3 Creating a Hello World Project

1. On the File menu, click "New → Project."
2. Select BlackBerry Project.

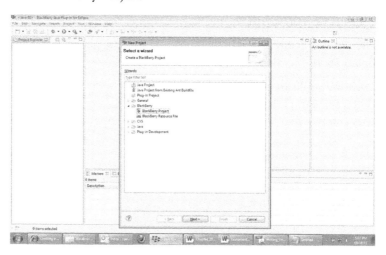

3. In Project name field, enter the name of the project.
   - ■ Select Create new project in the workspace.
   - ■ Select one of the below options.
     - – Select "Use a project specific JRE" to specify a specific JRE Version.
     - – Select "Use default JRE" to specify the default JRE in the workspace.

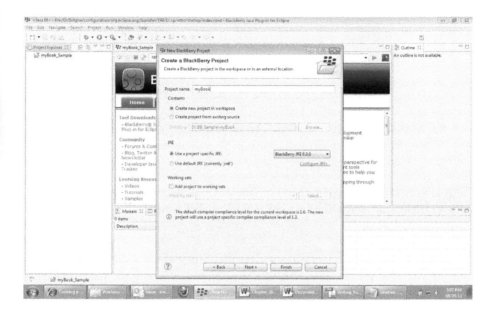

4. Click "Next."
5. Click the template that you want to use.
6. Enter the Application details and click "Finish."

A project will be created at this step. These steps will create a BlackBerry project with a UI element. We will now need to add a Label control to the code and then display "Hello World."

7. In BlackBerry, MainScreen is a class that provides a working area where all the data from the application can be displayed. We will add the below code to the class containing Application Class file: (MyApp.java in this case).

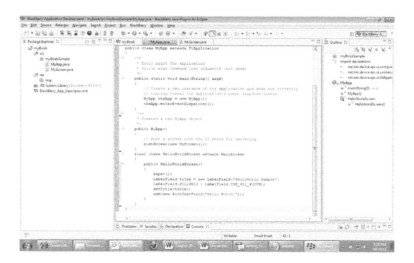

```
final class MyScreen extends MainScreen
{
public MyScreen ()
{
super();
LabelField title = new LabelField("HelloWorld Sample",
LabelField.ELLIPSIS | LabelField.USE_ALL_WIDTH);
setTitle(title);
add(new RichTextField("Hello World!"));
}
}
```
We will also need to add few imports
```
import net.rim.device.api.ui.component.*;
import net.rim.device.api.ui.container.MainScreen;
```
8. Run the application in the simulator.

20.5.4 BlackBerry APIs

20.5.4.1 Networking

The BlackBerry application platform offers different APIs that developers can use to create network connections from a code:

1. Communication API
   - The API encapsulates all the operations that are required to connect to a HTTP server located on the Internet or behind a firewall.

- It simplifies the process of interacting with web services and applications.
- The objects created using the API will handle identification of the available network transport, handling thread-safe connections, and negotiation of exchange of data with the URI or URL end point specified.
- The API is implemented in net.rim.device.api.io.messaging package.
2. Generic Connection Framework (GCF)
   - Creates network connections on devices that run previous versions of the BlackBerry Device Software.
   - Any code that is written using the GCF also runs on later versions of BlackBerry Device Software. GCF is implemented in the javax.microedition.io.Connector class.
   - Developers need to call Connector.open() to create a connection.
   - Parameters for Open() method includes a connection string that specifies the type of connection to make, the end point, and the optional configuration details for the connection.
3. Network API
   - Provides a simple interface for working with network transports and sets the variety of parameters for a connection.
   - Features provided by ConnectionFactory and TransportInfo classes.
   - Implemented in net.rim.device.api.io.transport and also in net.rim.device.api.io.transport.options packages.
   - The connectionFactory object returns a ConnectionDescriptor object containing a Connection object and information about the transport over which the connection was opened.

20.5.4.2 Location Services

The key features supported in the BlackBerry Location-Based Services APIs are as follows:

- Find a location
- Display information on a map
- Estimate the time and distance of a trip
- Perform geofencing

20.5.4.2.1 Finding a Location

Location information can be retrieved for a BlackBerry smartphone by using one of the following services:

1. Global positioning
   - Gives location information using GPS satellites.
   - Uses the JSR 179 Location API in the javax.microedition.location package.

- BlackBerry extensions to JSR 179 in the net.rim.device.api.gps package can also be used.
2. Geolocation
    - Provides location information using cell-tower positioning and WLAN access points.
    - GPS technology on the smartphone is not needed for using the geolocation service.
    - Geolocation can be used for applications that require an approximate location, and it can also be used indoors.
    - Can retrieve geolocation using the net.rim.device.api.gps package.
3. Geocoding and reverse geocoding
    - Provides geospatial coordinates for an address (geocoding).
    - Provides address for geospatial coordinates (reverse geocoding).
4. Display information in a map:

The information obtained from location-based APIs can be used to pass location information on to BlackBerry Maps from the application using the Invoke.invoke-Application() method with MapsArguments parameters.

5. Travel Time API:
    - Estimates the time and distance of a trip
    - Calculates the estimated time and distance to travel between two points on a given date and time
    - Provides estimates for automobile travel for selected countries
6. Perform geofencing:
    - Geofencing is the marking of a virtual geographic area of interest defined by a radius around a location or by the coordinates that define the border for the location.
    - Geofence class is provided in the net.rim.device.api.location package.

20.5.4.3 File System

Users can programmatically create and manage the files and folders on BlackBerry smartphones with the File Connection API.

File Connection API
- Introduced with BlackBerry Device Software 4.2
- Based on the GCF

The FileConnection API can be used to connect to the internal and external storages. Internal storage is the application storage or the built-in media storage. All BlackBerry smartphones have internal storage.

```
FileConnection fc = (FileConnection)Connector.open("file:///Store")
```

External media card storage is accessible only on smartphones with micro-SD cards.

FileConnection fc = (FileConnection)Connector.open("file:///SDCard")

The class javax.microedition.io.file.FileConnection is the main component of the File Connection API.

20.5.4.4 Sounds

BlackBerry Java SDK enables users to capture and playback sound files in their device application, which has the following features:

1. Recording audio
   - BlackBerry users can record audio by using the javax.microedition.media. Player class along with the associated RecordControl interface.
   - The recorded file is stored in built-in media storage, media card storage, or to a stream.
   - Different properties of the recording, such as the bit rate and the audio codec, can be specified while creating the player object.
2. Playback audio
   - The class javax.microedition.media.Player supports the playback of a stored audio file or generating a series of tones.
   - The BlackBerry browser instance can playback the audio file by passing the location of an audio file in the same format as any URI.

20.5.4.5 Sensors

BlackBerry devices with touch screen feature include an accelerometer designed to sense the orientation and acceleration of the BlackBerry device.

- Accelerometer APIs are in the net.rim.device.api.system package.
- net.rim.device.api.system.AccelerometerSensor.isSupported() API can be used by developers to check whether the device supports an accelerometer.
- AccelerometerData class can be used to identify the direction the user moves the BlackBerry device.

20.6 Conclusion

This chapter shows how to create the HelloWorld program for Android, iPhone, Windows Phone, Windows Mobile, and BlackBerry platform. The chapter also covers high-level details on the key APIs that can be used in the application development.

On comparing the different development environments, Visual Studio IDE is rated better than Eclipse-based Android and BlackBerry- and Xcode-based iOS application development. With Visual Studio and Expression Blend, amazing UIs can be designed in a short time. The amount of configuration that needs to be done for the application development is less in both Visual Studio and Xcode. With the advancement in HTML5 and jQuery, Mobile Web programming will slowly gain prominence over the App Store kind of business.

Additional Reading

Android: http://developer.android.com/index.html
iOS: http://developer.apple.com/devcenter/ios/index.action
Windows Phone: http://msdn.microsoft.com/en-us/library/ff402535(v=vs.92).aspx
Windows Mobile: http://msdn.microsoft.com/en-us/windowsmobile/bb264318
Blackberry: http://us.blackberry.com/developers/

TECHNOLOGY CONSIDERATIONS IN MOBILITY

Chapter 21

Mobile Security

One of the famous writers and freethinkers of the early 20th century, H.L. Mencken, said, "Most people want security in this world, not Liberty." Half a decade later, this quote still makes us think, and it is because of the ever-increasing need for security in all walks of life. As the current trend is to go mobile in all walks of life, security has become an inevitable component of any mobility solution. Smartphones are no longer phones but full-fledged mobile computers running an operating system and powerful applications.

According to the latest trends, the use of wireless network is proliferating, enterprises are going mobile, more and more business applications are ported to mobile platforms, diverse kinds of mobile devices need to be managed, personal devices are being used in the corporate environment, and the existing policies and management solutions are incapable of addressing the new mobile environments. All these developments in enterprise mobility have created a greater significance for mobile security and its emergence as the first priority in infrastructure design and formulation of business strategies. The leaders of the industry in the various sectors are formulating their mobile strategies considering the current trends in the field of consumer smartphones, enterprise mobile applications, tablet PCs, and slates, which are the preferred choice of people.

21.1 Introduction

According to Juniper Networks, the reports on malicious mobile threats for 2010–2011 have found a 400% increase in Android malware and targeted attacks over WiFi. According to a survey conducted on large businesses, 40% consider smartphones as the greatest security risk. About 17% of the security-breach cases reported was against short messaging services (SMS) Trojans, which send SMS to some premium-rated numbers, thereby causing monitory loss to users and businesses; 20% of teens are found to use mobile devices for sending explicit or inappropriate contents. Also mobile phones can easily escape security checks and are used to capture images and videos of confidential and private data. Capturing, marketing, and distributing porn videos using smartphones have become a social issue. The capability of smartphones to capture large amounts of data and transfer them to cloud or remote storage locations is a feature that is greatly misused by people. It is important for both consumers and enterprises to be aware of the security risks.

Mobile security solutions have become a booming industry now. Antivirus and antimalware products for securing devices against malicious spyware, malware, applications, SMS Trojans, and infected secure digital (SD) cards are increasing in the industry. Solutions to locate, lock, track, and procure lost and stolen devices are another class of software solutions. Solutions are available in the market to secure communication interfaces of smartphones such as WiFi, Bluetooth, universal serial bus (USB), and other interfaces. Statistics shows that in 2010–2011, 45% of companies expressed their willingness to invest in mobile security. Market trends show an increase in the demand of mobile device management solutions for mobile security from 13% in 2010 to 25% in 2011.

Consulting services are also seeing an increase in demand among organizations that seek assistance in formulating strategies for their mobility operations at an enterprise level and also in determining the right kind of mobile devices and technology platforms. Extending corporate security policies to mobility solutions is the primary focus.

21.2 Enterprise Mobile Management and Security

21.2.1 Defining a Mobile Strategy

For every enterprise, it is important to formulate a mobile strategy before considering the solutions for mobile device management. These strategies need to be revised periodically based on the latest developments in this industry. It should define a technology road map for implementing the strategies. For choosing the right solution, we need to consider factors such as the need for customer mobile application (i.e., whether to provide corporate mobile devices to employees or provide device management solutions to personal mobile devices), thereby reducing the operational cost and the costs on roaming and data charges. In the case of corporate devices, an organization has to use expense management solutions to settle the bills of corporate mobile device usage. Organizations also have to use solutions for security and policy deployment and management on the devices. Corporate mobile policies should have the following basic elements:

- Mobile security/access control policy
- Mobile device management and support
- Mobile framework

21.2.1.1 Mobile Security and Access Control Policy

21.2.1.1.1 Mobility Authentication and Authorization

The mobile security policy should consider enforcing the following approaches:

- A strong password policy: It includes authentication, administration, and user login.
- Allowing usage of the device in dual mode—both personal and corporate.
- Multifactor authentication: Additional authentication can be enforced by using hardware secure tokens that generate a key that needs to be provided for access to secure mobile applications. This is an effective mechanism against phishing and online identity theft. Different authentication factors that can be combined to provide multiple security layers are hardware-based tokens, user ID and password, biometric scan such as fingerprint, retinal scan, or voice print.
- Situation-aware authentication: Situation-aware authentication is achieved by using a cognitive process. A cognitive system could be a human controlling the system or a machine. However, the cognitive system should be aware of the available resources and its maximum and minimum limits, system configuration, previous system states, and other necessary information based on the type of system. An example of situation-aware authentication system is the Mobile *Ad Hoc* network. In addition to measuring the success ratio for determining the effectiveness of authentication, the system is designed to rely on the quality of authentication (QOA). QOA is defined as the confidence level of an authenticating entity on the target device. Combining success ratio and QOA processes would ensure complete evaluation of authentication.
- Lock-down devices to provide access to selected features and applications according to access permissions set for a user profile.
- Lock-down browser functionalities.
- Audit login for database or device resources such as registry.
- Device lock-down on any attempts to hack the device or multiple entries of invalid login credentials.

21.2.1.1.2 Mobile Identity Management

The mobile phone has acquired a new definition as the digital identity of a person. It is the digital signature of a person, which tightly associates the mobile device and the subscriber identity module (SIM) card with the user's credentials. It provides better security when compared with smart cards. The European Telecommunications Standards Institute has established a mobile signature service standard. The government of Finland has for the first time introduced "Certificate Authority" (CA) to issue digital certificates to link the digital key of a SIM card to a person's complete details. Many countries and consortiums provide digital certificates for creating mobile identities for their citizens and members.

21.2.1.1.3 Securing Data

Securing data involves the following approaches:

- Wipe all data and disable the device in case of a security threat even in case the device is not accessible over the network.
- Blocking Activesync or similar data synchronization and data access options. Activesync and BlackBerry Enterprise Solutions can be configured to meet most of the enterprise needs for Windows and BlackBerry phones and to meet the challenges of new security risks arising in the industry, enterprises prefer to go for sophisticated and dedicated mobile device management solutions.
- Usage of appropriate encryption protocols such as secure sockets layer (SSL) and transport security layer (TSL).
- Data and software recovery in case of malicious software attacks and periodic backup of data or snapshot of device registry and configuration settings.
- Blocking Bluetooth, WiFi, and USB and limiting the installation of applications not suggested by the organization. These features are permanently blocked in case the employees are provided corporate devices. In case of allowing the usage of personal devices for corporate purposes, these features are controlled and access to corporate data is restricted by creating an isolated virtual environment for the user to work on corporate data. Similar virtualization solutions are discussed in Chapter 26.

21.2.1.1.4 Tracking User and Device Activities

- Logging, retrieving, and analyzing user activities and important device events.
- Creating rules and alerts on configured activities happening on the device.
- Location-based tracking based on the telecom service provider or global positioning system services. It includes tracking of device movement, locating stolen or missing devices, and recording the location information history of devices.
- Option to select third-party solutions to further extend the security and enterprise requirements. This includes integration of third-party solutions for scripting, reporting tools, and device management.

21.2.1.1.5 Defining Security Models for the Application and Device

Depending on the enterprise requirements, a suitable security model needs to be defined for the mobile devices and mobile applications. Usage of security framework or third-party security tools should ensure controlled access to system resources and applications based on user roles and permissions set for the user. For example, Android is a privilege-separated operating system where each application has a unique system identity (Linux user ID and group ID), which is used by the framework to isolate the application space from conflicting with each other. Also every Android application must have an AndroidManifest.xml file in its root directory, which basically is a declaration by the application about its security permissions and the resources it has access to.

21.2.1.1.6 Securing Mobile Transactions (m-Commerce)

Previously, mobile devices handled data such as music, images, contacts, and ring tones, but the smartphones of today carry more sensitive data and perform financial transactions. Mobile banking has become wide spread. The new technology and market space that has recently evolved is m-Commerce (mobile commerce). Lack of established security practices has slowed down this field, but it has a great potential for growth according to the recent surveys conducted. The projected revenue from m-Commerce is $633.4 billion as indicated in http://www.nearfieldcommunicationsworld.com. The near-field communication (NFC) forum had established the standards for implementing the NFC support of the mobile devices.

NFC technology allows industrial players to enable payment from the mobile device of a customer by sending virtual cards (virtual credit and debit cards) and establishing payment gateways. Combining the mobile identity management technology with m-Commerce makes it more secure than the existing modes of financial transactions. An example of such an application is Google Wallet. It is an Android-based virtual credit card service offering from Google. The following security features are available for this service:

- Lock for wallet application using secure PIN.
- It stores the encrypted payment card credentials in a dedicated computer chip in the phone, which is called Secure Element. The Secure Element holds a separate memory in the mobile device, which can be accessed only by the Google Wallet application.
- There are multiple layers of security features with the collaboration between Google and MasterCard.
- Even if the device is stolen, the user can contact the corresponding bank and disable the card.

Other applications of m-Commerce are ticketing (purchase of rail, airway, and movie tickets), boarding pass (the NFC device acts as boarding pass), coupons, point-of-sale, tour guide, etc.

21.2.1.2 Mobile Device Management

Mobile device management should consider the following for enforcing mobile security:

- Support for diverse kinds of devices
- Management console to enforce security policies in devices and run scripts to schedule and configure events
- Central management of all devices and security policies
- Creating and deploying a master image for all devices
- Managing application versions in the devices and automating the process
- Remote execution of antimalware and antivirus applications
- Real-time push of data or installation packages to multiple devices
- Real-time monitoring and remote access to device desktop and device resources
- Broadcast messages to the device and interactive chat with the device from the control room
- Provide support and help to users; it includes providing training information and helping users remotely by accessing their devices over the network and providing education and demonstrations to users about using the security features.
- E-mail service management for devices
- Regular monitoring of devices and activities for identifying any potential security risks
  Refer to Chapter 29 for a discussion on mobile device management.

21.2.1.3 Mobile Framework

Managing mobile security without a well-defined framework is a tedious task.

This is equally true for different mobile platforms such as iOS, Windows Phone, Windows Mobile, Android, and other mobile platforms. Open-source platforms have greater flexibility to be customized for specific uses according to needs and requirements. However, with greater control there is greater responsibility, as users have complete access to system resources and application programming interfaces (APIs), which would provide unrestricted access to unknown and entrusted applications. It is the role of the mobile security framework to prevent such vulnerabilities of a platform. The security framework can be designed at the mobile operating system level and at the application level. A mobile security framework would help in the following areas:

- Automate tasks for prevention, monitoring, detection, and isolation of security breaches
- Ensure security at different levels of intelligence
- Create and manage scripts
- Ensure data security and encryption

When the number of devices to manage becomes huge, the automation of tasks makes the process easier. Automation provides the user tools to schedule tasks for a group of devices. Automation also helps in saving time. This also helps in reducing the costs on IT support and infrastructure. It automates the application versions, validates and upgrades security certificates, customizes profiles, and ensures compliance to policies. The ability to write and manage custom scripts by the framework allows users to schedule tasks to run the script for a set of devices for a specific day or a week over a period of time. The script can also make intelligent decisions for execution based on the battery level, connectivity, sufficient memory, etc. This improves the maintainability and scalability by adding more devices to the fleet.

Frameworks provide flexibility to ensure security at different levels of intelligence. They could perform integrity checks for the authenticity of executables at the boot-loader, kernel, and application levels. The framework could be used to map the source code with the executables using cryptography-based source authentication. Most of the highly targeted attacks on security modify the program logic in the executables. For example, the computer worm called Stuxnet is an APT-malware attack, which spreads across thousands of computers in a nuclear power plant. The attack was actually intended to modify the program logic of the Siemens code called Organizational Block 35 of the Siemens control system for nuclear power plants, which monitors critical factory operations. This was one of the most sophisticated attacks that we have seen in the history of malware attacks. Examples of security frameworks include Zenprise Windows Mobile Security Management Framework and Mobile Simplified Security Framework developed for Maemo and Meego platforms.

21.2.3 Mobile Management and Security Solutions in the Market

21.2.3.1 Zenprise Mobile Management Solution for iOS

It is available in the iPhone App Store by the name "Zenprise for Employees," which needs to be downloaded and installed in the iPhone. It could be used to establish a secure connection with your enterprise network by providing the server details and authentication data provided by your organization. It requires the user to install a corporate certificate that is validated with the enterprise network. It also requires the user to download, install, and provision a personal profile, which can be used to configure phone settings, password policy, e-mail account, WiFi, and virtual private network (VPN) settings.

21.2.3.2 MaaS360 Mobile Device Management Platform

According to the MaaS360 Mobile Device Management (MDM) architecture, the life cycle of MDM has been classified into provisioning, management, and deprovisioning of devices. Provisioning includes commissioning new devices under the management framework and applying rules, configurations, and security settings. Management mainly involves day-to-day IT management activities. Deprovisioning involves decommissioning devices from the service and wiping of data from the device in case the device is stolen. It can configure active sync in Windows devices and enable mailbox access to specific user(s) using the device. Maas360 is available for iPhone, Windows Phone, and Android devices.

21.2.3.3 SODA™

Secure-on-device API (SODA™) solution from Smith Micro software provides a single consistent secure interface for communicating across all types of mobile broadband devices, chipset suppliers, operating systems, hardware, and software (refer to the Section 30.7 for a discussion on some of the major solution providers for mobile antivirus and mobile VPN in the market).

21.3 Implementing Mobile Security by Developers

A developer should ensure that all known vulnerabilities and security issues are addressed in the design, coding, and testing phases. Some of the common vulnerabilities that need to be addressed are as follows:

1. Avoiding buffer overflows in stack-and-heap memory
2. Invalidated data input from untrusted sources
3. Race conditions
4. Insecure file operations
5. Access control
6. Secure storage and encryption of data
7. Social engineering where the user is tricked to provide sensitive data to the attacker

How to mitigate these basic and known vulnerabilities is provided in the developer guides available in the official web sites of Android, iPhone, Windows Phone, and other platforms. Usually the APIs and methods to address these basic vulnerabilities are provided in the platform level for the developers.

21.3.1 Android Platform

Android has a well-defined process and policies for third-party applications for defining the privileges and access to the user and device data and making the process transparent to users. By design, the Android kernel sandboxes applications from each other, and it does not allow the following:

- Applications to perform any operation that would overwrite into any other application's process space. Basically, security is enforced at the process level.
- Read-and-write operations on user's private data (contacts, e-mail, etc.).
- Accessing the network.
- Keeping the device awake.

AndroidManifest.xml can be configured to set the access permissions for each application. This file has to be present in the root directory of any application. In this configuration XML file, if the shared user ID attribute in the manifest tag is set for the same user ID, all such packages will be considered part of the same application and will have access rights to shared data and files across the applications or packages signed for that user ID. The file also declares the minimum level of Android APIs required by the application and also the libraries the application needs to be linked to.

We can create new tags by name <uses-permission> in the AndroidManifest. xml to define new permissions for the application, for example, permission to send and receive SMS. All Android applications have to be signed with a certificate. The private key for the certificate is held by the developer of that application. Details of all the Android APIs and help for developers are well documented in the official site for Android developers (http://developer.android.com).

21.3.1.1 Pluggable Authentication Modules

Android supports adding new authentication modules from third-party developers. For example, representational state transfer (REST) API can be used to create custom Android and hypertext transfer protocol (HTTP) authentication using REST services. Another example is RIFT Mobile Authenticator for Android devices, which can be downloaded from Android Marketplace. Some of these third-party pluggable authentication modules (PAMs) provide APIs to customize them to suit your Android application. A PAM is used to set up a workable environment for the user. On user lock-out, the PAM will dissolve the working environment.

21.3.2 Apple iOS Platform

There are lot of security features built into iOS, such as security APIs for cryptographic services, read-and-verify certificates, use of a "keychain" for secure storage of passwords and cryptographic keys, addition of a digital signature to data, and generation of cryptographically secure random numbers and APIs to transport data securely over a network using SSL or TLS. The security policies for iPhone are unique and are different from other platforms such as Android or Windows Phone. Apple has introduced a vetting process to prevent malicious applications. This vetting process ensures that all iPhone applications comply with Apple's privacy and security rules before they are distributed to users through the App Store. According to these policies, an application should get explicit consent from the user before sending any data to third parties. According to the policy, applications may ask for permission from the user only when functionality is dependent on the availability of data. But there were instances when Apple had to remove some applications from the iTunes App Store, which bypassed Apple's security policies for protecting customers. However, there are other unofficial application repositories such as Cydia mainly for jail-broken iPhones.

Applications are expected to respect personal identifiable information stored in the mobile devices as per the agreed policies. Such applications are scrutinized by Apple's vetting process and provided with a digital certificate, but there are few applications that were found to have leaked the personal information and unique ID of the device. This vulnerability has allowed third parties to track and create the user's preferences and application usage patterns. The basic flaws of the policies are as follows:

■ The policies are not enforced at a framework level and are only enforced by licensing agreements and digital certificates.
■ iPhone does not ensure that the data accessed by the application are relevant to its functionality.
■ The licensing agreement neither has precise definition for the scope of sensitive data nor enumerates functions that can be categorized as sensitive.

PiOS is a third-party iOS application that is capable of identifying breach of privacy policies and sharing of user-sensitive data to third parties without consent from the user. It also tracks access to sensitive data not relevant for the application (refer to the Secure Coding Guide provided in Apple's official iOS Developer Library and to "Additional Reading.")

21.4 Mobile Security from the Telecom Service Provider Perspective

21.4.1 History of Evolution of Security Threats

According to the history of evolution of security threats in the mobile telecom industry, there were only a few security threats in the period from 1998 to 2004. These threats were mainly spying on subscribers, spoofing of multimedia message services (MMS), and attacks specific to certain service providers, exploiting vulnerabilities specific to the service provider. In 2005, Bluejacking attacks emerged. This included attacks on mobile devices over Bluetooth, such as spamming and stealing pictures and contact lists stored in mobile phones. Attacks mainly targeted Bluetooth devices that had no password set and which were within the proximity of 10 m from the attacker. Common grounds of attacks were bus and train stations and people on travel. In the later half of 2005, viruses were spread over Bluetooth. Another development in 2005 was MMS exploits. MMS could do activities similar to an application, and it could send or receive phone calls automatically. The year

2009 witnessed messaging exploits that automatically sent messages from mobile devices. Carriers implemented the standards on their own, and this caused the MMS attacks to target specific carriers whose design had vulnerabilities. Another type of attack was the man-in-the-middle attacks where the proxy settings in the attacked devices are changed by the attacker, and the attacker could capture all the data and web traffic. The attacker could see the entire flow of actions from the user.

21.4.2 Latest Trends in Security Threats and Attacks

The year 2011 saw more sophisticated attacks such as base-band exploits, browser-based attacks, attacks at the radio level, and advanced persistent threats. Attacks such as the browser-based ones could affect devices from different manufactures. For example, Webcat is an open standard used by RIM and Android. For any vulnerability in Webcat, we have to change the Webcat for the target devices.

Advanced persistent threats have lots of potential and are a major challenge to the mobile security industry. These threats lay the foundation for cyber warfare.

21.4.3 Some Examples of Mobile Malwares

ZeuS in the Mobile (Zitmo) steals user inputs in the keyboard and sends the data over the network as SMS in the background; GoldDream, DDLight2, and "GoldDream" malware are found to be spreading through different applications; DroidDream and DroidDream Light family are malicious or infected applications.

21.4.4 Detecting Malware Attacks

Malware has a spreading mechanism to spread from one device to another, and usually, it is through messages, which are the most common medium of communication between people. Malwares send messages to all contacts in the address book of the affected device. When the person getting the message clicks on the link in the message, the malicious software gets downloaded to the device. One such solution implemented by service providers to detect such attacks is to have some hidden entries in the contact book that is not visible to the user. The user can never send messages to these hidden numbers but the malware can. The messages sent to these hidden numbers are monitored and tracked. Such messages can be blocked at the message center of the service provider itself to prevent spreading of the malware.

21.4.5 Mitigating Mobile Malware

Smartphones are no longer phones but full-fledged mobile computers running an operating system and powerful applications. Detecting malicious data traffic at the network layer has some advantages in identifying the affected device, preventing the malicious software from misusing the device and network resources, and cleaning up the malicious software from the device. A telecom provider can get the statistics about the infection in a greater geographic region.

The telecom service provider AT&T has implemented a solution to detect malicious data patterns, find their source device, and then corner down the malicious application running in the device. There is a mitigation engine at the command and control servers at the network layer to examine the data packets, and there is a trusted host component in each device to identify the suspicious behavior of the host and reach out to the application that launched the malware attack. The trusted component is part of a virtual environment on which the applications are running in the host device, where it can examine the data packets generated by various applications. In another model, where there is no virtual environment present, the trusted component is part of the device operating system that can intercept and examine the data packets. The malicious applications detected are further used to refine the algorithm to detect such data packets.

21.4.6 Advanced Persistent Threat Detection

Advanced persistent threats (APTs) are usually extremely targeted attacks to steal information. They are designed to survive and can reconfigure themselves to be adaptive to the actions taken by antimalware software. Malwares are built to be adaptable, so they can stay in the attacking environment for longer time when preventive actions are enforced upon them. These malwares are resilient, and these can detect the presence of reverse engineering and shut down. Also the malware gets stored in undetectable areas such as in system volume and system restore. This makes the malware come back after device clean-up and system restore. Application whitelisting by antimalware solutions has proved to be an effective counter measure for APT attacks.

21.5 Open Mobile Terminal Platform

Open mobile terminal platform (OMTP; http://www.omtp.org) is a forum formed by mobile network operators to discuss and define standards with mobile device manufacturers. Mobile device manufactures in this forum include major original equipment manufacturers (OEMs) companies such as Nokia, Samsung, Motorola, Huawei, Sony Ericsson, and LG electronics. Mobile operations in the forum include AT&T, Orange, Deutsche Telekom AG, KT, Vodafone, Smart Communications, Telecom Italia, Telefónica, and Telenor. The forum's major work was to standardize terminal requirements for mobile operators.

OMTP has a major contribution to mobile security. The BONDI project was started by OMTP, which has been later moved into the wholesale application community. This project is intended to standardize a set of key interfaces from web services to mobile devices and create a user-controlled security policy. Major activities of the BONDI project, according to http://bondi.omtp.org, are defining the following requirements:

- Interface requirements
- Security and architecture requirements
- Security policy document-type definition (DTD)
- Reference implementation (RI)
- Compliance criteria

21.6 Security in Next-Generation Mobile Networks

In this section, the security features in next-generation mobile networks (NGMNs) are very briefly discussed. The current generation network technologies are high-speed downlink packet access (HSDPA) and evolution-data optimized (EVDO). The NGMNs are said to be system architecture evolution or long-term evolution (SAE/LTE) by 3GPP and IEEE 802.16e or WiMAX. The NGMN alliance and the Institute of Electrical and Electronics Engineers (IEEE) are the major bodies involved in research and standardization of the mobile network. They have proposed several measures to ensure security for mobile users at the level of network service providers (Internet service providers), and the highlights of these measures are as follows:

- Providing secure access across the first hop provided by the operator
- Protection across all communication planes: the management plane, control plane, and user plane
- Deploying self-protection mechanisms at all levels of the network system to protect against external attacks and unauthenticated intrusions
- New ciphering mechanisms and built-in VPN encryption to protect mobile networks from attacks using viruses and spams
- Providing secure access to operator-provided services
- Secure mobility management of inter and intraradio access technology handovers
- Secure charging mechanism for services offered through third-party networks

More details on these measures may be found at http://www.ngmn.org.

21.7 Conclusion

Forthcoming years will witness a greater evolution of security systems in the context of newly evolving types of attacks. Future attacks would target specific users or information irrespective of the system in use, whether it is mobile devices or computers. New platforms such as iOS and Android are expected to face attacks. We will witness new combinations of end-point security and control solutions that will overlap with computer life cycle management solutions. Blacklisting and whitelisting of applications become equally important for antimalware applications.

21.7.1 Mobility Entering the Cyber Warfare

We have seen some of the recent cyber attacks, which highlight the potential damage that can be caused to an industry or a nation. Such attacks are highly targeted to attack a particular system at a specific time and place. Such attacking systems are capable of intermittently doing checks to determine whether the parameters for launching the attacks are met. Such a system can spread on its own and cleans up all the traces it followed. Such malicious programs are designed to mutate and make adaptive changes to resist counter measures taken against them. Such attacks could paralyze an entire state or a nation. Mobile devices are good carriers and triggers for similar kinds of attacks. One example is the computer worm called Stuxnet, which attacked the industrial nuclear power plant facilities in Iran in 2010. Stuxnet was designed to spy on industrial systems, gain privileged access to systems by hiding itself from administrators, steal data in industrial systems, reprogram external program logic controllers and hide the changes, and remote control, monitor, and sabotage industrial systems. The use of mobility in terrorist activities is also a major security concern for the governments of all nations. Overall, the ever-increasing challenges in the security space pave ways for more investments, researches, and the evolution of security solutions. The future of the mobile security industry is very promising.

Additional Reading

1. Forrester Research. *Fifteen Mobile Policy Best Practices*. Available at: http://www. forrester.com/rb/Research/fifteen_mobile_policy_best_practices/q/id/57709/t/2
2. http://www.mobilesecurityconference.com
3. http://www.jazdcommunications.com/commtech/leaf/Mobile-Applications-and-Content/Mobile-Security.htm
4. *Near Field Communications and m-Commerce*. Available at: http://www.nearfield-communicationsworld.com/2011/03/17/36483/mobile-payment-security-concerns -put-brakes-on-m-commerce-market
5. http://developer.android.com/guide/topics/security/security.html
6. *Develop your Own Pluggable Authentication Modules (PAM) for Android*. Available at: http://www.packtpub.com/article/development-with-pluggable-authentication-modules-pam
7. *Security Features for iOS Developers*. Available at: http://developer.apple.com/library/ios/navigation/#section=Topics&topic=Security
8. *Next Generation Mobile Networks and Mobile Security*. Available at: http://www. ngmn.org

Chapter 22

Mobile NFC

Near field communication (NFC) is a simple but profound technology that is fast evolving along with other mobile technologies in the market. This technology enables interaction between the virtual mobile world and the physical world. The concept of NFC was coinvented by NXP Semiconductors and Sony in 2002. At that time, the market was not ripe enough to leverage the full potential of this technology. The world is converging on the mobile space. Mobile devices are becoming more powerful in terms of their applications, bandwidth of communication channels, processing power, graphic user interface, and size, which have made these part and parcel of the life of common people. It is all about people's creativity to explore the possibilities of this technology for which the sky is the limit. NFC technology plays a pivotal role in the development of mobile commerce. It helps to reduce staffing, printing costs, and point-of-sale (POS) costs.

It is estimated that more than 70 million mobile devices manufactured in 2011 will have hardware and software capabilities to support NFC. A recent survey conducted by Mobio Identity Systems, a payment service provider, states that around 94% of the people who participated in the survey prefer mobile devices for payments if they could ensure adequate security. It is estimated that by 2016, 85% of the point-of-terminals worldwide would be providing contactless payments. Eric E. Schmidt, Google's chief executive, believes that wireless transactions enabled by the new generation Android smart devices with NFC capabilities would be a serious business for the company. Schmidt in his keynote presentation at the Mobile World Congress said that Google will be working with advertisers for extending offers to NFC-enabled mobile devices, which could offer POS. Google Android 2.3 and its higher versions in the market support NFC. Apple has been keen in investing in NFC and promoting mobile commerce. Apple has recently filed patents on iPay, iBuy, and iCoupons based on NFC technology. Apple also plans to integrate NFC features with its iAds program. We are seeing a whole new set of NFC-based features in iPhone 5. BlackBerry devices launched in the later half of 2011 have NFC capabilities for pairing, streaming control with accessories, and peer-to-peer data exchange. The market trends indicate that NFC is set to be widely accepted in the market and fully operational across all mobile platforms by 2012.

22.1 Introduction

NFC is a collection of short-range (4 cm or less) wireless communication technologies developed for enabling communication and data transfer between two devices that have hardware and software support for this technology. The NFC operating frequency is 13.56 MHz with speed ranging from 106 to 848 kbit/s. This technology is mainly intended for mobile devices. With the introduction of smartphones and new classes of mobile devices such as tablet PCs in the market, wireless data transfer mechanism has become a necessity for the communication of the device with other devices in the physical world. NFC filled this gap and serves as the communication mechanism. NFC would require appropriate hardware and software support in the device. Pluggable NFC modules are now available as micro-SD NFC devices and universal serial bus pluggable NFC devices.

22.1.1 NFC Standards

An NFC forum was formed in 2004 by Nokia, Sony, and NXP semiconductors (a Royal Philips Electronics Company) for setting industry standards for NFC. Now, it has over 140 members. The NFC forum (http://www.nfc-forum. org) defines the standards for implementing NFC hardware and driver software. There are specifications for the NFC antenna in a device, format of data, and data transfer rates. NFC implementation should support radio frequency (RF) requirements for International Standards Organization/International Electrotechnical Commission ISO/IEC 14443A, ISO/IEC 14443 B, and FeliCa as outlined in the ISO18092 defined by the NFC forum. FeliCa is Radio Frequency Identification (RFID) based contactless smartcard system developed by Sony, one of the coinventors of NFC. The following are the specifications listed down by the NFC Forum:

- NFC data exchange format (NDEF) defines the data format to be used in the communication between NFC devices.
- Record-type definition (RTD) for building standard record types.
- Four specific RTDs (text, uniform resource identifier, smart poster, and generic control) for building standard record types.
- Connection handover defines the rules for establishing a connection using other wireless communication technologies.

- Operations specifications for four tag types (1, 2, 3, and 4) enable core inter-operability between tags and NFC devices.
- Logical link control protocol (LLCP) to support peer-to-peer communication between two NFC-enabled devices.
- Digital protocol for communication between NFC-enabled devices.
- Signature RTD defines the format used when signing single or multiple NDEF records.

There are different NFC tag types defined by the NFC forum. A brief summary of the different tag types is given below:

- ISO 14443 is the standard defined for contactless integrated circuit (IC) cards and the transmission technologies used to communicate with the card. It has two types—NFC A (ISO/IEC 14443–3 A) and NFC B (ISO/IEC 14443–3 B). Both operate at 13.56 MHz frequency. The difference between both types is in the modulation methods, coding schemes, and protocol initialization.
- Type-1 tag is based on NFC A, and it has a read-and-write memory capacity of 96 bytes. Type-1 tags are the most cost-effective. The NDEF field of the tag occupies 6 bytes. It could provide a 16- or 32-byte digital signature.
- Type-2 tag is also based on the ISO/IEC 14443–3 A with 48 bytes of read-and-write memory, which is only half the memory capacity of the Type-1 tag. NDEF occupies 2 bytes of memory. Type-2 tags are usually used in unsecure mode, but they can support up to 48 bytes of digital signature. An example of a Type-2 tag is MIFARE UltraLight from Philips.
- Type-3 tag is based on NFC FeliCa (F) or Japanese Industrial Standard (JIS) X6319-4. Type-3 tags include a contactless IC chip, memory, and memory access functions. However, the physical shape is not defined in the specifications. The tag has more memory of 2 KB and higher data rate of 212 kbits/s. It could provide a 16- or 32-byte digital signature.
- Type-4 tags are compatible with ISO 14443A/B. These are more costly compared with Types 1, 2, and 3 because of their high-end security, higher data transfer rates, and faster electrically erasable programmable read-only memory (EEPROM). The memory is variable. The tag has higher read speeds in the range of 106–424 kbits/s. It supports a digital signature of variable length, for example, MIFARE DESFire tag from Philips.
- NDEF is a common data format defined by NFC forum to send data across devices, which is compliant with the standards defined by the NFC forum.

It is interesting to note that types 1 and 2 are of a similar group. Types 3 and 4 are of a similar group with different memory capabilities. The applications of each type of tag have very little overlap. Also Type-1 and Type-2 tags are dual state, which means that read and write operations are allowed on the tag. On the other hand, Type-3 and Type-4 tags are read-only tags. The user can write data and lock the memory. Once locked, the tag will become read only. NFC specifications can be freely downloaded from the NFC forum (http://www.nfc-forum.org/specs). The NFC forum provides a certification program for devices to ensure conformance with standards and interoperability with NFC devices manufactured by other original equipment manufacturers (OEMs). It allows the certified devices to use the NFC emblem to indicate NFC support.

22.1.1.1 Other Standards

There are other organizations involved in defining the standards for NFC. The European Telecommunications Standards Institute (ETSI) or the Smartcard Platform (SCP) defines the standards for the interface between the SIM card and the NFC chipset. Global Platform sets the standards for development, deployment, and management of smartcards. Europay MasterCard and Visa (EMV) are international standards for interoperability of IC cards, POS terminals using these IC cards, and automatic teller machines (ATMs) for authentication and authorization of debit and credit transactions. NfcV (ISO 15693) is the technology used for cards implementing ISO 15693 standards for vicinity cards. These cards can be read from a greater distance (1–1.5 m) compared with proximity cards and operate at 13.56-MHz frequency. The RF signal is used with amplitude shift keying with a modulation index of 10% or 100%.

22.1.2 NFC Modes of Operation

The basic architecture of an NFC system consists of an initiator and a target. The initiator is an active device with its own power. The target can be active or passive.

1. Passive communication mode or reader–writer mode (ISO 14443 and FeliCa schemes): In case the target is passive, the initiator will generate the active RF field, which will power the passive target. Here, the target device acts as a transponder. The passive target can modulate the input RF signal by generating power from the magnetic field of the initiator's RF field. This modulated signal is embedded with data and transmitted back to the initiator in the reader mode. The initiator receives the modulated signal and decodes the data. In the writer mode, the active initiator can write data into the passive target. An RFID tag is an example of a passive target. These features of passive targets make them very simple in design and allow them to take a very small form-factor. Another example is the card emulation mode in which the device acts as a contactless transit pass. The data in an RFID tag can wipe off or rewrite in the write mode of the RFID reader.
2. Active communication mode or peer-to-peer mode (ISO/IEC 18092 standard): In this mode, both the initiator and the target are active devices with their own power. Both generate their own RF field for transmitting data and have a receiver for receiving RF signals, which actively engages in

communication in a synchronous fashion. Based on these two modes, an NFC-enabled system can be designed to have one-way or two-way communication best suited for the purpose, for example, an NFC-based P2P system in which the devices transfer data files and photographs across the devices or share the same using Bluetooth or WiFi link setup parameters.

3. Card emulation mode: The NFC is used in contactless smartcards that are used as authentication devices used within a range of 10 cm. In this mode, there will be an external NFC reader, which will be an active device with power. There will be a contactless smartcard that acts as a passive device. The reader device will read the data from the smartcard and authenticate the user for applications such as contactless ticketing and electronic payments. Such smartcard systems mainly use RFID technology, which follows ISO/IEC 14443 and FeliCa.

22.2 NFC versus Existing Wireless Mobile Communication Technologies

22.2.1 Bluetooth

Even though Bluetooth and NFC operate in the RF range, both these technologies were introduced for different purposes and will not replace one another even though the user has a choice of which technology to be used while implementing a solution. Bluetooth was first introduced to replace cables between call phones and laptops within a short range of 10 m. NFC (106–848 kbit/s) operates at a lower speed compared with Bluetooth V2.1 (2.1 Mbits/s), consumes less power, and can be operated without pairing. However, Bluetooth V4.0 (~1 Mbits/s), which has a range of ~100 m, has low energy and operates at a lower power [<15 mA (transmit or receive)] compared with NFC [<15 mA (read)]. In the case of Bluetooth, both devices involved in communication need to be active devices, whereas NFC is a passive communication mode. In passive mode, NFC consumes more power compared with Bluetooth V4.0, as the active device has to provide power for passive devices for transmitting the signal back with data. The NFC can be used to substitute for Bluetooth pairing used to authenticate a device. Unlike Bluetooth, NFC authentication does not require pass code authentication. NFC bonding can be used to establish a Bluetooth connection between the two devices.

- WiFi: WiFi was designed to optimize local area network (LAN) and make the system wireless. It was designed initially to operate within the 100-m range. NFC bonding can be used to set up an *ad hoc* WiFi connection.
- ZigBee: Wireless technology is used for controlling and monitoring purposes of industrial and residential applications within a range of more than 100 m.

■ Infrared Data Association (IrDA): Wireless communication using infrared frequency within a maximum of 1-m range. Nowadays, this technology is not used in smart devices, and it has been replaced by Bluetooth, which offers a faster transfer rate.

22.2.2 Radio Frequency Identification

A RFID tag can be attached to a product, and an RFID reader can be used to read or write data in the tag using RF signals. RFID tags are passive, and they derive power from the RF field of an active reader.

22.3 Choosing the Right NFC Tag for Your Business Solution

As we have seen while discussing about the different NFC tag types, the four different NFC tag types have their own space of operation, and the applications based on these types have very little overlap. A designer should be fully aware of the merits and demerits of each tag type. Depending on the type of solution, the designer has to balance between cost and performance. If it is a low-budget, low-risk application, then Type-1 tag is best suitable. Specialist applications would require higher specifications for the tag to be used. Tags should have more memory if additional security features are to be implemented or data to be stored in the tag are of a greater size. We have to consider the short swipe-time period between the NFC device and an NFC tag. If the business use involves transfer of data as part of the NFC tag, then the data-read speed should be high to capture data within the short swipe-time. But if it could trigger other services such as Bluetooth for data transfer, then data transmitted in the NFC tag can be minimized. Some applications are best suited to use Type-1 tags, such as smart posters, short message service (SMS), phone number shortcut, and Bluetooth pairing. Here, the tags hold minimum data. Low cost and small size are best suited for this requirement. To select Type-1 or Type-2 tags, information on read and write capabilities is required. In case of read-only memory and faster memory access, types 3 and 4 are suitable. Applications such as ring tone or multimedia message service (MMS) can be triggered by the NFC tag. It would require greater data capacity and high data-transfer speeds. The following factors are to be considered when using tags:

■ Cost factor: The price of an NFC tag is determined by various factors such as the size of memory, IC microchip used, and read–write speed.
■ Tag size: The size of the tag is determined by the type of IC used. If the IC is of a new-generation compact design type, then the size will be drastically reduced. Another factor is the memory associated with the tag.

- Performance: The higher the data read–write speed the lesser is the chance for a data tear to occur within the swipe-time period. In most of the NFC applications, the NFC-enabled device will be in close proximity with the NFC tag only for a few seconds. The "read all" property in Type-1 tags allows the NFC device to read all data in the tag in one shot. This improves the read speed.
- Security: Security is an important consideration for choosing a tag type for your application. A digital signature provided will consume the available memory of an NFC tag. As the size of the certificate increases, the payload data that the tag can carry also reduces. A digital signature would require 16 or 32 bytes and a header field of a 6-byte header. A Type-1 tag having a 16-byte digital certificate would have 58 bytes left with. In case of Type-2 tags, the remaining memory allocated to data in this case would be 14. In case of a 32-byte signature, a Type-2 tag will have no data left for payload.

When writing to a tag, we can lock the tag so that nobody can rewrite the data in the tag. This will prevent malicious update of the tag data (refer to Section 22.5 in this chapter).

22.4 Applications of NFC

22.4.1 Transportation

NFC finds its application in contactless smartcards and readers. These payment mechanisms can be supported in conventional public transit payment systems that use smartcard swipe. There would not be any more paper tickets in buses, trains, or movie theaters. The user just needs to wave the NFC-enabled phone over an NFC tag, and the fare will be deducted from the user's account.

22.4.1.1 Case Studies

German rail operator Deutsche Bahn launched an NFC-ticketing pilot program in the year 2010, which was a great success. Passengers need to touch an NFC tag while boarding the train and while getting off the train, eliminating the need for the passenger to spend any time for buying tickets.

22.4.2 Ease of Use

The main advantage and distinguishing factor of NFC devices compared with other mobile wireless technologies is fast transactions with a single touch. It does not require complex authentication mechanisms as in the case of Bluetooth and WiFi. For example, you can touch your printer with the NFC-enabled device, and it would print the picture in the device screen, or you may touch two NFC devices to initiate a two-player game or touch a wireless headset with your device to use it instantly.

22.4.3 Smart Objects

Smart objects provide extended information to an NFC device about a product or service when the device is brought near the object. Objects can be anything that has a tag embedded in it with data.

- Two-dimensional (2D) barcode tags can be used for object hyperlinking. In this case, a 2D bar code has all the data encoded in it. A barcode reader can be used to scan the bar code or take a photograph of the bar code. These images can be sent over the Internet to a universal resource locator (URL) target and can get the stored data in return to the mobile.
- Direct dial: A phone number associated with a target object can be dialed to receive, and it can get voice information about that object. This has been a great success in public areas such as museums, where it could effectively guide people.
- Hardlink: It is similar to hyperlink, the difference being that it is an alphanumeric sequence associated with a target object. This code can be entered in a web-enabled mobile device, which in turn will download the information about the target object to the mobile device.

22.4.3.1 Case Studies

Objects (http://www.objecs.com) is an object-hyperlinking solutions provider that has introduced a methodology called "point-of-need learning," which provides users the necessary and sufficient information at the right time at the physical point of need. For example, a user brings his or her mobile device in proximity to a passenger bus, and all the route information of that bus is sent to the mobile device. The data may be locally stored in the object embedded in the bus or may be downloaded from a remote database. RosettaStone (http://www.personalrosettastone.com) is an RFID-based solution provider that provides microchips stored with information, which can be embedded in memorials such as graveyards, headstones, and monuments. The data are readily downloaded to a mobile device that comes within the proximity of the embedded microchip.

22.4.4 Social Media

We are familiar with social networking and the role of mobile devices in promoting this activity in the current world. We have a number of location-based tracking mechanisms integrated with social networking such as global positioning system (GPS) tagging, tagging based on nearest transmission tower information, SMS-based tracking, etc. It is an innovative idea that NFC can also be used for location tracking.

22.4.4.1 Case Studies

- Friendticker (http://en.friendticker.com) is a web site where users can create an account and download the applications suitable for their mobile platforms. The web site lists many shops in your locality that offer discounts and rewards. You can visit those stores and check-in yourself in the store using your mobile device, which makes you eligible for the reward or discount scheme. The application would also alert your friends who are nearby.
- NFriendConnector (http://www.nfriendconnector.net) is a prototype application, which was later integrated with Facebook. This mobile application integrates the user's off-line social interactions with online social networks using mobile phones. It allows people who meet at a physical place to exchange profile data with each other using their NFC-enabled phones. They just need to run the NFriendConnector application and make their mobile device touch their friend's device. It acts as a social searcher, and the users need not search the Internet to find out the friend's profile and add it to their Facebook account.
- Google Hotpot is a new marketing model introduced by Google as a pilot project in Portland, Oregon. A marketing firm that is participating in the program will have an NFC-enabled window sticker with the HotPot logo and caption "Recommended on Google." Users can wave their NFC-enabled phone on this sticker, which provides more information about the business. Google will be providing their clients with special Google Places Business Kits, which contain marketing materials that can be used for getting more exposure to potential customers and getting their business rated and reviewed among users browsing the Internet or swiping the Hotpot sticker. Hotpot is for users to share recommendations about a business to their friends. Some companies or programs participating in Hotpot are Voodoo Doughnut and Hotpot Jackpot.
- Social gaming: An example of a social gaming program is Scoreloop challenge.

22.4.5 Mobile Payments

The short range of NFC makes it best suited for secure transactions, and it will soon replace wallets with mobile devices and hard currencies with e-currencies. It will also replace plastic credit cards, loyalty program cards, and coupons. A Gartner report on market analysis states that by 2014, 340 million mobile users will use mobile payments, which total to around $245 billion. Major players in the credit card business such as MasterCard, Visa, and American Express have joined the NFC forum. Day by day, we are seeing other players in the market providing support for this technology. In the United States, AT&T, Verizon, Discovery, Barclays, and T-Mobile have formed an initiative called ISIS Mobile Wallet to launch an NFC-based nationwide mobile payment network in 2012. T-Mobile and Vodafone have joined with banks such as ABR AMRO, ING, and Rabo bank to provide NFC-based payments by 2012. Japanese mobile operators Softbank and KDDI have joined with South Korea's SK Telecom to provide NFC-based payment systems. There are a number of new developments, and every telecom service provider is keen to partner with other financial institutions to roll out NFC-based m-Commerce solutions. These solutions mainly include mobile banking, mobile payments, and money transfers.

22.4.5.1 Case Studies

- FeliCa is a contactless smartcard developed by Sony. The mobile version of FeliCa was developed by FeliCa Networks, which is a subsidiary company of DoCoMo and Sony. It has a strong authentication mechanism using mutual authentication based on a dynamic key. FeliCa card is a passive device. It generates power from the RF signal of a FeliCa reader. The new-generation FeliCa reader announced in June 2011 will have a microchip with encryption based on Advanced Encryption Standards (AES), better performance, and lower power consumption. FeliCa is considered one of the NFC forum's recommendation for contactless smartcards.
- Google Wallet is a Google initiative in partnership with Citi, MasterCard, Sprint, and FirstData to provide contactless payment options for the user using NFC-enabled mobile devices.
- Amazon is introducing NFC-based marketing services. Amazon already has e-payment applications for iPhone and Android.

Major players in credit-card market have established their own contactless payment terminals for NFC-enabled mobile devices. For example, PayPass from MasterCard, ExpressPay from American Express, and payWave are some of them. These terminals provide tap-to-pay feature in selected stores such as McDonalds, HomeDepot, and other merchant locations. Micro-SD based NFC cards are available, which can be used by a wide range of devices to make their devices NFC-enabled.

- ISIS (http://www.paywithisis.com) is e-wallet, which is a joint venture between AT&T, Verizon, and T-Mobile USA to provide a nation-wide mobile commerce network with support for NFC-enabled smart devices.
- NFC payment solutions: Some other companies that have NFC-based payment solutions are Bling Nation, Boku, Zetawire, Placepop, AisleBuyer, and Coupious, to name a few. Other industries are keen to adopt NFC-based payment options for their customers in collaboration with payment specialist vendors.
- Coca-Cola is partnering with the European payment specialist PingPing to provide NFC-enabled vending machines that will accept payments by just

bringing an NFC-enabled mobile phone near the vending machine. HTC has signed a deal with China's credit-card service provider UnionPay to provide NFC-based payment options using HTC mobile devices.

22.4.6 Peer-to-Peer Applications

When the data to be transferred to another device are of a few kilobytes, then the NFC service would transfer the data within the shot span of time when two devices are in close proximity. However, if the data to be transmitted are of a greater size, then the NFC could establish a separate wireless connection over Bluetooth or WiFi and initiate file transfer. For example, a user could select a photo or a folder and bring the mobile device in proximity of an NFC-enabled printer. The NFC service in the device would establish a connection with the printer over Bluetooth and then print the photo or contents in the selected folder (check the Apple solutions in peer-to-peer communication in Section 22.6).

22.4.7 Health Care

NFC tags can be used to track the monitoring of a patient. Doctors and nurses have to scan their NFC device or smartcard to register their actions. There are many uses of this in the medical field.

22.4.7.1 Case Study

NFC technology was used to track patients in a low-resource area. It has been used in Pakistan to study about pneumonia in young children. Each child was given an NFC-enabled bracelet with an RFID tag. When the child visits a health care center, these tags are scanned to keep records of the patients.

22.4.8 Accessibility

NFC can be used to simplify the communication for people with disabilities. NFC-enabled phone could be used to touch a person's photograph to automatically dial a previously configured cell phone number. The NFC device could read aloud when the camera of an NFC-enabled device is brought near a text.

22.4.9 Content Sharing

NFC devices can be used to share different types of mobile contents with other NFC devices. A contact from the contact book can be shared by bringing the devices in close proximity. The NFC application would trigger Bluetooth services to transfer the required content. Web pages of interest can be shared with friends. While playing a YouTube video, you can share it with friends by just touching their phone with yours and the same video starts playing in the other device. Similarly, applications can also be shared across devices.

22.4.10 Service Initiation

The NFC application would act as a trigger for other services. When the NFC-enabled device is brought near a poster or a signage that has an NFC tag embedded in it, then the NFC application in the device would trigger appropriate services or applications in the device; for example, it would start the Bluetooth services to transfer a media content, automatically play the content in the media player, or automatically load a promotional video about the product or services from YouTube, and update your recent purchase of a product on the social networking site. It could trigger the GPS service to tag your location in Facebook or Google Plus. The NFC application in a device could switch on WiFi and automatically set up an *ad hoc* network to stream promotional video when the user waves the device on a signage near a WiFi hot spot. It could automatically do the set up in your device to add your friends as co-players in a mobile video game. While entering a store, you could swipe your NFC-enabled device over a tag to trigger download of an application. The application could provide you guidance on which items are available in which all parts of the store. When the device is brought near an item for sale, the application could provide all the promotional offers and discounts offered for that product.

22.5 NFC Security Challenges

Similar to any other technology, NFC is also not free from security threats. NFC standards do not provide solutions to end-to-end security issues for NFC-based applications. Security needs to be ensured at multiple levels. At the device level, there should be strong cryptography and authentication; at the customer level, there should be protection for the device used, protection for data using password, and protection from spyware and malware using antivirus solutions. Some of the common security issues seen in NFC are as follows.

22.5.1 Eavesdropping

The RF signal sent between two NFC devices or tags is captured by an eavesdropping antenna. It will be difficult to eavesdrop passive devices, but active devices are more vulnerable to attacks. Proxmark III is a device that can read, sniff, and clone RFID tags.

22.5.2 Data Modification

In this type of attack, the data in the RF signal are modified or destroyed. An example is an RFID jammer.

22.5.3 Relay Attack

The attacker receives the RF signals from a reader and relays back a response to the reader in real time pretending itself to be the intended receiver. Relay attack is a type of man-in-the-middle attack on the communication channel between two devices. A demonstration of relay attack is available in www.lobnfc.org (http://www.libnfc.org/documentation/examples/nfc-relay).

22.5.4 Threat on Loss or Theft of the NFC Device

With an NFC-enabled mobile device, it becomes a single point of authentication for a variety of applications such as financial transactions, payments, access to a restricted or secure area, etc. Mobile phones are usually protected by a single authentication mechanism of a personal identification number. We should extend the security by introducing multiple physically independent authentication factors in case the mobile device gets stolen.

22.6 NFC Support for Major Mobile Platforms

22.6.1 Google Android

Google Android Gingerbread version 2.3.3 and later editions support NFC. Google is providing more and more NFC capabilities as part of the incremental releases of the Android operating system. According to Android developer's blog, Android has the following updates [application programming interface (API) level 10] for NFC capabilities:

1. A comprehensive reader–writer API for applications to read and write a standard NFC tag.
2. Advanced intent dispatching that can be used by applications to have more control over when and how to launch the application when an NFC tag comes within the NFC field of the device
3. Support for peer-to-peer communication with other NFC devices

Android software development kit (SDK) 2.3.3 has android.nfc and android.nfc. tech packages, which provide APIs for supporting NFC. The related classes in Android are as follows:

- NFCAdapter (to identify and interact with NFC hardware)
- NdefMessage (defines NDEF data message format)
- NdefRecord (defines the type of data shared across devices and the object also contains the actual data)

■ Tag (the type of tag scanned)
■ TagTechnlogy (class used to access tag properties and to perform input–output operations on a tag)

It is mandatory for all Android devices to implement the following tag technologies:

1. NFC A (ISO 14443–3A).
2. NFC B (ISO 14443–3A).
3. NFC F (JIS 6319–4).
4. NfcV (ISO 15693).
5. ISO DEP.
6. NDEF on tag types 1, 2, 3, 4-compliant tag formats defined by the NFC Forum.

Android 4.0 Beam for NFC-based sharing is a new feature in Android 4.0 to instantly exchange anything such as favorite apps, contacts, music, and videos across two NFC-enabled devices. The Beam application pushes a link to the application's details page in Android Market, and the other device launches the Market App to download the app. Developers can use Beam for passing game scores, initiating a multiplayer game, or chat with other NFC Android devices. The new NFC classes introduced for this application are NfcAdapter.CreateNdefMessageCallback, NfcAdapter.OnNdefPushCompleteCallback, and NfcEvent. There are also third-party NFC development kits in the market for faster development of NFC-based solutions (e.g., the NFC development kits for developers from Identive, http://www.identivenfc.com/nfc-software-development-kit-sdk.htm).

22.6.1.1 NFC in Microsoft Windows Phone

Microsoft has partnered with NXP for providing NFC capability for Windows Phone 8. The NFC features available in the platform are as follows:

1. Device pairing for pairing with Bluetooth headsets and speakers
2. Data sharing (e.g., sharing business cards)
3. Device control transfer (e.g., transfer of video call across two NFC devices)
4. Tag reading (e.g., use of smart posters and NFC-tagged devices)

According to sources, Nokia's Symbian and the new Windows Phone devices will also have NFC capabilities.

22.6.1.2 NFC in Apple Products

■ Apple NFC mobile payment solutions: Apple has filed patents on mobile payment concepts such as iPay, iBuy, and iCoupons for a comprehensive and end-to-end mobile payment solution. Apple's mobile payment-related patents filed are Peer-to-Peer Financial Transaction Devices and Methods, System and Method for Processing Peer-to-Peer Financial Transactions, Portable Point of Purchase User Interfaces, Portable Point of Purchase Devices and Methods, Smart Menu Options, and Real-Time Bargain Hunting.

■ Apple NFC-enabled home-networking device: Apple has plans to introduce applications that can use iPhone as an NFC-enabled home networking device using their patents on the systems and methods for simplified resource sharing. The idea is to use iPhone as a universal remote to control all home appliances.

■ Apple NFC-enabled touch screen will be in the market soon. Apple has filed a patent on the Touch-Screen RFID Tag Reader.

■ Apple NFC-based sync and file sharing technology is yet to come in future iOS handheld devices, which will be based on Apple's patent filed in the name "The Grab & Go" (patent application).

■ NFC used for access control: NFC-enabled Apple devices will have the capability to be used as a key for providing access to restricted areas.

■ Apple Trusted Service Manager based on NFC is a program to enable Apple devices to act as a trusted service manager for NFC-based secure payments and other mobile applications. The trusted service may be implemented based on NFC or other technologies. The idea has been patented in the name "iGroups."

■ Public Platform Independent NFC Library (http://www.libnfc.org): Libnfc is an open-source library that provides NFC SDK and APIs for programming a wide range of NFC devices such as desktop readers, dongles, Flat, and OEM readers. The APIs can be freely used under the GNU Lesser General Public License. It could be used for programming micro-SD-card-based NFC devices, which can be inserted to the micro-SD card slot of a mobile device to have NFC functionality. For programming an NFC device, the hardware should be compatible for libnfc APIs. Currently, these APIs are supported by Linux, Mac, and Windows.

22.7 Conclusion

NFC technology is opening up new revenue models. It will bring a revolution in every industry in different ways to interact with customers. There will be no gap between the virtual world and the physical world, and NFC acts as the link between them. Both public and private sectors will leverage the advantages. NFC technology is in its growth phase. Early adopters of this technology will be able to increase their market share in the highly competitive mobile market. Android seems to have an advantage as this technology has been introduced in Android phones before introduction in iPhone, through a series of intermediate releases of operating-system updates. The key areas where NFC will find wide application in the market are service initiation, payment and ticketing, and peer-to-peer communication. Mobile POS is becoming a hot trend in all industries, especially in retail. We will witness a greater evolution of NFC standards and specifications in the future to meet the demands of new innovative solutions using NFC technology. NFC will become more and more cost-effective. Security will be a major area where increased standardization is expected to happen. All telecom providers across the globe are keen in establishing partnership with financial institutions to roll out m-Commerce services to their customers.

Additional Reading

1. http://www.mobilenfc.eu
2. http://www.nfc-forum.org, http://www.nfc-forum.org/specs
3. http://www.nfc-forum.org/resources/white_papers
4. *Android NFC Support for Developers.* Available at http://developer.android.com/reference/android/nfc/package-summary.html; http://developer.android.com/sdk/android-2.3.3.html; http://developer.android.com/reference/android/nfc/tech/TagTechnology.html
5. *NFC Development SDK.* Available at http://www.identivenfc.com/nfc-software-development-kit-sdk.htm
6. *Security Challenges.* Available at http://www.proxmark.org/proxmark
7. Public Platform Independent NFC Library (http://www.libnfc.org)
8. http://www.nfcworld.com
9. http://www.paywithisis.com

Chapter 23

Device Capabilities Leveraged in Apps Location, Magnetometer, Motion Sensor, Touch, and Scanner

The world of mobility is evolving at a greater pace than ever before. Apart from the common user input methods such as keypads, keyboards, and stylus, different kinds of new-generation input methods are evolving, such as accelerometers, touch-screen gestures, capacitive touch, handwriting recognition, light sensors, and vibrators. With the new input methods, devices work magically on the shake, flip, flick, and shout features.

We have already seen the success stories of social platforms that are based on "who you know" (such as Facebook) and "what you are doing" (such as Twitter). With the invention of different kinds of sensors, a new platform based on "where you are" has evolved, which has given a boost to social networking platforms.

23.1 Introduction

In this chapter, we explore the different capabilities of modern mobile devices and how these can be leveraged to create useful applications. Here, the reader is introduced to the world of enormous opportunities for developing applications for various mobile platforms. We also investigate the possibilities of integrating different kinds of sensors, which will again open newer dimensions for application development.

The market trends show that real-world objects such as fridge, television, home appliances, and other electronic gadgets are becoming web-based, and the key technologies involved are smartphones, sensors, and radio frequency identification (RFID). The day is not far off when the household will be a network of Internet-enabled objects.

23.2 Sensors

There are different types of sensors for mobile devices. Some of the most common sensors used in modern devices are as follows.

23.2.1 Touch Sensors

This is the era of touch-screen devices. The present trend in the design of mobile devices is to have maximum display space for the device. Some of the devices have eliminated the use of hard buttons completely, and the user is presented with soft touch buttons and a soft QWERTY keyboard. Unlike the old-generation mobile phones, the new-generation touch phones play the role of a business phone and also as an entertainment device and have abilities to play music, watch music, surf the Internet, capture photos and videos, and much more. All these functionalities would require a wide screen with high screen resolution. According to the current standards, smart mobile devices come with at least 3.5-inch screen, 16-million colors, and touch-sensitive controls. A touch screen has mainly three components: a touch-screen sensor, a controller, and a software driver. A touch sensor is a glass plate that has a touch-sensitive surface, which is placed symmetrically over the display screen. There are different types of touch sensors. Popular sensor technologies used in touch screens are resistive or capacitive touch sensor. Touch can also be provided on surface parts of a mobile device other than the screen.

23.2.1.1 Resistive Touch

In the case of resistive touch screen, the user has to apply slight pressure on the screen for the screen to acknowledge the touch. Resistive touch screen usually comes with a stylus.

23.2.1.2 Capacitive Touch

In the case of a capacitive touch screen, a soft touch is only required to register a touch. There is a minimum touch area defined for a capacitive touch screen, and hence capacitive screens do not register a touch using a sharp stylus. Hence, while designing a display screen for capacitive screens, the buttons and controls should be big enough for finger touch.

23.2.1.3 Touch Controller

The touch controller converts the data from the sensor into information that the driver software can understand. The driver derives the coordinates of the points in the screen where touch has been registered and interprets it as a mouse click or key press. This emulation of a mouse driver avoids the need for specific programming for a touch screen. It is common during mobile application development to have a desktop version for the same application, and no additional programming is required for the user input.

23.2.1.4 Different Means to Input Data in the Device

Touch screen usually takes the user input in different ways such as a soft QWERTY keypad, a soft keypad similar to the conventional hard keypad of mobile phones, or a soft scratch pad where the user can write using fingers. Some of the devices support multitouch in the touch screen. Using two fingers, it allows zooming in and zooming out the display screen. Also, touch screens employ haptics or feedback, which means that there will be vibration of the device or movement of display associated with a touch, which will provide the user an acknowledgement that the touch has been registered.

23.2.1.5 Haptic Tactile Feedback

Haptic technology allows the user to feel different surfaces when the user moves a finger over the surface. Usually, this feel is generated by the vibrator in the device. Users often get a vibration as an acknowledgement for the user's action on the display screen. Numerous researches are going on in this field. Apple has come up with solutions for better usage of haptics. One solution is to have a grid of piezo-electric actuators that can be activated by commands. Users will get different touch sensations when a finger is moved across different parts of the screen. Users may even move fingers across the display without even looking at the device to sense the position of the controls to click.

23.2.1.6 Leveraging Touch Features for Developers

Mobile platforms provide developers the tools and application programming interfaces (APIs) for programming different touch features to provide powerful interactions and user experience. The tools provide stylus input events, pressure, tilt, and distance axes, and related motion event properties. Android 4.0 provides specific tool types for stylus, finger, mouse, and eraser. The platform now provides distinct primary, secondary, and tertiary buttons, as well as back and forward buttons for improved input from multibutton-pointing devices. It also provides support for hover-enter and hover-exit events for advanced navigation and accessibility. These features could be leveraged by the application developer to provide precise drawing and gesturing, shape and handwriting recognition, improved mouse input, and much more.

23.2.2 Accelerometer or Motion Sensor

An accelerometer is a device used to measure proper acceleration. Proper acceleration is the acceleration measured relative to free fall. The device obtains acceleration due to motion with respect to the earth, and for this, the acceleration is measured relative to a local inertial frame. The device can measure both the magnitude and the direction of the acceleration. Nowadays, the type of accelerometers used in mobile devices is the microelectromechanical systems (MEMS). It is capable of detecting free fall, motion, and wake-up. It has dedicated programmable interrupt lines. Mobile devices usually use a three-dimensional (3D) accelerometer capable of 360° motion sensing, which can be controlled by a software. iPhone uses the LIS331DL MEMS chip for acceleration. It measures acceleration in the range 2–8 g and has shock survivability up to 10,000 g per 0.1 s. Accelerometers are commonly used in modern personal electronic devices such as smart phones, personal digital assistants (PDAs), and digital audio players, tablet PCs, digital cameras, advanced video game consoles such as X-Box and PlayStation. It is mainly used as a motion sensor to rotate the screen in the portrait and landscape modes based on the position in which the device is held. It is used for recognizing tap gestures in the screen or on any part of the device. The accelerometer should be calibrated for optimal use. Usually, the devices will be provided with a calibration button, which when pressed will record new acceleration values. The recorded values are taken as reference for further acceleration inputs and finally normalized for optimum results.

23.2.2.1 Applications of Accelerometers

- Trigger actions: Sleep-phase alarm clocks, step counter or pedometer, volume control, tilt sensor in camera applications, image stabilization, antiblur capturing, motion-sensitive games, augmented reality (AR) applications using accelerometer and global positioning system (GPS).
- Enhanced user experience: Motion sensors can also be used to control basic phone features such as receiving and ending a call, writing a message, and activating and deactivating a ring tone. For example, the phone will remain in silent mode when the cell phone display is faced downward. The motion sensor makes the normal phone activities faster. The motion sensor can be used to move a map in the display screen based on how the user moves the device. The user may write a message in the air using the device and the motion sensor could capture it in text.

- Gaming: The motion sensor can take up the steering control of a car in a game. In future, this feature may be available on a car, and we may well drive the vehicle using our mobile device.
- Medical field: If patient remains motionless for a considerable time, the sensor in the mobile device can call for medical assistance.
- Security: When an object is moved from its place, a motion sensor can inform the owner.
- Detect acceleration: It can be used to alarm the user when an object being moved undergoes vibration greater than the allowable limit. A sensor in the electronic gadget can detect free fall and do a device power-off or park the hard-drive heads to prevent damage and data loss.

23.2.3 Gyroscope

An accelerometer measures the linear acceleration, whereas a gyroscope measures the orientation of the device. The gyroscopes used in handheld devices are MEMS-based devices. The main components of a gyroscope are gyroscope frame, gimbal, spin axis, and a rotor. For example, iPhone 4 uses a three-axis gyroscope. With the accelerometer, it could operate on a total of six axes. This makes the iPhone more sensitive and powerful for gaming.

23.2.4 Proximity Sensor

A proximity sensor by definition is a sensor that is capable of detecting a nearby object without any physical contact. Mobile devices mainly use an optical proximity sensor. An optical proximity sensor can be configured to automatically change from earphone to loudspeaker when the user moves the phone away from the ear. Also, it can be used to turn off backlight when the phone is placed near the ear, and the backlight is automatically turned on when the phone is moved away from the ear, thus saving battery power. It also prevents accidental button clicks when the phone is placed near the ear.

23.2.5 Ambient Light Sensor

This sensor can measure how much light is available at any point of time, and it can automatically adjust the display brightness and backlight settings to conserve battery power.

23.2.6 Sound Sensor or Microphone

A microphone is an inevitable component of a cell phone. It captures the voice for video and voice calls and is also used to record voice. Recently, some innovative applications in the market make use of this application for a variety of purposes.

For example, the microphone can be used to calculate the amount of noise in the neighborhood. One such application is Widenoise for iPhone. This application can be helpful in identifying a suitable house in a location where the average noise level is minimum. There are applications that help users to calculate their exposure to noise pollution. Also, a user can measure the amount of noise pollution (measured in decibels) in an environment. Also, with the help of GPS and general packet radio service (GPRS), the data collected by sensors will be available across the web. These data can be used to calculate the collective noise level. There are additional driver softwares to reduce noise in the call using noise-cancellation techniques. This is done by identifying the frequency of the caller's voice, and this specific frequency range is amplified. Also, the background noise is cancelled by using a negative-feedback mechanism.

23.2.7 Temperature Sensor

A temperature sensor, also called as an infrared (IR) sensor, consists of a sensor module, an electronic circuitry, and an optomechanical system. The optomechanical system directs IR radiation onto the sensor. For accurate measurements, the device should be thermally stable, and the device temperature should be lower than the temperature of the measurable targets. Basically, the sensor calibration and the temperature measurement is based on two signals, which are the thermopile and thermister voltages of the IR detector. A temperature sensor may be used to turn off the device if the temperature of the device exceeds the allowable safe limit. There are cases where the device battery had exploded due to an increase in device temperature. The temperature sensor that is kept near the battery can warn the user about a temperature rise and can close the device to avoid further damage. This sensor can be used for the thermometer display on the device. However, this sensor is usually exposed for developers to use it for their application, and it is mainly used for the projection of the device.

23.2.8 RFID

An RFID tag refers to a small electronic device that has a small chip and an antenna capable of carrying a maximum of 2000 bytes of data. An RFID reader is a device used to read or write an RFID tag.

23.2.8.1 Difference between RFID and Bar Code Use

RFID tags have many advantages over bar codes. However, it is not considered a replacement for bar codes, as bar code has its own unique and significant role in the consumer goods industry. An RFID reader does not require a direct line of sight. It can read an RFID tag at distances up to 300 feet. The read rate is much faster than that of barcode readers. The RFID tags are more rugged and may be covered in plastic. They are usually implanted inside the product. The RFID reader can do read–write operations on an RFID tag. Hence, the tags are reusable. However, it is more expensive than bar codes. RFID tags can even be implanted inside a living body.

23.2.8.2 Applications of RFID

These tags can be combined with other sensors and can be used to collect real-time information. For example, an RFID tag can pass on the rate of heartbeat at regular intervals for the last 24 h from a pacemaker to the RFID reader in a smartphone. In retail stores, customers can scan various products using the RFID reader in a smartphone to get detailed information about a product. These tags may be deactivated once the product is billed and moves out of the store. These kinds of RFID tags are called "zombie RFID tags." The dead tag can be reactivated if the product comes back to the store and reenters the supply chain. RFID is the underlying technology for the newly introduced near-field communication (NFC) standards, which is now extensively used in the field of mobility.

23.2.9 NFC Capability

NFC has become a widely adopted technology in mobile devices. This technology has redefined mobility by enabling interaction between the virtual mobile world and the physical world. Now, the mobile is no more a display and caller device but much more. NFC could be used as a trigger for launching a web page or initiating a Bluetooth connection and use appropriate Bluetooth profile to communicate with another device or peripherals (for more details on Mobile NFC, refer to Chapter 22).

23.2.10 Barcode Scanners

Retailers across the globe have adopted bar codes for their products. The popular two-dimensional (2D) bar codes can hold a large amount of data. Also, bar codes are cheaper when compared with related technologies such as RFID. Many of the consumers wish to interact with real-world products using their mobile phones. Consumers are looking to get the best deals, and for this, they have to compare different products. Barcode technology in mobile phones enables users to do product comparisons very easily while shopping. According to the current trend, barcode scanning applications are expected to see a growth in 2011, and more real-world data will be available to users through the Internet and accessible on mobile phones. Users just need to wave their phones before the products and get all data relating to comparative products.

Google's Favorite Places program leverages barcode technology to infiltrate the real world using bar codes, mobile coupons, and visual search. According to this program, Google will provide to local businesses stickers with Google's logo, a scannable bar code, and a message reading "We are a favorite place on Google." These stickers will be pasted in store windows for the consumers to scan, and the user will be taken to that store's "place page" where various details such as mobile coupons, promotional offers, menus (for restaurants), product details, and contact information will be available. Also, users can give star ratings to the product or business, and they may submit their reviews.

23.2.11 Camera

When camera was first introduced in phones, it was never expected to become a user data input source. However, in modern mobile devices, it has major roles to play such as high-definition image and video capture, video call, face recognition, and user authentication. Google's new visual search service allows users to take a photograph of a location and use it to perform a Google search. This service is intended to provide information on landmarks, businesses or associated locations, stores in those locations and products on store shelves, or in billboard advertisements in that location. Eventually, it could even identify people. Cameras can take snapshots of bar codes, and these bar codes can be read from the mobile screen using a barcode scanner. This idea has been used in one of the applications developed by Infosys to generate a paperless boarding pass for one of its client. Here, the user receives a soft copy of the boarding pass in the form of a 2D bar code. An agent at the airport scans the bar code directly from the mobile phone display screen and retrieves all the information about the passenger.

One emerging technology using camera is the AR facial recognition for mobiles. This technology makes use of video capabilities, geolocation features, processor speeds, and APIs from web services. It uses the face-recognition technique where it compares a 3D model of a face in live video feeds. For more information, check on the AR browser application called Layer for the Android platform. Wikitude is an AR application that provides a *Wikipedia* layer for Android. Another one is the TwittARound iPhone application, which finds out nearby tweets and layers over video feeds.

TEVA is an AR application for Nokia. It is a unique blend of user-generated content and alternate reality gaming (ARG). ARG is an interactive narration using real world as platform. The characters in this will appear to be realistic and might provide the data in a phone call. One such ARG is the game called *The Lost Experience*. According to current standards, the camera should be at least 5 mega-pixels, with autofocus and light-emitting diode (LED) flash, and should have capabilities for face and smile recognition and geotagging.

23.2.12 Voice Recognition

Voice recognition is considered to be an evolving next generation user data input method for mobile applications as it is the easiest and fastest way of data entry.

There are mobile applications in the market that translate voice commands into search queries. Google has introduced a search application based on voice recognition. For more information, check on goog-411 from Google, which provides voice search, voice input, and voice actions (such as making a call). A similar application is Say Where for iPhone.

23.2.13 Magnetometer

Magnetometer or a digital compass is an instrument used to measure the strength and direction of a magnetic field. It shows the direction that we are facing. When this instrument is used along with the accelerometer, camera, and GPS, it opens a new world of opportunities for developers to develop innovative applications. Accelerometer gives the input on the angle of vision (whether looking up or down). This gives information on where or what you are looking at. The camera could capture the exact scene you are looking at. The magnetometer determines the direction we are facing. The GPS tells the coordinates or position. That is, it gives information on where you are. All these real-time information along with predefined information from a cloud network or web service are used to create applications that will simulate the real-time environment so magnificently that the application could provide inputs to the senses for touch, vision, and hearing. Also using camera, it could recognize your friends nearby with the help of face-recognition technology, and your friends would be coplayers with you in the AR application. In future, AR applications might be able to simulate smell and taste also.

The AR application could arrange data in different layers of display and provide sufficient background information to the user or give pointers on the screen to users. Applications using magnetometers help users to reach a nearby destination such as automated teller machines (ATMs), shops where the commodity they are looking for is available, bars, cinemas, restaurants, and other hot spots. It can lead us through a path with the help of map and pointers. When the functionalities of the accelerometer and magnetometer are combined, the roll, pitch, and yaw can be measured. Combined with the features of the gyroscope, up and down, left and right, and forward and backward motions can be measured. Thus, applications using these three sensors can sense the motion in six axes (more details of some AR applications can be found in Section 23.2.11 of this chapter).

23.2.14 GPS: The Location Sensor

Information about "where you are" is very important for filtering data for social-networking platforms. The GPS is a space-based satellite navigation system that provides accurate information on the location and time across all weather conditions anywhere on the earth where the device is in line of sight with the satellite. The GPS sensor has a GPS receiver and a transmitter.

There are a number of third-party applications for mobile devices for location-tracking services. The GPS sensor could determine the coordinates of your location. When these coordinates are linked with the geographic map of your location, your position can be tracked. GPS-based applications could provide turn-by-turn directions with the help of maps, and it can help you find any specific hot spot such as shopping malls, hotels, and similar destinations. Examples of such applications are TeleNav, ViaMoto, GoogleMaps, and SmartToGo.

GPS is also used for emergency services. For example, after dialing 911, the GPS transmitter will transmit the location of the device to the Public Safety Answering Point (PSAP). Some companies use GPS to deliver promotional offers to users based on their location.

23.2.14.1 Cell-Tower Triangulation

Limitations for GPS are that it requires line of sight to a satellite, and hence it does not work indoors. RFID has only a short range. Bluetooth does not provide much information about location except that it is in the proximity of another Bluetooth device or dongle. WiFi does not carry any location data. Both Bluetooth and WiFi can be helpful in determining the device's location within a certain range using triangulation. This technique also works for Groupe Spécial Mobile (GSM) networks using cell-tower triangulation. Without using GPS, the location of a device can be tracked by the GSM network using the following information:

- Angle of approach to cell towers
- Time taken by the signal from the device to travel to the nearest tower
- Signal strength when the signal from the device reaches the tower

There are hybrid location-based services (LBS) using all these technologies. There are applications that use anonymous position data from different cell phones to check whether the traffic is still flowing in a particular region. Research is going on in this area by leading market players such as Nokia. The research analysis shows that majority of people spend at least 80% of their time indoors. Hence, a location-based indoor service using various technologies would be useful if used in places such as hospitals, shopping malls, and offices. There are applications in the market such as Google Latitude, which uses triangulation from cell towers of a GSM network for calculating the current location of the user within a 3.5-km radius.

23.2.15 Environmental Sensors

These sensors are used to collect the information about the environment around us. For example, there are sensors to measure radiation, carbon dioxide, ethylene, and methane. Weather sensors use the temperature sensor in the device.

23.2.16 Biometric Sensors

Biometric sensors are attached in mobile devices for user identification and authentication. Some common types of biometric sensors are fingerprint readers, face or iris recognition sensors, and sensors for voice recognition. The main challenge is to manufacture these sensors in small sizes so that these can be part of the compact mobile device circuitry. Researches are going on to study the use of fingerprint sensors to read fingerprint patterns and use these patterns to identify distinct fingers. This can be used for providing multiple functionalities for touch inputs, depending upon which finger is being used. For example, different fingers can be used in a touch area of the screen to perform different operations on a music player in the device. New kinds of sensors are available in mobile devices such as the cardiac sensor for iPhone. This sensor can identify the pulses and rhythm of the heart of the person holding the device and identify the person based on this input.

23.2.17 Liquid Sensor

This is used to determine whether the device has been exposed to water or any kind of liquid. This would help the manufacturers to decide on warranty claims.

23.3 Programming the Sensors

There are various mechanisms on a mobile application to trigger a sensor, and some of these are as follows:

■ The application can allow a user to manually trigger a sensor on any user action on the screen.
■ The mechanism programs the sensor application to automatically trigger on a configured time or time intervals.
■ The application can listen to different applications and operating–system level events. For example, when a Bluetooth device is brought in the vicinity of a mobile device, the corresponding Bluetooth profile identifies the class of the external device and notifies the application. Bluetooth health device profile (HDP) identifies a Bluetooth-enabled health device such as a blood-sugar monitor and automatically pairs with the device to receive notifications on its blood-sugar readings.

23.3.1 Android Platform

Android is an open platform, and it provides the developer direct access to the underlying driver level to access sensor hardware. A number of developer guides and sample applications are freely available for beginners in the Android application development. Android software development kit (SDK) exposes certain classes to work with each sensor, and some of the common classes are as follows:

Class	Description
Android.hardware.Camera	Interfaces to control the camera features such as photo, preview image, and flash light
Android.hardware.SensorManager	Generic control for different kinds of sensors
Android.hardware.SensorListener	Listens to sensor events to capture a real-time change in sensor values
Android.media.MediaRecorder	Class to handle media recording and used for recording and analyzing media
Android.FaceDetector	Class for handling face recognition from a bitmap image. The image can be used as a lock or password to authenticate user. It provides biometrics capability
Android.os	A package of different classes to directly interact with the Android operating system; provides access to operating-system features such as power manager, message classes, and similar features
java.util.Timer java.util.TimerTask java.util.Date	Classes useful for managing real-time activities. Sensors mainly deal with real time data.

23.3.2 *iPhone Platform*

The Apple development platform for iPhone provides a separate set of APIs for programming each sensor. Also it is advisable for developers to use OpenGL, 2D, and 3D graphics-rendering APIs and OpenAL 3D audio APIs. In iOS, any user action is an event that is nothing but an object (UI Event object) that is sent to an application to register the user action. The events generated by sensors are basically categorized into multitouch events, motion events, and remote control events. For example, the motion event is an event generated from an accelerometer. A remote control event is an event generated by an external device such as a headphone.

23.3.2.1 Multitouch Events

The iOS multitouch model design recognizes multiple touches as part of a multitouch sequence. For each touch of the multitouch sequence, the iOS records the characteristics of the touch such as location, time of touch, touch area, pressure exerted on the screen, and the orientation of the finger. The applications can recognize certain combinations of touches as gestures and respond to the user in different ways such as zooming in, zooming out, or scrolling through the content.

23.3.2.2 Motion Events

Motion events are created when users move the device. Motion events can be of different formats, and there are associated framework classes for handling them.

- Shaking motion: A shake of the device is evaluated by the accelerometer, and it creates a UI event object representing this gesture. This object is passed onto the currently active application for processing.
- Core motion: This kind of motion deals with a high rate or continuous motion data. Core motion defines a manager class CMMotionManager and three other classes to handle measurements of different types of motion. The basic input data comes from the accelerometer or gyroscope. These classes are as follows:
- CMAccelerometerData class records a measurement of acceleration along the three spatial axes.
- CMGyroData class records a biased estimate of the rate of rotation along the three spatial axes.
- CMDeviceMotion class provides algorithms to process the data to provide precise measurements on roll, pitch, and row, altitude, rotating rate of the device, direction of gravity, and the acceleration that the user is giving to the device.

23.3.2.3 Remote Control Events

These events allow users to control multimedia features such as audio and video recording or playing according to the user's commands (UI Events). The headsets or other external accessories should conform to Apple's specifications, and the control events are sent via the UI Kit framework. The commands or the UI event objects are sent to the first responder, and if the first responder cannot handle it, then it goes up the responder chain. A responder is a class inherited from the UI Responder of iOS, which can respond to events and is capable of handling them.

23.3.2.4 Core Motion Framework Reference

The core motion framework (CMMotionManager class) is used to handle motion data from an accelerometer or gyroscope. The main classes involved in the core motion framework package are as follows:

1. CMAccelerometerData
2. CMAttitude
3. CMDeviceMotion
4. CMGyroData
5. CMLogItem
6. CMMotionManager

Sample codes for the accelerometerGraph, GLGravity, and similar applications are available at the Apple Web site http://developer.apple.com.

23.3.3 Windows Sensor and Location Platform for Microsoft Windows 7 Operating System

Windows 7 operating system provides built-in support for a variety of sensors. The platform categorizes sensors mainly into orientation sensors (such as 3D accelerometers) and location sensors (such as GPS, WiFi, and tower triangulator). The other sensor types are biometric, electrical, environmental, light, mechanical, motion, and scanner. Windows 7 represents device categories and types using globally unique identifiers (GUIDs), and there is a predefined set of GUIDs. However, device manufacturers can create new categories by publishing new GUIDs.

23.3.3.1 Sensor APIs

Windows 7 provides a native set of sensor APIs, which provides the required functionalities through a set of component object model (COM) interfaces. Any device manufacturer should implement the interfaces to develop the driver for the device. To use the native sensor APIs, you should call the COM CoCreateInstance method to create a sensor manager object and retrieve a pointer to the ISensorManager interface. The sensor manager maintains a list of all available sensors and provides access to each sensor. A particular sensor can be accessed using its unique ID. Also, the sensor manager can be used to register a sensor to receive a notification when the sensor is connected to the platform. Each sensor is considered as an object, and it can be accessed using its ISensor interface to perform all read–write operations and handle specific sensor events.

23.4 High-Speed Data Transfer across Devices

Various device sensors or NFC sensors could trigger a Bluetooth or WiFi in the mobile device to search, discover, or pair with an external device to establish reliable streaming data channels and initiate transfer of data across devices. It could be used for transferring contacts from the address book, taking reading from a medical device, pairing and sharing data with a Bluetooth printer, sharing photos and videos, synchronizing address book or mail box with another device, and much more.

23.4.1 Bluetooth

Bluetooth is a wireless transmission technology widely used in mobile devices for exchanging data and voice over short distances to other Bluetooth devices. The standards are set by the Bluetooth Special Interest Group (SIG). Visit the official Web site (http://www.bluetooth.org) of SIG for the core specifications of the latest Bluetooth versions v4.0 with Hallmark feature, v3.0+HS, and v2.1 + EDR. Bluetooth operates in the unlicensed industrial, medical, and scientific (ISM) band at 2.4–2.485 GHz, using a spread spectrum, adaptive frequency hopping (AFH), full-duplex signal at a rate of 1600 hops/s. The AFH feature enables it to coexist with other wireless technologies such as WiFi without causing any interference. The range and power varies depending on the class of radio used. The class specifications are defined by SIG.

Class 1 Radio: Range is 100 m or 300 feet. It is used for industrial purposes.
Class 2 Radio: Range is 10 m or 33 feet. It is used in mobile devices.
Class 3 Radio: Range of 1 m or 3 feet. It is not commonly used nowadays.

Bluetooth profiles define possible applications of this technology and specify how Bluetooth devices should communicate in case of these applications. Commonly used profiles are as follows:

- Advanced audio distribution profile (A2DP): It is used to stream stereo quality audio from a media source to a sink. It may be used along audio–video remote control profile (AVRCP).
- AVRCP: It provides a standard interface to control audio–video devices. It may be used along A2DP or video distribution profile (VDP).
- Basic imaging profile (BIP): It is used to remote control an imaging device to perform actions such as print, copy image to storage devices, or resize images.
- Basic printing profile (BPP): It allows controlling a printer to print e-mails, vCard, text messages, or any unformatted data. It could edit or format data to the printer depending on the device used.
- Common ISDN access profile (CIP): It is used to access ISDN services.
- Cordless telephony profile (CTP): It is used in a mobile device to act as a cordless phone with respect to a base station.
- Dial-up network profile (DUN): It provides access to the Internet and dial-up services.
- Fax profile (FAX): It defines the usage of a fax device as a terminal device.

- File transfer profile (FTP): It is used for browsing files and folders and transferring files from a remote system.
- General audio–video distribution profile (GAVDP): It provides the basis for A2DP and VDP.
- Generic object profile (GOEP): It is used to send information or files across two Bluetooth devices.
- Hands-free profile (HFP): It defines how a gateway device can be used to place and receive calls. The gateway device could be a car kit, headset, mobile phone, or GPS system.
- Hardcopy cable replacement profile (HCRP): It provides driver-based printing over Bluetooth.
- Headset profile (HSP): It is used to operate a Bluetooth-enabled headset.
- Human interface device profile (HIDP): It is used for operating Bluetooth-enabled HID class devices such as mice, keyboards, joysticks, etc.
- Intercom profile (ICP): For communicating across two Bluetooth devices in the same network without using cellular technology.
- Object push profile (OPP): It is used by devices to act as push client or push server. It should interoperate with the server, and client roles are defined by GOEP.
- Personal area networking (PAN) profile: It is used to create an *ad hoc* network across different Bluetooth devices.
- Service discovery application profile (SDAP): It defines how SDP should be used to find the services available in another Bluetooth device.
- Serial port profile (SPP): It is used to define virtual serial ports and connect two Bluetooth devices over this port.
- Synchronization profile (SYNC): It is used with GOEP to synchronize address information (personal information manager [PIM] items) and calendar with another Bluetooth device.
- Video distribution profile (VDP): It defines how video can be streamed across Bluetooth devices.
- Bluetooth HDP: It is used to communicate with medical devices and sensors used in hospitals, health centers, home, and fitness centers.

Apart from these profiles, there are different protocols defined by SIG to extend the usage of Bluetooth technology. Core specifications for these profiles and protocols are available in the official web site of SIG.

23.4.2 WiFi

Bluetooth was initially introduced for making existing personal area network (PAN) to be wireless personal area network (WPAN), where as WiFi was introduced for making the wireless version (WLAN) of general local area networks (LAN), which is the common wired Ethernet. WiFi is the brand name for all products using IEEE

802.11 standards. WiFi operates in the same frequency range of Bluetooth but uses more power, higher bit rate, and greater range from the base station. There are various protocols defined for WiFi with the name IEE 802.11 followed by a character.

Android 4.0 has introduced a feature called WiFi direct to discover and connect with another WiFi device to establish a high performance, secure direct connection without using Internet or a hot spot. It enables developers to think wide on the possibilities of using this feature. The advantage is the dedicated channel fully utilizing the bandwidth to transfer a large amount of data at high speeds. Some of the applications are streaming media from a peer device such as audio player, digital television, and other gaming devices used in network gaming, etc.

23.4.3 Wired Transfer

There are different wired data transfer technologies such as universal serial bus (USB) and High-Definition Multimedia Interface (HDMI) used to transfer data, video, and audio to and from a mobile device. Thunderbolt is a new technology introduced by Intel to transfer any kind of data at around 10 Gb/s data transfer speeds.

23.5 Conclusion

The main areas of mobile technology advancement are in the areas of computing, communication, and sensor technologies. In the last decade, these different technologies have evolved separately. In future, computing, communicating, and sensing capabilities will all be encompassed in small mobile phones and handheld devices.

Additional Reading

1. Pachube (pronounced Patch bay): Creating a Network of Internet-Enabled Objects.
2. Alasdair Allan. *Programming iPhone Sensors*. Sebastopol, CA: O'Reilly Publications.
3. http://developer.apple.com
4. *Introduction to the Windows Sensor and Location Platform*. Available at: http://msdn.microsoft.com
5. IEEE 802.11 specifications. Available at: http://standards.ieee.org/about/get/802/802.11.html
6. http://www.bluetooth.org

Chapter 24

Mobile Application Porting

The demand for mobile applications continues to increase day by day. Mobile companies are benefiting from mobile convergence of business solutions and customer needs. However, there is a big challenge in this industry with the sheer number of different mobile operating systems (OSs), platforms, devices, screen resolutions, device features, programming languages, and the use of proprietary technologies from different vendors. This fragmentation in technology is the greatest challenge to mobile application porting. Consumer needs are also continually changing. There are additional development and porting efforts to roll out applications and services to different mobile platforms. Porting helps to expand the market for the product. Testing efforts for each platform are also huge. As there are more platforms to support, the development cost increases. Reducing porting efforts and the time to market is the need of the hour. If there is a common platform for application development for all the different mobile platforms, it would save lot of cost and efforts. This is the dream of the mobile industry.

24.1 Introduction

The different types of mobile devices are as follows:

- Java for Micro Edition (J2ME) devices: The J2ME concept was introduced with the aim of having a common Java platform for application development across all devices that have Java support. Unfortunately, there is considerable difference in standard J2ME functionalities between different vendors and between different devices of the same vendor. Customization and porting and testing efforts are required to deploy J2ME applications across different devices from different manufacturers. Hence, the vision of developing this technology has not yet been met completely.

■ Binary runtime environment for wireless (BREW) devices: BREW is an OS from Qualcomm mainly for code division multiple access (CDMA)-based phones. BREW provides its own development environment. J2ME application would require to be ported to BREW, which is almost equivalent to the development effort of the application in this platform.

■ Smart devices: This includes the second- and third-generation handsets such as BlackBerry, iPhone, Android, and Windows Phone (WP). Porting is a generic term that is used, and it could be among any of the following categories:

 – Cross-platform porting: For example, J2ME to BREW, J2ME to iPhone, and Symbian to WP.

 – Interplatform porting: It involves porting across different versions of the same platform such as upgradation of OS versions, which involves efforts in porting drivers and features to the new OS, addition of new features, changes in application programming interfaces (APIs), etc. For example, porting drivers across WinCE 5.0 to WinCE6.0, Windows Mobile to WP, migrating across different Android versions to make modifications corresponding to the features and API changes.

 – Operator- or carrier-specific porting: Porting applications to be compatible for different carriers in the United States (AT&T, T-Mobile, Sprint, and Verizon), Europe (Vodafone, Orange, and Virgin Mobile), Canada, and the carriers specific to each country. Porting across different platforms has its own life cycle stages similar to application development.

■ Requirement gathering: This phase involves identification of the type of mobile devices and platforms involved in porting.

■ Gap analysis: Gap analysis is done to evaluate the porting to be done.

■ Assessment of platform and device: This is to identify the risks and challenges. It analyzes the platform or device limitations that could potentially threat the application porting.

■ Development: It involves the necessary changes to be done by a developer, and this stage may involve code rewrite and code optimization for new platforms, graphical user interface (GUI) changes, etc.

■ Testing: In this stage, thorough testing is required for each feature of the application.

The advantages and disadvantages of native platform-specific apps are depicted as follows.

Advantages of Native Platform-Specific Apps	Disadvantages of Native Platform-Specific Apps
Fine grain control over APIs exposed by the platform to provide better user experience and better performance	Application limited to single platform
Apps developed by cross-compilers could serve multiple platforms and give better user experience than web apps	Additional cost involved if required for porting applications to other platforms. It may have to be rewritten for a different platform, which almost equals the development cost of a new application
	Cross-compilation across platforms has its own challenges, especially for complex solutions

The challenges in cross-platform development are as follows:

- Testing a cross-platform application in different platforms is complex, as there could be slight behavioral changes in each platform.
- Advanced features specific for a platform cannot be used due to incompatibility with other platforms. This could cause less flexibility and lower performance.
- Each platform defines its own GUI design specifications. Cross-platform development should align to the GUI specifications of different platforms at the same time.
- Virtual machines (VMs) and scripting languages have to be translated to native, executable binaries specific for each platform, which may negatively impact performance. The use of just-in-time compilation would alleviate this performance hit to some extent, but not completely.

24.2 Cross-Platform Porting

24.2.1 Porting Android, iOS, and WP7 Apps across These Platforms

Microsoft is one of the oldest players in the mobile market. It still holds the major market share in mobile enterprise solutions. Different mobile platforms from Microsoft are Windows CE, Windows Mobile, and WP. WP7 was released in 2011, and WP8 is expected to be released in 2012. For the WP application development, the Integrated Development kit (IDK) Visual Studio Express, user interface (UI) design tool called Express Blend, Silverlight, the tool for game development called XNA Game Studio, and the WP emulator for debugging and testing from the Microsoft Web site can be downloaded for free from http://create. msdn.com/en-US/. In the case of Android, the software development kit (SDK) for developers can be downloaded from http://www.android.com. The latest iOS SDK can be downloaded from http://developer.apple.com. In Android and WP, the user navigation across screens has a similar design. It is important to learn the similarities and differences between these platforms for a developer. For users, there is a considerable difference in the UI experience. Even though the controls have a different look and feel, they provide the same functionalities in these different platforms. The implementation of the controls is also totally different in each platform. A developer needs to learn the differences in the programming language used for each platform in order to port applications across iOS, Android, and WP. Microsoft has released an API Android to the WP7 mapping tool to help developers in porting applications to WP. There is an online tool (http://wp7mapping. interoperabilitybridges.com) that helps us to map similar APIs in WP corresponding to the APIs in iOS and Android.

A developer should keep in mind the following basic differences between various platforms for porting applications:

WP7	Android 4.0	Apple iOS
WP7 is based on Windows CE 6 kernel. It supports only managed code written in C#, Visual Basic.Net (VB.NET), or .Net Compact Framework (.NET CF) 3.7. The common language runtime (CLR) manages memory and garbage collection.	Each application has its own process space and has its own instance of Dalvik VM.	iOS supports objective C programming. The Core OS layer corresponds to the kernel of iOS.
Developer tools		
Expression blend and Visual Studio 2010 Express for WP For UI design, color gradients and animations	Primary UI design for color and gradient are defined using extensible markup language (XML). Any XML tool can be used.	Interface builder and other third-party tools for iOS

WP7	Android 4.0	Apple iOS
Visual Studio 2010 Express for application development XNA Game Studio for game development WP Emulator comes as part of Visual Studio 2010 Express	Android development tools (ADT) UI plug-in or third-party tool such as DroidDraw used for UI design Eclipse is a fully integrated development environment (IDE) used for application and game development Android Emulator available	Xcode for application and game development iPhone simulator for testing and debugging
WP7 Base Class Library	**Android core library functionalities**	**Core Services layer in iOS**
WP7 Base Class Library classes correspond to Android Core Library and it provides the following functionalities: • Language Integrated Query (LINQ) is used to query XML data in isolated storage or in a remote database such as SQL Azure. Only WP8 and higher versions support SQL data base. • Third-party library can be used to get SQL Lite functionality. • XNA for 2D/3D game development • Silverlight for visual effects and animation; provides components similar to Android Standard Widgets	Media framework for audio and video codec support • SQLite for database • OpenGL for embedded systems (OpenGL ES) for 2D or 3D games • Hardware-accelerated 2D drawing • Native APIs based on Khronos OpenMAX AL for low-level multimedia streaming. It can also be used along with open sound library for embedded systems (OpenSL ES) API supported in lower Android versions. • Scalable Graphics Library (SGL) for graphics and animation	The Core Services layer supports basic services listed below: • SQL Lite • OpenGL ES or Quartz for 2D or 3D games • File system • XML • Location • Networking • Foundation

(*continued*)

WP7	Android 4.0	Apple iOS
• Networking Stack: Hypertext transfer protocol (HTTP) 5 and Windows communication foundation (WCF) used for web-based applications; provides interface with XML and simple object access protocol (SOAP) services • .NET CF 3.7 CLR corresponds to Dalvik VM	• Networking stack • Libc for embedding with Linux kernel • Dalvik VM • WebP content • Streaming for VP8and Vorbis content • HTTP Live streaming protocol version 3 and encoding of audio data transport stream (ADTS)-contained advanced audio coding (AAC) content	
Application UI		
The application's UI can be developed using Silverlight or XNA frameworks. Generally Silverlight is used for consumer and business applications. XNA is used for game development. Silverlight provides touch and different multitouch interfaces. The Silverlight app UI uses pages connected by flows. UIs are specified by a declarative language called extensible application markup language (XAML). Code behind can be written in separate files using C# or VB.NET languages. The XML in XAML contains the actual code. Hence, it need not require transformation to code unlike in the case of	Android provides touch and different multitouch interfaces. UI uses widgets and navigation mechanisms across widgets. Android uses XML for mapping. During compilation, XML mappings are translated to generated Java byte code. While designing the UI, we need to set the layout XMLs as content view in Activity. 2D/3D graphics and game development use OpenGL ES. Android applications consist of various components, such as Activity, Services, ContentProvider, and Broadcast receivers. There is no corresponding component in WP except in the case of Activity, which can be mapped	The application's UI is developed using iOS Media layer framework. Cocoa Touch provides controls for touch and different multitouch UI interfaces (tap, double tap, pan, flick, touch and hold, pinch and stretch). The UI uses views and navigation across views in the apps. Quartz or OpenGL ES is used for 2D/3D game development. The iOS provides application-specific file storage.

WP7	Android 4.0	Apple iOS
Android. 2D/3D graphics are developed using XNA and are able to have Xbox connectivity. Silverlight supports vector and bitmap graphics with hardware acceleration. Silverlight provides isolated sandboxed storage for each application to store app-specific data. This is to ensure that one application cannot affect other applications running in the phone.	to the concept of Pages in WP. Android 4.0 introduced Modular Sharing Widget called ShareActionProvider to embed standard share functionality and UI in the Action Bar of their applications	
Design		
WP7 has an information-centric design where the start screen will have dynamic tiles for each application, which displays critical information at a glance to the user, which are relevant to the time. Users can personalize the dynamic tiles to arrange it in start-up screen. The UI with dynamic tiles is called "Metro." WP also has a concept called Hubs, which is used to bring related information together. There are six hubs, namely, People, Pictures, Music and Videos, Marketplace, Office, and Games.	Android has an application-centric design, and all the application icons are arranged on the main screen.	iOS also has an application-centric design, and all the application icons are arranged on the main screen.

(continued)

WP7	Android 4.0	Apple iOS
Development		
While designing the screen for WP, User Experience Design Guidelines for WP should be followed. This can be freely downloaded. It helps in providing consistent experience across applications. The Metro UI open interface design model provides guidelines for designing and using images and fonts. This design model places emphasis on contents rather than on the chrome. It recommends flat, monochrome images for standard application tiles and toolbar icons. WP images may be designed using Microsoft Expression Design or Adobe Photoshop	Android developers should follow the design guidelines specified by the Android developer community.	Applications developed should follow the iPhone Human Interface Guidelines. The application needs to be approved by Apple in order to share it using iStore.
Porting images		
Due to differences in image formats, size, and screen resolution supported in WP, images from iPhone or Android apps needs to be either redesigned or converted. Retina images need to be downscaled to be used for WP. Application icons also need to be redesigned. Redesigning would involve more efforts and time; hence, conversion is recommended. Silverlight supports only joint photographic experts	Android supports a lot of image formats specified in the class: android.graphics. ImageFormat.	iPhone image guidelines provide resolutions for images for iPhone 3 (or older versions) and iPhone4. Images for iPhone 4 and higher versions are called Retina images, which are high-resolution images. Xcode optimizes PNG images when bundling with the application.

WP7	Android 4.0	Apple iOS
group (JPEG)- or portable networks graphics (PNG)- image formats. ImageMagick is an open-source software suited to create edits, to compose, or to convert bitmap images. Microsoft's image converter tool is built over ImageMagick and can be used to migrate the images of an iPhone app to work in WP apps.		
Migrating Application Preferences		
The developer needs to implement the pages for accessing and manipulating application preferences. It requires that application settings need to be managed within the application. Settings page is no different from an application page. WP UI widgets can be used to manipulate the preferences. Application preferences of an iPhone app can be migrated to WP platform.	Application settings can be stored in SharedPreference memory.	iPhone provides a settings bundle to manage preferences from the Settings application. The settings page(.plist file) contains specifications for preference parameter types.
The XAML in WP acts as the actual code of the UI and need not be translated during compile time. For each UI control in Android or iPhone, there is a corresponding control in WP. The Tap bar and Tool bar in iPhone corresponds to the Application bar in WP. An application bar menu corresponds to Action sheets in iPhone.	In Android, screens are designed using XML layouts, which need to be set as content view in activity after defining the UI. This XML is translated during compilation and converted to Java. The Title bar shows the title for the application or activity, such as buttons and links for navigation.	Tap bar and Tool bar provides alternate views and actions in the current context. The Action sheets provide context-sensitive menus on the navigation bar.

(continued)

WP7	Android 4.0	Apple iOS
Controls		
WP has some additional controls that are unique. It does not have a corresponding control type in Android and iPhone. WP has some unique controls such as multiscale image control, which provides images of various resolutions when the user is zooming into a photograph, Panorama control, which allows a page to span beyond the width of the screen and across multiple screen pages horizontally, the People hub, which allows large amount of information to be displayed on the screen, and Pivot control, which manages views and display information in logically divided sections on the screen.		
Navigation		
There is a hardware back button to be used for back functionality and for closing menus and dialogs depending on the context.	Back button is used for navigation across pages of an application or across applications and is also used for closing menus and dialogs. The developer needs to override back-button functionality accordingly. Android also uses widgets.	The App developer should implement back functionality using navigation controls in iOS.

WP7	Android 4.0	Apple iOS
Notifications		
Status bar in Android corresponds to tile for notifications in WP. Toast notifications and title bar remain the same in both platforms. Alerts in Android and iPhone correspond to application notifications in WP.	Android has different notification mechanisms such as Status bar notification, Toast Notification, and Alerts.	iPhone uses an application badge on the application icons in iPhone, which corresponds to the tile concept in WP and status bar concept in Android. Toast notifications are not supported. Alerts in iPhone are similar to Alerts in Android and application notifications in WP.
WP Frame and Page structure	**Defining Layout**	**Defining Layout**
WP applications have a single frame that has areas for • Content area where widgets or graphics are rendered • Reserved space for system tray and application bar It also provides properties for orientation.	For a UI screen, the programmer needs to define the layout. It can be done by declaring the UI elements in XML or instantiate UI elements at runtime using View and ViewGroup objects.	The user will have to create a window and then add views (UIView class) to the window. The user can use standard views or define custom views.
Hardware buttons		
WP mainly has four hardware buttons: Back, Phone, Search, and Home. Search and Home hard buttons have fixed behavior.	Android may have soft or hard buttons for the same and uses widgets for buttons and links.	iOS devices have a single hard button that takes user to the device start-up screen with application icons. It is used for closing or minimizing apps.

(continued)

WP7	Android 4.0	Apple iOS
Templates		
Visual Studio provides application templates. XNA gives templates for developing games similar to game development using OpenGL ES used in Android. Data-bound application templates for information drill down apps. WP Application templates for utility apps. Windows-based iPhone application type template is available.	Eclipse does not provide application templates. Eclipse provides code snippets similar to code snippets in Visual Studio.	Xcode provides different application templates and OpenGL ES templates for games. Navigation-based templates in iOS correspond to data-bound templates in WP and view-based templates for utility apps.
Sensors		
Microsoft Push. Notification Service is used for interfacing with sensors such as accelerometer, camera, global positioning system (GPS), etc.	It is supported by Android classes for each type of sensor.	The Apple notification service is used for interfacing with sensors.
Advertisements		
Microsoft Advertising SDK for WP7 provides APIs to handle advertisements	It does not have an SDK for advertisement developers. Advertising can be done using third-party platforms such as AdMob to push advertisements to applications.	Apple's iAD network services is a platform integrated in iOS for developers to create advertisements and sell these through Apple's iAd service.
Multitasking		
Multitasking is not supported in WP7, and it is supported for WP8 and above. WP7 provides	Multitasking is possible with seamless navigation across applications. Android suspends an	Multitasking is possible in iOS4 and above. It allows only one

WP7	Android 4.0	Apple iOS
seamless navigation using application tomb-stoning. Here the application is deactivated and stores latest data accessed by the app. The user can reactivate this application any time. To save application state, we need to get the IsolatedStore of that app and then create a file in IsolatedStorage to save the persistent state. The user can use home or back button to navigate out of an application. The user can start a tomb-stoned application to load its previous state before it was tomb-stoned.	application when the user starts another application. The last state of the application is saved. The suspended application is still loaded in the memory. State information can be saved using SharedPreferences, using files in the internal and external storages or using SQLLite. Back button is present in all Android devices, which performs the same actions as in WP. On pressing home button for some time, the user can see all the running applications and the user can resume an application from this list.	application to run in the foreground. On clicking Home button, the currently running application is moved into the background running state. In iOS4 and above, audio, location, or voice over Internet protocol (VoIP) applications can be run in the background while running other applications in the foreground.
Programming languages		
WP has a managed programming environment. C# is a strongly typed object-oriented concepts programming (OOP) language. The .NET Compiler compiles C# or VB.NET code to an Intermediate language (IL) byte code and metadata. CLR executes the byte code and uses metadata for managing type safety, exception handling, memory, and garbage collection. The Debug and Trace classes can be used to write runtime debug messages to the output window. C# supports Assert statements, which are evaluated at runtime. If Assert statement returns false, then the program breaks into a debugger.	Java is a strongly typed OOP language. The Java code is compiled into a .class file, which is again converted into a .dex file, which is optimized for low memory foot print. The .dex file is converted into an apk file which is executed on an android platform. Memory management, garbage collection, etc., are automatically handled by the framework.	Objective C is not comparable to a managed environment. It is compiled into ARB (Architectural Review Board) binary code and is executed directly. Objective C is similar to C# in terms of OOP. Xcode provides access to assembly instructions, memory dumps, and various registers.

24.2.2 Porting Qt Apps to WP

Qt is the recommended cross-platform development framework for Symbian OS. Recently, Nokia Corporation has announced that Nokia devices are migrating to the WP platform, and they are stopping the production of Symbian-based devices. Hence, it is important to know the differences between Symbian Qt and WP framework, which are shown below.

Symbian Qt Features	WP Framework Features
For development of an app UI and device integration (sensors, camera, etc.), Qt Quick and Qt Mobility modules are used. Symbian apps generally use stack- or tab-based navigation between pages.	For UI and sensors, WP uses Silverlight and WP framework.
Declarative QML (Quest Markup Language) UI language is used in Qt.	Silverlight uses a declarative language called XAML to specify UIs. The code behind can be in C# or VB.NET.
For graphics, animation, and multimedia, Qt Quick, Qt Framework Graphics, and GUI modules are used, and Qt Mobility and Qt Quick uses Open GL ES for 2D or 3D graphics.	XNA framework for games, 2D, or 3D graphics and Silverlight for consumer and business apps.
For OS, networking, XML services, and for persistent storage, Qt Quick, Qt Framework Engine, and Core modules are used.	Uses Common Base Class Library.

24.3 Some Cross-Platform Mobile Application Development Tools

24.3.1 J2ME Polish

J2ME Polish is a suite of tools for application development for mobile devices across a variety of mobile platforms that support Java. There are four categories of components in the tool suite, which are as follows:

1. Build framework for building J2ME applications
2. Client framework for providing APIs to improve applications
3. IDE plug-ins for Eclipse IDE for ease of development
4. Other stand-alone tools

The main features of J2ME Polish are as follows:

- Lush UI Toolkit: J2ME Polish allows the UI design, animation, and effects to be specified in cascading style sheet (CSS) files similar to the web page design. This provides options to customize an application without changing the source code. What You See Is What You Get (WYSIWYG) designer can also be used for the UI design. The tool provides different design options. The J2ME resource-assembling feature can be used to make the application screens adapt to different screen resolutions.
- Janus Toolset: J2ME Polish is platform-independent and is based on Ant (Java standard for application building). Hence, it can be used as a plug-in to any Java-based IDE. It runs on all mobile information device profile (MIDP) supporting devices. It can be used for porting to all mobile platforms including iPhone, Android, BlackBerry, and Windows Mobile.
- Touch technology: The Remote Method Invocation framework provided by J2ME Polish provides communication with the server by calling domain-specific methods. It also supports remote procedure call using XML standards. Touch technology can be used to display hypertext markup language (HTML) or RSS contents in mobile applications.
- Trunk solution: It is used for storage and handling of application-specific data. Automatic and manual data serialization is supported. Any application-level objects or complex tree structures can be serialized using this solution.
- Marjory device database: It provides information to developers regarding how to adapt the applications for a target platform. The database can be queried during the build phase, and necessary modifications can be made to the design, code, resources, and configurations.

24.3.2 PhoneGap Used across Six Different Mobile Platforms

PhoneGap (http://www.phonegap.com) is an open-source application development tool under the license of the Massachusetts Institute of Technology. It uses HTML 5, JavaScript, and CSS3 to create full-fledged web apps. It can also be used to even program for device sensors such as GPS, accelerometer, vibration, etc. There are more web developers than mobile application developers, and PhoneGap would equip web developers to create native apps across various mobile platforms. Currently, it supports application development that can be commonly used across six mobile platforms. PhoneGap Build is a service for developers for rapid development of App Store-ready versions of web apps compatible across different platforms.

24.3.3 Mobile Distillery

Mobile distillery (http://www.mobile-distillery.com) is a company that provides solutions and services in mobile technologies. The company also provides cross-platform porting of mobile applications and application testing. It has introduced a JavaME-based development platform called Celsius, which could be used to develop applications across a wide variety of mobile platforms such as iPhone, JavaMe, BREW, Windows Mobile, BlackBerry, Symbian JavaME, HTML, and Android. The unique features the tool set provides are as follows:

1. One-time development effort for applications that run across different mobile platforms.
2. Ability to adapt to each type of mobile platform for optimum performance and better usage of OS features.
3. Native look and feel specific to each platform.
4. Porting existing apps across platforms. The tool supports automatic porting.
5. Leverages all hardware features such as Bluetooth, camera, video, accelerometer, near-field communication (NFC), multimedia devices, etc.
6. It maintains and constantly updates its database with new mobile platforms that come in the market to provide application porting to the new platform.
7. Porting would handle security modules similar to the subscriber identity module (SIM), microsecure digital (SD) card, external Bluetooth-connected secure elements, and other embedded security modules.
8. Faster UI development using the tool with the help of multiresolution screen layout with drag-and-drop controls feature.

24.3.4 RhoMobile

Rhomobile (http://rhomobile.com) offers a development tool for developing and porting applications across different mobile platforms. The advantage of Rhomobile is that it allows the development of the application in Ruby, which can be deployed across multiple mobile platforms.

24.3.5 Titanium Tablet Platform from Appcelerator

Appcelerator, a web-based solution provider, has introduced a web application development platform called the Titanium Tablet intended to help iOS developers to create cross-platform web apps using Javascript, CSS, HTML 5, and scripting languages such as Ruby and Python to create native apps for iOS, iPhone and iPads, and Android platforms. The API support for native apps, along with web-app development features, gives advantage to developers to have good control over platform-specific features.

24.3.6 Brief Overview of Other Platforms and Tools

■ Cairo: It is a free device-independent software library that provides vector graphics-based functionalities. Cairo is in C programming language and can be bound to many other programming languages.

- Mono: It is an open-source version of Microsoft.NET frame work, which is a cross-platform framework.
- Mozilla: It is an open-source platform for application development in Mac, Windows, and Linux.
- Smartface platform: Cross-platform tool kit for Windows, which is used to develop mobile applications.
- For J2ME, Symbian, Android, and BlackBerry.
- Adobe integrated runtime (AdobeAIR): This is a cross-platform deployment tool for iOS, Android, and BlackBerry using programming languages such as Action Script, HTML, CSS, and JavaScript. It can be used with other integrated IDEs such as Flash Builder and Flash Professional.
- AirPlay SDK (Marmalade): It is used across iOS, Android, BlackBerry, Maemo, Palm/webOS, Samsung bada, Symbian, Windows Mobile 6.x, and desktop. The programming languages used are C and C++. It can be integrated with Visual Studio and Xcode IDEs.
- appMobi: It is used for application development in iO, Android, HTML5 Web Apps, and HTML5 Hybrid Apps. Programming is done using Javascript, CSS3, and HTML5. It can be integrated with any SDK.
- JMango: It is used for the cross-platform application development for J2ME, Android, Bada, BlackBerry, iPhone, Windows Mobile 6, and WP7 using C/C++. It uses JMango Flash IDE.
- Aqua: It is used across Android, iOS, Samsung Bada, Windows Mobile 6.x, BlackBerry Playbook Palm/webOS Windows Desktop using C, C+, and Javascript, and it can be plugged into Visual Studio, Eclipse, and Xcode.

24.4 Going Web

It is a good option to consider having a web application instead of platform-specific applications or native applications. Web apps run in the browser, most likely in Webkit. Webkit is an open-source web browser engine. Following are the advantages and disadvantages of web apps.

Advantages of Web Apps	*Disadvantages of Web Apps*
Available across all different mobile platforms	May not be able to leverage the full potential of the platforms, and the UI may not be as good as that of native apps
They are stand-alone apps even though they depend upon browser services	Certain stand-alone native apps are unique and does not match with a web-based app

(continued)

Advantages of Web Apps	Disadvantages of Web Apps
Less expensive	
The developer is not limited by the requirements of any particular app market place	
Could provide cloud-based storage and utilize the processing power of a virtual environment	The device would require Internet connection always to work with the app.
HTML 5 is a game changer when combined with Javascript and CSS3. Leading platforms such as Android, iOS, HP/Palm, BlackBerry, and WP7 (Internet Explorer 9) uses Webkit as their bases. The code for web apps is intended for desktops and can be reused for mobile versions also	
Could provide dynamic content creation to be compatible across devices and platforms with different form factors.	

24.4.1 Qt Webkit

Qt Webkit is a port of Webkit over the Qt platform. Currently, the Qt Webkit compiles and runs on Windows, Mac OS X, Symbian, and Linux (including Maemo and Meego). It relies on the public APIs of Qt. Hence, it can be used across platforms that have support for Qt. Nokia provides the Qt development kit for creating rich apps for the Symbian platform. There are a number of web-based application frameworks that are written as embedded dynamic web sites to support multiple mobile platforms and at the same time leverage native platform features. The advantage of a dynamic web page is that the content or layout of the page is not static, and it is dynamically created based on a combination of parameters such as content, user preferences, user interaction (e.g., web games), or context (such as parametric customization). Some other major players, to name a few, in providing web-based application framework are iUI (iui-js.org), QuickConnectFamily (quickconnect-family.org), Rhodes (rhomobile.com), iPFaces (ipfaces.org), Jmango (j-mango.com/web), Appcelerator Titanium (appcelerator.com), and NEXT (http://nextinterfaces.com/).

24.5 Conclusion

Forthcoming years will witness a greater evolution of web-based applications, which are independent of mobile platforms, along with the evolution of faster wireless communication technologies, which will enable faster web operations. HTML 5 plays a major role in developing web-based cross-platform applications. HTML 5 has an advantage over Flash or Silverlight as it is widely accepted across all mobile platforms such as Android, iOS, and WP. Cross-platform solutions that offer application development and porting across multiple mobile platforms will be the preferred choice for enterprises and application developers.

Additional Reading

1. *J2ME Polish*. Available at: http://www.enough.de
2. *Porting Applications to WP*. Available at: http://windowsphone.interoperabilitybridges.com
3. *Android to WP Porting*. Available at: http://windowsphone.interoperabilitybridges.com/media/49652/wp7_guide_for_android_application_developers.pdf
4. *iPhone/iOS to WP Porting*. Available at: http://windowsphone.interoperabilitybridges.com/media/1254/wp7%20dev%20guide%20for%20iphone%20app%20developers.pdf
3. http://create.msdn.com/en-us/home/getting_started
4. *Learn Similarities and Differences between Java and C#*. Available at: http://www.25hoursaday.com/CsharpVsJava.html
5. *SQL Lite for WP7*. Available at: http://sqlitewindowsphone.codeplex.com
6. http://www.mobile-distillery.com
7. http://www.webkit.org
8. *Web Applications for Multiplatforms*. Available at: http://en.wikipedia.org/wiki/Multiple_phone_web-based_application_framework

21.5 Conclusion

Chapter 25

Mobile Cloud Computing

As societies evolve, sharing resources in common will provide sufficient resources to everyone in the society to overcome scarcity. Our societies share electrical energy from a network of power stations (power grids), and very few generate electricity of their own. This is a great leap for mankind, as groups of people are learning to utilize resources efficiently. Today, the world is recognizing that computing power is also a shared resource.

25.1 Introduction: Inventing the Future

The future of cloud computing depends on the developments in the Internet, technologies that enable sharing such as sharing software through multitenancy and sharing hardware through virtual machines, services-oriented interfaces, the automation of cloud for the expected behavior, and the developments in the field of mobility. According to a survey conducted by IBM, mobile and cloud computing are the emerging technologies that will dominate application development and the information-technology (IT) infrastructure of enterprises. Surveys show a steady increase in the percentage of people preferring tablet personal computers (PCs) and smart phones in the place of laptops. Cloud computing has changed peoples' thoughts about mobile computing. Gartner research predicts that global cloud computing services market could reach $29.5 billion by 2013 and $150 billion by 2014. There will be over 20 times the amount of mobile cloud applications in 2014 than it is today. According to ABI research, a telecom analysis firm in Oyster Bay, New York, by 2014, cell phones and mobile devices will send and receive data each month that will be more than that it did in 2008. Three-fourths of the data will be from Internet access and rest of the data from audio and video streaming. Most

Figure 25.1   Mobility solution deployed in a cloud environment.

of the data transferred through the Internet is by cloud-computing applications. Leading utility applications will be Global Positioning System application with maps, productivity tools for sales and data sharing, social networking and search, and online gaming.

In future, cloud computing will make computing more collaborative, intelligent, and available. We are witnessing applications of cloud computing that otherwise would never have been possible. So cloud computing is not only a different way of doing things but also a window for newer dimensions of innovation. Mobile cloud computing refers to an IT infrastructure in which the data processing and data storage happen outside the mobile device. The outside mobile infrastructure virtually has infinite processing power and memory, and the mobile device communicates with the cloud using a very high-speed data channel literally making a mobile device capable of processing and rendering heavy applications (refer to Figure 25.1, which shows a mobile cloud application environment). This technology could make applications independent of mobile platforms.

25.1.1 Tiers of Cloud Computing

There are basically three tiers to cloud computing as shown in Figure 25.2.

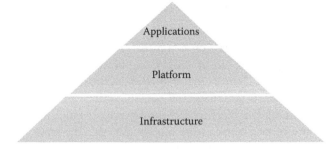

Figure 25.2   Different tiers of cloud computing.

25.1.1.1 Applications

For applications, the customer depends on companies that provide software-as-a-service (SaaS). SaaS allows users to run existing online applications over the Internet. These SaaS applications are either free or paid for a subscription. These applications are accessible anytime and anywhere over the Internet and facilitate collaborative working. For example, document-editing applications such as Microsoft office web apps, Google docs, image-editing applications such as Pixlr, Jaycut, or Aviary and business applications such as Employease, Netsuite, and Salesforce. For any enterprise mobility application availing customized SaaS, the mobile device provides the end user with authentication and graphical user interface to access back-end servers. More than 90% of the processing of business request happens in the servers. The performance of the mobile application mainly depends on the performance of the servers and the data transfer speed on the communication channel. One disadvantage of SaaS could be that sometimes these generic applications may not be suitable for custom needs.

25.1.1.2 Platform

There are service providers who offer platform-as-a-service (PaaS). It allows users to create custom cloud applications using supplier-specific tools and services at lower costs. These applications can be deployed in the service provider's infrastructure either for private or for public usage. An example is the Oracle platform for SaaS, which provides Oracle Database and Application Grid Middleware. Another example is Google AppEngine. It allows users to create and maintain web applications on Google's infrastructure. Microsoft Azure allows users to develop and maintain applications in the cloud. www.Force.com from SalesForce provides tools to build and host applications for free.

25.1.1.2.1 Telecom Operators Providing Cloud-Based PaaS

Verizon is offering cloud-based web hosting along with the high-speed Internet and phone connection. For creating e-commerce web sites faster, Verizon provides different templates that can be easily customized to suit the business needs. Vodafone 360 is another cloud-based web application provided by Vodafone in which phone subscribers can manage and control address book, e-mail, and photos online. Users can update their contact books online, which automatically synchronizes with the contact book in the mobile devices. The service also provides users online shopping facilities stores for music, games, and applications from where these can be downloaded directly to the mobile phones. It also brings all the social networking links together in the Vodafone 360 web application. The disadvantages are that users have limitations to use provider-specific tools and languages. Also, the applications developed in one provider's tool cannot be moved to another service provider.

25.1.1.3 Infrastructure

Infrastructure refers to the physical environment for hosting the application. Before the invention of cloud computing, infrastructure had to be managed by the company who owned the application. The main challenge is to keep the hardware equipments updated based on demands. High load during peak business seasons makes the services slow down, and to meet the demands, additional hardware needs to be purchased. Usually, the companies depend on third-party hardware vendors to provide hardware infrastructure. The maintenance cost for these owned assets is huge, and it also takes a considerable time to set up the infrastructure. There will be maintenance costs irrespective of the usage of the infrastructure, and when business is low, these maintenance costs affect the profit badly. With cloud computing, cloud service providers offer infrastructure-as-a-service (IaaS). This layer provides the physical hardware for storage and networking. IaaS allows users to run any application of their choice on the service. This overcomes the limitation of PaaS. It also includes technologies such as virtualization for servers and storage. The server virtualization enables isolation, resource pooling, and easy application deployment. It allows different users to share the same physical server. Using this technology, cloud service provider offers broadly four kinds of cloud infrastructure based on the type of service:

1. Private cloud: This is the most secure and costly option. Here, a definite number of physical services are allocated to a customer.
2. Dedicated hosting: In a dedicated hosting service, customers can get custom-configured cloud infrastructure for your enterprise. Here, customers have the option of specifying any particular configurations for the dedicated cloud.

Customers can also buy preconfigured dedicated servers in cloud, which could deliver the required performance.

3. Hybrid hosting: Here, a mix of physical services and virtual server instances are rented on a monthly basis to customers. This model of cloud hosting combines both in-house servers and cloud services. The advantage is that customers can still have dedicated servers and all the flexibilities it provides along with the benefits of the hosted services from a cloud service.

4. Public cloud hosting: Here, the customer avails virtual server instances on monthly or hourly basis.

An example of IaaS includes products from Amazon web services such as Amazon Elastic Compute Cloud (EC2), which provides different kinds of virtual server instances for purchase per hour. These server instances can be launched within minutes using Amazon Machine Image (AMI). Another cloud provider for various types of cloud-hosting services is GoGRID (http://www.gogrid.com). GoGrid provides provisioning tools and a set of GoGrid application programming interfaces (APIs) that can be used to directly or programmatically access the GoGrid portal and tightly integrate the application with the cloud services. The portal also provides services that allow tracking of previous usage, reviewing invoices, placing order for additional Internet protocol (IP) addresses, managing users, and setting roll-based access controls.

25.1.2 Cloud Management

Managing a cloud infrastructure involves managing platform and application deployment from the setup, maintenance, and decommissioning. This can be again categorized into the following:

- Life cycle management
- Configuration management
- Performance management
- Quality management

The strategy of managing the cloud varies from one service provider to the other.

25.2 Benefits of Cloud Computing

The benefits of cloud computing are as follows:

- Performance: The most attractive benefit of cloud computing is its speed, agility, and ability to move into and move out of the provider of business, eliminating the need to buy dataset equipments and security.

- Cost based on usage: Also the user can buy the processing capacity, memory, and data transfer in units or per-hour usage rates, and some cloud providers charge the user only for the capacity that they used.
- Scalability: A user has complete control over the computing resources and has the option to quickly scale the capacity up or down.
- Instant access: Cloud hosting is instant. It would take only a few minutes to add additional memory or processing power. These can be customized and configured through web sites.
- Saves money: Cloud computing saves a lot of money spent on network administration, server, and database maintenance, and there is no need to employ additional employees for maintenance of hardware. This enables them to remain competitive. In case of majority of enterprise mobility solutions, initially the application will be small and less complex but as the business requirements change, the application becomes huge and demands more memory and processing power. To accommodate these changes, companies have to replace the entire set of devices. Unfortunately, this cycle keeps repeating. Cloud-based applications provide a permanent solution to this issue.
- Saves time for building the business: The key with cloud computing is to focus on the web or device application development and not to bother about the hardware.
- Essential for next-generation technologies: The augmented reality applications that run on small smart phones relay on cloud data. We get more understanding about the need of cloud by examining some of the new generation augmented reality applications such as:
- Google Goggles can identify any object and provide overlay visual search results in smartphones.
- Layer browser can superimpose augmented reality cloud data on real-time view of the world.
- Google Translate is a cloud-based language translator that can convert a web site to another language in seconds (check for some interesting augmented reality applications in Chapter 30).
- Developments in artificial intelligence also depend on cloud data.

25.2.1 Synchronization between Applications Developed for Different Platforms

There are different mobile platforms such as Android, iPhone, WindowsMobile7, BlackBerry, bada, MeeGo, and others, which are totally different. Synchronization between applications across different platforms is one of the biggest challenges in mobile cloud computing. There are innovative solutions in the market to address these areas. One example is the Google Docs. It allows users to upload, download, edit, sync, and share any kind of files across different platforms. These files can be downloaded to any platform and is ready to use.

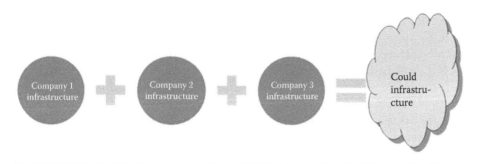

Figure 25.3 Cloud computing optimizes the use of infrastructure.

25.2.1.1 Security and Privacy

The clould service provider guarantees data security and privacy of the data. It would be difficult for a hacker to break the security of the cloud compared with hacking of PCs. A word document sent over Internet from a personal PC through e-mail is no more secure than a document prepared and shared in GoogleDocs. In case of forwarding documents over e-mail, we trust the communication channel provider and the e-mail server providers. Surveys shows that IT infrastructures are able to use only up to 30% of their infrastructure capacity, whereas a cloud can make use of at least 80% of its capacity, thus reducing carbon footprint. Hence, cloud computing is Green technology (Figure 25.3). Cloud environment could bring down the power consumption to 75%. Cloud tools allow people to access resources from anywhere and facilitate working from home and reduce business travel.

Cloud infrastructure is shared by multiple companies; hence, we may consider a cloud as physically the sum of infrastructures of shared companies. In reality, the cloud does more things than the sum of work done by the infrastructures of individual companies. Here, the whole is bigger than the sum of parts. With new standards evolving in communication technologies, such as 3G, 4G, WiFi, and WiMax, which provide data transfer speeds greater than 3 Mbps, the mobile application gets the performance of a high-end desktop application.

25.3 Mobile Cloud Applications

The applications based on cloud computing can be broadly classified into the following categories:

1. Productivity
2. Utilities

3. Search
4. Games
5. Social networking
6. Enterprise business solutions

Applications based on mobile widgets are becoming popular. Mobile widgets are basically web applications built on web technologies such as cascading style sheets (CSS), hypertext markup language (HTML), and JavaScript. This widget is downloaded by a device from the web and is installed locally. Widgets are the simplest form of client-side applications that can be used to talk to the server over the Internet. Google entered into enterprise mobile cloud computing with the release of Android 2.2. This version of the operating system (OS) provides security for enforcing the security policies for enterprise through the mobile.

- Google's Gmail and Google Voice are cloud-based services.
- Google cloud picker is an application that provides storage in cloud. The products link together several other Google services such as YouTube, Maps, Docs, and Picasa photos.
- Soonr is another cloud-based web application that provides secured file storage in the cloud, version control of documents, and setting access rights, and it also provides online work spaces for working as a team.
- Apple's MobileMe and iCloud application stores contacts, mails, calendars, eBooks, music, documents, apps, and shared files in the cloud and make them available across all the apple devices such as Notebook, iPhone, iPad, and other devices. It also provides tracking for any lost apple device registered in the cloud.MobileMe. These services provide storage of files in the cloud using a concept called iDisk. The MobileMe can be accessed anywhere over the Internet through the Me.com web site. This is a typical example of SaaS-based application.
- Funambol is an open-source mobile cloud sync software. It is similar to MobileMe and is available for all the different mobile platforms such as iPhone, Android, BlackBerry, etc.
- eDiscovery software from CaseCentral is a cloud-based application for corporate councils and law firms. CaseCentral supports both garden variety and bet-the-company litigation and regulatory matters for corporate and law firm clients.
- Mobile voice over Internet protocol (VoIP) is another emerging application based on mobile cloud. There are many cloud-based VoIP service providers such as Skype.
- Netflix is a cloud application for renting a DVD library.
- Salesforce.com provides a cloud-based online customer relationship management (CRM) solution.

25.4 Impact of Cloud Computing on Mobile Application Development

In the context of cloud, developers should be aware of the new set of opportunities that has increased the scope of application development. The applications no longer have dependency on the device for processing power and data storage. Most mobile cloud applications would have browsers that are independent of the OS of the device. This will bypass the restrictions or limitations of mobile OSs. The building cost of the application will reduce as most of the business logic is migrated to the server-level business implementation. While developing services over cloud, we should decide at which level we need to engage with the cloud service provider, and this depends on the focus area of the application such as tuning the OS, working on application platforms, or writing business applications. After choosing a suitable cloud service provider, an organization should plan to move some computers or people as a pilot project to work out the cloud service offerings and then migrate completely to the cloud. The pilot phase would help to identify the costs that are involved in migrating to the cloud. Signing the agreement for security of data with the cloud provider is important. Different clients have different services for data security. Some providers would use your data for advertising purposes and may use data unless it is blocked in the agreement. Some cloud service providers provide the following services:

1. Work-flow management services to create and manage development, test and stage environments, and help replicate the production environment to do proper load and performance testing. An example for such a tool is Citrix VMLogix.
2. Application life cycle management services that provide source control, version control, testing tools, and load generation tools. If the enterprise chooses to have some of the application life cycle management stages such as source and version control within the enterprise premises, then the cloud provider provides cloud-bridging services to provide integration of cloud and enterprise data centers. An example of this tool is Citrix VMLogix.
3. Application development: Cloud offers agile development methodologies and platforms for rapid application development. They provide tools for pushing various components of the application to different application topology tiers such as app tier and web tier. The tools can also be used for provisioning infrastructure components for load balancing and firewall configurations. An example of such a tool is WaveMaker.
4. Cloud framework, access, and bridging services provide tools and access for provisioning and controlling in multitenant shared infrastructure and interfaces shared with other cloud provider services. Access services help to extend the policy frame work of an enterprise infrastructure to the cloud infrastructure. Bridging services provide persistent and secure connection between the enterprise and the cloud data centers. It helps in establishing a network across

physical and virtual topologies. Specific tools are available from Citrix for cloud framework, access, bridge, and networking services.

25.5 Factors Influencing the Development of Cloud Computing

25.5.1 HTML5 Technology

The HTML5 technology that is redefining the web markup language in future will create a stable backbone for cloud computing as it offers off-line data caching. This would enable the cloud-based mobile applications to work in off-line mode and later work with the data changed in the server for the period in which the device was off-line. This will drastically reduce the server load. Also, this provides services from the cloud servers, even in cases where the Internet connectivity is poor.

25.5.2 Browser-Based Applications

There are hundreds of browser-based applications available from major market players such as Firefox, Google, and others, which can be operated anywhere with an Internet connection. The major target of these applications is the smartphones and mobile devices that do not have much processing power.

25.5.3 Thin Client-Based Applications

Thin client is emerging as a new form of desktop computing. It runs at very low power in the order of 10–15 Watts of power compared with the normal desktop PC, which runs on an average power of 90 Watts. It comes with OSs such as Windows Embedded systems or Windows XP Embedded. It comes with basic hardware with a display screen. The OS image will be burned to the read-only memory (ROM). This will drastically bring down the hardware costs of IT departments of all companies. It may also include solid-state memory for caching the data from cloud for performance. It utilizes the whole processing power of the cloud. In December 2010, Google unveiled a notebook computer Cr-48, which relies on web for all its applications to compete with desktop PCs with all installed softwares. It runs on Google's new Chrome OS. Google has provided a Chrome App Store in which different cloud-computing applications are available to install in the Chrome browser or to Chrome OS.

25.5.4 Thick Client-Based Applications

Some technology experts predict that even though thin client applications would hit the market of most of the rich thick client applications, still there would be applications that require rich client. Enterprise mobility applications may come in this space, as the processing power of the device is also a deciding factor for its success. Hence, it is said that both think and thin client technologies will coexist in its own space.

25.5.5 Evolution of Cloud Standards

The Open Grid Foundation has a working group for setting standards for cloud-computing infrastructure called Open Cloud Computing Interface (OCCI). They provide API specifications for different cloud services such as IaaS, PaaS, and SaaS. You may visit the official site of OCCI at http://occi-wg.org/ for more information. It is a basic trend seen in Internet-based technologies that they enter the market as closed and proprietary, but in the long run if the technology is not open, cheap, and available, it would cease to exist. When the technology attains maturity, the technology will be freely available to all and the quality of service is what matters. Cloud is no exception to this trend, and in this regard going for an open-cloud technology has its advantages in the long run. The organizations that bring out the standards have a major role in this phase shift, which is the case for the introduction of any technology. Going for open cloud provides customers the flexibility to change their SaaS, PaaS, or IaaS providers at any time. Customers have full control over their IT assets. In case of proprietary services, the customers get locked up with the service provider. Portability includes the following:

1. Portability of data and code
2. Programming language and libraries
3. Ownership of IT assets

25.5.5.1 Some Case Studies for SaaS

Force.com has the proprietary Apex programming language, which will not work outside their service.ware; GoGrid and Amazon have some proprietary stuffs in this level of service, and Google App Engine supports common languages such as Java and Python, but to access BigTable, which is a proprietary database for Google file system, we have to depend on Google proprietary libraries.

25.5.5.2 PaaS and IaaS

Most service providers allow customers to download the virtual machine image, which can be directly applied to the customers' own infrastructure, for example, the AMI. Still the major providers such as VMware, GoGrid, and Amazon have some proprietary tools used in their services. Since the invention of standards such as OCCI and virtual machine portability, many providers are planning to adopt them. The importance of open standards is self-evident if we see the case study of how Google Android has captured the mobile market in a short span of time when there was strong competition from Apple iPhone, BlackBerry, and Windows Mobile. The disruptive innovations of this decade are social networking, cloud services, and mobile computing. In the future, we can see the maturity of these technologies and its integration into a common platform.

25.6 Challenges

25.6.1 Connectivity

Cloud-based applications will have drastic performance hit if the connectivity is poor as the application depends on connectivity over Internet to the cloud servers. When data transfer speed is low due to less connectivity, the mobile devices would retry sending the packets over the air several times, which could drain out the batteries. Also, the end users of cloud applications have to bear the data transfer charges over the Internet. This limitation is not there for cloud web hosting and services offered by the network service providers. When the device is outside the service provider's network, additional roaming charges may apply for using the cloud application. In most of the developing countries, the network infrastructure has not developed enough to provide sufficient network bandwidth to support cloud applications over the Internet. Hence, it would take some more time for market readiness in developing economies.

25.6.2 Security

Different security-related questions are still open for cloud-based services, and service providers are in an effort to address these concerns. End users completely rely on the security offerings by service providers, and if any security breach occurs, then the customer may end up losing the entire business and trust, for which no amount of compensation can make up the loss, and it may lead to complex legal issues. This is still an emerging technology; new vulnerabilities may arise, and it may take time to test and prove the system.

25.6.3 Cost

There will be additional cost for data transfer over the Internet.

25.6.4 Difficult to Change the Service Provider

The customers are highly dependent on the cloud service provider. If the customer has to change the service provider, it may take a lot of effort to migrate the whole data to the new environment. Most of the PaaS and SaaS services are built on tools provided by the service providers, and it may not be compatible to use with other service providers. Hence, changing the service provider may have the cost of new application development for a new platform. As discussed, the evolution of open cloud standards would revolutionize the cloud industry.

25.7 Conclusion

Cloud computing have opened up new relationships between service providers and enterprises. This new technology has opened up new kinds of business and has also changed our perspectives on mobile application development. It has also integrated different technology streams such as social networking, mobile computing, and online file sharing into a common integrated platform. The core processing power and storage has migrated to the servers in cloud from the desktop PCs and mobile devices. In future, information about every person will be available in cloud. You may probably walk into a restaurant, get a seat, and place your hands over the glass desk. The biometric reader in the desk surface identifies you and gathers information about you such as the kind of food you prefer that is available in the menu. Wherever you go, the cloud is all around you to help you in all ways. Also, it is seen that there is a trend for cloud to become open, such as the Internet, and it will be a purely service-oriented business.

Additional Reading

E-Reading

http://en.wikipedia.org/wiki/Cloud_computing http://www.vmware.com/solutions/cloud-computing/
http://www.redhat.com/solutions/cloud/
http://www.citrix.com/English/ps2/products/product.asp?contentID=1681633 &ntref=hp_cat_cloud
http://www.ubuntu.com/cloud
http://aws.amazon.com/ec2/
http://www.microsoft.com/windowsazure/
http://www.vmware.com/products/mobile

Books

Anthony T. Velte, Toby J. Velte, and Robert E. Peter. *Cloud Computing, A Practical Approach.* New York: McGraw Hill, 2010.
George Reese. *Cloud Application Architectures: Building Applications and Infrastructure in the Cloud—Theory in Practice.* Sebastopol: CA O'Reilly, 2009.

Chapter 26

Mobile Virtualization

As a technology is evolved, it is important to introduce different layers of abstraction to hide the complexity of one layer to the other and to have common interfaces to talk to similar layers of other systems. We can see this abstraction in any technology. For example, high-level languages provide an abstraction layer to hide the complexities of machine language, which in turn provides a layer of abstraction to control hardware, which understands only high and low of a clock cycle. Mobile technologies are providing an abstraction for all the tasks that were previously possible only in desktop machines. Virtualization brings about abstraction between different layers of hardware and software. Virtualization is the technology that is the skeleton of cloud computing, which is a very promising field for mobile applications in future.

26.1 Introduction

Virtualization is a technique for hiding the physical characteristics of computing resources to simplify the way in which other systems, applications, or end users interact with those resources. Virtualization is a layer of abstraction that hides the complexities of the underlying layers. Virtualization not only defines the abstraction between different layers but also reduces the requirements for physical hardware. It also brings the scalability of processing power based on the requirement. Replacement of hardware is also easy. Virtualization implemented in data centers show that using virtualization could bring consolidation of servers, thereby bringing down the cost of maintenance, heating and cooling costs, costs on power, cost on space, and other management costs. On an average, virtualization would replace four server racks with one. Virtualization is now being applied to mobile and server technologies. Mobile devices are no longer stand-alone devices; rather, they are becoming enterprise application end points. The different types of virtualization are operating system (OS), hardware, and applications virtualization. Classification of virtualization is based on the application (i.e., the different contexts in which the term "virtualization" is used in the embedded space).

- OS virtualization
- Platform virtualization
- Workspace virtualization
- Network virtualization
- Environment sharing virtualization
- Application virtualization
- Paravirtualization
- Virtualization using emulator
- Management virtualization
- Grid virtualization
- Other virtualization products

Virtualization is a vast domain, and here we focus on the applications of virtualization relevant to mobile applications and embedded space.

26.2 OS Virtualization

In OS virtualization (Figure 26.1), there are multiple OSs running on the same physical hardware. Each instance of OS does not know that it is virtual, and there are other virtual OSs running at the same time.

OS virtualization creates isolated containers on the hardware, and each of these containers run different instances of OSs. There are common virtualization layers for all the OSs, which allocate resources to virtual servers, which are also called as containers. It has advantages over hardware virtualization in which the hardware

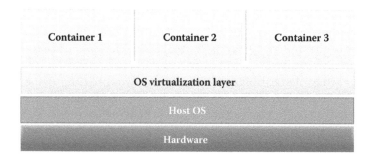

Figure 26.1   OS virtualization.

resources are duplicated for each OS. The advantages of OS virtualization are as follows:

1. Maximum server or container performance.
2. Ease of management of the virtualization environment.
3. Very less overhead on the hardware (approximately 2%).
4. Efficient utilization of processing power and memory.
5. Faster context switching, central processing unit (CPU) load balancing, and efficiency.
6. Complete isolation of different virtualization environments for preserving the integrity of data.
7. Better management of optimization of application and database.
8. Reduces the cost of purchasing new equipment.
9. Lower energy consumption.
10. Lower support cost.
11. Virtualization solutions offer a common platform to control and configure different OSs.
12. Users can fine-tune the maximum and minimum limit for usage of CPU, memory, and other resources by each OS. It can be configured to alert the user if an OS requires resources more than the maximum limit allocated. The resource requirements of each container can be scaled without a server reboot or user impact.
13. Any OS update can be automatically propagated from the virtualization layers to the containers.
14. OS virtualization can be used to allocate a finite number of hardware resources to a large number of people.

Unlike the case of hardware virtualization, there is no emulation of a complete set of hardware resources and hence no overhead of translating the host and virtual machines (VMs). This enhances the performance compared with hardware virtualization. Virtual machine managers (VMMs) manage each VM individually. Each OS instance allows multiple user-space instances such as virtual environments (VEs), virtual private server (VPS), or containers, for example, mobile hypervisor.

26.3 Hardware Virtualization

A hardware virtualization (Figure 26.2) layer is also called as a hypervisor. It provides a layer of abstraction between virtual systems and physical hardware. Different VMs that run over the hypervisor are OS agnostic, which means that it is unaware of other VMs, and it assumes that it has dedicated hardware resources (CPU, memory, and network). For running 10 OS instances, the hardware virtualization platform should provide 10 OS files and hardware configurations. Each

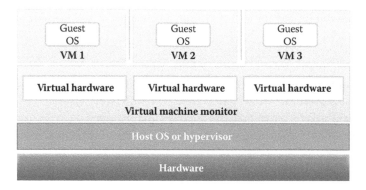

Figure 26.2   Hardware virtualization.

VM has to request the hypervisor for getting the hardware resources. A hypervisor is a thin layer of software that pretends to be hardware.

In order to manage the multiple clusters of hardware, there are virtual center management solutions that coordinate the working of different VM monitors. One such monitor is the vCenter from VMware. Some of the hardware virtualization platforms available in the market are as follows:

Microsoft virtual server
VMware server
VMware ESX

26.4 Paravirtualization

This is similar to OS virtualization (Figure 26.3). Paravirtualization offers a special set of application programming interfaces (API) to interact with the host OS. The main advantage is improved performance compared with OS virtualization. However, the OS needs to be customized to support this API. An example of the paravirtualization solution is Xen.

26.5 Platform Virtualization

Platform virtualization abstracts applications from the platform by encoding it in a common format. It provides run-time environment for a specific platform. The run-time environment for each platform knows how to convert the common format to a code that can be executed on the platform, for example, Java Micro Edition (Java ME), is the Java platform for embedded systems and mobile devices, personal digital assistants, set-top boxes, and printers. Applications developed in Java ME are

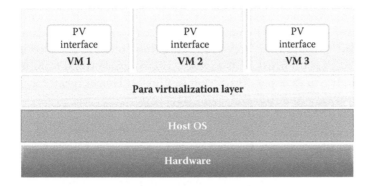

Figure 26.3 Paravirtualization

portable across devices as the Java ME is available for different platforms. The Java ME provides developers a flexible user interface, security features, and built-in network protocols.

26.6 Workspace Virtualization

Workspace virtualization is a fast-evolving architecture aiming to move the application workspace along with the application so that it can be run on multiple machines that may not have the application workspace to run a specific application. The information technology (IT) workplace is dynamic. If organizations want to provide their workforce with instant access to IT resources and data from the field or a remote location, they have to embrace workspace virtualization. There are a number of such solutions in the market, but many of the enterprises do not have a clear roadmap to develop a mobile strategy to provide a virtual workspace for providing employees access over the cloud. One of the cost-effective models of workspace virtualization is the virtualized desktop, which provide employees access to their business desktop machine from any mobile device anytime and anywhere, for example, Smart Drive and Ceedo Virtualization software for mobiles.

The desktop virtualization solution from Ceedo enables users to have a desktop work environment in portable devices such as pocket hard disks, universal serial bus flash drives, mobile devices, or a network drive in the cloud. The Ceedo solution for mobiles is unique compared with other desktop virtualization solutions in the market, as it does not require virtualization of the mobile OS.

26.7 Network Virtualization

Virtual network is a software-based administrative entity, which combines software and hardware network resources. Network virtualization includes platform virtualization and sometimes resource virtualization. A virtual network provides a proxy server that acts as a front end to get requests and sends data to multiple embedded systems in the back end. The virtual interface provided by a proxy, often referred to as a Virtual IP, is exposed to the outside world from multi-input to multi-output, for example, Cisco Mobile Wireless Home Agent, for roaming in different networks (front end) and giving data to different embedded systems (back end).

Network virtualization can be classified as external or internal virtual networks based on its implementation. In external network virtualization, one or more local networks in a corporate or data center is grouped or divided into virtual networks using virtual local area network (VLAN) and network switch technology. An example is the service-oriented network architecture solution from Cisco. Another example is the solutions based on Hewlett Packard's X Blade Virtualization technologies such as Virtual Connect, which combines local area networks (LANs) and storage networks under a single administered virtual network.

In internal network virtualization, a single system is configured with pseudo-interfaces and containers to create a virtual network within a system. Examples of solutions in the industry are as follows:

- Solaris Open Network Virtualization and resource Control solutions
- Microsoft Virtual server
- Virtual Network Stack from Citrix and Vyatta
- Virtual Network from VMware

26.8 Environment Sharing Virtualization

An embedded system provides the CPU and the random-access memory (RAM) required to run the software, but nothing is installed locally on the system, which includes applications such as terminal services and browser-based applications. All of these implementations depend on the virtual application running locally and the management and application logic running remotely, for example, Terminal Services Client in Windows Mobile 6.0, which comes as a built-in application.

26.9 Application Virtualization

Application virtualization is a way to encapsulate an application in such a way that it could achieve the following objectives:

1. The application is running in a virtual and isolated environment.
2. By configuring the virtual environment, the application should be able to utilize system resources.

3. The OS should not interact with the application directly. The installation of the application should have no impact on the configurations of host OS.

As the application is fully encapsulated in such a way that it has no dependency on the host OS, the application need not be installed in the system. The virtualized application can be streamed to the client just in time. The components of the application are downloaded as and when required. Some of the virtualized applications come with an automatic request system, which will stream the application and check out to the client when required and check in the application back when it is no longer in use. This feature of virtualization provides a business model in which user can subscribe to the application and pay according to the usage. Users need not worry about the application versions and licensing. Application virtualization can be used for sharing the application and remote login to a virtual environment. It differs from server-sharing virtualization, in that each client has its own version running in the server for server-sharing virtualization, while the same instance of the server is viewed by the clients in application virtualization, for example, virtual network computing (VNC) and Putty in Windows mobile. Some of the application virtualization solutions in the market are as follows:

- Citrix Streaming Server
- Thinstall Virtualization Suite
- Altiris Software Virtualization Solution
- Microsoft SoftGrid
- VMware ThinApp

26.10 Application Server Virtualization

This type of virtualization was invented to provide a virtual interface to the end user as its front end, and in the back end, it load balances multiple servers. Application server virtualization is also called as load balancing or reverse proxy. This provides a load balancer the capability to manage multiple web services in a single instance. One of the major providers of application-server virtualization solutions is f5. Some of the popular tools from f5 in the application server virtualization technology space to offer application delivery networking solutions are BIG-IP Local Traffic Manager, BIG-IP Global Traffic Manager, wide area network and LAN application delivery controllers, and virtual private network solutions.

26.11 Virtualization Using Emulator

This involves emulating an application or its work environment. It has a variety of uses that are detailed as follows.

26.11.1 Windows Mobile Emulator

It is a virtual hardware platform that mimics the behavior of different Windows mobile hardware platforms. It supports various features such as configurable screen resolution, serial port mappings, storage card emulation, networking support, and management of host key combinations. These emulators are mainly used for application development and testing for specific hardware platforms, for example, emulator for devices to be launched (T-mobile G1 emulator) on the Android platform.

26.11.2 Mobile Browser Emulation

Mobile browser emulators are used for developing and testing mobile web applications in a desktop machine. Emulators for different mobile OS platforms can be downloaded from http://www.mobilexweb.com/emulators.

26.11.3 Emulating Home Computer in Mobile

This type of emulator can be used to access home personal computers remotely and work on it. This has been covered as part of workspace virtualization. Some of the solutions in the market are the XenDektop from Citrix and VMware View from VMware.

26.12 Management Virtualization

This virtualization technique is used to define segmented administrative roles for one platform. This is achieved by creating virtual users. Each virtual user can be configured to provide or deny access to specific server resources. On the same server, different users have different experiences based on their roles. An example of management virtualization is the group policies in Microsoft windows XP, 2003, or Vista. An example of the management virtualization solution is BIG-IP Product auth domains from a company called f5 Networks. Another example is f5's device management platform, which can be used to manage multiple devices from a common platform with the same ease as handling a single device.

Another major player offering management virtualization solutions for enterprise mobile device management is SOTI (visit http://soti.net). Some of the products of SOTI in this domain are MobiControl, MobiAssist, and PocketController applications for different mobility platforms such as Windows mobile, BlackBerry, iPhone, and Android.

26.13 Grid Virtualization

Grid virtualization is a collection of mobile nodes sharing resources to create an infrastructure to run complex computing tasks, for example, Mobile grid. Mobile Grid is a second life messaging client for Android. Grid-In-Hand is the mobile grid client for iOS. The mobile grid provides open simulator messaging viewer and client, which supports voice chat with one or more persons, teleport to different locations, inventory management, global positioning system–based maps, and precise information for each of the avatars. So, many other real-world objects can be mapped to the grid.

The mobile grid client also supports second life, which is an online virtual world with over 25 million people registered in it. The grid client is also used for collecting data using a barcode reader for small business needs. The data can be stored in a file transfer protocol server or in a cloud-based storage.

26.14 Mobile Virtualization Platforms

Presently, organizations provide employees smartphones to access corporate resources at any time to increase the productivity and availability of people anytime and anywhere. Current market studies show that more than three-quarters of corporate employees have personal smartphones, and they prefer to have access to corporate resources from their smartphones. Virtualization solutions can provide corporate data security and, at the same time, provide freedom for employees to choose the smartphone of their choice. Users can switch between the personal mode and corporate mode environments, which are isolated from each other in the same device. As the virtualization platform is independent of the mobile OS, corporate organizations can provision, manage, and update the devices remotely.

Apple's iOS running in iPhone, iPad, and other mobile devices does not provide third-party solutions and access to the OS layer. Meanwhile, Android and Windows Phone 7 are emerging as preferred OS platforms for providing mobile virtualization platform (MVPs) solutions. These OS flavors are available for a variety of devices from different original equipment manufacturers (OEMs), which is also a reason for these platforms to be the platform of choice. MVP also enables semiconductor suppliers, OEMs, and network operators to reduce operating and manufacturing costs with the help of hardware consolidation, portability, and reliability. Examples are the MVP solution from VMware and SecureIT Mobile solution from Open Kernal Labs. Mobile service providers also provide similar virtualization products, for example, Nice Office and XORA workforce management products from AT&T. Another innovative product is the Nirvana Phone, which is a joint venture of Open Kernal Labs and Citrix. The phone has Citrix receiver software. It provides an extended workplace environment for corporate employees.

26.15 Challenges in Mobile Virtualization

Mobile OEMs are facing the challenge of introducing new cost-effective handsets in the market with more features, processing power, and memory. Because of the high competition and increased number of innovations in this field, the time to market the products is very less. Technologies are getting outdated at a fast pace as new technologies are invented. Limited and smaller memory capacity of mobile devices demand slimmer mobile hypervisor or microvisor footprints. Most mobile processors are outdated as they do not have virtualization support at the hardware level to support paravirtualization. Hardware manufacturers are working with VM developers to address the new scenarios, which have emerged with the invention of virtualization.

One challenge faced by virtualization is reliability. Numerous researches are going on to improve mechanisms in hardware to be able to recover from faults, and if it is unable to recover from the fault, it should notify the VMM. The VMM could identify which VM caused the fault and avoid sharing tasks with that VM. The hypervisor could restart the VM that caused the fault. Thus, hardware and software can coordinate to make the system more reliable. There are some security challenges when we have multiple OSs and services on a single platform. There are well-defined boundaries between the VM and the system, and it should be ensured that the boundaries are not breached. One such mechanism is the platform technology developed by Intel called the VT-d to check how direct memory access (DMA) and interrupts are processed. Another is the trusted execution technology by Intel, which validates whether the VM is trusted to run on the hardware. Most security systems are developed in collaboration with hardware and VM manufacturers.

The hypervisor can ensure that it boots up securely, and it can pass on the information to the auditing software, which logs it in a remote data center. The hypervisor can make use of the VT-d technology to ensure that VMs cannot infect each other and cannot infect the hypervisor. VT-d can be used to protect hypervisors to prevent wrong DMA. Tools to perform audits to provide compliance report is one area that is still in research. Graphics processing unit (GPU) virtualization is one challenging area because the GPU hardware software interfaces are more frequently changing. To do a VM migration, the VM has to capture the state that is more complex when compared with normal CPUs. VM ware has some GPU virtualization products that are based on API proxying and intercepting OpenGL directex calls.

26.15.1 Limitations

As the size of the VMs grows and when the VM migrate the tasks at run time between two physical CPUs, it has to move huge size of physical memory pages of data between hardware, which takes a long time. The pages that are migrated could be eavesdropped by an intruder and hence the pages should be encrypted, and this also adds on to the time taken for migration.

26.16 Conclusion

Virtualization is finding its application in more areas to bring about horizontal and vertical slicing of platforms. This means the OS becomes independent of platforms, and the applications also become independent of the OS. Virtualization applied to run-time environments is an emerging field in which a running application is switched to a different hardware platform. Mobile virtualization products are widely gaining popularity in the market. Live data and application migration between a virtualized desktop and a mobile is one of the key areas of focus. The current trend is that hardware and software manufactures are working together to develop virtualization products. GPU virtualization is an emerging field in which the collaboration between hardware and software vendors is more eminent.

Virtualization is spreading to more markets, and now it has become a standard practice for companies to adopt virtualization for better performance. This trend is seen not only across different industries but also for mobile applications also. The emergence of Mobile Virtualization Platform solutions from VMware is one of the products of this kind in the market. New x86-based low-power processors in mobile devices such as Intel Atom make it easier to develop VMs, which can take over the task done in a desktop environment. The Google Android platform is emerging as a platform of choice for mobile virtualization mainly due to the fact that it is open source, and third-party developers have more access to the OS internals to develop virtual environments. Also Android supports hardware from multiple OEMs.

Additional Reading

1. http://www.mobilexweb.com
2. Maximiliano Firtman. *Programming the Mobile Web*. Sebastopol, CA :O'Reilly.
3. http://www.vmwareintelalliance.com
4. Thomas Phan, Rebecca Montanari, and Petros Zerfos. *Mobile Computing, Applications, and Services*.

Chapter 27

Mobile 3D Solutions

As technology is converging toward mobile applications, handheld devices such as cell phones and tablet PCs are the hot cakes in the market today. The market is expecting mobile devices to have the capabilities of high-power desktop applications. Selection of hardware for the mobile device is an important step if the business solution to be implemented requires high graphics and 3D capabilities. With the invention of organic light-emitting diode screens, the percentage of the surface area of devices having user interface (UI) display is also increasing. This chapter gives an overview of the hardware selection criteria for 3D support and also the various programming options available to developers of various platforms for working with 3D solutions, and some of the 3D-enabling platforms and tools are dealt in detail.

27.1 Introduction

Processor speeds of more than 1 GHz are now available for mobile devices, which open up the scope of 3D solutions in the mobile world. Mobile OSs are being reworked to support more application process space and multiprocessor support. A separate graphic processing unit (GPU) is required for better 3D capabilities. The major original equipment manufacturers (OEMs) in the 3D graphics arena are NVIDIA, ATI (recently acquired by the semiconductor giant AMD), Samsung, and Qualcomm. Most leading OSs in the mobility market are working toward continuous improvements to overcome the limitations and bottlenecks for supporting 3D solutions. For example, Windows CE 6.0 supports only a single processor and a hard limit of 512 MB of physical memory. These limitations are being addressed in the new upcoming Windows Mobile 7, which also supports a separate GPU. The limitations can also be addressed by the use of a hardware platform with dedicated GPU and application programming interfaces (APIs) for accessing the GPU functionalities. The limitations in the maximum-allowed process space for Windows Mobile versions with Windows CE 5.0 kernel are also being addressed in the new Windows CE 6.0 kernel-based mobile OS. Also, the day is not far for having multicore processors for handheld mobile devices and personal digital assistant phones. The areas of technology in 3D solutions, which are evolving at a great pace, are as follows.

27.1.1 3D HD Imaging

Three-dimensional (3D) solutions are also evolving in the field of 3D high-definition (HD) imaging. Mobile hardware has the capability of high-definition 3D photo and video and a corresponding encoder–decoder support. 3D images are composed of two views taken by two different cameras with a separation of ~63 mm, which provides an accurate simulation of human eyes. Nowadays, mobile devices have video and photo editors to trim or join video clips, add sound tracks, and stabilize images to provide special effects and file-sharing support. Fast processing of video is also required for video calls and for operating future social networking web sites. There are hardware and software vendors for providing 3D solutions for HD video or image capture and processing. For example, the Movidius MA1101 video editor and A/V decoder for mobile phones deliver high-quality 1080i Moving Picture Experts Group-2 decoding for Integrated Services Digital Broadcasting-T Full-Seg reception and a unique video-editing effects suite.

27.1.2 3D Stereoscopic View

The human eyes are separated by about 6.3 cm, and the views from the two eyes are slightly different. This difference between the images is known as disparity. Also, our eyes can pivot inward or outward for viewing nearby and far-off objects. The brain interprets the angle of convergence of the eyes and the disparity to give us the perception of depth in the images and to give an effect of stereoscopic view. This processing of the brain is called retinal rivalry. As the distance of the object from the eyes increases, the disparity reduces, and hence the brain is not able to calculate the depth accurately. Beyond 100 m, the human eyes cannot have the perception of depth of the objects viewed. The stereoscopic view has been developed as a technology and has been recently introduced in a Google Android handset from LG named as Optimus 3D, which is powered by a dual-core Omap4430 chipset, by Texas Instruments, with a dedicated graphics accelerator. This breakthrough in technology has set new standards for mobile users' experience and gaming. The technology provides 3D view to users without the need to wear any special glasses. The device comes with 3D-capable touch screen and also has the ability to turn the stereoscopic effects on or off. It can also capture 3D videos and can upload the videos to a dedicated 3D YouTube channel. Qualcomm has also introduced a powerful Snapdragon quadcore chipset that is 2.5 GHz per core for new-generation 3D tablet and smart devices. 3D stereoscopic games have become an emerging market for game developers. A few examples of such games are Let's Golf 2, Asphalt Origins, and Near Orbit Vanguard Alliance.

27.1.3 Mobile Television

Mobile television is another area in which 3D mobile solutions are used. Third-party solutions are available for providing high-quality upscaling or downscaling of HD contents to fit to the screen resolution, increase the frame ratio for action programs such as sports, and reduce the broadcast noise, video stabilization, and slow motion (more details can be found at http://www.movidius.com).

27.1.4 3D Biometric Authentication

3D face recognition and biometric scans are available on mobile phones, according to the latest trends. With the invention of biometric digital signatures and mobile point-of-sale, the field of 3D face recognition and biometric scan has a great scope in the mobile market. Nowadays, 3D signature (vector representation of 3D facial image) has evolved. Elements of the vector correspond to fixed points in the face-centered coordinate system.

27.1.5 3D Navigation

Mobile devices require high-processing power and 3D graphics to display high-resolution 3D maps in the device. Apart from the 3D map being displayed on the device, the navigator application may show routes overlaid on 3D satellite maps, indicate current traffic along the route, visualize turns with street view imagery, navigate to destination based on voice input, and search for any kind of business, stations, or parking along a specific route. Some products in the market are AT&T's Internet-based TeleNav navigation service. Urban Horizon's 3D Navigation for Windows Mobile operates with or without Internet connectivity.

27.2 Choosing Hardware for Mobile Platforms

Some of the most popular and leading hardware vendors in the mobility market are QualComm and Samsung. QualComm, one of the leading OEM players in the manufacture of mobile processors, has come up with a "system on chip" with snapdragon processor and Andreno 205 GPU. This processor series starts with a minimum of 1.3-GHz processing speed. This GPU features dedicated 2D Open

VG graphics hardware along with 3D hardware, which provides faster, higher quality 2D rendering, simultaneous use of 2D and 3D, and lower power use. The latest iPhone 4 comes with A4 processor, which runs at 1-GHz frequency. iPhone has a separate GPU. Samsung is another major player in the OEM segment for the manufacture of semiconductors for mobile devices. It also has a strong footing in the mobile phone manufacturing industry. Samsung's most popular mobile processor for 3D support is the Cortex A8 processor, which is coupled with a PowerVR SGX540 GPU, and other features include the following:

- Hardware-accelerated scalable vector graphics (SVG) and Adobe Flash®
- Significant improvements in shader performance
- Streaming textures that can combine video, camera, SVG, and other image surfaces with 3D graphics with supported APIs such as those listed:
  - OpenGL for embedded systems (OpenGL ES) 2.0
  - OpenGL ES 1.1
  - OpenVG 1.1, EGL 1.3
  - Direct3D Mobile
  - SVGT 1.2
  - Direct Draw
  - GDI
  - Concurrent central processing unit (CPU), digital signal processor, graphics, and MDP

This hardware platform is mainly used by Windows Mobile 7 and Android mobile OS. Another major player in the market is NVIDIA. The latest series from NVIDIA is the NVIDIA® Tegra™, which is a full HD ultralow-power mobile web processor. It comes with a dual-core ARM® Cortex-A9 MPCore™ processor, up to 1.0 GHz, and a separate GPU designed to power the new generation of tablet PCs, slates, mobile Internet devices (MIDs), e-readers, automotive safety and entertainment solutions, and Internet television boxes. NVIDIA Tegra delivers an uncompromised web experience, including ultralow-power Flash 10.1 acceleration, 3D touch-screen UI support, 1080 pixel video playback, and unmatched battery life.

27.2.1 Tegra Development Kit

The development kit provides OS images for Microsoft Windows CE, Ubuntu Linux, and Google Android platforms. It can be used to customize the OS shell according to customer needs. AMD has announced a suite of tools for the company's next-generation graphics parts for mobile devices. Handheld game development is one of the focus areas. The Rendermonkey shader tool that comes with this suite allows developers to write the graphics code for devices that support OpenVG, OpenGL ES, and Unified Shader Architecture technologies. ATI's Unified Shader technology powers the graphics in Xbox 360. AMD's Imageon processor is a GPU for mobile devices that provides support for 3D and 2D graphics, video and digital cameras, video recording with image stabilization, video transcoding, television out, and other multimedia features.

27.3 APIs for Developers

27.3.1 Mobile 3D Graphics API (M3G) for J2ME

The Mobile 3D Graphics API or M3G is a specification defined for developing 3D graphics for JavaME. It was developed under the Java Community Process as Java Specification Request (JSR) 184. It is totally different from Java 3D. M3G is primarily used for 3D Java game development. Android supports M3G. The background images and textures can be provided in portable network graphics format, or data files can be included as M3G files to convert texture maps to PNG format. The set of APIs can be used to draw complex animated three-dimensional scenes. It has plug-ins for 3D modeling tools, which can be used to create 3D model assets. For asset creation, there are different 3D modelers available with 3G plug-in, such as Lightwave, Maya, 3D Studio Max, and Softimage|XsI. M3G provides two modes of development of 3D graphics: immediate mode and retained mode. In the immediate mode, the graphics commands are directly sent to the graphics pipeline and then executed by the rendering engine. In this mode, a developer has to tell the rendering engine what to draw for an animation frame. The camera and set of lights are not necessarily part of the animation frame.

In the retained mode, a user can use a scene graph. A scene graph links all geometric objects in a well-defined tree structure. It also has the information about the background and camera lights. The high-level information (geometric structure and position) is retained from frame to frame for each graphics object. For example, Sony Ericsson supports different 3D engines (software engine, which renders real-time 3D graphics). Sony Ericsson Windows Mobile Java platform, Sony Ericsson, Symbian OS Java platform, and Mascot Capsule V4 are used to implement JSR-184. The engine is Mascot Capsule Engine and is also known as Micro3D. In some high-end phones, JSR-184 APIs run the NVIDIA graphics accelerator. The JavaME platform is seamlessly integrated with these 3D engines (Figure 27.1). JSR-239—Java binding for the OpenGL® ES common profile API—allows rendering of low-level graphical objects in JavaME. The OpenGL ES provides two profiles: the common profile that supports floating point and the common-lite profile that is a 32-bit fixed-point profile. The latest M3G API version can be downloaded from http://www.forum.nokia.com/main/resources/technologies/java/.

The API takes the form of an optional package expected to be used with MIDP and version 1.1 of the Connected Limited Device Configuration (Figure 27.2).

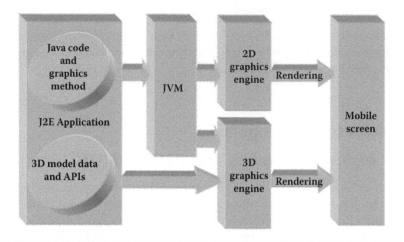

Figure 27.1   3D image rendering in J2ME.

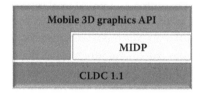

Figure 27.2   Software stack for mobile 3D graphic APIs.

27.3.2 Java 3D

Java 3D is a set of scene graph–based APIs. A scene graph is used for vector-based graphics editing, a technology commonly used by applications such as AutoCAD, Acrobat 3D, and Coral Draw tools. Also, Java 3D offers spatialized sound support. The official site for Java 3D (http://www.java3d.org) provides more details.

27.3.3 Direct3D® Mobile

Microsoft® Direct3D® Mobile is an API that provides support for 3D graphics applications on Windows CE-based platforms. It has multitype architecture, and it supports both floating-point and fixed-point values.

27.3.4 Silverlight, XNA, and the .Net Compact Framework for Windows Mobile 7

There are three main development frameworks on Windows Mobile 7 platform for developing 3D rich Internet application (RIA), 3D games, and 3D support in consumer applications. These platforms are Silverlight, XNA, and the .Net Compact Framework 3.7 (and above), respectively. Note that Silverlight and .Net CF can be used together, whereas Silverlight and XNA UI cannot be mixed for the development of applications. However, the common services are common and are available for the three frameworks. The common services include the accelerometer, microphone, location, sound, media, networking, etc. There are third-party tools in the market, which provide rich UI controls for application development. These tools provide advanced multipouch and 3D features for the application. One such tool is the Resco Mobile Forms Toolkit for Windows Mobile, which comes as a plug-in for the Visual Studio integrated development environment.

27.3.5 OpenGL ES for 3D Application Development across All Mobile Platforms

OpenGL ES is a royalty-free, cross-platform API for full-function 2D and 3D graphics on embedded systems, including consoles, phones, appliances, and vehicles. Figure 27.3 demonstrates the different mobile platforms supporting OpenGL. OpenGL ES 1.X is for fixed function hardware and offers acceleration, image quality, and performance. OpenGL ES 2.X enables full programmable 3D graphics. OpenGL SC is tuned for the safety critical market. Anyone can download the OpenGL ES specification and implement and ship products based on OpenGL ES. OpenVG is a set of royalty-free APIs for consumer electronics devices enabling them to have hardware-accelerated 2D vector and raster graphics. It provides interfaces for vector graphics libraries such as Flash and SVG. OpenVG is targeted for handheld devices such as portable mapping applications, e-book readers, gaming devices, and low-level graphics devices, with small screens that require portable acceleration of high-quality vector graphics. OpenVG works perfectly for the

Figure 27.3 The OpenGL ES cross-platform APIs for different platforms.

hardware accelerator, which will reduce the power consumption up to 90% compared with the software engine.

Imagination Technologies is a multimedia chip manufacturing company that has come up with PowerVR SGX series of the graphics core, which has passed the Khronos conformance tests for OpenVG. COLLADA from the Khronos group is an XML-based schema to transport 3D assets between applications. This intermediate language provides encoding of visual scenes such as geometry, shaders and effects, animation, physics, and kinematics (http://www.khronos.org/opengles/).

27.3.6 3D Programming for iPhone

For developing 3D applications for iPhone, a Mac OS with iPhone software development kit (SDK) installation is required. iPhone's public APIs are categorized into four layers: Cocoa Touch, Media Services, Core Services, and Core OS. All of the iPhone graphics technologies are the customized versions for Mac OS X. Both iPhone (Figure 27.4) and OS X (Figure 27.5) have the same kernel architecture and core OS. The shared components are collectively known as Darwin. The difference between both the platforms is the way in which they handle OpenGL. Max OS X supports full features of OpenGL, whereas iPhone is based on more svelte OpenGL ES. The graphics technologies for iPhone include the following:

1. Quartz 2D Rendering Engine: Quartz is a powerful graphics technology on which the foundations of 2D imaging model are built for Mac OS X. This engine provides a vector-based graphics library with support for alpha

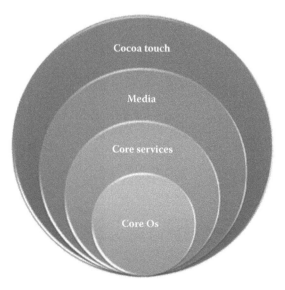

Figure 27.4 iPhone programming stack.

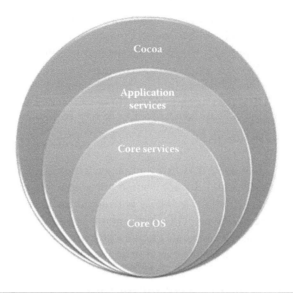

Figure 27.5   Mac OS X programming stack.

blending, layers, and antialiasing. The applications need to reference the Quartz Core framework that is a collection of libraries and resources.

2. Core Graphics: Vanilla C interface to Quartz. This is a trimmed down version of the interface available on Mac OS X.

3. UI Kit: Native windowing framework for iPhone. Among other things, the UI Kit provides a wrapper to Quartz primitives using Objective-C classes. The Mac OS X counterpart for these native frameworks is called App Kit, which is a component of Cocoa.

4. Cocoa Touch: Cocoa Touch for iPhone is the conceptual layer in the programming stack that contains the UI Kit along with a few other frameworks. The UI Kit provides tools to develop event-driven graphics applications for iOS. The UI Kit also provides access to the photo library using photo picker interfaces and interfaces to control the camera. Cocoa Touch is a collection of frameworks. The framework for audio and video has the following components: core audio, open AL, media library, and AV . The framework for graphics and animation has components for core animation, OpenGL ES, and Quartz 2D. For data management, the framework supports core data and SQL lite. For networking and Internet, tools are available, such as Bonjour, Webkit, and Berkeley Software Distribution sockets. Bonjour is the zero configuration protocol from Apple to automatically detect systems and services in a network.

5. Core Animation: It handles the layout and rendering of animations. The Objective-C framework facilitates complex animations. The basic building blocks of this framework are layers that provide transparency, filter effects,

and automatic transitions between states. It supports different media types such as texts, OpenGL, video, and 2D graphics.

6. OpenGL ES: It provides hardware-accelerated C APIs for rendering 2D or 3D graphics. iPhone relies on the more svelte OpenGL ES.
7. EAGL: It provides APIs that interact between the UI Kit and the OpenGL ES. Some EAGL classes (such as the CAEGL layer) are defined in the Quartz Core framework, whereas others (such as EAGL Context) are defined in the OpenGL ES framework.

Even though OpenGL ES has many implementations, it has the same set of APIs. This makes the OpenGL ES application portable across different platforms. Basic knowledge in C++ and Objective-C is required for working with OpenGL for iPhone development. iPhone 3GS and the above versions have a programmable graphics pipeline because of a separate graphics processor support for these devices. These hardware features enable these devices to use OpenGL ES 2.0.

27.3.7 3D Application Development for Android Platform

Google Android has support for high-performance 3D graphics using the OpenGL ES APIs. Android currently supports OpenGL ES 1.0, which corresponds to OpenGL 1.3. Android supports Java programming and is based on Dalvick Java virtual machine. Android also supports a new programming language called GO, which is supposed to be a cross between C++ and Phython.

27.3.8 3D Applications for the BREW Platform

Binary runtime environment for wireless (BREW) is a UI framework from QualComm, which provides user themes, form management, a rich new set of UI controls, and a model-view-controller. The BREW platform basically uses C or C++ for application development. The platform has extensive support for 3D graphics using OpenGL ES.

27.3.9 3D Application Development for Linux-Based Mobile OS

There are many Linux-based OSs for mobile devices in the market. The most popular among them is the Android platform (with Dalvick Java virtual machine). Other customized Linux platforms include UBUNTU and MAEMO. These platforms depend on OpenGL ES for 3D graphics.

27.3.10 3D Application Development for Symbian

Symbian mobile OS has provided a software-based implementation of the OpenGL ES 1.0 standard since the launch of Symbian OS v8.0a. Both S60 3E and UIQ

1.0 SDKs provide plug-ins to upgrade it to OpenGL ES 1.1.2. In fact, the S60 3E FP1 SDK includes the OpenGL ES 1.1 plug-in by default. Most of the latest Symbian devices have support for hardware-accelerated 3D graphics. The major market players in the Symbian market are Nokia and Sony Ericsson. Nokia devices have PowerVR MBX graphics processor from Imagination Technologies, and most Sony Ericsson devices contain the lite version of the same processor. Nokia is the biggest promoter of Symbian OS development.

27.3.11 3D Application Development for Bada

Samsung introduced a new mobile development platform called Bada in late 2009, and devices with this OS hit the market in 2010. It is a platform that runs on mobile OSs such as Android and Windows Mobile. The first device was Samsung phone WAVE GT S8500 with a 1-GHz strong ARM Cortex-8 CPU and in-built PowerVR SGX 3D graphics engine. Bada is an open platform. The Bada architecture consists of a Bada kernel, and it has three layers (i.e., device, service, and framework layers) over the kernel. It supports application development in C++.

27.3.12 Adobe Footprint in 3D Mobile Application Development

There is an industry-wide initiative lead by Adobe called the Open Screen Project™. Android, the BlackBerry® platform, Symbian® OS, Palm® web OS, and Windows Mobile® support this initiative. As part of this initiative, Adobe® Flash® Platform and Adobe® AIR® on mobile devices provide consistent run time for stand-alone applications across multiple platforms. Flash Player 10.1 optimized for mobile is the first release of the Open Screen Project enabling web browsing of expressive applications and support for content and high-definition videos across various kinds of mobile devices, mobile OSs, and browsers in the market. The Open Screen Project enables developers to develop RIAs with 3D support.

27.4 3D Mobile Benchmarking

Benchmarking gives a normalized mean for comparing different hardware configurations for GPUs, especially for gamers and overclocking enthusiasts for asserting end-user performance capabilities. Some of the mobile 3D benchmarking products in the market are as follows:

1. GLBenchMark: Provides benchmark suite for OpenGL® ES 1.x/2.0 compatible Linux, OpenKode, Symbian, and Windows Mobile devices. http://www.glbenchmark.com/

2. 3DMarkMobile: The 3D benchmark software for mobile devices from Futuremark is intended for use on development hardware to assist in product development, design evaluation, and for mobile hardware media reviews of next-generation devices. The latest version available in the market is 3DMarkMobile JSR 184.

27.5 Conclusion

There is a new traction seen in the market with respect to mobile solutions to go 3D. Major software vendors are getting service requests to improve the application UI to have 3D features across different platforms. There are independent third-party solutions emerging in the market providing toolkits for application development with rich UI components. The fast market acceptance of iPhone is the best example of the influence of a rich UI and 3D solutions for mobile applications. 3D stereoscopic view is the next step in the user experience of the next generation of handset.

Additional Reading

1. *iPhone 3D Programming*. Available at: http://developer.apple.com/devcenter/ios/index. action
2. *3D OpenGL programming for Android*. Available at: http://developer.android.com/guide/topics/graphics/opengl.html
3. *Windows Phone 7 3D programming, Visual Studio Tools and Features for 3D Programming Using .Net, Silverlight, and XNA*. Available at: http://www.microsoft.com/visualstudio/en-us/products/2010-editions/windows-phone-developer-tools
4. Balder. *3D Engine for Silverlight, Windows Phone 7, XNA and OpenGL*. Available at: http://balder.codeplex.com
4. http://www.glbenchmark.com
5. http://www.khronos.org/opengles/
6. http://www.java3d.org
7. *Mobile TV*. Available at: http://www.movidius.com
8. *M3G API*. Available at: http://www.forum.nokia.com/main/resources/technologies/java/

Chapter 28

Mobile Signage

For any business venture, it is very important to advertise the products and services. Advertising is done for the following reasons:

- Creating awareness among people to make them know about "who you are," "what you do," and "what you can offer."
- Differentiating yourself from your competitors. This is to address the question "why you." Here, the aim is to inspire a customer to opt for your product and services compared with that of your competitor and to tell them what difference your product or service can do for them.
- Branding to create a positive image in the minds of the customer, which will give them a feeling of trust and familiarity with your brand.

The mobility space opens up vast opportunities to enterprises to reach out to people. It opens up new faces of advertising. The statistics of Internet application downloads and hits to mobile advertisements shows that mobile signage is becoming popular, and it has the potential to exponentially increase the sales of products and services. This is due to its unique features over personal computers (PCs), and it can provide unduplicated access to customers. In this chapter, we explore the vast possibilities and opportunities of mobility in digital signage.

Mobile advertising has become the key for the success of any enterprise in today's world. It is the first step in m-commerce. Mobile marketing requires marketers to engage with customers at every stage of the life cycle of a product or a service, from awareness to brand-building advertisements, prospecting, lead generation, customer relationship management, up-selling, customer care, engaging social media, and retirement stages.

28.1 Introduction

Because of the unique advantages of the mobile platform over conventional advertising platforms such as television (TV), posters, and computer screens, there needs to be a different operating model for mobile advertisements. Conventional advertisement platforms broadcast advertisements to a variety of customers. When there is too much of information before a customer, a large amount of advertisements gets unnoticed by the customers. Hence, it is very important to deliver the right kind of advertisement to the right kind of customers at the right time by considering the location and the taste of the customer. Current trends show that people in public places are either in conversation with friends or family, or they are plugged to mobile headsets. The consumption of digital content is ever increasing with the Internet and mobile technologies. The use of social networking sites also shows an exponential increase. Mobility has the following advantages over other advertising options:

- Mobile devices are aware of the customer's location. This provides additional information such as what the customer is seeing now, and this provides creative opportunities to divert the customer's attention to what we want him or her to look at.
- Mobile screen stays with the user throughout the day, unlike any other medium of advertising. This provides the opportunity to expose an advertisement to the user for a longer duration of time.
- Mobile devices are highly personalized. This would provide information about the taste of the customer.
- Digital signage can quantitatively and qualitatively measure and analyze the user's reaction to the advertisement, which is not possible with conventional signage solutions.
- It would provide data on the paid signage services to help in calculating how much of the profit margin is worth to be invested in advertisements.
- Digital signage can measure the performance of advertisements. It could provide statistics on how well the advertisements are accepted in the market, how many hits are received in a time frame, etc.
- The cost associated with mobile advertisements is calculated per click on the advertisement, which directs the user to buy or download the product.

The digital signage industry is driven by three economic models. First is the advertisement-funded digital signage, where a third party provides content management system, display system, media layer software, and hardware to a venue at no cost. Revenue is generated for showing the advertisement on the display screen. The second model is the traditional digital signage, wherein the venue owner purchases the signage system as done by hotels, casinos, banks, corporations, etc. In the advertisement-supported model, the venue owner purchases the system but sells the advertising to generate revenue to make profit or meet the initial expenses. However, the mobile convergence of digital signage has created a new economic model and integrated the features of all the previous three economic models. The analysis done by Fortune shows that in July 2010 advertisement requests in Android have grown by 47% month after month, iOS advertisement requests have grown by 24% every month, and for RIM and iPAD, the figures are 24% and 18%, respectively. On a yearly basis, this had accounted for a growth of more than 690%, 15%, 66%, and 327% for Android, iOS, RIM, and iPAD, respectively.

28.1.1 Mobile Marketing Association

The Mobile Marketing Association (MMA) is a nonprofit organization that has proposed best practices and guidelines for promoting mobile marketing and developing marketing solutions for mobiles (visit http://mmaglobal.com for more details).

28.1.1.1 Mobile Entertainment Forum

The Mobile Entertainment Forum (MEF) is the global community to promote and guide mobile content and m-commerce. It helps in shaping the commerce industry in adopting mobile-based technologies and solutions (visit http://www.mefmobile.org for more information). A digital signage system basically has the following components:

1. Content design: It includes the design of screen layouts, scheduling time, and dates.
2. Content management: It is used for facilitating content delivery to various network end points.
3. Playing the media: It determines the format of media content.
4. Display: It is the presentation of contents to the end users.

Mobile technologies deliver value-added services to digital signage in the following convergences through mobile devices:

1. Dial tone mobile frequency (DTMF)
2. Proximity marketing services
3. Short messaging services (SMS)
4. 2D bar codes
5. Graphic recognition
6. Mobile web
7. Mobile application
8. RSS feeds

28.1.2 Dial Tone Mobile Frequency

DTMF uses the touch tones on mobile key pads to control the content presented on a screen. The touch tone interactions can be recorded and analyzed to quantify the viewership of the digital signage and content. It also provides information about the response time between call and action. For example, Nike used this feature in one of their promotional campaigns in New York's Times Square, where a Nike shoe was shown on an electronic billboard, and users could use their mobile phones to customize and personalize the style of the shoe.

28.1.3 Proximity Marketing or Mobile Marketing

By 2011, more than 80% of the population of the United States has used cell phones, and out of this, more than 50% has used smartphones. People have a second thought when they have to replace a PC. These figures are increasing as people are replacing PCs with smartphones and tablet PCs. Also about 98% of mobile phones have Bluetooth and about 35% of phones have WiFi; hence, these wireless technologies are the preferred mediums for delivering digital signage to customers. These wireless technologies do not require the customer to share personal information or cell phone numbers in order to access digital signage contents. Proximity marketing provides digital content to brands and agencies to reach out to customers through mobile phones. The digital content includes any type of file format that the mobile device can play. Proximity marketing service providers will identify the specific type of mobile device a customer is using and deliver the digital content accordingly. This makes it a power tool to deliver advertisements and other digital contents to smartphones and traditional phones based on the handset types. For example, customers can freely download the digital signage displayed on an advertisement screen in a shopping mall to get attractive offers. Some examples of digital contents used are as follows:

- Videos: This includes short films, advertisement videos, movie and video game trailers, interviews, and animated videos.
- Images: Images include wall papers, brand logos, and photos of celebrities and brand ambassadors.
- Ring tones: This includes tailored character, actor, and actress voice tones, sound tracks, audio tunes, or short video clippings (video ring tones) of the video advertisements.
- Mobile applications: Some of these apps can be downloaded for free from marketing web sites. For example, an airline would provide the customer an application to download that will help them know the departure or arrival details of specific flights and help them to check-in or track their luggage
- Mobile games: Free-download games are tailored to provide partial free play, and the customer can purchase them for full-play features. Also, the game could be full play but with a minimum number of trials.

- Mobile games are now recently used for promoting new movies. Mobile games and comics are launched with the characters in the movie.
- Coupons: These provide discounts and offers on specific products. Based on the location of the customer, coupons are provided that are valid for a limited time period.
- Calendar appointments: These provide reminders of product launches or future events.

Proximity marketing could deliver contents based on highly targeted locations such as shopping malls, bars and clubs, cafes and delis, and movie theaters. The contents are delivered using transmitters set up in or near to digital signs. An example of proximity marketing is the demonstration by Blue Bite, a New York-based interactive mobile marketing firm to deliver the content of Reach Media Group's (RMG) NYTimes.com. RMG delivered digital contents from New York Times to digital signs located across New York. The Blue Bite's solution embedded in the digital signage systems delivered the contents to the smartphones and smart devices of people on an opt-in basis.

28.1.4 Short Messaging Services

SMS, also called text messaging, allows users to send or receive text messages. All the mobile phones in the market have support for these services, and hence, it is the fastest way to reach people. Statistics shows that people prefer SMS compared with call most of the time.

Customers can subscribe to SMS from a digital content provider through their web site or texting a message to a specific number called short code to register for subscribing marketing materials from different brands or marketers. Users can provide inputs through texting to these short codes as per the guidelines of the brand that offered the short code in order to receive offers sponsored by the brands.

28.1.4.1 SMS-Based Convergence

SMS-based convergence can be classified into the following categories:

- Signage as recipient: Signage viewers can send SMS to a short code, which is then broadcasted to all viewers. Viewers can respond to the text messages by replying to the short code with a text message.
- Content selection: Viewers can control the display of a signage screen by texting predefined commands or keywords to a short code. There will be specific keywords or commands recognized by the content manager for controlling the signage, such as changing the display or selecting a choice from the menu to play a video or music. The system can track and analyze user preferences.

- Content control: Viewers can control the contents on the screen, such as rotate or zoom the screen in or out, show text messages in display, and move pieces in a game, etc. This is mainly used to entertain a group of people with the signage content. It can be used to analyze user preferences.
- Promotional: Viewers can text in keywords to short codes to participate in a lucky draw or win discount coupons. The promotional offers are texted back to the user by the content management system. For example, a Norwegian-based interactive solutions firm, Never.no, in collaboration with the e-clothing manufacturer Diesel had introduced a signage system, where users can send their photographs to a special short code. These photos were displayed in Diesel's Copenhagen retail stores, and these pictures were also included in the mosaic hosted on Diesel's Facebook page.

28.1.4.2 Applications of SMS Convergence

- Ring tones and wallpapers: SMS can be used to subscribe for specific ring tones from the telecom service provider. It is mainly used for the promotion of the brand, for getting people engaged with the brand, or selling ring tones and wall papers.
- Alerts and subscription list: The alerts could be updates on traffic, weather, share price, movies, or anything. Users can simply register to a web site or text in an SMS to a number provided by the marketer or the brand.
- Text to vote: Text to vote is used for engaging customers and conducting surveys for getting votes and feedback from people to know the reaction of the public to the usage of a brand. It is also used to get public opinion on specific issues or decision taken by the government. This feature is getting popularity in democratic countries.
- Text to win: SMS counts in favor of a candidate are taken into consideration to determine the winner of an event. This feature is used in an engagement stand point to interact with customers.
- Donations: Marketers can accept donation from people by asking them to send an SMS to a specified number. The donation amount will be accounted in the periodic service bill to the customer.
- Alerts and subscription: Subscription includes updates on the price of a commodity, share market prices, weather, traffic, movies, art, or music.
- E-mail capture: Users are asked to reply back through SMS with their e-mail address to receive brochures and other details about a product. The SMS can be taken to newer levels to extend its roles in reaching out to people delivering digital signage. Some of the new features evolving are as follows:
  - Text to screen and pictures to screen: The customers of a product can text in messages to specific contact numbers about how much they like the product or other comments about the product to get engaged in contests such as gaming, lucky draw, or other exciting events. Pictures to screen is

similar to text to screen in which people can send a picture to a web site, a ribbon board, a moving display, or a display screen in a TV channel.
- Content selection and modification by the user over SMS: We have multiple content selections that can be controlled over SMS. The user can select the particular content on the display screen or bill board. Also, the user can use SMS to change different attributes of the display contents such as the color and size.

28.1.4 3 Factors to Be Considered for Choosing SMS

The factors to be considered for choosing SMS are as follows:

- Goal setting: There could be different goals for using SMS, such as branding, engagement, acquisition, or fun. There are different tactics for using SMS as the medium of signage. We need to determine the goal and check whether the channel of communication selected aligns to the goal.
- Budget and time: It is important to narrow down the features to be used based on budget and time constraints.
- Getting help: It is an important step to associate with a technology partner to layout a road map and to determine the right technology, features, and functionalities to be used. This will ensure that the choice of SMS for achieving the goal is justified.
- Experiment and evolve: Based on the new trends in the market, initial feedback from the end users and considering the emergence of new technologies and features, appropriate modifications on the plan should be made.

28.1.4.4 2D Bar Codes

2D bar codes are displayed along with digital signage in a screen. Users can capture this bar code using the barcode reader equipped devices or photograph the bar code. The application in the mobile device would decode it to get additional information related to the signage and display it on the device's screen.

28.1.5 Graphic Recognition

The basic idea of graphic recognition and bar code in the field of digital signage is the same. In the case of bar code, the additional information about a product or services is embedded in the bar code, which can be translated using common algorithms, whereas in graphic recognition, users can capture the image of an object or graphics or the entire digital signage and get additional information by querying the image in a remote database or with the usage of software applications to decode the contents. Additional information about the object is delivered to the mobile phone from the remote server. The system helps in recording, analyzing, and quantifying the usage and viewership of the signage. An example of this is the U-Snap application from the company called JCDecaux, which delivers the signage contents based on the photograph of digital signage posters, billboards, etc., photographed by a mobile device. Another example is Nokia's Point & Find application in Nokia phones, which can be used to capture the photo of an object to receive content information about that object.

28.1.6 Mobile Apps

Mobile apps are digital signage delivery platforms in which one of the display components of the signage system is the mobile screen. This form of convergence is applicable only to second- and third-generation smartphones. Mobile apps are more popular among users as the smartphone usage is exponentially increasing year by year. Mobile apps are more interactive to users compared with other signage systems. They provide image, voice, and text at the same time to the user. One of the first mobile apps used as digital signage was the signage application called InView, developed for iPhone to deliver scores and details of the Wimbledon Championship. It could deliver interactive real-time contents based on the geographic location of the user. The content was delivered by the same content management system used to provide contents to the other types of display systems such as display boards. The app was able to provide complete tracking of the number of downloads, location of the user, number of views, and statistics on the user's actions upon viewing the contents.

28.1.7 Mobile Web

In this method, the digital signage provides or acts as a web URL, which takes the user to a phone-optimized web content. The interactions of viewers with the web site are tracked and analyzed to quantify viewership and find out user choices.

28.1.8 RSS Feeds

A digital signage system has a content manager that is remotely located. The digital signage contents are delivered to different kinds of signage systems. Each signage system has its own technology to receive and update the contents. The technology chosen is based on whether the digital signage network is a closed (without Internet access) or an open network (with Internet access). Open networks can receive updates in real time and stream data from other Internet sources. RSS (RDF site summary) is a family if web formats used in an open network to publish and update at real-time contents such as news headlines, blog entries, audio, and video. This is a widely accepted and popular technology. RDF stands for resource description framework, which is a family of World Wide Web Consortium (W3C) specification for meta-data models. The advantage of using this technology for delivering digital signage is that we can deliver the contents to specific customers who are interested as they have registered to receive the RSS feeds. The RSS reader installed in a mobile device will check for the user's subscribed feeds periodically for any latest updates or downloads.

28.2 Other Emerging Mobile Signage Trends

28.2.1 Location-Based Services

Location-based convergence of digital signage has recently emerged since the introduction of global positioning system (GPS)-based services to smartphones and mobile devices. This approach leverages the capabilities of the device to determine its geo-coordinates (longitude and latitude of the specific place) to deliver location-based content and services to the user. Similar to all other convergent solutions, this also helps in collecting data to extrapolate the viewership of a digital signage content and derive statistics on the common interest of the viewers for market study. For example, InView is a location-based digital signage delivery application from Symon Communications. This solution has been presented as a case study under Section 28.4 in this chapter.

28.2.2 Augmented Reality-Based Services

Augmented reality makes use of different mobile convergent services such as location tracking using GPS, camera, gyrosensor, Internet access, etc., to create an augmented reality experience in which the viewer instead of just watching a signage plays as an actor in the signage. This has huge potential, and lots of signage applications are using this to attract viewers. Augmented reality solutions often combine with other technologies to create a better user experience such as facial analytics, 3D Graphics, etc.

28.2.3 Digital Out-of-Home Services

Digital out-of-home (DOOH) signage represents all forms of digital signage that are used to reach out to potential customers out of their home. It mainly has two categories. The first category is called Glance Media, which attracts mass audiences. This includes signage systems such as bill boards on the road and digital location-based contents. The second category is targeted more toward niche customers, and it provides highly customized contents and promotional offers to the users. These customers are selected based on the history of their transactions. DOOHs, in its current form, are generally passive systems. In future, more importance will be given to interactivity with the users. One of the easiest ways to interact with people is to provide them access and control to the signage through their mobile phones.

This can be done over text messaging, Bluetooth, or WiFi. There are standards defined to measure the audience and the number of hits to a DOOH signage, such as the Canadian Out-Of-Home Digital Association (CODACAN). CODACAN suggests the following factors to be considered for measuring the audience:

1. Opportunity to see: This determines the number of people whose attention was caught by the signage.
2. Dwell time: This determines the time a user spent with the signage system and how much time the user was present in the vicinity of the signage system.
3. Within what interval does the advertisement get repeated.

28.2.4 Mobile Media

The latest paradigm shift in the field of media and entertainment is the emergence of mobile media. Mobile media has become more popular than conventional TV channels and news papers, mostly because of the changing lifestyle of the people and people want everything while on the move and need real-time update of news. The means through which people acquired information has changed from newspapers and TV channels to wider options of social media such as Facebook, Google+, Twitter, YouTube, Orkut, FourSquare, and other similar social networking solutions. Some examples of digital marketing intelligence solutions for leveraging mobile media are provided in Section 28.4.

28.2.5 Mobile-Enhanced Customer Care

Industries are realizing the potential of an effective mobile customer care. It provides an opportunity to interact with the customers and offer services and market new solutions. User can do interactive chat with a customer-care representative through the mobile device. This will improve customer satisfaction and reduce support costs. Kaiser Permanente, a leading healthcare provider based on California, had saved $275000 a month after launching an SMS-appointed remainder service.

28.2.6 Loyalty Programs

Marketers use loyalty programs to engage customers. These programs bring value to customers such as access to exclusive contents, VIP access to programs and events, special discount coupons, vouchers, and more (e.g., My Coke Rewards program from Coca-Cola Company).

28.2.7 Engagement Solutions

Engagement solutions include products and services for conducting market research, interviews, surveys, polling for campaigns, mobile ethnography, and digital diary services. These solutions are of two types. The first approach is to directly engage with customers through SMS, multimedia message services, voice, Internet, e-mail, applications, and proximity channels. It can be again classified into marker-initiated or consumer-initiated solutions. Interviews and survey solutions provide tools for customizing survey questioners, face-to-face and on-site surveys as a service to brands for analyzing the acceptance of any product among users.

28.2.7.1 News and Reviews

For example, IPSOS & Techneos created a news and review service for different mobile platforms, which was used to collect public opinion on how people felt about the royal wedding in the United Kingdom. There was another mobile application used across all mobile platforms to conduct reviews during the TV coverage of the Oscar Awards. Diary solutions provide users to input feedbacks on a service or product. These signage mechanisms are presented to the users based on the context. Users are prompted with reminders and self-initiated feedback about the products. Such solutions can record the voice or video of users who are willing to share their experience about using the products. Consumer engagement applications provide value-added services to customers when they choose to download small applications in their mobile devices that provide two-way interactions such as chat and call facilities. For example, a retailer called Starbucks provides a free downloadable application. Users can download and install these applications to register in a coffee club. The application delivers discount coupons and promotional offers to customers. The application can tweet in Twitter or update your preferences in your social networking sites such as Facebook or Google+. For example, check for the Techneos mobile platform solution offered by Techneos Systems Inc. (http://www.techneos.com), which provides engagement services through mobile devices.

28.3 Measuring Mobile Signage Success

One of the commonly used currency metric for measuring any advertising media such as mobile signage is the audience. The costs involved are accounted in thousands to calculate the cost per impression (CPI). The digital signage solutions based on mobile devices can easily measure the audience and CPI. However, signage solutions such as DOOH find it difficult to gather details of audience. Integrating DOOH to user interactions over the Internet would enable measurement of the audience. As mobile devices are becoming the face of the Internet, every signage solution is converging to mobile devices. comScore AdEffx™ is an advertising effectiveness solution for measurement of effectiveness of an advertising campaign over the Internet (http://www.comscore.com/Products_Services/Product_Index/Ad_Metrix_Mobile).

28.4 Mobile Signage Solutions

We examine a handful of mobile signage solutions in the market: InView Mobile™ is a media player application from a company called Symon. This application delivers real-time, interactive multimedia content to mobile devices from Symon's centralized content management system (http://www.symon.com/mobility.shtml). Solutions to leverage mobile media are available from comScore, a leading market player in digital marketing. Ad Metrix Mobile™ is a mobile advertising intelligence solution from comScore. For advertising agencies, this product helps in identifying and choosing among the different advertisement formats, gather information about other competitors in the advertisement market, find new publishers and servers for advertisements where there is a potential for delivering the advertisements to possible candidates and for future customers, and discover sites that are most valuable to the growth of the business. For publishers and advertisement networks, this product analyzes advertisement servers for new tractions and potential clients, identifies when and where inventories are sold in large numbers, how different advertisers are performing in their campaign in mobile advertising, and how the campaigns are running across various publishers, and analyzes and watches specific advertisement servers.

28.4.1 Advertisement Services for Mobile Devices

iAds service is an advertisement placement service offered by Apple for Apple device users. Developers of mobile applications can integrate the iAd services to their applications. Apple generated around $60 million revenue in the first 60 days from the launch of iAd. Apple has plans to integrate near-field communication (NFC) capabilities to its iAds program. Apple's recently filed patents on iPay, iBuy, and iCoupons indicate the latest trends of combining mobile advertisements with mobile point-of-sales (POSs). AdSense is the advertisement placement service offered by Google for mobile applications. It supports various types of conventional advertisement formats such as banner, text, and search advertisements. AdSense is available for application developers of all different platforms.

Google Adwords is the service offering from Google, which allows customers to create and customize their own advertisements. Customers can choose the keywords relevant to their business. When people search with these keywords, then Google shows the advertisement along with the search results. If the user chooses to click on the advertisement, then he or she is redirected to the customer's web site. Adwords provides tools to create reports and fine tune the search criteria to improve the hits on the ad. It also provides features to customize advertisements for a specific region or time period. Google charges only for the user clicks on these advertisements and no charges for displaying the advertisement. Google has launched a web site (http://www.ourmobileplanet.com) providing mobile consumer data resource. The site provides interactive tools for marketers for understanding mobile consumers. Similar to the advertising business model for Google, we have similar business models from Microsoft (Microsoft Ad Center), which provide advertising options in Microsoft Bing and Yahoo search engines. There are other service offerings from search engine providers that provide application programming interfaces to place advertisements on the web site and generate revenue if people visiting the web site click on these advertisements.

AdMob is an advertisement service from http://www.admob.com. Developers can develop custom advertisements in Android and use third-party services to push them to multiple devices.

Twitter ad is an advertisement service provided by Twitter to its customers in an innovative way. If one chooses to follow, for example, Walmart, then all tweets, announcements, and offers related to Walmart will be displayed on the user's Twitter pages.

28.5 Signage Support in Mobile SDKs

An application developer can provide advertisements that are sources for generating additional revenue. The advertisement business over the Internet is a billion-dollar market, and we have the success of major players such as Google in the market.

28.5.1 Windows Phone Advertising SDK

Microsoft is providing an advertisement software development kit (SDK) for Windows Phone. SDK provides Silverlight and XNA controls, which can render and display advertisements from Microsoft's real-time advertisement exchange for mobiles. This advertisement platform supports advertisement networks that could provide real-time bid on impressions generated by the users. On click of the advertisement, it could take the user to a web page, marketplace, or initiate a call to customer services. It can also be integrated with the Microsoft Pub Center, which provides reports on how effective an advertisement is for the application.

28.5.2 Advertising SDKs for Android

Android provides support for third-party advertisement platforms to push advertisements to an application. An example for such a platform is AdMob from http://www.admob.com. It fully utilizes the potential of Google's AdSense services. Adsense maximizes profit by using the cost per thousand impressions business model. Using Google Adwords helps us to progressively improve the search criteria to increase the number of hits for the advertisement.

28.5.3 Advertising Platform for Apple iOS

Apple provides support for providing advertisements in devices running iOS using Apple's iAd network. iAd platform is integrated with iOS and does not require a separate SDK. It helps in developing advertisements with rich media contents. An advertisement can be developed for your application, and iAd network can be used to deliver the advertisements to the application running in other iOS devices. Apple will sell the advertisement, and the application owner would receive 60% of the revenue generated on that advertisement.

28.6 Conclusion

The growth of digital signage directly depends on the growth of the Internet and the common medium used by people for Internet access. Most widely used and preferred Internet devices are mobile phones and tablet PCs compared with laptops for personal needs. We have seen how digital signage has converged to mobility in recent times. It has become inevitable for an enterprise to adopt mobile technology for advertisements. Mobility has increased the average time spent by a viewer on a signage. The latest paradigm shift in the field of media and entertainment is the emergence of mobile media. It is much more than the convergence of media in the mobile space. The new source of gathering information is through the social networking applications in the market. Mobile media has gained wide acceptance because it suits the busy life style of the people who crave for better technology solutions in a highly dynamic and evolving market.

An enterprise needs to define its strategy for advertising considering the emerging advertising ecosystem. The key to adopt the right strategy to advertise the products lies in the understanding of the emerging complex relationships between consumers, media, mobile devices, and technology. Industries have to depend on technology solutions to measure the effectiveness of advertisements and to study the market and in-flight optimization of the advertising solutions. Often, signage solutions are integrated to other solutions such as Mobile POS, wherein the user can immediately purchase the product if inspired by the signage. In light of this, Google has a lot of advantages as it provides multiple services using a single account, which includes services such as social networking (Google+ and Orkut), e-mail (Gmail), payments (Google Wallet), selective advertisements based on the taste of the viewer and previous browsing history (Google Ads), and search for product and offers (Google shopping). All these services are by default integrated in Google Android devices, and the user can integrate these services for other mobile platforms. The latest trends show that in future, signage solutions will combine different mobile signage convergent models. Augmented reality solutions seem to have a bright future. It is also seen that the integration of different technologies would provide new business models. Mobile signage would be integrated with mobile

POS business models, and users can make payments using their mobile devices using NFC technology. Mobile advertisements have become a booming industry. The latest statistics on the number of advertisement hits in Android, iOS, Windows Phone, and other mobile platforms shows that the day is not far away when every citizen would have a mobile phone, and matters of public interest are voted by people using their mobile devices. Mobile engagement solutions are effective tools to reach out to the masses within a short time.

Additional Reading

E-Reading

1. MMA. Available at: http://mmaglobal.com
2. *The Global Community for Mobile Content and Commerce*. Available at: http://www.mefmobile.org
3. *Google's Guide for Mobile Marketing*. Available at: http://www.ourmobileplanet.com
4. http://www.symon.com/mobility.shtml
5. http://www.digitalsignagetoday.com
6. http://en.wikipedia.org/wiki/AdWords
7. *Consumer Engagement Solutions*. Available at: http://www.theopenexchange.org/category/mobile/ and http://www.knowledgenetworks.com
8. *Apple iAds*. Available at: http://developer.apple.com/iad/

Books

1. Keith Kelsen. *Unleashing the Power of Digital Signage: Content Strategies for the 5th Screen*. Burlington, MA: Elsevier, 2010.
2. Cindy Krum. *Mobile Marketing: Finding Your Customers No Matter Where They Are*. Indianapolis, IN: Pearson, 2010.
3. Michael Becker and John Arnold. *Mobile Marketing for Dummies*. Indianapolis, IN: Wiley, 2010.

Chapter 29

Mobile Device Management

As the number of devices to be handled by an organization increases, the need for a device management (DM) solution becomes inevitable. Managing mobile devices is more tedious than managing personal computers (PCs) within an organization as the devices may operate out of the secure corporate environment. If corporates want to provide employees access to corporate data and e-mails in their own personal devices, then the DM solution has to address a new set of challenges. Mobile device management (MDM) solutions help in creating an extended workplace and redefining mobility in the corporate world. They have broadened the class of mobile workers to include more job profiles other than that of managers and executives who are usually on the move rather than being confined in an office.

29.1 Introduction

As mobile devices are becoming part and parcel of our personal and business needs, we are facing new challenges at the corporate and consumer levels. Before the introduction of iPhone and Android in the mobile market, very few smartphones were used by employees for corporate work. RIM's BlackBerry was popular for secure corporate e-mail, and corporate mail access was mostly limited to the smartphones provided by the corporate. With the introduction of third-generation smartphones and the new class of mobile devices such as tablets and notebooks, employees are using their personal devices for accessing corporate network and data, even if the employers may not be fully aware of it. Gartner has classified MDM market players into four categories:

1. Challengers who provide solutions to cater to the need of basic functionalities of MDM. They often focus on a specific area of MDM and may challenge the market players in terms of cost and mainly target small enterprises (e.g., Tangoe).
2. Market leaders who have demonstrated a balanced progress in their vision and all areas of MDM, for example, Sybase, AirWatch, MobileIron, and Good Technology.
3. Niche players who often have a self-limiting business model and offer solutions within the boundary of the industry or geographical location. SOTI, Motorola, Fiberlink Communications, Boxtone, McAfee, Mobile Active Defense, and Excitor are a few examples.
4. Visionaries who offer long-term vision accomplishments and also provide other services for catering to the needs of the changing market, for example, Zenprise and Symantec.

MDM solutions have a wider scope of functionalities to offer, and again the features offered may be limited for certain mobile platforms. In general, you should be aware of the following facts while choosing the appropriate solution for your enterprise:

■ MDM solution may not support all device platforms in the same way. This could be due to limitations of the device or the platform. So, check the feature availability for each mobile platform. For example, iOS devices have restrictions on manipulating the kernel level. Hence, some of the security features available for Windows mobile devices may not be compatible for iOS devices.
■ Android has recently stepped into enterprise solutions. Hence, most of the MDM features may still be in the development phase for this platform.
■ Not all MDMs support BES integration. Check for the availability of this feature. Most of the solutions offer their own enterprise services.
■ Ensure how good the reporting and business intelligence tools supported by the solution are. It is important to have support for text and graphical reports as well as canned and customized reports.
■ The architecture of an MDM solution should be flexible enough to integrate with an organization's legacy life cycle management systems, and specific services on MDM should be available for reuse. MDM and life cycle management solutions have the potential for generating huge revenues in consulting services.

29.2 Device Management Specifications

Open management alliance (OMA) is a standards body that was created in 2002. Members of this alliance include industry players in mobile equipments and systems manufacturers, mobile operators, and different software vendors. OMA has specified a DM protocol called OMA-DM for interoperability between product implementations from different vendors. This protocol is platform independent. It can be freely downloaded from http://www.openmobilealliance.org. The specification includes an OMA-DM specification and an OMA data synchronization (DS) specification. OMA-DM provides specifications for provisioning, configuring, fault management, and software updates of mobile devices with small memory footprints and constrained wireless bandwidth. The specification also addresses security. OMA-DS specifies how to synchronize data during operations such as over-the-air updates of software and firmware. Some vendors have even extended the OMA-DM specifications. For example, Microsoft has extended some parts of this standard for their Windows Mobile platform, which can be referred in MSDN.

29.3 Defining Mobile Strategy for Enterprise

For every enterprise, it is important to formulate a mobile strategy before considering solutions for MDM. These strategies need to be revised periodically based on the latest developments in this industry. It should define a technology road map for implementing the strategies. For choosing the right solution, we need to consider factors such as the need for customer mobile application, whether to provide corporate mobile devices to employees or provide DM solutions to the personal mobile devices, thereby reducing the operational cost and reduce costs on roaming and data charges. In the case of corporate devices, an organization has to use expense management solutions to settle the bills of corporate mobile device usage. Organizations also have to use solutions for security, policy deployment, and management on the devices. Corporate MDM solutions should have at least three of the following basic elements:

- Software distribution
- Mobile inventory management
- Policy management
- Mobile security and access control policy
- Service management

29.3.1 Software Distribution

Software distribution includes the ability to manage mobile application across different devices and provide support for the applications deployed. It should support various phases of deployment such as installation, updates, block, and uninstall. It is also used by original equipment manufacturers (OEMs) for updating over-the-air firmware.

29.3.2 Mobile Inventory Management

Mobile inventory management should consider the following:

- Provisioning and support for diverse kinds of devices
- Management console to enforce security policies in devices and run scripts to schedule and configure events
- Central management of all devices and security policies
- Creating and deploying a master image for all devices
- Managing application versions in the devices and automating the process
- Remote execution of antimalware and antivirus applications
- Real-time push of data or installation packages to multiple devices
- Real-time monitoring and remote access to device desktop and device resources
- Broadcast messages to device and interactive chat with the device from the control room
- Provide support and help to users, which includes providing training information and help remotely to the device users

29.3.3 Policy Management

In general, policy management defines the development, control, and operations of enterprise policies for mobile devices.

29.3.4 Mobile Security and Access Control Policy

The security policy should consider the following:

- A strong password policy. It includes authentication, administration, and user login.
- Blocking Bluetooth, WiFi, and universal serial bus (USB) and limiting the installation of applications not suggested by the organization. These features are permanently blocked in case the employees are provided corporate devices. In the case of allowing the usage of personal devices for corporate purposes, these features are controlled, and access to corporate data is restricted by creating an isolated virtual environment for the user to work on corporate data. We have seen similar kind of virtualization solutions in Chapter 26.
- Allowing the usage of the device in dual mode, both personal and corporate.

- Blocking Activesync or similar DS and data access options. Activesync and BlackBerry enterprise solutions can be configured to meet most of the enterprises' needs for Windows and BlackBerry Phones, but to meet the challenges of new security risks arising in the industry, enterprises prefer to go for sophisticated and dedicated MDM solutions.
- Usage of appropriate encryption protocols such as SSL and TSL.
- Lockdown devices to provide access to selected features and applications according to access permissions set for a user profile.
- Lockdown browser functionalities.
- Audit login for database or device resources such as registry.
- Device lockdown on any attempts to hack the device or multiple entries of invalid login credentials.
- Wipe all data and disabling the device in case of a security threat even in case of device not accessible over the network.
- Data and software recovery in case of malicious software attacks and periodic backup of data or snapshot of device registry and configuration settings.
- Logging, retrieving, and analyzing user activities and important device events.
- Creating rules and alerts on configured activities happening on the device.
- Option to select third-party solutions to further extend the security and enterprise requirements. This includes integration of third-party solutions for scripting, reporting tools, and device control.
- Location-based tracking based on the telecom service provider or global positioning system services. It includes tracking of device movement, locating stolen or missing devices, and recording location information history of devices.

Enterprises should ensure that security is not compromised with the introduction of new type of devices. As each type of device is different in their platforms, operating system (OS) and other capabilities, an enterprise should ensure that the security policy is defined for each type of device or platform.

29.3.5 Service Management

Service management refers to the rating of telecom services. It includes e-mail service management for the devices. Telecom service providers can control device configurations and firmware updates across a wide range of devices using MDM solutions. It also helps them to roll out new services similar to mail services. It could be used to remote wipe or lock stolen devices. It also helps in providing helpdesk services. Device manufacturers are also thinking of having MDM solutions for the devices they manufacture for their customers. This helps in providing helpdesk services for complaints raised on devices.

29.3.6 Support for Cost-Effective Communication Infrastructure

Unlike computers in the conventional enterprise workplace, mobile devices are used in extended workplaces. They will have additional costs for cellular services for trunk calls, SMS, and other types of telecommunication. An MDM system should be smart enough to reduce the cost of communication. It should be able to automatically switch between the corporate WiFi network and the cellular or vice versa automatically based on the environment. It should be able to initiate data transfer through low-cost mechanisms such as Bluetooth or Internet in extended workplaces outside the corporate network. There are third-party solutions, which provide the right kind of communication infrastructure to have cost-effective communication and data traffic (refer to mobile unified communication solutions in Chapter 30).

29.4 MDM Considerations for Some Major Platforms

29.4.1 MDM for iOS Platform

Apple has very strict rules for enterprise solutions in the iOS platform. Apple controls the way applications are developed and deployed. For rolling out enterprise solutions, an organization should first register for the iOS Developer Enterprise Program (iDEP). Once it is approved by Apple, then Apple will provide a push notification service certificate to the organization. The certificate allows application deployment without the use of iTunes. This certificate needs to be loaded into an in-house MDM server or a third-party MDM solution used by the organization in order to enroll, configure, query, and manage hosted applications on Apple devices. If the application has implemented simple certificate enrollment protocol, then iDEP is not required. Enrolling can be done by connecting a device via a USB or can be enrolled over the air through a secure web portal. Enrolling will establish a relationship between the device and the server so that the server gets control to manage and provision the device remotely. The various steps involved in enrolment are user authentication, certificate enrolment, and device configuration. At the end of the enrolment process, the device will show an installation display screen with the access rights of MDM server on the device. The user will have to accept the access rights to automatically enroll the device.

■ Configure: The server sends XML files called configuration profiles to the devices, which are automatically installed in the device. It contains account information, pass- code policies, restrictions, and other device settings. Configuration profiles can be signed, encrypted, and locked so that it cannot be manipulated by an intruder.

- Query: MDM servers can query the devices for retrieving a variety of information related to device, network, applications or compliance, and security.
- Manage: MDM server can remotely manage and administered using specific set of actions such as remote wipe, remote lock, clear password, configuration, and provisioning profiles.

Because of the well-defined rules set by Apple, all MDM solutions offer similar features for managing Apple devices.

29.4.2 Device Administration in Android

Android provides device administration application programming interfaces (APIs) for supporting enterprise applications. These APIs can be used for providing administrative features and security settings for the development of an in-house MDM dashboard with rich controls. Security policies can be hard coded in device or can be pushed from a third-party server. Android does not have an automated provisioning. An administrator can deploy applications in devices through the following options:

- Android Market
- Nonmarket installation
- Distribution of application through e-mail, web sites, and other means

Once the application is deployed, the user will have to enable an administration application, where the user has to specify the settings for the policies. Until the administration application is configured, the user will not be able to use full features of the deployed application. When an application connects to a server that requires validation of policies and if the policies are not supported in the administration API of the device, then the connection request from the client will be denied by the server. It is up to the application in the device to handle any violations of the policies defined through the device administration APIs. In case of multiple enabled administration applications in the device, the policies will be strictly enforced. Android's in-built e-mail application and associated APIs can be used to provide exchange support for MDM solutions and features such as e-mail password policy enforcement and synchronizing e-mail and calendar.

29.4.3 MDM for Microsoft Windows Mobile and Higher Versions

Before iPhone and Android came to the mobile market, Microsoft's Windows mobile was holding the major market share in mobile enterprise solutions. WM 5.0 and above has support for messaging and security feature pack (MSFP), which push security policies. These policies are pushed from an Exchange 2003 or Exchange

2007 server to the device. MSFP can be used to perform remote wipe of devices, device lockout, and remotely configure the device.

29.5 Some MDM and Security Solutions in the Market

29.5.1 MDM Solutions from SOTI

SOTI (http://www.soti.net) is one of the major players in the market. They have a range of products for providing solutions to different aspects of MDM for mobile devices and desktop machines. The products from SOTI cover Android, iOS, Windows Mobile, and BlackBerry devices. The following sections will have a brief overview of some of their products.

29.5.1.1 SOTI MobiControl

It is a cloud-based enterprise MDM solution from SOTI. The key features are as follows:

1. Secure e-mail access: It ensures that the device accessing corporate mail is a trusted device. It could be configured to send or receive mail to a list of trusted devices only. It could provide an additional layer of security at the device level over the security features at the user level provided by mail services.
2. Sophisticated dashboard: User-friendly dashboard for administrators with animated screens, graphs, security features for devices, device activity, remote viewing, and controlling of devices and much more. Tools for helpdesk management.
3. Access point management: It provides the access point management features by integrating with the Aruba Airwave solution.
4. Security features: It could enforce a well-defined enterprise security policy. It could restrict devices to run only a specific set of applications, disable cameras and sensors within a secure area, encryption and decryption of files transmitted across devices, identify digital certificates, and configure secure network connections such as WiFi, APN, or virtual private network (VPN).
5. It could also limit and control the applications running on desktop machines.
6. It provides cloud-based solutions. SOTI provides agent builder services to build custom device agents, which could interact with cloud-based service to manage the device.
7. Messaging service to message across devices of various platforms that are added onto Mobicontrol.
8. It can be integrated with third-party life cycle management solutions.
9. Geo tagging and geo fencing: Device can be tracked over GPS and can be configured to generate alerts when it goes outside a defined boundary of GPS coordinates.
10. Asset management and application management.

11. Reporting of various live information from a fleet of devices like battery information, application information, collecting application logs or data files from devices and much more.

29.5.1.2 SOTI MobiAssist

This is another cloud-based solution from SOTI intended for administrators, help-desk managers, and technicians to provide support for a fleet of devices. The tool helps in reducing operating costs, resolution of issues within a single customer call, and speedy resolution of issues. The tool provides these features across devices running various platforms such as Android, iOS, Windows Phone, and BlackBerry. Some of the key features are as follows:

1. A powerful console for technicians to work on devices provides features to take remote control of a device, edit registry, record macros, record videos, take screen shots, download event logs, and view BlackBerry service books.
2. Remote diagnosis of devices by collecting device information and using tools to manipulate services, tasks, and applications remotely.
3. Instant chat facility with the device user or with other technicians.
4. Hotline access to helpdesk for users by configuring helpdesk number in the device registry.
5. Manage session and session history so that technicians can view or review their own session history or share it with other technicians for review. Technicians can transfer a session to another technician. Sessions can be recorded for training purposes. Session history can be used for analyzing any security breach.
6. The tool provides advanced features for security. It supports 256-bit advanced enterprise security (AES) or 128-bit Triple DES algorithms for data encryption. Technicians should get end-user permission for resetting the device or editing registry remotely. The end user of the device can terminate the session at any time.

29.5.2 AirWatch

Airwatch has been there in the MDM market since 2003 and is a niche player in the industry. Key features that distinguish it from other products are as follows:

■ Support for Android, iOS, Symbian, BlackBerry, and Windows platforms
■ Range of products and services to cater to a variety of needs and provides SaaS hosted on a cloud or user site
■ Multitenant support for improved scaling can provide selective isolation for large installations

▪ Rich policy management for e-mail server environments such as Post Office Protocol, Internet Message Access Protocol, SMTP mail servers, Lotus Domino, Gmail, and Novell GroupWise

29.5.3 Afaria from Sybase

Sybase is an SAP company that has well-established DM platforms for managing PCS since 1980. Sybase released the first version of MDM for Palm and Windows Mobile platforms in 2000. Now, it is a full-fledged MDM solution capable of catering to diverse kinds of needs in the industry. Sybase has partnered with the company SAP, which is the inventor and giant of the SAP industry. Sybase Unwired Platform can be used to develop a wide range of SAP-based mobility applications including mobile ERP and mobile customer relationship management solutions. Sybase Unwired mobile platform comes integrated with Afaria MDM. Details of this platform have been covered in Chapter 30. Key features that distinguish Afaria from other products are as follows:

▪ Support for Android, iOS, Symbian, BlackBerry, Palm, and Windows platforms
▪ Provides life cycle management
▪ Support and integration with Sybase Unwired platform
▪ With the integration of Mobile Office, it provides wireless e-mail and a mobile application integration framework
▪ Well-established software distribution functionalities
▪ Support for helpdesk management and expense management functionalities
▪ Embedded VPN in e-mail client along with a sandbox architecture to isolate and control access to business data and VPN connections
▪ Afaria AES for Android has more than 80 MDM features for Samsung Android devices

29.5.4 Zenprise Mobile Management Solution for iOS

It is available in iPhone App Store by the name "Zenprise for Employees," which needs to be downloaded and installed in iPhones. It could be used to establish a secure connection with the enterprise network by providing the server details and authentication data provided by your organization. It requires the user to install a corporate certificate, which is validated with the enterprise network. It also requires the user to download, install, and provision a personal profile, which can be used to configure phone settings, password policy, e-mail account, WiFi, and VPN settings.

29.5.5 MaaS360 MDM Platform

According to MaaS360 MDM architecture, the life cycle of MDM has been classified into provisioning, management, and deprovisioning of devices. Provisioning includes commissioning new devices under the management framework and applying rules, configurations, and security settings. Management mainly involves day-to-day information technology (IT) management activities. Deprovisioning involves decommissioning devices from service and wiping of data from the device in case the device is stolen. It can configure active sync in Windows devices and enable mailbox access to specific user(s) using the device. Maas360 is available for iPhone, Windows Phone, and Android devices.

29.6 Some Telecom Service Management Solutions in the Market

Telecom service providers are looking for MDM solutions for a wide range of purposes such as inventory, expense, asset, deployment, circuits, and security management. Tangoe (http://www.tangoe.com) is one company involved in providing communications life cycle management solutions. It includes the following:

1. Telecom expense management: For managing the expenses of services, contracts, and rates
2. MDM: For managing mobile inventory registering, provisioning, application management, etc.
3. Strategic consulting: Another example is the product and service offerings from Teligistics (http://www.teligistics.com). It provides features such as MDM, invoice management, vendor management, wireless policy, technology strategy, and strategic sourcing

The Mobile Network Director Application from SmithMicro allows telecom operators to optimize network traffic based on load by directing the traffic of data between 3G, 4G, and WiFi networks. It also provides IPSEC security features. Telecom operators are also partnering with vendors in MDM and mobile ERP companies to create mutually beneficial business models. Telecom providers could provide seamless wireless Internet connectivity for mobile devices, which would provide the basic infrastructure for deploying MDM and ERP solutions. It provides a huge opportunity to sell voice and data plans to support a fleet of enterprise mobile devices.

29.7 Importance of MDM in the Mobile Workforce Management Solutions

Mobile workforce management solutions automate daily tasks of a business process to eliminate manual inefficiencies and paperwork, improving and adhering to business process, reducing operating cost, saving time, sending or receiving work orders electronically, providing guidance to complete a job, and many more similar functionalities. These solutions also include fieldforce automation also. Such workforce management solutions depend on MDM solutions for deploying applications across devices in the field, version control, extending application support to users in the field, scheduling scripts to update application settings, or copying files to or from the devices in field, etc.

29.8 Mobile Connectivity Management Solutions

Connectivity for the fleet of mobile devices is one of the preliminary requirements for deploying an MDM solution. A connection management framework or solution should automatically work in the background to provide seamless connectivity over the wireless and wired network. The solution should be able to provide "connect and forget" user experience. It should switch to the best available connection mode such as WiFi when the device is used within the enterprise, the cellular network when the device is outside the enterprise wireless network, and Ethernet when the device is cradled. It should also establish a VPN over unsecure channels such as cellular network and provide data security. It should be able to manage network profiles and maintain sessions and other features. QuickLink Hot Spot Manager and SODA (secure on-device API) provide a consistent, safe way for communicating between devices and hot spots. Some players and their solutions in the market are as follows: NetMotion Wireless Mobility XE is an advanced mobile VPN from a company called NetMotion wireless. It has some add-on modules such as the following:

■ Policy management: Creating and managing policies for security or for better control
■ Analytics: For managers to view the historical data of the application or network
■ NAC ensures advanced data security

Some other solutions are QuickLink Mobility and Quicklink Hot Spot Manager from SmithMicro software (http://www.smithmicro.com), Mobile Net Switch (http://mobilenetswitch.com), and MOBILEwise from netwise applications.

29.9 Integration of MDM with Other Enterprise Solutions

MDM solutions fetch or send data to devices locate, enforce security policies, or device lockdown. An MDM solution does not have the intelligence to interpret the data to identify a business process.

29.9.1 Integration with Legacy Systems

Enterprises will have different solutions within the organization such as the service life cycle management to track customer management, asset management, service management, forward and reverse logistics management, mobile workforce management and optimization, servicing and renewing damaged devices. Such life cycle management solutions require to be integrated with MDM solutions in order to gather data for analysis and interpretation. An example is the Astea Service Lifecycle Management solution that is integrated with the MDM solution from another company called SOTI and both the solutions are sold together. This is a good example of a business partnership, and MDM solution providers would be looking at providing end-to-end solutions to customers.

29.9.2 Integration Using Middleware Applications

Companies providing IT services have opportunities to provide integration of MDM solutions with the life and asset management solutions used by an organization. Companies such as Infosys provide market-ready asset management solutions and middleware applications, which can be integrated with any MDM solution in the market at minimum cost and also provide lifetime support and maintenance services.

29.9.3 Integration with SAP and ERP Solutions

Another challenge of the mobile industry is to integrate mobility solutions including MDM solutions with SAP-based business models and ERP solutions (refer Chapter 30, Section 30.8 on mobile ERP solutions in the market in this business segment).

29.10 Conclusion

MDM solutions are evolving to catch up with the new challenges created by the fast-growing mobile market. It has evolved from managing physical devices to the management of applications in devices. Enterprises even want to integrate life cycle management solutions with MDM solutions. These integrated management solutions are intended to enforce workflow within the organization to manage the allocation, deallocation, or associating the cost of the device with a particular department. Integrating solutions to meet end-to-end processes of organizations will be a new expectation from MDM solutions in the market. Service companies also have opportunities to offer Software-as-a-service (SaaS) solutions to integrate different management solutions within an organization. Because of the increasing demands for MDM solutions, more and more players who offer solutions for managing PCs are also looking into the MDM space. MDM solutions for the telecom industry are seeing good traction and industry-wide adoption. They have lot of potential to expand their scope for managing different processes associated with mobile management. This technology provides a lot of business opportunities for MDM product companies and IT service companies. Consulting is another booming revenue-generating business in this industry. Enterprises need guidance on choosing from MDM as a service or as a product. Services usually charge per device. There are life cycle management solutions in the market, which offer MDM along with a set of services, which are priced per user. It is up to the enterprise to evaluate the best and cost-effective model.

Additional Reading

1. GartnerReport_MDM_MQ_April2011
2. *OMA DM for Microsoft Mobile Platforms*. Available at: http://msdn.microsoft.com/en-us/library/bb737369.aspx
3. *MDM for Apple Devices*. Available at: http://www.apple.com/iphone/business/integration/mdm/
4. *Device Administration in Android*. Available at: http://developer.android.com/guide/topics/admin/device-admin.html
5. *Afaria from Sybase*. Available at: http://www.sybase.com/products/mobileenterprise/afaria
6. *Airwatch MDM Solutions*. Available at: http://www.air-watch.com
7. *Absolute Software*. Available at: http://www.absolute.com
8. *AetherPal Solutions*. Available at: http://www.aetherpal.com
9. *Lifecycle Management Solution*. Available at: http://www.tangoe.com

Chapter 30

Popular Mobile Solutions in the Market (Anti Virus, ERP, SAP, SCM, etc.)

The definition of mobile application has become highly volatile. It is redefined every day as new innovative applications are launched for various types of mobile devices. This trend is common for enterprise business solutions and for consumer applications. The question of the hour is, "What else can we mobilize?" As mobile devices are becoming more powerful in terms of processing power, memory, and Internet bandwidth, the line drawn across desktop and mobile applications is becoming narrow. With the invention and wide adoption of cloud-based applications, mobile applications and services have overcome the limitations of handheld devices. Information technology (IT) departments of every industry are driven to integrate mobility into their system, as it has brought about an unprecedented boost in employee productivity, fast returns on investment, the ability to directly interact with the customer, and the availability of real-time or recorded business information anytime and anywhere to make critical business decisions.

30.1 Introduction

In this chapter we discuss on the major mobile solutions in the market and some of the emerging trends that are revolutionizing the mobile industry. Mobile market is growing in an ever increasing pace and a reflection of this can be seen in the increase in the number of applications in App Stores of different mobile platforms.

In this chapter we will have a glimpse through emerging solutions in the enterprise in m-commerce, mobile marketing, ticketing, banking, security, Push mail services, SAP, ERP, supply chain, MSCM, UC, BI applications, MDM, and mobile media management.

30.2 M-Commerce Solutions

Mobile commerce (m-commerce) refers to all solutions in the mobile market, which facilitate commerce using mobile devices. These solutions facilitate transactions involving the transfer of rights or the ownership of goods and services. M-commerce is one of the fastest evolving industries and provides great opportunities for business enterprises, software and telecom service providers, and application developers. Any goods or service can be sold through m-commerce. M-commerce is a broad classification, and it involves many different business areas that are as follows:

1. Software vendors
2. Infrastructure equipment vendors
3. Content providers
4. Content aggregators
5. Mobile portals
6. Billing and payment

Some of the m-commerce applications are as follows.

30.2.1 Mobile Signage and Marketing Solutions

Mobile marketing is the first step in m-commerce. The first step toward mobile marketing is to optimize your website for mobile devices. Next step would be to enhance user experience by adding richer contents, video and user interactive features to bring life in your website. Literally any website can go mobile and that is the beauty of mobile marketing. Next comes advertising your website, services or products through mobile ads. Mobile Marketing is an emerging business that covers areas like Media Delivery services, Content Management, Mobile Delivery, Web acceleration for optimizing dynamic contents for improving user experience, cloud-based services for on demand content storage, traffic management, and content delivery. We have covered different mobile marketing solutions in detail in Chapter 28.

30.2.2 Mobile Ticketing

Some of the NFC-based mobile ticketing services are discussed in Chapter 22. NFC is one of the many technologies that are used for mobile ticketing. There are solutions based on short message services (SMS), multimedia message services (MMS), enhanced message services (EMS), wireless application protocol (WAP)-based push, online purchase, or dedicated mobile applications. Some of the solution providers in this domain are Bissano Software Ltd., Mobile Tickets Ltd., codeREADr, Eagle Eye Solutions Ltd., Impact Mobile, NTT DoCoMo, ScreenTicket, Wayin Solutions, and mticket.

30.2.3 Mobile Banking

Mobile banking is an extension of Internet banking that enables banking operations from mobile devices using thick and thin client applications installed in the mobile device. These applications provide enhanced security, functionalities, and portability. They allow customers to check the balance, transfer funds, receive alerts, pay credit cards and utility bills, and much more.

30.2.4 Mobile Payments and Money Transfers

Here, the mobile device acts as a payment device for transfer of value from one party to another. There are different mechanisms for enabling payments from the mobile device. There are pluggable card readers, which can be used for swiping credit cards. The latest trend is to embed payment features within the mobile device. NFC-based mobile devices acting as point-of-sale (POS) terminals are detailed in Chapter 22. We are witnessing a number of partnerships between telecom service providers and financial institutions to provide m-commerce solutions. Telecom service providers can generate additional revenue by selling data plans for providing Internet bandwidth, premium SMS services, and WAP billing. Examples of such billing solutions include Sybase 365 Operator Charging Gateway, Ericsson Internet Payment Exchange (IPX), PayFort in United Kingdom, and Simpay in Europe. mPayConnect (mpayconnect.com) offers mobile payment services. The following list provides a brief overview of few of the mobile payment solutions:

■ NFC-based mobile payment solutions (details can be found in Chapter 22).
■ Square credit card reader is a pluggable card reader for Android and iOS devices, which can be plugged in the telephone jack. This saves the investment in credit-card terminals, but there is a service charge associated with each transaction.
■ Eagle Eye Solutions (http://eagleeyesolutions.co.uk) provides the design, development, and implementation of mobile-based solutions for retail for business-to-business and business-to-consumer. Eagle Eye Solutions is the leading player in mobile voucher technology.
■ GSM Association's (http://gsmworld.com) Mobile Money for unbanked program provides financial services to the unbanked, low-income class population.

- Sybase 365 is an end-to-end m-commerce solution with SMS, MMS, GRX, IPX interoperability, mCRM, mMarketing, and content delivery services. Sybase is the biggest player in SMS-based mobile payment service.
- iTunes from Apple also offers payment mechanisms based on the credit stored in the iTunes account. Apple has filled multiple patents on NFC-based payment technology.
- Mobile POS service offerings from major IT players such as Infosys and IBM
- mConnect from Infosys is a real-time enterprise middleware solution that provides mobile services for web sites and e-commerce platforms. It can be used to reach out to mobile customers in real time. The solution helps enterprises to extend their eCommerce solutions to different mobile platforms.
- Mobile billing services provide the feature of purchasing goods and services by charging the mobile account. This is an alternative to NFC. Major players are BilltoMobile, Boku, and Zong.

30.2.5 Mobile Location-Aware and Context-Aware Personalized Applications

Retail is one of the areas that leverage the uses and advantages of location-based services for a variety of purposes such as advertising, in-store shopping, and post–customer relationship management (CRM). These services are used in mobile signage, searching for products and availability of stocks, comparing prices, managing loyalty programs, promoting mobile coupons and POS applications, and enabling customers to do shopping, getting information on a product, payment, and checkout all at one go. Such applications are designed to be context-aware; for example, it will show the advertisements of those products that are placed in the section of the store where the customer is using the POS application. Another example is an application that provides specific services depending on the nearest WiFi hot spot. Enterprises, governments, and small consumer enterprise solutions are also going mobile.

30.3 Major Mobile Push E-mail Services

BlackBerry services, from Research In Motion (RIM), are one of the oldest push e-mail services for mobile phones since 2000. It uses a wireless mail user agent and a BlackBerry enterprise server (BES) over a traditional e-mail system. iOS mobile platforms support push e-mail services from Yahoo push e-mail, Hotmail, Gmail push e-mail via Google Sync and Microsoft active Sync services, and Direct Push Technology used for push e-mails in Windows phone and Windows Mobile phones. The Google Android mobile platform uses in-built Gmail client, which uses Google's Syc services for push e-mail. Nokia Messaging push e-mail services support Hotmail, Yahoo, and Gmail. Other third-party push e-mail solutions in the market are Emoze, NotifyLink, Mobiqus, SEVEN Networks, Atmail, Good Technology, as well as Synchronica.

30.4 Application Distribution

Day by day the number of mobile applications developed for each platform is growing high.

Distribution of applications can be achieved in various ways. One option is to preload applications and make them available from a trial version to full version when customer is paying for it. Application developers can create widgets that will redirect users to sites or links of correct version of application where users are encouraged to download applications that enhance their current functionalities in device. These widgets can be linked with channels operated by developer in facebook Twitter, Youtube or similar social networking sites where user will find useful information about the applications they are using and can download new application versions. Another way to get your applications distributed is through specialist press who review applications. Developers can also use Ad networks for directing users to App download sites. Another option for App distribution is to use pay per install like Getjar. Getjar offers pay per download ads where users can bid a price for a download in Getjar site. Some time they provide offers like free App down load when user purchases a minimum number of applications.

Ads in TV is also a widely used and older way of promoting a product. One of the effective medium of App distribution is App market place.

30.4.1 Application Market Places Specific for Native OS

For distributing mobile applications to mobile devices of consumers, each mobile platform has different digital distribution platforms. Some of these platforms are provided by the mobile manufacturer or OS manufacturer or sites recommended by them.

The application distribution systems native to each mobile platform are as follows:

Market Place	Device Platform	Owner	Web site
Android Market	Android	Google	https://market.android.com
App Store	iOS	Apple	http://store.apple.com
Windows Phone Marketplace	Windows Phone	Microsoft	http://www.windowsphone.com/en-US/marketplace

(continued)

App World	BlackBerry	RIM	http://us.blackberry.com/apps-software/appworld/
Ovi Store	Symbian	Nokia	http://store.ovi.com
App Catalog	Web OS	Palm/HP	http://www.hp.com/united-states/webos/us/en/apps.html
Samsung Application Store	Bada, Symbian, Java, Windows Mobile	Samsung, Handmark	http://www.samsungapps.com

A few third-party platforms are as follows:

Market Place	Device Platform	Owner	Web site
Amazon Appstore	Android	Amazon	
Fasmicro Android Store	Android	Fasmicro Ltd.	http://apps.fasmicro.net
App Centre	Multiple	Nukona, Inc.	http://www.appcenter.com
Cellmania	Multiple	General Software	http://www.cellmania.com
Software Store (Sprint)	Multiple	Sprint Nextel, Handmark	http://sprintmobile.handmark.com/phones
VZAppZone	BlackBerry OS, BREW, Windows Mobile	Verizon Wireless	http://support.verizonwireless.com

30.5 Cross-Platform Application Development Solutions

Nowadays mobile applications are developed focusing on specific business use cases rather than on specific mobile device. This will ensure application developed is available across different mobile platform and reduces the cost of developing same application separately for different mobile platforms. The HTML 5 standard introduced for this purpose has been a trend setter for the industry. This topic has been covered in detail in Chapter 24.

30.6 Mobile Business Intelligence Applications

Business intelligence (BI) applications are used for the distribution of business data to mobile devices followed by data analysis. There are various mechanisms through which BI applications fetch data in a device. It could use static data push using SMS or text messages or use a mobile web browser. The BI application running in the device would process the data. BI applications can be categorized into the following applications:

■ Mobile Browser Rendered app: These are basically web-based thin client apps with hypertext markup language (HTML) support. These apps are static and provide little data interactivity.
■ Customized app: These apps render data in device-specific format to best suit the screen size, screen resolution, support for device-specific navigation control (such as thumb button, rotating ball in BlackBerry, gestural manipulation for iPhone, arrow keys for Palm, and so on).
■ Mobile Client App: These can be applications designed for a mobile platform or web-based application that could run across different mobile platforms. These applications mainly process business data specific to a context and provide immediate results to the user. It could also cache data and analyze it offline.

Some examples of BI application vendors are Cognos, Business Objects, iVEDIX, MicroStrategy, Transpara, Yellowfin Business Intelligence, QlikView InetSoft, and eQube BI. SAP Business Objects Mobile is a BI solution, which is discussed in detail in Section 30.8.

30.7 Mobile Security Solutions

The following list provides some examples of mobile security solutions:

■ Mobile antivirus software products: Kaspersky Mobile Security (http://www.kaspersky.com), McAfee Virus Scan Mobile, McAfee Enterprise Mobility Management Suite, Symantec Mobile Security, and Mobile Security for Android from TrendMicro
■ Mobile virtual private network solution providers: NetMotion Wireless, NeoAccel, Columbitech, Radio Internet Protocol (IP) Software, ERICSSION, and Birdstep Technology (refer to Chapter 21 for more information)

30.8 SAP-Based Mobile Solutions

SAP mobile solutions help in mobilizing existing business solutions by making use of the existing IT infrastructure and extending the business processes for the mobile world. SAP Business Objects Mobile is a BI solution that provides reports and metrics in the mobile device. SAP Netweiver Mobile is part of SAP xApp's solution for mobilizing business processes. It has the following components:

1. Data orchestration engine is a middleware providing data consolidation, data realignment, and data staging for handling huge volumes of business data in mobile devices.
2. Mobile client is a device-based thick client application that provides the capability to work on business data in an off-line mode, when only intermittent connectivity is available to download business data.
3. Mobile administration and monitoring provides a set of specialized tools and procedures for administering a large group of mobile devices.
4. NetWeaver Developer Studio is used for modeling mobile applications for catering business requirements.

ITSMOBILE is another solution for accessing ABAP DYNPRO-based SAP applications from different mobile devices. It has the following major features:

1. It requires Internet connectivity to network.
2. Web browser with native web application support is required as ITSmobile is based on browser-based technology, and it requires support for hypertext transfer protocol (HTTP).

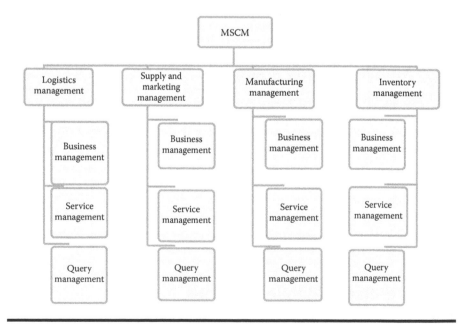

Figure 30.1 MSCM architecture.

3. It has a very low total cost of ownership (TCO) technology that makes it easy to mobilize new applications.
4. It is an open framework and can easily adapt to business needs and requirements.
5. It supports mobile hardware features such as camera, RFID reader, and barcode reader, etc.

ITSmobile finds its usage in warehouse management and in its extended applications, such as SAP Retail and AutoID Infrastructure. SAP Business Objects Mobile is used to remotely access BI reports, metrics, and right-time data over a wireless network. It extends the availability of BI desktop solutions to mobile devices to enable sales and field service staff to deliver products and work order information to a customer anytime and anywhere. Syclo SMART Mobile Suite is another SAP-based solution for mobile devices for mobilizing asset maintenance, operator rounds, time and attendance tracking, and materials management.

30.9 Mobile Enterprise Resource Planning Solutions

Enterprise Resource Planning (ERP) solution automates and integrates internal and external management information across an organization. Any system such as manufacturing, finance, customer relationship management (CRM), human resource management, manufacturing, supply chain management, access control, project management, or sales and service within an organization can be brought under ERP. ERP systems are designed to run across different hardware and network configurations. The challenge of the mobile industry is to integrate any mobility solution with the existing ERP solutions used by a business enterprise. One of the latest trends in the industry is SaaS on demand ERP, which has brought down the TCO to one-tenth of the cost of traditional ERP systems. The next latest trend in the industry is its expansion into the mobility space. Mobile ERP revenue has reached over $35 billion in 2011, and we are seeing a good traction in future. Mobile operators are partnering with mobile ERP vendors to capture the market share and generate new sources of revenue to increase average revenue per user. Revenue from voice services is declining compared with the growth in revenue from ERP-based services and e-mail services. Major players in the ERP solutions market are PeopleSoft (one of the original ERP system vendors), Oracle, SAP, Microsoft, Sage, Epicor, and CDC. These players have extended their existing ERP solutions to mobile devices. Oracle and SAP share more than half of the market share.

SAP, the greatest player in the industry, has partnered with Sybase and introduced a mobility enterprise application platform for SAP-based ERP solutions known as Sybase Unwired Platform. It has support for many tools such as 4GL tooling environment and IDEs such as Eclipse for faster mobile application

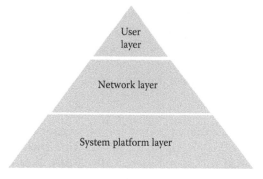

Figure 30.2 MSCM structure.

development. It supports Windows 32 platform and diverse mobile platforms such as Windows Mobile, iPhone, and BlackBerry. It can be integrated with Afaria mobile device management (MDM) and mobile security solution. The capabilities of Afaria MDM have been covered in Chapter 29. @hand is a company providing enterprise mobility solutions for SAP-based customers. Their solutions combine information from multiple systems and provide a common interface. This common interface could provide mobility-based applications and services. Hence, the solutions are independent and also provide a standard interface to interact with existing ERP systems. @hand provides field mobility solutions for mobile field service, mobile asset management, and mobile inventory management. @hand also provides mobile solutions for SAP environments in the fields of mobile ticketing, job management, and equipment maintenance. The PeopleSoft Mobile Inventory Management application performs inventory transactions across mobile platforms.

30.10 Mobile Supply Chain Management Solutions

SCM involves transportation and storage of raw materials, work-in-process inventory, and finished goods from the point of finding raw materials to the point of consumption. Mobile supply chain management (MSCM) is an expansion of m-commerce in managing the supply chain, which helps in performing warehouse and shop-floor transactions from any location in real time. The developments in high bandwidth with 3G and 4G networks and technologies such as RFID in mobile devices and global positioning system (GPS) for location tracking has revolutionized this industry. SCM involves the following basic processes: plan, source, make, deliver, and return. MSCM extends specific areas of an SCM only to mobile devices and does not use the entire process modes. The MSCM architecture consists of three layers:

1. The user layer corresponds to the terminal user of the mobile in the supply chain. The terminal user could be the end consumers of products, second-tier suppliers or distributors, retailers or merchandisers, people working on products and maintaining warehouses or people in sales.
2. The network layer is involved in the transfer and distribution of data across mobile devices and the SCM system. The network could be the telecommunication network from a service provider, Internet, or a unified communication (UC) solution.
3. The system platform layer makes the major business decisions for managing areas in logistics, supply and marketing, and manufacturing and inventory in a mobile supply chain. Each of these areas has various modules such as business management, service management, and query management. The system platform layer also does the management of the user layer and the network layer.

30.10.1 Major MSCM Solutions in the Market

Some of the major MSCM solutions in the market are as follows:

- Oracle Mobile Supply Chain: This solution is part of the Oracle E-Business Suite, which provides a complete set of tools for automating business processes.
- MSCM solution from Manhattan Associates. This mobility product suite has different solutions such as distributed order management, hub management, store commerce activation, supply chain intelligence, and warehouse management.
- MSCM solution from Lawson Software: This solution has key features such as delivery management and verification, package receiving, activity tracking and reporting, par and cycle counting, and receiving and delivery.
- Kronos solutions for warehouse management: These solutions are for managing the movement and storage of goods. They also offer CRM and ERP solutions that can be integrated with the warehouse management solution.

30.11 Mobile Field Service Providers

For any industry implementing mobile-based solutions, one challenge is to provide service for the devices in the field and have a field service management (FSM) solution that suits their field requirements. There are key players in the mobile industry who provide field services. Stratix Mobile Field Service Software provides functionalities for managing and optimizing various business processes to be carried out in the field such as sales order management, invoicing, inventory, asset management, and customer management. METRIX (http://www.metrix.com) offers the following solutions in mobile field services: field service software, mobile work force automation, service parts and logistics, return service management, warranty asset management, advanced scheduling, and contact center solution. Another solution is the FSM solution from Astea.

30.12 Mobile Device Management Solutions

In the evolution of mobile device from a simple gadget to make phone calls to a multipurpose and vital tool for running daily business in the enterprise world, the need of the hour is to manage a fleet of devices ensuring seamless availability and security. Here comes the importance of Mobile Device Management (MDM) solutions. MDM solutions offer device and data security, authenticate user, restrict user access to configurable number of devices, end to end version management and deployment of mobile applications, handle device theft, device tracking, geo fencing, remote control, customer assist and much more. This has been covered in detail in Chapter 29.

30.13 Mobile-Based Home and Remote Control Solutions

Gmote is an Android application used to control home personal computers using the Android phone. A Gmote client application needs to be installed in the Android phone, and the Gmote server needs to be installed in the desktop or laptop machine. The client and server can be configured to control the PC from anywhere over the Internet using the phone. Other solutions are RemoteDroid from http://remote-droid.net/. Google introduced the Android@Home solution during Google I/O Conference for controlling all electronic devices and home appliances. It uses an open protocol to control all closed systems such as Apple and Windows devices. Android@Home concept was introduced as a home theater proof-of-concept in the name of Project Tungsten. It can control all devices of the home theater system and also download and play music and videos from Google's cloud-based services. Apple has plans to introduce applications that can use iPhone as an NFC-enabled home networking device using their patents on "Systems and methods for simplified resource sharing." The idea is to use iPhone as a universal remote to control all home appliances.

30.14 Mobile UC Solutions

Mobility has redefined the workplace and has extended it to literally anytime and anywhere and from any device and equips people to take business decisions while they are on the move. People prefer to access and work on corporate data while at home or during travel in a secure way. Chapter 29 discusses how MDM solutions help in building an extended workplace. The challenge is to provide seamless connectivity at a low cost. Mobile voice-over protocol (VoIP) solutions play a major role in providing UC. UCs also have within its scope communication over VoIP, presence, video, and audio conference, data share, and chat capabilities. It will reduce costs associated with PSTN calls, international and domestic calling charges over 3G and 4G or cellular. Important traits required for such solutions are efficient battery power management, WiFi handling, secure device data, data transmission, support for all mobile platforms, easy integration with other PBX and UC systems, integration with corporates, and seamless connectivity under adverse conditions. Major players in UC solutions are as follows:

■ ShoreTel mobility solutions for UC from ShoreTel is a good choice for corporates to extend the workplace to mobility by integrating with the existing PBX and UC systems. It provides reverse dialing and SIM swap features to reduce call costs and provides platform agnostic capabilities. It supports all mobile platforms.

■ OpenScape UC Suite 2011 from Siemens has advanced features such as call swipe wherein call can be seamlessly transferred from a mobile device to a desktop phone while moving from the cellular network to WLAN using SIP-based voice-over WLAN. It supports all mobile platforms.

■ Microsoft Lync UC solution has the advantage of having smooth integration with other Microsoft products such as Microsoft Exchange, Microsoft Office Suite, etc. It has integrated capabilities for instant messaging, rich presence, search capabilities, support public IM services such as Windows Live, AOL, and Yahoo! Using single work identity, it allows building social connections, face-to-face meeting with video application and desktop sharing

■ Avaya UC solutions have the advantage of a wide range of product suites carefully crafted to suit specific requirements and provide value for money as we subscribe for minimum and necessary features.

■ Cisco UC solutions: Cisco is a major player in the communications market and has a wide range of UC products under the categories of conferencing, customer collaboration, IP communications, messaging, mobile applications, presence, and clients.

There are many other solutions also in the market from AlcatelLucent OmniTouch, AT&T, etc.

30.15 Mobile Content or Media Solutions

Mobile content refers to any type of media used or viewed in mobile phones such as graphics, ring tones, images, games, movies, GPS navigation apps, Mobishows, and Cellsodes. It also includes voice and data streaming applications such as radio, television (TV), and live shows. There are thousands of mobile content applications for each mobile platform. The following categories of applications for different mobile platforms are available in the market: antivirus, books and reference, business, comics, communication, education, entertainment, finance, health and fitness, library, lifestyle, live wallpaper, media, medical, music and audio, magazines, personalization, photography, productivity, security, shopping, social, sports, tools, transportation, travel and local, weather, and widgets. Despite this, the mobile platform provides options to download or buy music, videos, create play lists, and share with friends. Some innovative media solutions are discussed in the following sections.

30.15.1 Interactive Solutions

MyCityWay mobile application from BMW is an interactive tool for exploring a city or location in order to discover, connect, and share in real time. It provides a common interface for different applications providing location-based services. The tool provides detailed information about each nook and corner of a city, different shopping and dining options, and much more. Siri from Apple is an interactive voice response application that is intelligent enough to interpret voice commands and interact with the user verbally. The application makes mobility an integral part of life. It could act on voice inputs to send text messages and e-mails to people in address book, set reminders, play music, search for anything such as dining options, restaurants, and best options available in the locality.

30.15.2 Augmented Reality Solutions

Augmented reality solutions make use of location-based services, GPS data, compass, camera accelerometer, and other device sensors to create better user experience. There are a number of augmented reality games developed for mobile devices.

- Google Goggles can identify any object and provide overlay visual search results in smartphones.
- Google Android Layer browser allows developers to superimpose augmented reality cloud data on real-time view of the world.
- TwitARound application overlays live video around your tweets. People tweeting are shown in varying distances based on how far they are located from your location.
- Nearest Tube is an iPhone app that could show directions within a city by superimposing text and images over live video from the camera of the mobile phone. It integrates itself with location-based services.

- TAT augmented ID application uses Flickr facial recognition technology of Polar Rose to recognize a person's face and pull information from that person's online flicker profile.
- Wikitude AR Travel Guide application acts as a travel guide. Holding the mobile camera at a site will bring up Wikipedia information about that site.

30.15.3 TV Applications

The following are mobile TV applications from Apple and Google:

- Apple TV: It is a service offering from Apple to provide TV channels online in high-definition video and audio. There are a number of features available for the customers, such as recording a movie and storing it in iCloud (cloud-based storage service) or book-marking videos to be watched later. The application called Camera for Apple TV for iPhone or iPad can be used to play video captured in iPhone to be played on a bigger screen using Apple TV. Apps are available to remote control Apple TV using iPhone or iPad.
- Google TV: Google has introduced Google TV similar to Apple's Apple TV to provide high-definition movies and TV channels through the Internet and cloud-based services. It works on the Google Android platform. The greatest strength of this platform is the ability to search within TV channels and video contents using Chrome browser. Also Google TV can directly access market apps for downloading interesting apps. Multiple vendors such as Sony, Logitech, Samsung, and Vizio have rolled out products based on Google TV.

30.16 Conclusion

We are witnessing a number of tractions in enterprise mobility solutions. Cloud-based mobility applications are one of the emerging markets. In the field of mobile media solutions, there are plenty of small and large applications coming into the market. In a way it is increasing the choice of customers to choose the best while flooding the market with so many solutions that it becomes less maintainable in mobile devices. According to the market trends, people prefer application platforms that integrate multiple applications and provide a common interface. Such applications are more accepted and are becoming an integral part of peoples' life. SCM has huge opportunities to mobilize more areas and identify new application areas.

Additional Reading

E-Reading

1. http://www.sybase.com/mobileservices/financial-services
2. *m-Connect Middleware for M-Commerce Solutions from Infosys.* Available at: http://www.infosys.com/products-and-platforms/mConnect/Pages/index.aspx

3. *SAP-Based Mobile Solutions.* Available at: http://www.sdn.sap.com
4. http://www.erp.com
5. http://www.hand.com/mobile_for_sap
6. http://www.sap.com/solutions/mobility/sybase-unwired-platform/index.epx
7. *MSCM Solutions.* Available at: http://www.lawson.com, http://www.oracle.com/us/products/applications/ebusiness/logistics/053335.html, and http://www.manh.com/solutions/mobile-supply-chain
8. *Mobile Field Service Solutions Field Service 2011: Trends in Work Force Management.* Available at: http://www.aberdeen.com/Aberdeen-Library/6837/RA-field-service-management.aspx
9. *Google AppGalaxy Helps to Build and Market Your Own App.* Available at: http://www.guidetotheappgalaxy.com/?utm_source=admob&utm_medium=web&utm_campaign=ag#/developersguide/1

Books

1. Norman Sadeh. *M-Commerce: Technologies, Services, and Business Models.* Canada: John Wiley & Sons, 2002.

Index

Milton Keynes UK
Ingram Content Group UK Ltd.
UKHW030902141024
449569UK00025B/1271